Hijacking America's Mind on 9/11

Hijacking America's Mind on 9/11

Counterfeiting Evidence

Elias Davidsson

Algora Publishing
New York

Library of Congress Cataloging-in-Publication Data —

Davidsson, Elias, 1941-
  Hijacking America's Mind on 9/11: Counterfeiting Evidence / Elias Davidsson.
    pages cm
  Includes bibliographical references and index.
  ISBN 978-0-87586-972-8 (soft cover: alk. paper) — ISBN 978-0-87586-973-5 (hard
cover: alk. paper) — ISBN 978-0-87586-974-2 (ebook: alk. paper) 1. American Airlines
Flight 11 Hijacking Incident, 2001. 2. American Airlines Flight 77 Hijacking Incident,
2001. 3. September 11 Terrorist Attacks, 2001. 4. Terrorism—Government policy—United
States. 5. Conspiracy theories. I. Title.
  HV6432.7.D3836 2013
  973.931—dc23
                          2013009044

Front Cover: Drawing by Klaus Uhlig (Germany)

Printed in the United States

"In a time of universal deceit, telling the truth is a revolutionary act."

— George Orwell

TABLE OF CONTENTS

An old saying goes: "The Devil is in the details."

Most people, busy making a living and caring for their families, have not felt they had any particular reason to study the details of 9/11.

It's not surprising. On that fateful day average citizens everywhere in the world were presented, usually via TV, with shocking events in a framework constructed by the media, a framework that made horrible sense. The constructed official version explained immediately what happened and who did it. Within that, the spectacular images seemed cut and dried. The Twitterlike TV crawl said it all: "America Under Attack."

The narrative presented everywhere in the media was so overwhelming as to mask from our minds even what our own eyes were seeing—for instance, giant steel skyscrapers collapsing at freefall speed in the time it takes a telephone to ring twice—although such structures never before (or since) have succumbed to even much longer lasting and much more intense infernos. We were mesmerized, traumatized, infanticized, tricked.

The official narrative is too well known to repeat here. Let us say only that crazed Muslims were said to have done it. Everything else followed: the "war on terror," huge arms buildup, the 9/11 wars in Afghanistan and Iraq, and vastly increased surveillance, "security" forces and routines everywhere.

Back to details: those painstakingly amassed by Elias Davidsson in this book reveal, one by one, that the events of 9/11 were a sordid false flag terror fraud.

Considering the continuing expensive, bloody and fascistic fallout from 9/11 it's not intemperate or unreasonable to suggest that every citizen of the world should have an opportunity to see the details in this book and ponder the implications.

What the author offers in these pages for any reasonable person is indubitable, irrefutable proof that thousands of details put forward by the US government and subservient media are fake threads that make up a Big Lie tapestry.

After tracing the genesis of the official narrative on 9/11 to political decisions made on the very day of the events and reflected in a Congressional resolution adopted within a mere 24 hours, Davidsson shatters to pieces the myth of 19 Muslim hijackers by demonstrating the failure by the US Government to produce evidence that those accused had even boarded the aircraft they allegedly hijacked: Their names do not appear on authenticated passenger lists; no one saw them board the aircraft; no authenticated CCTV tapes have been produced to prove that they were in the airports; and their bodies were not formally identified. Davidsson for a few years offered a generous cash prize to anyone, including prestigious journalists, who would successfully debunk his findings. There were no takers.

Having disposed of the foundational myth of 9/11, Davidsson disposes of another myth, namely that the aircraft assigned to flights AA11, UA175, AA77 and UA93 crashed at the known landmarks.

He finally tackles one of the remaining mysteries: The fact that passengers and crew members of these flights made telephone calls in which they specifically talked about hijackings. Such effort required a minute deconstruction of every phone call "made from the aircraft," to which Davidsson devotes no less than four chapters. Readers might initially wish to skip these detailed chapters and go directly to Chapter 11, which sums up this meticulous analysis in the guise of 12 inexplicable omissions by callers, seven calls that "didn't make sense," six calls reporting "puzzling conduct" and five calls that revealed "unexplained contradictions." Readers may consult the detailed chapters for corroboration.

Among inexplicable omissions Davidsson mentions that no caller reported how the "hijackers" took over the plane and broke into the cockpit. No caller either mentioned the foreign accent of the "hijackers" or what they allegedly said. Surprisingly, even flight attendants who made calls did not mention these basic facts.

It does not make sense to Davidsson that, according to Barbara Olson who called her husband Ted at the Department of Justice, the pilot of flight AA77 was actually aware of the "hijacking" but did not inform the ground about this fact; or that Peter Hanson, a caller from flight UA175, claimed to have overheard the "hijackers" say (in Arabic?) that they intend to fly into buildings.

Davidsson considers it "puzzling conduct" that Betty Ong, a veteran and respected flight attendant, after reporting with a serene voice that her colleague "was being" murdered a few feet away, continued to chat on the phone for another 20 minutes; or that none of the 80- odd passengers of flight AA11, having presumably witnessed a passenger (Daniel Lewin) being murdered and overcome by mace, should have done anything to overcome the attackers, or call their families.

These incongruities led Davidsson to search for and develop a compelling theory explaining the phone calls. This theory is presented in the last, and arguably the most sinister, part of the book under the heading "The Deception."

The Devil in these pages is left with nowhere to hide. We are confronted with a corrupt US-centered war-based global apparatus, an historically unprecedented confluence of military and money power operating through vast calculated deceptions so ubiquitous that I call it the *diaboligarchy*.

But there's an oddly parallel saying: "God is in the details." Which is it? Well, if scrupulously-documented truths are the best means of exposing the Devil, the two concepts are reconciled.

Davidsson's approach—using official government documents to undermine the assertions of the governments themselves—was pioneered to great effect by the award-winning Indian journalist and author Palagummi Sainath when he was editor of *Blitz*.

The "technique" requires a lot of work, but leaves prevaricating governments gratifyingly speechless because they can hardly deny their own words and statistics. (Although they are very prone, as this book shows, to repeatedly altering records, hiding information and changing their stories.)

This book is populated by as scrofulous a band of phantom witnesses, lying witnesses, bullied witnesses, lying officials, planted "evidence," fake documents, bogus reports up to and including the official 9/11 Commission Report, compromised organizations including airlines, police forces and insurance companies, corrupted officials including police officers in the FBI and elsewhere, corrupted politicians up to the White House, corrupted judges, juries, courts and court systems as you could imagine, and many you couldn't until you see them in the glare in these pages.

The FBI alone stands revealed as a massively corrupt outfit that would make the old KGB look like a Boy Scout troop.

The evidence Davidsson marshals comprises a catalogue of how wrong minded is the "apologist community" for the 9/11 fiction. As he notes, that community includes almost all in the groves of academe, in the coffee shops and union halls of the Left, and in the executive suites and newsrooms of the media, including the so-called "alternative media." With these institutions in league to squelch the truth and even the questioning of the official line, it's a wonder that as many ordinary people as there are have decided there's something very rotten in the state of Denmark.

That there would be so many media outlets in so many countries conspiring to censor out questions about the Big Lie of 9/11—that there would be an almost universal squelching of reviews of all 9/11Truth books such as this one—no matter how evidence-based and intellectually sound they may be—is a testament to the unbelievable number of gatekeeper moles at work, following their handlers' instructions to spin or "disappear" the issues, persons and movements that most threaten the power elites.

Of Darwin it was said that he "saw what everyone saw and thought what no one thought." There's a parallel contemporary variation. In today's world virtually everyone saw—on TV on 9/11—two massive skyscrapers in New York City fall, allegedly due to impacts of hijacked airplanes followed by fire. (A third skyscraper, WTC building 7, also came down at freefall speed, at 5:20 p.m., even though not struck by an airplane.)

In today's world we have not one but tens of millions of Darwins thinking what we're not supposed to think. Our existence is censored out of the media except for a rare mention of public opinion polls proving our numbers. But the mention is almost always in the context of a story about the inexplicable persistence of "conspiracy theorists."

This book confirms that our disbelief of the official 9/11 story is justified. That our theory of a criminal conspiracy is fact-based. That the 9/11 story is not even a theory, but simply a big lie. It was Adolf Hitler, the evil genius of war propaganda, who said a Big Lie is more likely to believed than a small one. The events of 9/11 were not a tragedy, but a crime of mass murder and treason.

This book confirms that exploring for ourselves and applying our skeptical powers is the first step toward achieving a safer, saner world, to engage in the kind of revolution Davidsson calls for:

> It appears to me that only a revolution can save our civilization from a terrible ordeal; not a revolution by an enlightened minority who has found "the truth;" nor a suicidal armed insurrection; but a cultural revolution based on moral integrity, refusal to obey immoral orders, grass-root solidarity across the globe and genuine commitment to a social order in which human dignity and compassion prevails over greed and the quest for power. Such a revolution can only be achieved by peaceful means.

This book does not purport to cover all aspects of 9/11, but it contains such a large chunk of the Devil's DNA—and God's truth, if you will—that you need, if you wish, go no further.

Barrie Zwicker
Author, *Towers of Deception: The Media Cover-Up of 9/11*
Toronto, Canada

PART I. THE FOUNDATIONAL MYTH

INTRODUCTION

By way of introduction, I have chosen to quote a prophetic statement made in 2004 by former LAPD officer Michael Ruppert, long before his view was espoused by a large and respectable 9/11 truth community:

> "Events in the five-year period that began on September 11, 2001, will determine the course of human history for several centuries to come. The fall of the World Trade Center buildings and the Pentagon attack were not isolated events. They were one predictable outcome of an economic system whose pressures necessitated murder in the judgment of those who perpetrated it."[1]

In the present book, I intend to present evidence that largely supports Ruppert's conclusion. And while Ruppert's book focused on the subject-matter from the perspective of an American citizen, his conclusions are equally applicable to citizens of other countries, whose governments continue to collude in suppressing the truth on the mass-murder of 9/11.

Numerous excellent books have been written from a critical perspective on the issue of 9/11. I wish first to cite two remarkable individuals, who already early on recognized the deceptive nature of the official account of 9/11: Thierry Meyssan, the French director of voltaire.net, who published two important eye-openers in 2002 and 2003 that have been translated into 26 languages;[2] the other is Andreas von Bülow, former German Minister of Research and Technology, who

---

1   Michael C. Ruppert, *Crossing the Rubicon: The Decline of the American Empire and the End of the Age of Oil* (Canada, New Society Publishers, 2004)
2   Thierry Meyssan, *L'effroyable imposture* (France, Editions Demi-Lune, 2002) and *Le Pentagate* (France, Editions Carnot, 2003)

while being a member of the German Bundestag (Parliament) served on the parliamentary committee that supervises German intelligence agencies. Von Bülow made waves in Germany in 2002 after stating in an interview that "planning [and executing] the attacks was a master deed, in technical and organizational terms, unthinkable without backing from the secret apparatuses of state and industry."[1] He later published a book about the role of secret services in international terrorism.[2] Both von Bülow and Meyssan were demeaned by mainstream media for daring to question the official account and ultimately were excluded from media coverage.

Prof. David Ray Griffin, who only became a 9/11 skeptic a couple of years after the event, has become the undisputed leading scholar in 9/11 studies. He has written more than ten books on this subject, each with a different slant. Some of his books focus on particular aspects of 9/11, such as the dereliction of the 9/11 Commission, while others contain a heterogeneous collection of articles on important facets of 9/11. His first book, *The New Pearl Harbor*, served and continues to serve as an excellent introduction to critical studies of 9/11. I concur with Professor Richard Falk's assessment of this book:

> David Ray Griffin has written an extraordinary book. If carefully read with even just a 30-percent open mind, it is almost certain to change the way we understand the workings of constitutional democracy in the United States at the highest levels of government.... It is rare, indeed, that a book has this potential to become a force of history.[3]

Other authors, such as Webster Tarpley,[4] Michael Ruppert,[5] Peter Dale Scott,[6] and David MacGregor,[7] attempt to shed light on covert aspects of US governance that might underlie and explain the mass-murder of 9/11. These authors contend that there exists a deep and hidden structure ensconced within the official state apparatus of the United States, which wields far greater power than is generally suspected. Their view has been partly vindicated by revelations made in Europe concerning similar structures operating during the Cold War under

---

1   "Da sind Spuren wie von einer trampelnden Elefantenherde," *Tagesspiegel (Germany)*, January 13, 2002, #930

2   Andreas von Bülow, *Die CIA und der 11. September: Internationaler Terror und die Rolle der Geheimdienste* (Germany, Piper Verlag, 2003, 2004, 2011)

3   Richard Falk, Foreword to David Ray Griffin, *The New Pearl Harbor: Disturbing Questions about the Bush Administration and 9/11* (Olive Branch Press, 2004), vii

4   Webster Griffin Tarpley, *9/11 Synthetic Terror Made in USA* (Progressive Press, 2006)

5   Ruppert, Op. cit.

6   Peter Dale Scott, *Deep Politics and the Death of JFK* (University of California Press,1996); *The Road to 9/11: Wealth, Empire, and the Future of America* (University of California Press , 2008) and; *American War Machine: Deep Politics, the CIA Global Drug Connection, and the Road to Afghanistan* (Rowman & Littlefield Publishers, 2010)

7   David MacGregor, "September 11 as 'Machiavellian State Terrorism'" in *The Hidden History of 9/11*, edited by Paul Zarembka, Research in Political Economy, Vol. 23 (Elsevier, May 2006)

the name of Stay-Behind Armies or Gladio.[1] Tarpley has also sketched a theory of *synthetic terrorism*, including a taxonomy of the actors involved. Other authors, including Barrie Zwicker, a veteran 9/11 researcher and producer of one of the best early documentaries on this issue,[2] have focused on the role of media in covering up the crime of 9/11 and that played by leftist gate-keepers in maintaining the belief in the so-called blow-back theory.[3] Specific aspects of 9/11 have been dealt in depth by several authors. Rowland Morgan, for example, provides an excellent critical analysis of the facts and myths surrounding flight UA93.[4] Political scientist Nafeez Mosaddeq Ahmed provided a fresh and critical evaluation of the Al Qaeda network and its covert links to Western intelligence agencies.[5] Aidan Monaghan has elicited important information by persistently and judiciously using Freedom of Information (FOIA) requests.[6]

A number of serious 9/11 researchers have preferred to present their findings in the form of articles, blogs or video documentation posted on internet forums. Among those are groups entitled Scholars for 9/11 Truth and Justice.[7] The main focus of Architects and Engineers for 9/11 Truth[8] is to produce studies on the mysterious disintegration of the World Trade Center (WTC). The association Pilots for 9/11 Truth[9] focuses on anomalies and contradictions in official reports concerning the four flights. Other fine examples of web-based sources are writings by bloggers *Killtown*, *Woody Box* and *Shoestring*, whose ground-breaking analyses based on verifiable and quoted reports, illustrations and photographs have been very helpful.[10]

One name that deserves special praise among 9/11 truth activists is Paul Thompson, whose encyclopedic data-base on 9/11 is universally acclaimed as the best resource available to researchers about this subject: It is extensive, objective, fabulously well sourced, accessible to everyone and free of charge (Thompson *does*, however, appreciate donations).[11] The results of his almost single-handed efforts surpass greatly in quantity *and* quality those of the official 9/11 Commission.

---

1   Operation_Gladio, *Wikipedia*
2   Barrie Zwicker, *The Great Conspiracy: The 9/11 News Special You Never Saw* (2004) [DVD]
3   Barrie Zwicker, *Towers of Deception: The Media Cover-Up of 9/11* (New Society Publishers, 2006)
4   Rowland Morgan, *Flight 93 Revealed: What really happened on the 9/11 'Let's Roll' Flight?* (Robinson publishers, 2006)
5   Nafeez Mosaddeq Ahmed, *The War on Truth and the Anatomy of Terrorism* (Olive Branch Press, 2005)
6   Aidan Monaghan's Blog: ‹911blogger.com/blog/2074› (last visited March 8, 2013)
7   Scholars for 9/11 Truth and Justice: ‹stj911.org› (last visited March 8, 2013)
8   Architects and Engineers for 9/11 Truth: ‹ae911truth.org› (last visited March 8, 2013)
9   Pilots for 9/11 Truth: ‹pilotsfor911truth.org› (last visited March 8, 2013)
10 Killtown's (pseudonym) webpage: ‹killtown.blogspot.de/› (last visited March 8, 2013)
11 The Complete 911 Timeline: ‹historycommons.org› (last visited March 8, 2013)

None of the aforementioned researchers, nor myself, could achieve what we do, without drawing on Paul's gold mine.

I feel deeply indebted to all aforementioned persons, to Dr. Ludwig Watzal, who was kind enough to provide helpful comments regarding the original manuscript and to others, unnamed, who have contributed significantly and sometimes against heavy odds, to the deconstruction of the official myths and deceptions surrounding 9/11 and to our understanding of the phenomenon designated as "false-flag" or "synthetic" terrorism.

After these words, readers might rightfully wonder what one more book on 9/11 can add to these efforts. While deferring with deep respect to the work of the aforementioned and other unnamed researchers, I believe that the approach followed herein does not duplicate what has been done but complements or corroborates it.

Some aspects of 9/11 have been extensively investigated. These include particularly the destruction of the Twin Towers of the WTC and of building WTC 7 by explosives and the failure of the 9/11 Commission to establish the facts on 9/11. This book deals with three aspects of 9/11 that have remained less investigated: The boarding of the four flights, the phone calls, and the flight paths of the four 9/11 flights. The inquiry takes the form of three questions:

1. Is there concrete evidence that Muslim hijackers boarded the four flights of 9/11?

2. What is the reason for the numerous anomalies and contradictions encountered in analyzing the phone calls that were reportedly made from the four flights?

3. Did the four flights crash at the known landmarks, and if not, what happened to them?

The two first questions will be treated exhaustively, leaving no stone unturned. Much of the underlying research will be published for the first time. I will provide definite answers to these questions. The third question cannot yet be treated in a definitive manner, absent access to information suppressed by the authorities. The work herein merely extends original research by Pilots for 9/11 Truth and others.

Although no great admirer of President George W. Bush, I believe that he unwittingly made an important point when he said at the United Nations on November 10, 2001:

> "We must speak the truth about terror. Let us never tolerate outrageous conspiracy theories concerning the attacks of September the 11th; malicious lies that attempt to shift the blame away from the terrorists, themselves, away from the guilty. To inflame ethnic hatred is to advance the cause of terror."

The events of 9/11 were obviously a massive act of terror. It was used to "inflame ethnic hatred" of Americans and Europeans against Arabs and Muslims and "advance the cause of [state] terror" as reflected in the wars conducted by the US government and NATO states against Afghanistan, Iraq, Libya and their own populations. For that reason, we "must speak the truth" about terror and "never tolerate outrageous conspiracy theories concerning the attacks of September the 11th." The primary purpose of this book is, therefore, to heed President Bush's good advice

The first central tenet of the official 9/11 account is that the mass-murder of 9/11 was executed by 19 Muslims, acting pursuant to an alleged Islamic terrorist conspiracy plotted in Afghanistan. In Part I of this book, entitled *The Foundational Myth*, I will describe its political birth (chapter 1) and attempt to demolish it by demonstrating that there exists no evidence that America was attacked by foreign hijackers (chapter 2).

Numerous readers might still wonder what they are to make out of the crashed airliners, one of which was seen by the entire world, on television, as it crashed into the South Tower of the WTC. Part II provides evidence that the US authorities failed to identify the debris of the four 9/11 airliners which departed as flights AA11, UA175, AA77 and UA93 and produced a dubious transcript of the cockpit voice recorder from flight UA93. At least two of the four flights will be shown to be airborne past crash time at great distance from their alleged crash sites. Circumstantial evidence suggests, furthermore, that each of the four flights was doubled by a "phantom" flight.

The lack of concrete evidence regarding the boarding of the four flights, and the failure to identify their debris, justify an examination of the phone calls made by passengers and crew members to report hijackings. Part III of the book constitutes an exhaustive analysis of all known phone calls reportedly made from "hijacked aircraft." This voluminous analysis leads to one irresistible conclusion: That no real hijackings took place.

Part IV, the shortest of this book, attempts to explain what may have really happened with regard to the four flights. This explanation will have to be regarded as my best hypothesis.

The absence of hijackers does not mean that no aircraft crashed on 9/11. It only means that if aircraft actually crashed on 9/11, it is not known what type of aircraft they were and how they were made to crash. The theory according to which four trained pilots might wish to simultaneously sacrifice their lives in times of peace and kill thousands of innocent strangers for some vague idea, defies belief. There is, in fact, no concrete evidence that any of the 19 alleged hijackers had suicidal tendencies or terrorist intentions. Whatever has been presented by the US authorities about their alleged intentions remains highly speculative.

If pilots did not steer aircraft into buildings, such an operation could have been accomplished by remotely controlling aircraft. Such technology has existed for decades.

A practical note for readers

The Memoranda For the Record (MFRs) and FBI 302 forms referred to in this book are, for the most part, found in the 9/11 Commission Records, stored at the National Archives (NARA) [see ‹www.archives.gov/research/9-11/commission-memoranda.html›]. Where a document lacks a MFR or 302 serial number, its location (Team and Box number) be provided in order to expedite the reader's access to the document.

Following a source, the reader will find in most cases a number preceded by the #-sign. This number refers to the document number in my personal archive. Most of these documents are also posted at ‹www.aldeilis.net/english/fake/nnn›, where 'nnn' is the given number. I also maintain a paper copy of virtually all MFR's and FBI 302 forms referred to in the book, with few exceptions that are clearly indicated.

Some methodological observations

The overwhelming majority of sources for this study can be classified into two categories: (1) documents and statements issued by the U.S government, its agencies, its officials, members of Congress, courts and private entities acting at the behest of government authorities; and (2) reports from mainstream media. At times, credible monographs and blogs are cited.

Without access to authenticated documents held by U.S government agencies, and without the ability to forensically examine them, the authenticity of such documents and their *integrity* can only be inferred from indices.

As for the *credibility* of statements found in reports or documents, I assign more probative value to statements made on record by identified individuals than to indirect attributions. Statements made by unidentified individuals will be referred herein, as needed, but will be treated with the appropriate circumspection.

A particular problem arises with respect to FBI documents, including so-called 302 forms, which "report on and summarize an FBI agent's interview of a witness".[1] These documents are never authenticated by a signature or by disclosing the names of the interviewing agent(s). In many cases, even interviewees' names are redacted. These reports do not represent a verbatim transcription of

---

1   *United States v Skilling*, 554 F.3d 529, 577-78 (5th Cir. 2009) (describing these Forms and noting that the government disclosed them in that case)

what witnesses have said. They are thus not considered as "statements" by the witnesses within the meaning of the Jencks Act.[1] They consist of an edited version of the interview and contain what the interviewing agent noted down during the interview from what the witness had said. Interviewees are not given an opportunity to review the accuracy and completeness of this summary. Readers of these reports cannot, therefore, ascertain what questions were asked by the interviewing agent(s), how the questions were formulated, what was not asked, and what the witnesses actually stated. Omissions of every kind are legion in these reports. Some omissions are glaring, even to uninformed readers.[2] While such documents *may* represent, in substance, what witnesses have told the agent(s), the reformulation of witnesses' statements in summary form and the lack of transparency regarding the elaboration of the reports leaves a wide margin for omissions, and erroneous or deliberate misrepresentation. Apart from these overt deficiencies, there exists no reason to presume the integrity and truthfulness of documents produced by the FBI.

It must be added that it has been extremely difficult to obtain through Freedom of Information (FOIA) requests the release of even the most innocuous 302 forms regarding the 9/11 events, namely documents that do not relate in any way to security matters or that would breach privacy.

It cannot be excluded that some 302 forms may represent outright forgeries. Yet, referring to the publicly released 302s allows independent investigators to build their case on official documents. Some 302s also contain facts overlooked by the censors. Using official documents provides, additionally, a baseline on which an analysis can be grafted.

In order to verify statements included in FBI 302 documents, statements quoted by media or statements made to the staff of the 9/11 Commission, I have tried to locate witnesses. Where I succeeded in locating and contacting witnesses, they often expressed apprehension to talk, or even to confirm their erstwhile testimonies.

Anyone attempting to investigate possible US government complicity in the events of 9/11 is essentially engaging in *intelligence analysis*, namely sifting large amount of data, including deceptive data, in order to discover what is relevant. James R. Schlesinger, former US Secretary of Defense, and thus a person with the proper background, explained to a Congressional Committee in 2004 the difficulties facing *intelligence analysis*:

---

1   Title 18, Part II, Chapter 223, $3500. Demands for production of statements and reports of witnesses

2   Here just one example: Document FBI 302-86822 of September 18, 2001, contains an interview with Henry J. Wnuk, pilot for Northwest Airlines regarding an occurrence aboard Northwestern flight no. 36. The report does not mention on which date the reported event occurred.

[I]ntelligence is inherently a difficult business. Intelligence targets naturally seek to conceal what they are doing, and have a strong tendency to mislead you. A central problem in intelligence is to discern the true signals[1] amidst the noise. The relevant signals may be very weak...Countless events are being recorded each day, and countless events are failing to be recorded, or are deliberately hidden. Moreover, false signals are deliberately planted.[2]

A further methodological observation relates to the concept of "intent," which applies directly to the issue of 9/11. Intent cannot usually be determined on the basis of self-incriminating statements made by suspects. Statements by suspects and apparent confessions are not reliable, even if they appear to incriminate the speaker. They can be made for a variety of reasons and purposes, including maltreatment, threats and intimidation, or conversely, financial or other inducements, as well as the urge of suspects to brag or be viewed as heroes. Sometimes suspects may believe that they are guilty while actually being innocent. Courts generally infer intent from the overall circumstances, of which statements made by suspects are only one part. Although this book is mainly concerned with concrete evidence, or the lack of it, there will be cases where inferential reasoning can help explain puzzling facts. Where the case arises, presentation of concrete evidence and inferential reasoning will be clearly distinguished.

As will be noted throughout this book, even a cursory examination of the 9/11 case would reveal to the student a bewildering number of anomalies, contradictions and unanswered questions that in the language of intelligence analysis may amount to "noise." I have aimed to draw a distinction between noise and significant information.

In mathematics, equations with one or several unknowns are solved by various mathematical operations. The solution may be a single number or a set of numbers. When attempting to solve a criminal mystery, formal operations are also used to discover the unknowns. These operations include deduction, induction, tests of logical coherence, tests of reliability and plausibility, sensitivity tests, Occam's razor, etc. Where major pieces of evidence are either inaccessible or have been destroyed, the solution to a criminal mystery may not yield a precise answer, but can provide an approximation, adequate for policy purposes. As will be shown herein, the mass-murder of 9/11 may never be solved to a sufficient degree of precision necessary to make the case for a criminal conviction of any individual participant. However, it can be solved to an adequate degree of preci-

---

1   By the term "signals" the speaker is evidently not referring to a limited technical meaning, as in "electronic signals" but to the informational value of any data item, regardless of the form in which it is obtained.

2   James R. Schlesinger, in "Hearings before the Committee on Armed Services," United States Senate, August 16 and 17, 2004 (Senate Hearing 108-875)

sion for questioning the legitimacy of the institutions who have prevented the establishment of the truth on 9/11.

I wish, therefore, to follow Nafeez Ahmed's wise approach to the presentation of facts on such a highly sensitive issue. Introducing his own study he wrote:

> Due to the controversial nature of the subject matter, I have chosen quite deliberately to attempt to grant as much space as possible to my sources to allow them, effectively, to speak for themselves. Simultaneously, I have avoided overemphasis on my own personal conclusions, preferring instead to assess rigorously the factual record and its most immediate implications. The method minimizes the possibility that I have misrepresented crucial data that is often stunningly at odds with the conventional wisdom. Thus, although I attempt to outline what seem to me the most obvious deductions from the available facts, the actual value of my work is in the facts themselves. The readers, ultimately, are free to draw their own overarching conclusions.[1]

---

1   Ahmed, Op. cit. pxiii

Chapter 1. Establishing The 9/11 Myth

A unique, unambiguous, official account of the events that took place on September 11, 2001, emerged within days. It can be summarized in the following terms from numerous reports issued by the three branches of the US government and by the media:

> On the morning of September 11, 2001, four civilian airlines with dozens of passengers and crew, designated as flights AA11, UA175, AA77 and UA93, were hijacked by teams of four or five Muslim fanatics. Each team included one trained pilot. The hijackers took control of the airliners and flew a Boeing 767 assigned to flight AA11 into the North Tower of the WTC in New York, another Boeing 767 assigned to flight UA175 into the South Tower and a Boeing 757 assigned to flight AA77 into the Pentagon. The fourth airliner, a Boeing 757 assigned to flight UA93, presumed to have been destined to crash on the White House, did not reach its target. It crashed in an empty field in Pennsylvania after the passengers rose up and tried to seize control of the aircraft.
>
> As a result of the impact of the aircraft on the Twin Towers and the ensuing fires, both towers collapsed soon afterwards onto their own footprint, causing massive deaths. Almost 3,000 people died in the attacks. Osama bin Laden and his al-Qaeda network were shortly thereafter blamed for conceiving, planning, financing and coordinating the attacks.

Every major historical event is sooner or later narrated in a simplified and easily apprehended manner. What distinguishes the official narrative of 9/11 from most historical accounts is the surprising speed with which it took its definitive form. This narrative was not elaborated on the base of a forensic investigation but by politicians. It was the type of evidence the US government had presented on alleged Iraqi weapons of mass-destruction.

(1) Osama bin Laden was named after 15 minutes

The name of Osama bin Laden, as a suspect, surfaced on CBS News within 15 minutes of the crash of the second aircraft into the South Tower. His name remained from that time grafted onto the semi-official account of 9/11, notwithstanding the lack of any concrete evidence linking him to the mass-murder.

(2) Bush determined within twenty minutes that "America is under attack"

Approximately 20 minutes after being informed that a second aircraft had crashed into the World Trade Center (WTC), President George W. Bush announced to the world that an "apparent terrorist attack on our country" had taken place.[1] This expression implied that the United States had been attacked from abroad. Such wording was not in any way self-evident, for at the time neither President Bush nor his aides possessed any evidence, whatsoever, that the two aircraft that hit the WTC were piloted by foreigners, let alone that the aircraft came from abroad.

(3) WTC demise explained within six hours

The official explanation for the demise of both Twin Towers of the WTC in New York was established within six hours of these events, unprecedented as they were in the history of high-rise buildings. When asked in a press conference on September 11, 2001, at 2:30 p.m. EST, whether the demise of the skyscrapers had been caused by the planes "or by something else," New York Mayor Rudy Giuliani answered, muttering:

> "We believe, we believe that it was caused by the after-effects of the, of the planes hitting the...buildings. We don't know, we don't know if there were additional explosions"[2]

Experts invited by national television networks to comment felt surprisingly confident in explaining—within hours—why the Twin Towers disintegrated, although they had no precedent to rely upon. Jim DeStefano, from the National Council of Structural Engineers, for example, explained to CNN at approximately 4:20 P.M (EST)—relying exclusively on what he had seen on television—that

1   *CNN*, September 11, 2001, at 9:30 AM, September 11 Television Archive, ‹http://archive.org/details/sept_11_tv_archive› (last visited March 8, 2013)

2   Ibid. at 2:37 PM

the impact [of the aircraft] was sufficient to cause damage to the columns and the ... systems supporting the building. That couples with the fire raging and the high temperatures softening the structural steel that precipitated a destabilization of the columns and clearly the columns buckled at the lower floors causing the building to collapse.[1]

(4) Main "facts" established by Congressional vote within 24 hours

On September 12, 2001, shortly after 10:00 a.m., the following Draft Resolution, containing multiple factual allegations, was presented by Senator Daschle to the US Congress:

H.J. Res. 61

Whereas on September 11, 2001, terrorists hijacked and destroyed four civilian aircraft, crashing two of them into the towers of the World Trade Center in New York City, and a third into the Pentagon outside Washington, D.C.;

Whereas thousands of innocent Americans were killed and injured as a result of these attacks, including the passengers and crew of the four aircraft, workers in the World Trade Center and in the Pentagon, rescue workers, and bystanders;

Whereas these attacks destroyed both towers of the World Trade Center, as well as adjacent buildings, and seriously damaged the Pentagon; and

Whereas these attacks were by far the deadliest terrorist attacks ever launched against the United States, and, by targeting symbols of American strength and success, clearly were intended to intimidate our Nation and weaken its resolve: Now, therefore, be it

Resolved by the Senate and House of Representatives of the United States of America in Congress assembled, That Congress—

- condemns in the strongest possible terms the terrorists who planned and carried out the September 11, 2001, attacks against the United States, as well as their sponsors;

- extends its deepest condolences to the victims of these heinous and cowardly attacks, as well as to their families, friends, and loved ones;

- is certain that the people of the United States will stand united as our Nation begins the process of recovering and rebuilding in the aftermath of these tragic acts;

---

1 Ibid. at 4:20 PM

- commends the heroic actions of the rescue workers, volunteers, and State and local officials who responded to these tragic events with courage, determination, and skill;

- declares that these premeditated attacks struck not only at the people of America, but also at the symbols and structures of our economic and military strength, and that the United States is entitled to respond under international law;

- thanks those foreign leaders and individuals who have expressed solidarity with the United States in the aftermath of the attacks, and asks them to continue to stand with the United States in the war against international terrorism;

- commits to support increased resources in the war to eradicate terrorism;

- supports the determination of the President, in close consultation with Congress, to bring to justice and punish the perpetrators of these attacks as well as their sponsors; and

- declares that September 12, 2001, shall be a National Day of Unity and Mourning, and that when Congress adjourns today, it stands adjourned out of respect to the victims of the terrorist attacks.

In the debate that ensued, Senator Lott said:

> I just want to say also—and I will have more to say about the resolution in a moment—how much I appreciate the work yesterday that was totally nonpartisan, totally cooperative from the leadership on the Democratic side of the aisle and with the House of Representatives. That was the right thing to do. It was done. Senator Daschle was there. He made decisions that were appropriate after consultation—and some of them were tough—that even sometimes had to be modified later because events kept changing. I express my appreciation to him for that.[1]

Though expressed in deliberately vague terms, Senator Lott's statement indicated that the draft Resolution had been already in the works on the very day of the events. He did not reveal, however, what "tough" decisions Senator Daschle had to make and what modifications were made to those decisions.

At first, the Resolution appears reasonable. A detailed analysis of the Resolution reveals, however, a number of surprising features.

The Resolution includes factual allegations for which the drafters and members of Congress could not at the time possess reliable evidence, namely:

- that the events of the previous day constituted "attacks against the United States" (Operative paragraph 1);

- that terrorists had "hijacked" and "destroyed" four civilian aircraft (Preambular paragraphs 1 and 2);

---

1   Congressional Record, 107th Congress (2001-2002), September 12, 2001, page S9283, #1060

- that the "attacks" attributed to these terrorists "destroyed both towers of the World Trade Center"(Preambular paragraph 3); and

- that the operation was intended "to intimidate our Nation and weaken its resolve" (Preambular paragraph 4).

A perusal of the debates in Congress on September 12, 2001, reveals that no member of Congress asked for evidence in support of the above allegations.

"Attacks against the United States"

By this expression, the Congress excluded from the outset, and without the slightest reason, the possibility that the operation might have been of domestic origin. Yet, at the time the Resolution was drafted and adopted, there was no evidence of any foreign involvement in the operation.

"Terrorists hijacked and destroyed four civilian aircraft"

During the morning hours of September 11, 2001, numerous individuals re-ported in phone calls that they were sitting in aircraft that had been hijacked. There was no apparent reason to distrust the reports by the recipients of the calls. During the morning two airliners crashed into the Twin Towers in New York City, one airliner crashed into the Pentagon and a fourth airliner is said to have crashed on a field near Shanksville (PA).

While it was unwise for members of Congress to adopt factual statements regarding the events before these had been investigated, they could be forgiven for concluding in good faith, on the basis of the phone calls, that airliners had been "hijacked" by "terrorists."

It was, however, premature to claim that the "terrorists" had destroyed civil-ian aircraft, because at the time it was not yet determined which aircraft had crashed where. American Airlines, for instance, issued a press release at 5:56 p.m. on the day of Operation 9/11. In this press release the company confirms that "two American jets...were lost in apparent terrorist attacks," yet the location where and the reason why they were lost is not mentioned. As shown in a later chapter, general confusion existed on 9/11 regarding the number and identities of allegedly hijacked planes. The claim that "terrorists" had "destroyed" four air-craft by flying them at the known landmarks was thus, at best, a supposition, not a proven fact.

"The attacks by the terrorists destroyed both towers of the World Trade Center"

This allegation rested on a chain of inferences. First, it was assumed that terrorists had "hijacked" aircraft; on that basis it was further assumed that they "destroyed" aircraft by flying them into the WTC; and finally it was assumed that the impact of the airliners (and the ensuing fires) *caused* the destruction of both towers. The problem here was not only the reliance on a set of inferences, but that persons endowed with normal intelligence would consider it possible for three skyscrapers (the North and South Towers and WTC 7) to undergo complete collapse due to fire in a single day. Those members of Congress who watched the television coverage could not have failed to notice that some commentators compared the demise of the buildings to a "controlled demolition" with explosives and that some witnesses interviewed during these TV broadcasts actually reported having experienced, heard or seen numerous explosions shortly before or during the collapse. Such observations, let alone the complete collapse of WTC 7 which was not hit by an aircraft, should have been sufficient to deter Congress members from jumping to conclusions about the cause for the buildings' demise. Determining the causality of the Twin Towers' demise in a congressional resolution was not only uncalled for, but incomprehensible, unless the inclusion of this determination was prompted by political considerations.

"The attacks were intended to intimidate our Nation and weaken its resolve"

By this factual allegation the drafters went one step further: They purported to have the Congress actually read the minds of the unidentified perpetrators and determine their motives. This was, evidently, beyond their capabilities. The inclusion of such an allegation, again, suggests the existence of a hidden purpose, which bears no relation to the actual facts.

Operative paragraph (8)

According to operative paragraph (8) of the Resolution, the Congress declared its support for "the determination of the President, in close consultation with Congress, to bring to justice and punish the perpetrators of these attacks as well as their sponsors." This paragraph, which appears innocuous on its face, contains two puzzling features.

First, it should be noted that by this provision, the Congress did not commit itself to support efforts "to bring to justice and punish" the perpetrators and their sponsors. It merely declared its support for the "determination of the President, in close consultation with Congress" to do so, whatever that means. One is entitled to wonder why this provision was couched in such a convoluted language. Why didn't the Congress, for example,

> demand that no stone remain unturned in efforts to identify, prosecute and punish the perpetrators, planners, facilitators, and sponsors of the attacks; and pledge its determination to provide to the Government all means necessary for this task?

The second puzzling fact is the relegation of this provision to the penulti-mate position in the Resolution, instead of placing it directly in the second posi-tion, where it would logically belong. It leaves the observer with the impression that the drafters did not wish to emphasize law-enforcement aspects, possibly in view of the decision by the White House to frame Operation 9/11 as an "act of war." That hypothesis finds support in statements by several members of Con-gress, made during the debates of September 12, 2001, who warned against treat-ing the events of 9/11 as a crime.

A hidden agenda?

There was nothing extraordinary in the Congress condemning the mass-murder of 9/11, express its sympathy to the victims and their families and com-mend the valiant efforts of rescue teams and first responders. Numerous govern-ments and international bodies did so in the following days without suggesting how, by whom and why the mass-murder was executed. What distinguished the congressional resolution from numerous similar resolutions was the specificity of the factual allegations it included.

Congressional resolutions do not emerge in a void. Each resolution has a drafting history and is adopted to serve a purpose. The drafting history of the above resolution is not known. It was only alluded to in Senator Lott's address.

One must, therefore, presume that the inclusion of specific allegations in the above resolution had a *purpose*. The most plausible explanation for including these factual allegations is, that the US government wanted to cast in stone the foundations of the 9/11 account. Securing a Congressional imprimatur to that ac-count and linking it to the ensuing war, ensured that questioning the official ac-count would be regarded as a betrayal of the victims and as unpatriotic. Indeed, despite ample time for debates on September 12, 2001, members of Congress dis-played a surprising lack of curiosity about the actual events of the previous day: No member of Congress demanded concrete evidence in support of the factual determinations he or she was asked to approve. Instead, one after the other rose to pledge his or her allegiance to the US flag, invoked the grace of God and ex-pressed unreserved loyalty to the President, a scene reminiscent of a ritual from bygone days.

(5) FBI releases the names of the alleged hijackers

On September 14, 2001, the FBI released the names of 19 individuals whom it *identified* as hijackers aboard the four airliners that crashed on September 11, 2001, into the North and South Towers of the WTC in New York, the Pentagon, and Stony Creek Township, Pennsylvania.[1] For unknown reasons, the original press release no longer appears on the website of the FBI, having been replaced by a virtually equivalent press release dated one day earlier.[2] No reason was given for this replacement. While the 19 "hijackers" are listed there as "identified," for many of them no birth date is given, giving rise to the question how these individuals could be identified.

(6) Paul Wolfowitz's evasive answer

On September 26, 2001, Deputy Secretary of Defense Paul Wolfowitz was asked at a press conference held at the NATO headquarters in Brussels,[3] "Sir, two weeks into the crisis, is the United States incapable of telling its allies precisely what the findings are in regard to *evidence* related to Osama bin Laden or other terrorists that you might think were behind the attack?" Wolfowitz' answer: "I think the *evidence* is there for the whole world to see. I think many of the people in this room watched *it* live on television, watched the two towers of the World Trade Center coming down. If you want evidence I'll be happy to—oh, I can't, I guess. The FBI controls it."[4]

(7) FBI releases photographs of the alleged hijackers

On September 27, 2001, the FBI released photographs alleged to be of the 19 individuals mentioned in the September 14 press release. These individuals were no longer designated as "identified" but merely as "*believed* to be the hijackers of the four airliners that crashed on September 11, 2001, into the North and South Towers of the World Trade Center in New York, the Pentagon, and Stony Creek Township, Pennsylvania."[5] Emphasizing the by now tentative nature of the identification, the press release added the following caveat:

> It should be noted that attempts to confirm the true identities of these individuals are still under way.[6]

Apparently these "attempts to confirm the true identities" of the alleged hijackers are still "under way" as these lines are written, for this press release has not been superseded in any way by the FBI. As will be shown in this book, it is

---

1   US Department of Justice, FBI Press Release, *FBI National Press Office*, September 14, 2001
2   FBI Announces List of 19 Hijackers, *FBI National Press Office*, September 13, 2001, #065 (emphasis added)
3   Press Conference of Paul Wolfowitz, *NATO headquarters*, September 26, 2001, #578
4   Ibid. Emphasis added
5   "The FBI releases 19 photographs of individuals believed to be the hijackers of the four airliners that crashed on September 11, 2001," *FBI National Press Office*, September 27, 2001. #002
6   Ibid.

far from proven that these individuals had anything to do with the mass-murder of 9/11.

(8) No known links between the alleged hijackers and Afghanistan

On September 28, 2001, Attorney General John Ashcroft was asked whether the US was able "to trace any of the 19 hijackers back to Afghanistan." His response: "I don't think I'm capable of answering that question."[1]

(9) The US government: "We have no obligation to prove our case"

In a message sent by the State Department on October 1, 2001, to all US embassies around the world, embassy officials were requested "to [orally] brief senior host government officials" about al Qaeda, Osama bin Laden and the events of 9/11 and "NOT leave the document (with the foreign officials)."[2] The message also emphasizes that "the United States is not obliged in any way to make any kind of showing as a prerequisite or precondition to the exercise of its right of self-defense under Article 51 of the UN Charter, whether now or in the future".[3] This convoluted formulation means in ordinary English that the US authorities declare themselves under no obligation to prove their case to the world and reserve themselves the right to provide bogus evidence to justify their wars.

(10) Donald Rumsfeld's evasive answer

On October 2, 2001, before he embarked upon a tour of the Middle-East, Secretary of Defense Donald Rumsfeld was asked in a Press briefing: "Will you be sharing with the leaders [you plan to visit] any evidence of Osama bin Laden's connection with the [9/11] attacks?" He answered:

> I think that I will not be sharing the evidence. I would be happy to, but I think that has been done amply. The evidence of the attack is on television every day. The linkages between the terrorist networks involved are on television every day. And it strikes me that anyone who is slightly interested has a very clear idea of what took place the fact that a terrorist organization that's being harbored by more than one country, and has relationships with other terrorist organizations, was directly involved. I don't

---

1   "Transcript from Press Briefing," Attorney General Ashcroft and FBI Director Mueller, FBI Headquarters, September 28, 2001, #576

2   "Declassified fax from the US Department of State to US embassies around the world," October 1, 2001, Nr. 170698, Subject: "September 11: Working together to fight the plague of global terrorism and the case against al-Qa'ida," #279

3   Ibid.

know if we need any more evidence, or do I think that anyone is asking for any more evidence, except the Taliban.[1]

Rumsfeld's answer does not need comments.

(11) US government does not formally link Afghanistan to 9/11

Unnoticed by most observers, when President Bush addressed the American people on October 7, 2001, to announce the initiation of the bombing campaign against Afghanistan, he did not link that country in any way to the events of 9/11. These events were not mentioned in his speech. The reason he offered for his war was the alleged refusal of the Taliban government to "close terrorist training camps; hand over leaders of the al Qaeda network; and return all foreign nationals, including American citizens, unjustly detained in your country."[2]

On the same day—October 7, 2001—the US Representative to the United Nations John Negroponte delivered a letter to the President of the UN Security Council[3] in which he listed the reasons for what he described as US "military operations" against Afghanistan. In that letter the representative of the United States claimed that the mass-murder of 9/11:

"was specifically designed to maximize the loss of life";

"resulted in the death of more than five thousand persons, including nationals of 81 countries"[4]; and that

"my government has obtained clear and compelling information that the Al-Qaeda organization, which is supported by the Taliban regime in Afghanistan, had a central role in the attacks."

Ignoring the exaggerations included in that statement,[5] readers are invited to take note that the US did not herein state that the mass-murder of 9/11 had been conceived, planned, directed or financed from Afghanistan, or that the Taliban government had in any way supported this deadly operation. This official letter to the highest executive body of the United Nations did not include evidence linking Afghanistan to 9/11. Donald Rumsfeld admitted in a press conference on October 7, 2001, that the Taliban who ruled Afghanistan at the time, "do not have armies, navies and air forces" and could thus not threaten the security of the United States.[6] The bombing campaign against Afghanistan was thus a plain

---

1   "Secretary Rumsfeld En Route to Saudi Arabia," *Press Briefing*, October 2, 2001, #574
2   George W. Bush, "Address to the Nation" (on the Use of Force in Afghanistan), October 7, 2001, #1059
3   Letter of John Negroponte to the President of the Security Council, October 7, 2001. #569
4   These figures were deliberately inflated.
5   The number of victims was approximately 3,000 and the number of nationalities was less than fifty.
6   Transcript of Defense Secretary Donald Rumsfeld's news conference with Gen. Richard Myers, chairman of the Joint Chiefs of Staff, *The Washington Post*, October 7, 2001, #1036

act of aggression that should have triggered action under Chapter VII of the UN Charter and constituted a crime of aggression under customary international law.[1] NATO members and other governments are undoubtedly aware that the US failed to prove a link between Afghanistan and 9/11 and that it acted unlawfully, but for political expediency, they have hitherto failed to spell out this blatant violation of the international order and to undertake appropriate measures against the violator.[2]

(12) The FBI admits possessing no evidence that Osama bin Laden was involved in 9/11

On June 5, 2006, a journalist by the name of Ed Haas contacted the FBI after having noticed that the Wanted poster for Osama bin Laden posted by the FBI on its website did not mention bin Laden's suspected links to 9/11.[3] Haas asked for an explanation. Rex Tomb, Chief of Investigative Publicity for the FBI responded, "The reason why 9/11 is not mentioned on Osama bin Laden's Most Wanted page is because the FBI has no hard evidence connecting bin Laden to 9/11."[4] This answer explains why US leaders refrained from directly accusing Osama bin Laden over 9/11. One has to read twice the FBI answer in order to fully digest its meaning. As was to be expected, most corporate media suppressed Haas's report as a news item.

Conclusion

Students of international affairs will already at this point realize that the definite official account on 9/11 was established politically before the facts were determined, that the US government attacked Afghanistan without any justification, that the US government has neither accused Osama bin Laden over 9/11 nor determined the identities of the alleged hijackers, and that allies of the US have closed their eyes to these facts. These conclusions alone justify a thorough and independent investigation of the mass-murder committed on 9/11.

---

1   Wikipedia: War_of_aggression
2   Hans-Christian Andersen's tale "The Emperor's New Clothes" applies perfectly to this conduct by the world's governments.
3   FBI: Usama bin Laden (FBI Ten Most Wanted Fugitives), Poster on FBI website revised in November 2001 (i.e. after 9/11), #910
4   Ed Haas, "FBI says, it has 'no hard evidence connecting Bin Laden to 9/11'," *Information Clearing House*, June 18, 2006, #853

Chapter 2. Shattering The Myth Of 19 Muslim Hijackers

Introduction

The official account of 9/11 is based on a hijacking narrative according to which 19 individuals, whose names and photographs have been posted on the website of the FBI,[1] *boarded* aircraft designated as flights AA11, UA175, AA77 and UA93 on the morning of September 11, 2001, hijacked those aircraft and crashed the aircraft in a suicide operation into symbolic landmarks in the United States.

According to the official account an aircraft designated as flight AA11 was flown into the North Tower of the WTC in New York; shortly thereafter an aircraft designated as flight UA175 was flown into the South Tower of the WTC. At 9:37 a.m. an aircraft designated as flight AA77 is said to have impacted the Pentagon in Washington, D.C. As for the fourth aircraft, designated as flight UA93, it is said to have crashed in an empty field near Shanksville, Pennsylvania, after the passengers had risen up against the alleged hijackers and attempted to retake control of the aircraft. It was later surmised that the aircraft was intended to crash on the White House or the Capitol.

Within hours of the operation, the FBI confiscated all known CCTV recordings and interviewed dozens of airline and airport employees who could provide information about what they had experienced on that morning before and during boarding. It must therefore be assumed that all *available* evidence about the boarding of the four aircraft is stored in the archives of the FBI.

---

1   "The FBI releases 19 photographs...,", Op. cit., #002

The present chapter deals with one, and only one, question, namely: Were the individuals designated by the US government as the hijackers of 9/11 present at the scene of the crime? In other words, did they board the four aircraft that allegedly crashed with passengers on that day.

Shortly after the FBI released names and photographs of the alleged hijackers, questions about their identities began to emerge. The family of Hamza Alghamdi, one of the alleged hijackers, said the photo released by the FBI "has no resemblance to him at all."[1] CNN showed a picture of another alleged hijacker, identified as Saeed Alghamdi. That man, a pilot, was alive and working in Tunisia.[2] The photograph of a Saudi pilot by the name of Waleed Al Shehri was released by the FBI as one of the alleged hijackers: he protested his innocence from Casablanca, Morocco.[3] Two people with the name of Abdulaziz Alomari presented themselves, surprised to see their names on the FBI list of suspected hijackers. One of them, a Saudi engineer, said he lost his passport while studying in Denver, Colorado, in 1995. Of the FBI list, he said: "The name is my name and the birth date is the same as mine. But I am not the one who bombed the World Trade Center in New York."[4] Another Abdulaziz Alomari was found working as a pilot with Saudi Airlines.[5] Salem Alhazmi, also listed by the FBI as an alleged hijacker, was indignant at being named as a suspect for a mass murder. He said he was working in petrochemical plant in Yanbu (Saudi Arabia).[6] Abdul Rahman Al-Haznawi, brother of another suspect, said, "There is no similarity between the photo published [on Thursday] and my brother." He said he does not believe his brother was involved in the crime: "He never had any such intention."[7] Gaafar Allagany, the Saudi government's chief spokesman in the United States, said in an interview in Washington that the hijackers probably stole the identities of legitimate Saudi pilots.[8] The FBI disregarded these stories and maintained the names and photographs it originally posted on its website as those "believed to be the hijackers" of 9/11,[9] including those of living individuals. The 9/11 Commission did not address these conflicting identifications. The passive and tentative formulation used by the FBI in attributing the crime to particular perpetrators remains the official position of the agency.

1   Caryle Murphy and David B. Ottaway, "Some Light Shed on Saudi Suspects," *The Washington Post*, September 25, 2001, #1061
2   "Hijack 'suspects' alive and well," *BBC*, September 23, 2001, #231
3   Ibid.
4   Nick Hopkins, "False Identities Mislead FBI," *The Guardian*, September 21, 2001, #538
5   Ibid.
6   Ibid.
7   Jamal Khashoggi and Badr Al-Nayyef, "Hanjour family denies Hani's involvement in crime," *Arab News*, October 1, 2001, #100
8   Kevin Cullen and Anthony Shahid, "Hijackers may have taken Saudi identities," *Boston Globe*, September 15, 2001, #950
9   "The FBI releases 19 photographs....," Op. cit., #002

One basic goal of a criminal investigation is to identify the perpetrators. In order to prove that particular individuals could have hijacked an aircraft, it must be first demonstrated that they boarded that particular aircraft. In order to demonstrate this, the following five classes of evidence should have been produced by the US authorities in September 2001 or shortly thereafter:

1. *Authenticated* passenger lists (or flight manifests), listing the names of all the passengers and crew members, including those suspected of hijacking;

2. *Authenticated* boarding cards (or their detached coupons), on which the names of all the passengers and crew members figure, including those suspected of hijacking;

3. *Authenticated* security videos from the airports, which depict the passengers (and the alleged hijackers) arriving at the airport, in front of check-in counters, passing security checkpoints and boarding the aircraft;

4. *Sworn testimonies* of personnel who attended the boarding of the aircraft;

5. Formal identification of the bodies or bodily remains from the crash sites, including *chain-of-custody reports*.

It is, however, important to remember that even if such evidence had been produced and found reliable, it would not necessarily prove that these 19 individuals had perpetrated the crime attributed to them. They could have been innocent passengers on those flights, or patsies in a plot of which they knew nothing. If it is proved that they were present at the scene of the crime, they *could* in theory have perpetrated the crime.

The scope of this chapter is limited to examining whether the US government has produced the five classes of minimal evidence mentioned above and if so, whether that evidence is admissible, relevant and compelling. If such evidence does not exist or is deemed to lack credibility, it is likely that these individuals did not board the aircraft and that, consequently, no "Islamic hijackings" took place.

In theory, it is impossible to prove a negative. It is thus impossible to prove that the evidence in support of the official allegations does not exist in some hidden government safe.

In the present case, the US authorities claim that 19 named individuals boarded four aircraft on 9/11 and committed mass-murder. In law, the *burden of proof* lies with a party that levels accusations. The US government could not discharge its burden of proof, if it failed to produce *clear and convincing evidence* in support of its accusations. In the present chapter I go beyond demonstrating that there is a "reasonable doubt" as to the complicity of the 19 alleged hijackers, for I intend to show that the evidence produced by the US government does not even reach *probable cause*, relatively easy test used in the United States to determine whether a search, or an arrest, is warranted.

(1) No authenticated passenger lists

The primary source used by airlines after aircraft crashes to locate the next-of-kin of victims is the passenger list (also designated as the *flight manifest*). A passenger list is also a legal document proving—for insurance purposes—that particular individuals boarded an aircraft. This is why airlines are required to check the identities of passengers who board the aircraft. In order to serve as legal documents, passenger lists must be duly authenticated by those responsible for their accuracy.

With regard to the four 9/11 flights, American and United Airlines have consistently refused to demonstrate that they possess authenticated passenger lists of these flights. This refusal alone ought to have prompted serious questioning by the media and the 9/11 Commission. Surprisingly, neither corporate media nor the 9/11 Commission demanded the release of these documents.

Between September 11 and September 14, 2001, mainstream media published names of alleged hijackers and passengers, which were then deleted and replaced by other names. These irregularities are examined below.

(a) Adding and deleting passengers' names after the crashes

On September 13, 2001, Attorney General John Ashcroft announced that "[b]etween three and six individuals on each of the hijacked airplanes were involved" in the hijackings.[1] Later at a press briefing, Ashcroft specified that there were exactly 18 "hijackers", five on each of flights AA11 and UA175 and four on the others.[2] On the same day FBI Director Robert Mueller also said that a "preliminary investigation indicated 18 hijackers were on the four planes, five on each of the two planes that crashed into the World Trade Center, and four each on the planes that crashed into the Pentagon and in Pennsylvania."[3] A day later the number of alleged hijackers grew to 19.[4]

On September 14, 2001, the name of *Mosear Caned* (phonetic) was released by CNN as one of the suspected hijackers on "a list of names...that is supposed to be officially released by [the Justice Department] sometime later today."[5] His name disappeared a few hours later from the list of suspects and replaced with that

---

1   "FBI: Early probe results show 18 hijackers took part," CNN, September 13, 2001, #045

2   Department of Justice, Briefing by Attorney General John Ashcroft and FBI Director Robert Mueller, September 13, 2001, Transcript, #464

3   Ibid.

4   "FBI Announces List of 19 Hijackers," Op. cit, #065

5   Kelli Arena (transcript), CNN, September 14, 2001, #066

of *Hani Hanjour* when CNN posted a new list of suspects released by the FBI.[1] It was never explained where Caned's name came from in the first place, who this person was supposed to be, or why the name was later replaced by Hani Hanjour.[2] No other passenger (or "hijacker") had a name resembling Mosear Caned.

The *Washington Post* revealed that the original passenger lists did not include the name of *Hani Hanjour*, who was later named as the pilot of flight AA77. In its final edition of September 16, 2001, the paper explained that his name "was not on the American Airlines manifest for [flight 77] because he may not have had a ticket."[3] For its information, the *Washington Post* relied almost exclusively on the FBI. This report would fit with the declaration by Attorney General Ashcroft of September 13, 2001, that only four "hijackers" had been on flight AA77.[4] Counsel for American Airlines, in a letter to the 9/11 Commission of March 15, 2004, appears to confirm the absence of Hanjour, writing, "We have not been able to determine if Hani Hanjour checked in at the main ticket counter."[5] Yet Hanjour's name appeared later on an unauthenticated but official passenger of flight AA77 released at the Moussaoui trial, indicating that the latter list did not reflect the original version of the passenger list.

According to CNN on September 14, 2001, "[f]ederal sources initially identified [*Adnan*] *Bukhari* and *Ameer Bukhari* as possible hijackers who boarded *one* of the planes that originated in Boston" (emphasis added). Yet, a few hours later, CNN issued the following correction: "Based on information from multiple law enforcement sources, CNN reported that Adnan Bukhari and Ameer Bukhari of Vero Beach, Florida, were suspected to be *two of the pilots* who crashed *planes* [plural - E.D.] into the World Trade Center. CNN later learned that Adnan Bukhari is still in Florida, where he was questioned by the FBI...Ameer Bukhari died in a small plane crash" on September 11, 2000. These names disappeared from later published but unauthenticated passenger lists and were replaced by new names. The above facts were attributed to "federal sources," most probably the FBI. This means that the FBI either suspected these individuals to have been pilots who had crashed planes into the WTC, *because* their names were listed on the *original* versions of the passenger lists, or was simply inventing the names of suspects.

1   "FBI list of suspected hijackers," *CNN*, September 14, 2001, 2:00 PM, #067

2   Xymphora, "Mosear Caned," June 14, 2005, #1062

3   "Four Planes, Four Coordinated Teams," *Washington Post*, 16.9.2001, #080. Indeed, the only name missing from a report compiled by G. Bartulevicz (American Airlines) on September 11, 2001, about American Airlines bookings of the alleged hijackers, is that of Hani Hanjour, #150

4   Department of Justice, Briefing by Attorney General John Ashcroft, September 13, 2001, Op. cit., #464.

5   Condon & Forsyth LLP, Letter to Mr. John Raidt, 9/11 Commission, March 15, 2004, on behalf of American Airlines, in response to February 3, 2004 requests, p. 11, #318

On the very day of 9/11, the FBI, "which has been combing the passenger manifests of all four planes, was already focused on [Amer] *Kamfar*" as a suspected hijacker.[1] On the morning of September 12, eight FBI agents arrived at the door of Kamfar's neighbor, Henry Habora in Vero Beach, Florida, waiving a photograph of Kamfar, and asked Habora if he knew him.[2] If the FBI suspected Kamfar to have been one of the hijackers and informed the media about its suspicion, it could only credibly do so if it had found Kamfar's name on the original passenger list. Yet that name disappeared from computer print-outs released later that purported to represent passenger lists and was replaced by another name.

According to Terry Tyksinski, a veteran flight attendant with United Airlines, a customer service supervisor told her that he had observed two passengers leave flight UA93 after hearing an announcement that there would be a five-minute delay in the plane pushing back from the gate. The two first-class passengers were reportedly of dark complexion, "kind of black, not black." According to Tyksinski, the supervisor noted their names and was subsequently interviewed twice by the FBI.[3] No other accounts, including the 9/11 Commission Report, mention this incident. I could find no FBI document related to this incident. As these individuals presumably checked in with a ticket, their names should have been found on the *original* passenger list of Flight 93. This fact further strengthens the hypothesis that the computer print-outs released later as "passenger lists" are fake.

According to a report by American Airlines to the 9/11 Commission dated March 15, 2004, "some passengers" had boarded AA11 "after the aircraft had pushed back from the gate." I could not find out who these passengers were, whether they were listed on any version of the passenger lists, and particularly how they could board the aircraft after push-back.[4]

On 12 September 2001, various newspapers published partial passenger lists of the crashed flights. These reports included the names of *Jude Larson*, 31, and his wife, *Natalie*, 24, as passengers aboard flight AA11.[5] As example thereof, here is an excerpt from a news report published by the *Honolulu Star Bulletin* on September 12, 2001:

> Also among the confirmed dead was Jude Larson, the 31-year-old son of Maui artist Curtis Larson, who was aboard American's hijacked Flight 11.

1   Naftali Bendavid et al, "Officials scour US for clues," *Chicago Tribune*, September 13, 2001, #523

2   Ibid.

3   Jere Longman, *Among the Heroes: The True Story of United 93* (Harpers Collins Publisher, New York, 2002) p. xiii-xiv

4   Staff Report of the 9/11 Commission ("The Four Flights"), 26 August 2004, Note 31

5   "Partial list of terror victims," CBS, September 12, 2001, #814; Rod Antone and Helen Alton, "At least 2 from isles killed in attacks," *The Honolulu Star Bulletin*, September 12, 2001, #046; "American Airlines Partial Passenger List," *The Washington Post*, September 13, 2001, #815

Jude Larson and his wife Natalie were en route to the University of California at Los Angeles, where he was attending college...Larson's wife Natalie,
whose family lives in Boston, was a rising fashion model and had been to
Italy four times in the last 18 months to work for Gucci.[1]

A person presented as a friend of Jude's father, Steve Jocelyn of Lahaina, told
the *Honolulu Advertiser* on September 12, 2001, that Jude "was an amazing guy, a
cool kid. He was a fun-loving, happy-go-lucky guy with a good heart."[2] He said
that Jude visited Maui often, was working as a horticulturist in Washington
State but decided to enter medical school a few years ago. A week later, the same
newspaper reported that it had been "unable to confirm the identity of...Steve
Jocelyn," and was unable to locate him.[3]

On September 18, 2001, the *Honolulu Star Bulletin* reported that the newspaper had received an email from Jude, giving notice that he and his wife were
alive.[4] According to the paper, "a person claiming to be with the airlines" had
called Jude's father and told him that his son and daughter-in-law had been passengers on flight AA11.[5] The *Honolulu Advertiser* of September 20, 2001, which
published a detailed report on this apparent hoax, wrote that Curtis Larson, a
"sculptor and jewelry maker," now claimed he had been duped, but that it was
Curtis Larson who initially told reporters that "his son was in medical school at
UCLA, that his daughter-in-law was pregnant and that the couple had visited
her family in Boston." According to Jude, the report continued, his real name
is not Larson but Olsen. He also said he is 30, not 31, years old, that he does
not study in Los Angeles but works as a landscaper in Olympia, Washington
State, and that his wife is not pregnant.[6] The names of Jude and Natalie Larson
then disappeared from publicized passenger lists. Assuming that a prestigious
news agency such as Associated Press would check with American Airlines and
the FBI whether the Larsons were passengers on flight AA11 before releasing its
story, it would follow that the Larsons were listed on the original passenger list
of flight AA11 but later had to be removed from the official list of dead passengers
or their names had to be changed.

The story becomes even more bizarre. The names and photographs of Jude
and Natalie Larson, no longer officially listed as flight AA11 victims, in March

1   Ibid. (Rod Antone and Helen Alton)
2   Christine Snyder, "Five from Hawai'i may be victims," *Honolulu Advertiser*, September 12,
     2001, #822
3   Timothy Hurley, "Maui man says misinformation led to false report of son's death," *Honolulu
     Advertiser*, September 20, 2001, #824
4   Gary T. Kubota, "Maui man discovers son still alive," *Honolulu Star Bulletin*, September 18,
     2001, #1063
5   According to Anand Vaishnav ("Pair believed dead very much alive"), *Boston Globe*,
     September 19, 2001, the father was told that Jude and Natalie had been on flight United
     Airlines 175, #821
6   Timothy Hurley, Op. cit., #824

2013 were still listed on the National Obituary Archive list of those who died on 9/11. Jude Larson's obituary includes his photograph:

> Jude Larson, 31, of Los Angeles, CA, died Sept. 11, 2001, a victim of the coordinated terrorist attacks against the United States in New York, Washington, D.C., and elsewhere. Jude was a student at the University of California at Los Angeles. He and his wife, Natalie, were returning from visiting her family near Boston. Natalie Larson, four months pregnant, was a fashion model who had modeled in Italy.[1]

Natalie Larson's obituary, which does not include a photograph, reads:

> Natalie Larson of Los Angeles, CA, died Sept. 11, 2001, a victim of the coordinated terrorist attacks against the United States in New York, Washington, D.C., and elsewhere. Natalie and her husband, Jude, were returning from visiting her family near Boston. Natalie was four months pregnant and was a fashion model who had modeled in Italy.[2]

According to the webpage of the National Obituary Archive, the list "is based on authoritative sources, The Associated Press and funeral home records."[3] In order to include an obituary, the managers of the Archive say they request submitters to ask their "funeral director to submit the obituary."[4] Submitters are required to supply documentation of the death which is reviewed by the Archive's

---

1   "Jude Larson," *National Obituary Archive*, #580 (emphasis added)
2   "Natalie Larson," *National Obituary Archive*, #581 (emphasis added)
3   "List of 9/11 victims," *National Obituary Archive*, as of June 26, 2012, #1064
4   "Add an Obituary," *National Obituary Archive*, #1065

staff. It is not known who supplied the above information to the National Obituary Archive, or when this was submitted.[1]

Another website dedicated to the victims of 9/11 includes the following photograph, said to be Natalie Larson (Los Angeles), Jude's wife. The photograph is credited to the Associated Press and to the *Boston Herald*.[2] Yet the file containing the photograph is entitled lasden_natalie.jpg. Natalie Lasden was another passenger on flight AA11.

Various attempts were made to provide an innocuous explanation for this story.[3] David Hoff, news editor of the *Maui News* in Hawai'i, said the paper was trying "to make every local connection" it could: "When it appeared we had a local resident who lost his son and daughter-in-law, it was something that we went with."[4] Kelly Tunney, director of corporate communications for Associated Press, said, "We picked [the story] up from the papers [*sic*] and didn't follow our own stringent guidelines in this case."[5] Lynn Shue, a friend of Curtis Larson said, "He has been on medication and has a penchant for exaggerating... I can't believe he brought it all on himself."[6] Natalie Olsen, contacted in Olympia, confirmed the couple were alive but declined further comment.[7] Jude Olsen acknowledged that Curtis Larson was his father, denied studying medicine and said he saw Maui for the first time in the summer of 2001, "when he surprised his father during his first visit to Hawai'i."[8]

---

1   I sent a request for clarification to the editor of the National Obituary Archive on February 2, 2012 but received no response

2   "Photographs of AA11 victims," *myfriendsphotos.tripod.com*, #1066

3   Anand Vaishnav, Op. cit, #821

4   Ibid.

5   Ibid.

6   Ibid.

7   Ibid.

8   Timothy Hurley, Op. cit., #824

The original source for the Larson story—Curtis Larson—described as a "well-known local artist" in his community, apparently cannot be located.

(b) Curious discrepancies in names

According to the *Boston Globe*, one of the passengers on flight AA11, suspected to have been a hijacker and sitting next to Mohamed Atta, was *Abdulrahman Alomari*. In the Justice Department list of hijackers released on September 14, 2001, Alomari's first name is spelled *Abdulaziz*. Federal investigators "said they could not explain the discrepancy between the American Airlines passenger list and their list."[1] The name *Abdulrahman* Alomari was also mentioned by the *Washington Post* on September 14, 2001, as one of the "five hijackers who took over American Airlines flight 11, according to a source familiar with FBI's list of the hijackers."[2]

As early as September 12, 2001, NBC displayed a photograph of Mohamed Atta and mentioned his name, but no other suspects.[3] On the late afternoon of September 13, 2001, various American TV networks displayed photographs of "Mohamed Atta" and "Marwan al-Shehhi," designated as suspects in the mass-murder of 9/11. Surprisingly, ABC News (September 13, 2001, 7:02 p.m. EST of that day) captioned Atta's photograph with the name *"Amanullah Atta Mohammed."*[4] It was not explained from where "Amanullah" was gleaned. Was there another person impersonating Mohamed Atta, using Amanullah as first name?

On September 22, 2001, T.A. Badger of Associated Press reported that one of the alleged hijackers whom he named as *Ziad Jarrahi* (with a final "i") had been seen in San Antonio, California, in mid-June 2001.[5] Who was the Jarrahi who was repeatedly[6] mentioned by the American media? Was he another person, distinct from Ziad Jarrah (without final "i") who is alleged to have piloted flight UA93? Perhaps, if one believes the testimony of Charles Lisa, the landlord of an apartment he rented to a certain *Jarrahi* and who told *The Miami Herald* that this *Jarrahi* and his friend *Alhaznawi* had "German passports."[7] Ziad Jarrah, who had studied in Hamburg (Germany) was, however, a Lebanese citizen and is not known to have obtained a German passport. Was *Jarrahi* perhaps the assumed

1   Kevin Cullen and Anthony Shahid, Op. cit., #950
2   Dan Eggen and Peter Slevin, "Armed men held at NYC airports," *Washington Post*, September 14, 2001, #955
3   September 11 Television Archive, ‹http://archive.org/details/sept_11_tv_archive›
4   Ibid.
5   T.A. Badger, "San Antonio rental agent says he recognized hijacker," *Associated Press*, September 22, 2001, #1076
6   Andres Viglucci and Manny Garcia, "Hijack plotters used S. Florida as a cradle for conspiracy," *The Miami Herald*, September 15, 2001, #777; Nicolaas van Rijn, "Hijackers set down roots, blended in, then attacked," *The Toronto Star*, 15 September 2001, #081
7   Andres Viglucci and Manny Garcia, Ibid.

name of an unidentified German citizen whose role was to impersonate Ziad Jarrah? According to Elizabeth Neuffer in a detailed report on Ziad Jarrah and his family printed in the *Boston Globe* of September 25, 2001, "FBI agents, reviewing flight manifests, found a Ziad Jarrahi, the 'i' in the last name a possible misspelling, on United Airlines Flight 93."[1] Yet, the computer print-outs released later as passenger lists spelled his name without final 'i.' Elizabeth Neuffer, incidentally, died on May 9, 2003, in Iraq in what was reported as a car accident.

The aforementioned fluctuations in the number and names of the alleged hijackers could not have occurred if these various statements had been based on authentic passenger lists.

(c) Releasing bogus passenger lists five years later

In 2006, a seven-page set of faxes, purporting to represent the original passenger lists, was published in a book by Terry McDermott.[2] These released images, of which one page is shown below, were of bad quality and do not appear to be authentic copies of the original passenger lists (or flight manifests): (1) The published lists appear to have been pasted together from various computer print-outs;[3] (2) The lists are not authenticated by any airline or law-enforcement official; (3) It is not clear when the lists were printed out; (4) Ziad Jarrah's name is spelled correctly on the list of flight UA93, whereas as described above, the FBI referred to him initially as Jarrahi;[4] (5) The name of Hani Hanjour appears on the AA77 list, whereas the *Washington Post* reported that his name did not appear on the original American Airlines list for the flight (see above); (6) The list does not include names originally claimed as suspected hijackers; (7) Neither the FBI nor the airlines have been willing to confirm that these lists represent true copies of the original passenger lists (or flight manifests).

The FBI, responding on April 4, 2007 to my FOIA request for the release of the original passenger lists, wrote that the requested passenger lists of flights AA11, AA77, UA93 and UA175 were "available publicly through the internet at the US Department of Justice website."[5] The website to which the FBI referred, contains numerous exhibits, produced at the Moussaoui trial. An examination of Exhibit P200054, to which the FBI provided a link, revealed that it does not display the passenger lists released in McDermott's book and mentioned above, but

---

1   Elizabeth Neuffer, "Hijack suspect live a life, or a lie," *Boston Globe*, September 25, 2001, #902

2   Passenger Lists : Victims Lists, Passenger Manifests, and the Alleged Hijackers , *9-11 Research* (undated), #1075

3   See example of a non-authenticated passenger list on #872

4   See Elizabeth Neuffer, Op. cit, #902

5   Letter in my possession, #094

graphic layouts of the seating arrangements.[1] In its response to me, the FBI did not engage in a direct lie. It merely attempted to mislead me into believing that authentic passenger lists were "available publicly," and thereby avoid to admit in writing that it will not release a copy of the original passenger lists.

Illustration of a released, non-authenticated, passenger list from flight UA93

(d) What lists did Bonner and Clarke see?

Robert Bonner, former Administrator of the Drug Enforcement Administration (DEA) and former Commissioner of US Customs and Border Protection, testified before the 9/11 Commission, that

> "On the morning of 9/11, through an evaluation of data—by the way, this was the passing through manifest, which US Customs was able to access from the airlines—I would say, within about an hour of 9/11 US Customs

---

1   See the first pages of chapters 7-10

Office of Intelligence had identified the 19 probable hijackers as well as the complete list of the passengers on the aircraft."[1]

This observation piqued the curiosity of Commissioner Ben-Veniste, who a short while later asked Bonner, "How are your people able to [identify the 19 probable hijackers within about an hour]?" Here is what Bonner answered:

"Well, it was pretty simple actually. We were able to pull from the airlines the passenger manifest for each of the four flights. We ran the manifest through the TECS/IBIS system. This is essentially the lookout system that both US Customs and INS use but it's maintained by Customs. We ran it through the system. Two of the passengers on those aircraft were hits for having been entered on the watchlist in August of 2001. That was al Mihdhar and I forget the other one's name but they were the two people that had gone to Singapore that the CIA had identified. But they actually were put on the watchlist in August of 2001 by the FBI. So they hit on those two.

"Just using those two hits and taking a look at some other basic data about the flight manifest, both in terms of—I don't want to go into a lot of detail—but where they were seated, where they purchased their tickets, you could do just a quick link analysis and essentially, I remember I was at Secret Service headquarters, as I said, but I would say whether it was 45 minutes, I don't know but my recollection is that certainly by 11:00 a.m., I'd seen a sheet that essentially identified the 19 probable hijackers. And in fact, they turned out to be, based upon further follow-up in detailed investigation, to be the 19."[2]

Ben-Veniste then asked: "Was this more than looking at the two who were hits and then checking out the other Arab names?"

Bonner:

"It was partly that, by the way, but it was more than that. No, it was seat location, ticket purchase information. Again, I am on public record here. I don't want to go into exact details since we use some of this information in terms of targeting today for potential terrorists. We actually use, as I was saying, advance passenger information to identify beyond just who's on the watch list by biography to try to do a more intelligent job as to who, as the combined immigration inspection and Customs inspection, Customs and Border Protection who would you ask a few questions to as they're arriving in the United States.

"So you're doing more than just looking at a watch list. You're looking at a lot of data and trying to figure out who to look at, just as in the same way we're looking at what cargo to look at by examining a multitude of factors. That is, to some extent, strategic intelligence driven. So it was looking at a bunch of relational data. Obviously, more refinement of that occurred later

---

1   Statement of Robert C. Bonner to the National Commission on Terrorist Attacks Upon The United States, January 26, 2004, #1077
2   Ibid.

but it was—it didn't take a lot to do, just sort of what I'd say a rudimentary link analysis to identify essentially all 19."[1]

The question arises why Robert Bonner, who mentioned in his testimony that on 9/11 he had "not been confirmed yet as Commissioner of Customs,"[2] was able to obtain the flight manifests on the morning of 9/11. Furthermore, it must be remembered that, according to official reports, both the Federal Aviation Administration and the US Military did not know for many hours how many and which aircraft had been "hijacked." Bonner did not actually say that he personally carried out the research he described: He used the plural "we": "We were able to pull from the airlines the passenger manifest for each of the four flights"; "We ran the manifest...," "We ran it through the system," etc.

He said that "by 11:00 a.m." he had personally "seen a sheet that *essentially* identified the 19 probable hijackers" (emphasis added). Apart from the fact that a "sheet" listing the 19 "probable hijackers" could not have constituted an original flight manifest, only a compilation based on other documents, he did not say who handed him that "sheet" and who compiled it. That "sheet" was, furthermore, never released.

Richard Clarke, who served under both President Clinton and George W. Bush as National Coordinator for Security and Counterterrorism, said that he was informed by Dale Watson, counterterrorism chief at FBI, on the morning of 9/11 through a secure telephone line that, "We got the passenger manifests from the airlines. We recognize some names, Dick. They're al Qaeda." Clarke: "I was stunned, not that the attack was al Qaeda but that there were al Qaeda operatives on board aircraft using names that FBI knew were al Qaeda."[3] The documents on which Robert Bonner and Dale Watson based their statements were never released.

The above accounts by Robert Bonner and Richard Clarke make it imperative that they should testify under oath from where and on what statutory basis they obtained the "passenger lists" so early on 9/11, explain how they could identify the names of 19 alleged hijackers, and indicating what became of these lists. Their unverified statements cannot supplant the release of authenticated passenger lists.

(e) The airlines' refusal to release authentic lists

I attempted in 2004 to obtain authenticated passenger manifests for the two American Airlines flights of 9/11. Karen Temmerman, Customer Relations, American Airlines, wrote to me on September 9, 2004:

---

1   Ibid.
2   Ibid.
3   Richard A. Clarke, *Against All Enemies* (Free Press, 2004), p. 13

> At the time of the incidents we released the actual passenger manifests to the appropriate government agencies who in turn released certain information to the media. These lists were published in many major periodicals and are now considered public record. At this time we are not in a position to release further information or to republish what the government agencies provided to the media.[1]

The airline did not explain why it was not in a position, at this time, to confirm what had already been for a long time in the public domain.

On November 29, 2005, I tried again to obtain the passenger list of AA77 from American Airlines.[2] The first response by Sean Bentel from the airline was to send me a typed list that consisted of nothing more than the first and last names of 53 passengers from that flight. The list did not contain Arab names. Asking again the airline for "something more authentic," Sean Bentel responded that "the names I sent you are accurate...There may have been a formatting problem." In turn I wrote that the problem was not the formatting of the data:

> What I am asking for is a replica of the original passenger list (either a scan of the original, or at least a document faithfully reflecting the contents of that list)...[namely] the list of the paying passengers who boarded AA77. Can I take it that the list you sent me faithfully reflects the names of the paying passengers who boarded AA77?

Within hours Sean Bentel answered in the most laconic manner: "Mr. Davidsson, Names of terrorists were redacted. Sean Bentel." Asked in return, "Why can't you send me a facsimile copy of the passenger lists, including the names of the terrorists," Sean Bental answered, "This is the information we have for public release." That was the end of this exchange.

I asked United Airlines on October 21, 2004, why the original flight manifests have not yet been publicized and whether United Airlines had provided some media with a copy of the original flight manifests. The airline answered that "[a]ll matters pertaining to the September 11th terrorist attacks are under the investigation of the US Federal Authorities. Please contact the FBI." That was it.

Numerous individuals have attempted without success to obtain authentic passenger lists from the airlines, among them Thomas R. Olmsted, M.D. He wrote, for example: "I attempted on three occasions to obtain a final passenger list from American Airlines. They refuse to give a list and in fact won't even verify

---

1   Email communication to the author from Karen Temmermann, American Airlines, September 9, 2004
2   Exchange of letters between Elias Davidsson and American Airlines regarding 9/11, November 2005, #926

that they gave the first list to CNN. Since the list is in the public domain, I find it curious that they would not take ownership nor provide a current, 'correct list'."[1]

(f) No plausible reason for secrecy

I requested through FOIA in February 2012 from the FBI form-302, serial 7134, which contains "flight manifests for hijacked flights" and "information related to manifests."[2] The request was denied. As the names of all victims and alleged hijackers were publicized within days after 9/11, I could not identify any plausible reason for the refusal of the airlines and the FBI to confirm information that already exists in the public domain by releasing the original documents or certified copies thereof. Authenticated passenger lists were not provided to the Congressional Joint Inquiry of 2002 or the 9/11 Commission and were not presented as evidence in the trial of Zacarias Moussaoui. It must therefore be presumed that no authenticated passenger lists for the four 9/11 flights exist or that whatever lists the airlines and the FBI possess do not correspond with the official allegations.

(g) No legal proof that Muslim terrorists boarded the 9/11 aircraft

To sum up this section: No authenticated passenger lists of flights AA11, UA175, AA77 and UA93 have ever been produced by the airlines or the FBI. It is therefore not possible to confirm the *names*, let alone the identities,of the persons (including those of alleged hijackers) who checked in and boarded these flights.[3]

(2) No authenticated boarding passes

To ensure that all checked-in passengers actually boarded the aircraft, in 2001 American Airlines used boarding cards with a stub to be torn-off at the gate by airline employees. These stubs normally include passengers' names and seat numbers. A report by the 9/11 Commission staff ("Staff Report") mentions specifically that Mohammed Atta received a boarding pass at Portland airport from where he reportedly flew on the morning of 9/11 to Logan Airport, Boston. The report surprisingly does not mention anyone handing out, or the handling of, boarding passes for flights AA11, AA77, UA175 and UA93, the so-called "death flights." In footnote 62 to Chapter 1 of its Final Report, the 9/11 Commission mentions having received "copies of electronic boarding passes for United 93," whatever the term "copies of electronic boarding passes" means, and in footnote 74 it refers to "copies of boarding passes for United 93."

---

1   Thomas R. Olmsted, "Autopsy: No Arabs On Flight 77," June 9, 2003, *Physics 911*, #107
2   This report is referred to in the 9/11 Commission's released Team 5, Box 62, Aliases and IDs folder - Doc. Req. 43, p. 2, #1162
3   Passengers can and do sometimes board onto airplanes under assumed names.

The only mention of boarding cards in connection with one of the 9/11 flights is a third-hand account presented in a book by Tom Murphy:

> Terri Rizzuto is the United Airlines station manager at Newark Airport, from where Flight UA93 departed. Some time after hearing that this plane had crashed, she speaks on the phone with the FBI, which is requesting the plane's manifest and its Passenger Name Record (PNR). After arranging permission to release these, she goes to gate 17, from where Flight 93 had departed, in order to talk to her staff there. Approaching the gate, an unnamed supervisor hands her four boarding passes. Rizzuto: "What are these?" Supervisor: "The men, who did this maybe." Rizzuto: "What? How do you know?" The supervisor pointed to one of the unnamed gate agents who had boarded the passengers onto the flight. When Rizzuto asks the gate agent again: "How do you know?" he replies: "They were too well-dressed. Too well-dressed for that early in the morning. And their muscles rippled below their suits...Yes, and their eyes."[1]

This report was not corroborated elsewhere. Ms. Rizzuto was interviewed by unnamed FBI special agents on September 11, 2001[2] and again on December 6, 2001.[3] In none of the FBI interviews—released in 2009 together with 9/11 Commission documents—did she mention the above episode. According to an FBI document dated September 11, 2001, Ms. Rizzuto provided to an unnamed FBI agent "38 airline boarding passes used by passengers to board United Airlines flight 93 on 9/11/2001 at Gate 17 of terminal A at Newark International Airport."[4] The document lists the names of these 38 individuals and includes the names of the four alleged hijackers. The document does not include an explanation from where Ms. Rizzuto obtained these "boarding passes," which were later described by the 9/11 Commission as "electronic" boarding passes. These boarding passes were not submitted as evidence in the Moussaoui trial. The aforementioned FBI document states that the documents provided by Ms. Rizzuto "are being maintained as evidence at the Newark office of the FBI."

On March 21, 2012, it was pointed out to me that a file posted on the website 911myths.com contains photocopies of a fax depicting boarding cards from flight UA93. The file appears to have been created on December 15, 2011 and, according to the website, was obtained from the National Archives and Records Administration (NARA), where the documents from the 9/11 Commission are

---

1   Tom Murphy, *Reclaiming the Sky* (AMACOM Books, 2007), p. 72-73
2   FBI NK-745. September 11, 2001. In this report Ms. Rizzuto merely provides names of employees who were working at Newark International Airport on 9/11. #1163
3   FBI 302-90747. December 6, 2001. In this report Ms. Rizzuto provides "a general understanding of the boarding procedures that were in place on 09-11-2001 for UAL Flight 93." She does not provide the time of the check-ins.
4   FBI NK-744. September 11, 2001. List of 38 boarding passes and 40 flight coupons provided to an agent by Ms. Rizzuto. #1163

stored.[1] The fax and the copies of the boarding cards do not carry any authentication and are not accompanied by a chain-of-custody report. It is not clear who was the sender and the recipient of the fax. The circumstances of their sudden, belated and discreet release and the lack of authentication inspires the same lack of confidence in their authenticity as the computer print-outs of passenger lists referred to above.

(3) No one saw the hijackers at the security checkpoints and at the boarding gates

(a) Security personnel

According to the 9/11 Commission, ten of the 19 suspected hijackers were selected on 9/11 at the airports by the automated Computer Assisted Passenger Prescreening System (CAPPS) for "additional security scrutiny."(Final Report, 451, n.2) Yet none of those who handled the selected passengers, or any of the numerous airline or airport security employees interviewed by the FBI or the Federal Aviation Administration (FAA) on or after 9/11 is known to have seen these suspects. As for flights AA11 and UA175, which reportedly left from Logan Airport, Boston, the 9/11 Commission found that "[n]one of the [security] checkpoint supervisors recalled the hijackers or reported anything suspicious regarding their screening."[2]

As for flight AA77, which reportedly left from Dulles Airport, Washington, D.C., the 9/11 Commission wrote that "[w]hen the local civil aviation security office of the FAA later investigated these security screening operations, the screeners recalled nothing out of the ordinary. They could not recall that any of the passengers they screened were CAPPS selectees."[3] As for flight UA93, which reportedly left from New Jersey International Airport, the 9/11 Commission indicated that the "FAA interviewed the screeners later; none recalled anything unusual or suspicious."[4] According to an undated FBI report, the "FBI collected 14 knives or portions of knives at the Flight 93 crash site."[5] Yet no screener is known to have mentioned coming across a single knife that morning.[6] To sum up

---

1   Images of boarding passes, allegedly from Flight UA93, as faxed by United Airlines, #904

2   Ibid. Chapter I, p. 2. In support of this statement, the Commission refers to interviews with six named individuals

3   Ibid. Chapter I, p. 3. In support of this statement, the Commission refers to an interview made on April 12, 2004 with Tim Jackson, a person whose role is not indicated

4   Ibid. Chapter I. p. 4. In support of this statement, the Commission refers to an unreleased FAA report, "United Airlines Flight 93, September 11, 2001, Executive Report," of Jan. 30, 2002

5   Ibid. Note 82, p. 457

6   Staff Statement No. 3 to the 9/11 Commission made at the 7th Public Hearing, 26-27 January 2004, p. 9-10

this sub-section, no airport security employee has testified to have actually seen any of the alleged hijackers.

(b) Boarding gate personnel

Normally there would have been airline employees tearing off the stubs of passengers' boarding cards and observing the boarding of the four aircraft at the departure gates. Under the circumstances of 9/11, one could have expected to read interviews with some of these airline employees, under headlines such as "I was the last person to see the passengers alive" or "I saw TV commentator Barbara Olson board the doomed flight."[1] Yet no such interview is known to have taken place. The 9/11 Commission does not mention the existence of any deposition or testimony by airline personnel who witnessed the boarding of the aircraft. As a response to my request to interview American Airlines gate agents of flight AA77, the airline responded that their identities cannot be revealed for privacy reasons.[2] Among the documents from 9/11 released in 2009, two FBI 302 forms were discovered which contain interviews with Liset Frometa (conducted on September 11, 2001)[3] and Maria Jackson (conducted on September 22, 2001),[4] who testified to have worked at gate 32 for flight AA11, and one FBI 302 form recording an interview with an unidentified female employee of American Airlines who testified on September 11, 2001, to have "worked the gate for AA flight 11" on 9/11.[5] The 302 form does not indicate at which gate number she worked. Neither of these ladies recalled any of the alleged hijackers. Maria Jackson was shown a "photo spread of subjects" but did not recognize anyone from the photo spread. The 302 form records her saying that she "took the tickets for [Flight 11] from AA Flight Attendant Karen Martin and brought them to the ticket lift and deposited them in the safe." These documents were never released as evidence.

---

1 Barbara Olson, a passenger on Flight AA77, was a known, conservative, television commentator who appeared on CNN, Fox News Channel and other media outlets (Source: Wikipedia)

2 Exchange of emails between myself and American Airlines, Op. cit., #926. On May 25, 2009, I discovered on the internet a declassified FBI document no. 302-1805 relating an interview with an unnamed American Airlines employee who advised she had "worked the gate for AA Flight 11" at Logan airport on 9/11. The interview was taken by an unidentified Massachusetts State Trooper and summarized in the document three days later. According to the interview, the employee "boarded the passengers" for Flight AA11 but "did not observe any suspicious people or notice anything out of the ordinary." She also said that "three or four passengers flew standby on this flight." She did not mention the gate number from which the passengers left.

3 FBI 302-522. September 11, 2001. Interview with Lisa Frometa, Logan Airport

4 FBI 302-18941. September 22, 2001. Interview with Maria Jackson, Logan Airport

5 FBI 302-1805. September 11, 2001. Interview with unidentified employee of American Airlines, Logan Airport

(c) The testimony of Marsha L. Smith

Marsha L. Smith, an American Airlines employee, told FBI on September 11, 2001[1] that she was assigned by the airlines as the "standby stewardess for Flight 11" and was "called to monitor the gate while loading and if the population in coach class was over 70 people then she would be added to the flight crew." She said that when she arrived at the gate "most of the people were already on the plane." She stated she did not observe anything suspicious and apparently she was not presented with photographs. According to the 302 form, she did not mention the gate number, the exact time she arrived at the gate, nor who else was at the gate.

(d) The testimony of Manuel Carreiro

Manuel Carreiro, a customer service representative for United Airlines at Logan Airport, told the FBI on September 11, 2001, that an unnamed man with dark olive skin approached him and presented a "certificate" that he was unfamiliar with. He said he did not see this individual with anyone else. He then sent him to see Gail Jawahir (see below).[2] Carreiro was again interviewed by the FBI on September 28, 2001.[3] On that occasion he reportedly said that "suspected terrorists Hamzah [*sic*] and Ahmed Alghamdi checked in for flight 175" and that "one of the men" had presented to him a "certificate" that he was unfamiliar with. Carreiro was shown by the FBI agent a photo lineup of twelve individuals believed to have been involved in the events. After reviewing the photo lineup, he said that the photograph of Abdul Alomari resembled the man he talked to on 9/11. According to the FBI, however, Alomari did not fly with United Airlines.

(e) The testimony of Gail Jawahir

Gail Jawahir, a customer service representative at the United Airlines ticket counter at Boston's Logan Airport was interviewed three times by the FBI. In the first interview, conducted on September 11, 2001,[4] she said that "shortly before 7:00 a.m....two well dressed Arabic males approached her ticket counter....Subject #1 indicated that he wished to purchase a ticket." She "observed that Subject #1 had a United Airlines envelope with a UA itinerary in hand." She informed the person that he did not need to buy a ticket, for he already had one. Manuel Carreiro to whom she sent them, sent the men back to her. She said they had problems answering standard security questions. She was then asked if she would recognize the names of the passengers from the UA manifest for flight 175 and answered that she would be able to do so, because they had the same last name.

---

1   FBI 302-37123. September 11, 2001. Interview with Marsha L Smith, Logan Airport
2   FBI 302-1169. September 11, 2001. Interview with Manuel Carreiro, Logan Airport
3   FBI 302-29690. September 28, 2001. Interview with Manuel Carreiro, Logan Airport
4   FBI 302-19081. September 11, 2001. Interview with Gail Jawahir, Logan Airport

Jawahir "was shown a [flight] manifest and immediately indicated that Hamed Alghamdi and Hamza Alghamdi were the two Mid Eastern individuals who checked in with her at the ticket counter." She added that she "was positive that those were the names utilized by the two men.." On September 25, 2001, Jawahir was shown by an FBI agent a photograph of a passenger on flight 175 but did not recognize it as either one of the two males she had checked in.[1] Interviewed again by the FBI on September 28, 2001, she said she had checked in Hamza and Ahmed Alghamdi into Flight 175.[2] But when shown a photo lineup of twelve individuals believed to have been involved in the 9/11 events, she commented that the photo of Mohand Alshehri resembled one of the men she had checked in and that the photo of Saeed Alghamdi looked like the second man she had checked in.[3] According to the 9/11 Commission, however, she suggested that the two may have been Mohand Alshehri and Fayez Ahmed Banihammad.(Final Report, pp. 2,451, Staff Report). Jawahir did not board the passengers. Her testimonies were contradictory. Why was she repeatedly interviewed?

(f) The testimony of Janet Padilla

According to Janet Padilla, described in a FBI document as a Regional Reservations Manager located in Chicago, Illinois, and interviewed sometime on September 11, 2001, Gail Jawahir (in Newark International Airport) had earlier in the day checked in Fayez Ahmed, Mohand Alshehri, Ahmed Alghamdi for flight UA175.[4] In this FBI document the name(s) of the person(s) who allegedly checked-in Marwan Alshehhi for flight UA175 as well as the name(s) of the person(s) who checked-in Ahmed Alnami, Saeed Alghamdi, Ahmed Alhaznawi and Ziad Jarrah for flight UA93, are redacted. It is not known why the names of these employees were redacted while Gail Jawahir is mentioned. As she was working in Chicago, Ill., Ms. Padilla's testimony was no eyewitness to the check-in by Gail Jawahir.

(g) Secret identities of boarding gate employees

Remarkably, in a letter dated March 15, 2004 from Condon & Forsyth LLP, representing American Airlines, to the 9/11 Commission, the names of most of the 28 agents who worked at that airline's *check-in counters* at Logan and Dulles airports on 9/11 are listed, but the names of the agents who boarded passengers onto the aircraft at the respective *gates* are redacted.[5] No explanation was provided for this redaction.

---

1   FBI 302-37858. September 25, 2001. Interview with Gail Jawahir, Logan Airport
2   FBI 302-29693. September 28, 2001. Interview with Gail Jawahir, Logan Airport
3   Ibid.
4   FBI 302-51589. September 11, 2001. Interview with Janet Padilla
5   Letter from Condon & Forsyth, Op. cit., #318

(4) No authenticated CCTV of the hijackers at the departure gates

Apparently none of the three airports from where the 9/11 aircraft reportedly departed (Boston Logan, Newark International and Dulles Airport, Washington, D.C.) had surveillance cameras above the boarding gates. There exists neither eyewitness testimony nor a visual documentation of the boarding process.

The *Boston Herald* reported a few weeks after 9/11:

> In perhaps the most stunning example of Massport's lax security safeguards, Logan International Airport is missing a basic tool found not only in virtually every other airport, but in most 7-Elevens.... While Massport does employ cameras in parking garages, ramp areas and on Logan's roadways to monitor traffic, there are none to be found in the terminals, gate areas or concourses. "You have names (of hijackers), but the FBI has said it hasn't been able to match the faces of those who were on the flights," said Charles Slepian, a New York security consultant.[1]

Logan officials acknowledged this 'deficiency.' This is significant because two of the 9/11 flights originated from Logan airport.[2]

According to the 9/11 Commission's staff, Newark International Airport, from which flight UA93 reportedly departed, did not have such equipment.[3] According to the 9/11 Commission's Final Report, "there is no documentary evidence to indicate when the hijackers passed through the [security] checkpoint[s], what alarms may have been triggered or what security procedures were administered."(Final Report, 4)

Yet public opinion remains convinced that surveillance videos of the suspected hijackers have been shown on television. Indeed, something was shown around the world on television, but not the boarding process of any of the four aircraft. What was shown were two short video clips of people passing a security checkpoint, one reportedly from the Portland (Maine) Jetport and the other from Dulles Airport in Washington, D.C.

The video from Portland Jetport purports to show suspected hijackers Atta and Alomari passing the security checkpoint before they board a flight to Boston on the morning of September 11, 2001. Its authenticity has been disputed for two reasons: (1) Michael Tuohey, who checked in Atta and Alomari at the Portland Jetport, said on CNN that during check-in that they "had on ties and jackets." Shown the security video, he discovered that "they both have, like, open collar. They have like dress shirts with open collar." No one could explain what hap-

---

1   Doug Hanchett and Robin Washington, "Logan lacks video cameras," *The Boston Herald*, September 29, 2001 (article not accessible anymore on internet)
2   Staff Statement No. 3, Op. cit., p. 18
3   Ibid. p. 35

pened to their jackets.[1] (2) The security video displays two different recording times, as shown below.[2]

According to Kenneth R. Anderson, the pilot of Colgan Air flight 5930 from Portland, Maine to Logan Airport, Boston, on the morning of 9/11, he also served there as the flight attendant. He said he remembered two Arabic or Mid-Eastern males who were passengers on that flight. They were the last to board the aircraft and the last to exit the aircraft and sat in the last row of the plane. He described one of the individuals as wearing glasses,[3] yet neither Abdulaziz Alomari nor Mohamed Atta wore glasses. Anderson also said that one of them was 5'9" and the other 5'11" tall. According to an FAA certified copy of Atta's airman file, Atta's height was 5'7."[4] No information is available on Alomari's height.

"Mohamed Atta and Abdulaziz Alomari" at Portland Jetport on September 11, 2001

But even if the video recording from Portland were authentic,[5] in the sense of depicting two persons resembling and purporting to be Mohamed

1   See Paula Zahn Now, *CNN*, March 2, 2006

2   Rachel Gordon et al, "Security high but inconsistent at US airports," *San Francisco Gate Com*, September 20, 2001, #1067

3   FBI 302-23367. September 11, 2001. Interview with Kenneth R. Anderson

4   Airman Records for Alleged 911 Hijacker Mohamed Atta, *Federal Aviation Administration*, #1068

5   Mohamed Atta's father emphatically denies that the video depicts his son. Betsy Hiel, "Hijacking suspect's father says son 'hates bin Laden', isn't terrorist," *Tribune-Review*, September 25, 2001, #545

Atta and Abdulaziz Alomari, it does not prove *what* these persons did after they arrived in Boston.

The other security video recording purports to depict the alleged hijackers of flight AA77 pass through the security checkpoint at Dulles Airport, Washington, D.C. This recording was not voluntarily released by the US government, but was forced out in 2004 by the Motley Rice law firm representing some survivors' families, under the Freedom Of Information Act.[1] Zacarias Moussaoui was induced by the government and his defense lawyers to "agree to the authenticity" of that security videotape "without any further foundation."[2] This video recording was released as an exhibit in Moussaoui's trial, but it is cumbersome to download from that source.[3] It is however available on various websites.[4] According to the Final Report of the 9/11 Commission, the video "recorded all passengers, including the hijackers, as they were screened."(Final Report, 3) Yet none of the released versions of this recording shows any of the over 50 "passengers" from flight AA77, some of whom were well known nationally.

Jay Kolar, who published a critical analysis of this video recording,[5] made an important point: He pointed out that the recording lacks a camera identification number and a time stamp (date : time clock). Joe Vialls, who also analyzed this video recording in 2004, wrote, "Just this single terminal at Dulles Airport has well over 100 such cameras, every one of them with an individual camera identification number and date-time clock of its own."[6] He elaborated the point: "On-film data [such as camera number and date-time stamp] is essential of course, because it would be extremely difficult to track a target around the airport without these basic tools and absolutely impossible to sort out the precise time and date of an event that occurred more than two years before, which is exactly what the 9-11 Commission now claims to have done."

According to Vialls, the video recording could not have been made on the morning of 9/11 because the light suggests that it had been made around noon. He urges viewers to "play back a full size copy [of the video recording]...and

---

1   Nick Grimm, "Commission report finalized as 9/11 airport video released," *ABC.net.au*, 22 July 2004, #087

2   Supplemental Stipulation between the United States of Amereica and Zacarias Moussaoui, Government Exhibit ST00002, United States District Court for the Eastern District of Virginia, Alexandria Division (undated), #1135. Zacarias Moussaoui was not in a position to know the truth of the factual allegations he stipulated. A sane person or a person not subject to pressure would not stipulate factual allegations that would facilitate his/her conviction

3   United States v. Zacarias Moussaoui, Criminal No. 01-455-A, Prosecution Trial Exhibits, ‹http://www.vaed.uscourts.gov/notablecases/moussaoui/exhibits/›

4   See "9/11 hijackers at Dulles Airport," #1069

5   Jay Kolar, "What we now know about the alleged 9-11 hijackers," in *The Hidden History of 9-11-2001*, Research in Political Economy, Vol. 23, 3-45, Elsevier Ltd. (2006), p. 7-10

6   Joe Vialls, "Clueless 9-11 Commission Cheats American Public," July 23, 2004, #1070

freeze-frame at the appropriate points," pointing out the "footprint size shadow underneath the cab, and the brilliant sunshine streaming in through the open doors. On a full-screen picture you can even see the minuscule short [near vertical] shadows of the people standing outside the doors."

A strange story about the Dulles security video, suggesting that it was fabricated before 9/11, was told by airport security manager Ed Nelson of Dulles Airport, to authors Susan and Joseph Trento. Nelson said that shortly after arriving at the airport on the morning of 9/11, FBI agents confiscated a security tape from a checkpoint through which he believed the alleged hijackers had passed before boarding the plane. He then described the scene and expressed his surprise that the FBI agents could already at that time pick out on the security tape "the hijackers" from hundreds of other passengers:

> They pulled the tape right away.... They brought me to look at it. They went right to the first hijacker on the tape and identified him. They knew who the hijackers were out of hundreds of people going through the checkpoints. They would go 'roll and stop it' and showed me each of the hijackers.... It boggles my mind that they had already had the hijackers identified.... Both metal detectors were open at that time, and lots of traffic was moving through. So picking people out is hard.... I wanted to know how they had that kind of information. So fast. It didn't make sense to me."[1]

Aside from the dubious source of this recording and the likelihood that it was made before 9/11, it does not show who *boarded* an aircraft but provides only blurred images of individuals who pass a security checkpoint at an unknown time and location.

(5) No positive identification of the hijackers' bodily remains

According to the official account, the 19 alleged hijackers died in the crashes at the WTC, the Pentagon and at the crash site near Shanksville, Pennsylvania.

The *Pittsburgh Tribune* of September 13, 2001—two days after the events—reported that the

> remains from the main crash site [of flight UA93] have been taken to a makeshift morgue at the Pennsylvania National Guard Armory near the Somerset County Airport. State police escorted a tractor-trailer truck into the back of the armory late yesterday evening, according to a resident who lives nearby. The lights were turned off briefly as the truck was directed to the rear of the armory. A short time later, the lights were turned on as the police cars and the truck left, said the man who declined to be identified.[2]

1   Susan B. Trento and Joseph J. Trento, *Unsafe at any Altitude: Failed Terrorism Investigations, Scapegoating 9/11, and the Shocking Truth about Aviation Security Today*, (Steerforth Press, October 2006), p. 37

2   Robin Acton and Richard Gazarik, "Human remains recovered in Somerset," *Tribune-Review (Pittsburgh)*, 13, 2001, #386

Unidentified officials spoken to by *The Times* (U.K.) in October 2001 said they expected that the bodies of the 9/11 suspects would be identified 'by a process of elimination'.[1] They did not explain why they did not expect the bodies to be positively identified, one by one.

Chris Kelly, spokesman of the Armed Forces Institute of Pathology (AFIP), where the identification of the victims' remains from flights AA77 and UA93 took place, said that the authorities were reluctant to consider releasing the hijackers' bodies: "We are not quite sure what will happen to them, we doubt very much we are going to be making an effort to reach family members over there."[2] Neither did he explain why no efforts would be made to locate the families of the alleged hijackers, nor why AFIP could not use comparison DNA samples from known locations in the US where the alleged hijackers had lived. According to Llonald Mixell, landlord of one of the alleged hijackers, Alomari, in Vero Beach, Florida, the FBI "searched the Omari home [and] agents left a list of materials seized, including hair samples and air conditioning filters."[3] There were more such samples available from the alleged hijackers' hotel rooms and cars they had left at the airports. Yet, according to Dr. Jerry Spencer, a former chief medical examiner for AFIP, cited by CBS News, "the terrorists are usually not in our possession in the United States like this,"[4] implying that no DNA comparison samples were available to identify their remains. According to Jeff Killeen, spokesman for the FBI field office in Pittsburgh, "there haven't been any friends or family members to try to claim the remains of [the hijackers]."[5] Yet the family of alleged hijacker Ziad Jarrah in Lebanon was reported as early as September 16, 2001, to be "ready to cooperate with the authorities."[6] The US authorities did not respond to this offer of cooperation.

In mid-August 2002, a news report on the victims' remains noted that the DNA of the alleged hijackers still had not been checked, because "little attention has been paid to the terrorists' remains."[7] While the AFIP announced it had positively identified the human remains of all "innocent" passengers and crew from the flights, they did not identify the remains of any of the alleged hijackers. Kelly said later: "The remains that didn't match any of the samples were

---

1   Damian Whitworth, "Hijackers' bodies set Bush grisly ethical question," *The Times (U.K.)*, October 6, 2001, #092

2   Ibid.

3   Amy Goldstein and Peter Finn, "Hijack Suspects' Profile: Polite and Purposeful," *Washington Post*, September 14, 2001, #068

4   Brian Dakss, "Remains of 9 Sept. 11 hijackers held," *CBS News*, August 17, 2002, #526

5   Jonathan Wald, "Remains of 2 Sept. 11 hijackers identified," *CNN*, February 27, 2003, #1071

6   Robert Fisk, "Stunned into disbelief as their 'normal' son is blamed," *The Independent*, September 16, 2001, #1072

7   "What to do with hijackers' remains?," *Associated Press*, 16 August 2002, #052

ruled [by default] to be the terrorists."[1] Tom Gibb, of the *Pittsburgh Post-Gazette*, wrote, perhaps with tongue in cheek, that "air pirates have been identified as Ziad Jarrah, Ahmed Al Haznawi, Saeed Al Ghamdi and Ahmed Al Nami—but not so positively identified that officials will list the names in official records." Somerset County coroner Wallace Miller said that the "death certificates [for the suspected hijackers] will list each as 'John Doe'."[2] Under a ruling issued on October 11, 2001, by a Somerset County judge, everyone who died aboard flight UA93 "except the terrorists" will get death certificates. At the "insistence of the FBI, the terrorists won't be getting them because investigators *aren't sure of their identities*."[3]

The AFIP was at the time a joint entity of the three military departments, subject to the authority, direction, and control of the Secretary of Defense.

In a letter from the AFIP dated June 20, 2003, to Thomas R. Olmsted, MD, of Harahan, LA, in response to his FOIA request of April 3, 2002, where he requested copies of the final list of bodies identified by the AFIP at the Pentagon crash of flight 77 on September 11, 2001, Bonnie S. Short responded: "Attached file contains the names of the 58 victims of AA flight 77 that were identified here at the Armed Forces Institute of Pathology."[4] The list did not include any Arabic names.

According to the AFIP, bodily remains from virtually all passengers of flight AA77, which allegedly crashed at the Pentagon, could be identified, despite the impact of the aircraft crash and the ensuing fire. Yet representatives of the Department of Justice and the FBI told the staff of the 9/11 Commission that the contents of the cockpit voice recorder (CVR) for that flight "were destroyed by the intense heat it had been subjected to."[5] Such devices are, however, constructed to resist far greater impact and temperatures than human DNA.

Among documents transmitted to the 9/11 Commission and released in 2009, one document contains the claim by the FBI that DNA profiles of Ziad Jarrah provided to the FBI by the German Federal Police (BKA) from the apartment of his fiancée in Germany "matched the sample of one of the sets of unknown human remains."[6] The aforementioned FBI document was not signed, dated or

1   Brian Dakss, Op. cit., #526; Tom Gibb, "FBI ends site work, says no bomb used," *Post-Gazette*, September 25, 2001, #238

2   Tom Gibb, "Flight 93 remains yield no evidence," *Post-Gazette*, December 20, 2001, #073 (emphasis added)

3   Tom Gibb, "Judge OKs certificates of death in Flight 93," *Post-Gazette*, October 12, 2001, #762

4   Thomas R. Olmsted, Op. cit., #1073

5   MFR 04020027. May 13, 2004. Briefing by Department of Justice and FBI to staff members of the 9/11 Commission

6   "How FBI determined the 19 hijackers' identities", in NARA, Team 5 Box 24 Copies of Doc Requests File 2 Fdr - DOJ Tab, p. 129, #1074

otherwise authenticated. The US authorities have not relied on this document to claim that Ziad Jarrah's remains had been identified.

At this point, it might be useful to point out that at the reported crash site of flight UA93, no bodies or blood were sighted by eyewitnesses.

As for the remains of the suspects who allegedly hijacked flights AA11 and UA175, a spokeswoman for the New York Medical Examiner's Office, where the identification of the victims from the WTC took place, said she had received from the FBI in February 2003 profiles of all ten hijackers who allegedly died at the WTC, so "their remains could be separated from those of victims." She added, however: "No names were attached to these profiles. We matched them, and we have matched two of those profiles to remains that we have."[1] It was not indicated from where these "remains" had been brought. Dr. Lawrence Kobilinsky, professor of forensics at New York's John Jay College of Criminal Justice commented that this discovery is "extremely significant." He added: "This is the first confirmation that these individuals were on those planes."[2]

In 2005, the number of matched samples from New York increased to three.[3] Robert Shaler's forensic unit in New York City could not, however, identify the three by name. In an essay entitled "Who They Were," Shaler set down his inside account of the identification effort: "No names, just a K code, which is how the FBI designates 'knowns,' or specimens it knows the origins of," he wrote, adding, "we had no direct knowledge of how the FBI obtained the terrorists' DNA."[4] His statement was echoed in 2009 by his deputy, Howard Baum, in a *Newsweek* interview: "We had no idea where the profiles came from or how they were developed."[5]

It was not revealed from where and how the FBI secured the "profiles" of the ten individuals, designated as "hijackers," why it took so long to submit them for identification and why they could not be identified by name. The FBI had, according to its own records, collected numerous hair samples from cars, hotel rooms and apartments used by the suspects, from which DNA profiles could have been extracted to permit at least the positive identification of some of these individuals. The lack of identification could not, therefore, be imputed to the lack of comparison samples.

The lack of positive identification of the alleged hijackers' bodily remains, compounded by the absence of chain of custody reports regarding these remains,

---

1   "Remains of 9/11 hijackers identified," *BBC*, 28 February 2003, #053
2   Jonathan Wald, "Remains of two Sept.11 hijackers identified," *CNN*, February 27, 2003, #056
3   Paul D. Colford, "9/11 parts split by good and evil," *NY Daily News*, October 12, 2005, #1078
4   Ibid.
5   Eve Conant, "Remains of the day," *Newsweek*, January 12, 2009, #716

means that the US authorities have not so far proved that the alleged hijackers died on September 11, 2001, at the known crash sites.

Conclusions

The United States government, through its agencies and particularly the FBI, confiscated immediately after the events all available documentation regarding the boarding of the aircraft. Dozens of witnesses from the airlines and the respective airports were interviewed by the FBI. All existing evidence regarding the boarding of the four 9/11 flights must therefore be in the hands of the US authorities.

A government innocent of mass-murder would be expected not only to seek the truth about this crime, but show particular zeal in doing so, including by presenting the most incriminating evidence it possesses. It would do so both to satisfy a legitimate expectation of its population (and in the case of 9/11 of the world community) and to dispel any existing suspicions of its own complicity.

On the base of evidence provided in this chapter, the following inescapable and unassailable conclusions impose themselves:

1. Due to the lack of concrete and verifiable evidence that the 19 alleged hijackers boarded the four aircraft, it is unconscionable and slanderous to accuse these individuals of participation in the mass-murder. Such accusations constitute a grievous attack on their dignity and that of their families.

2. By consistently refusing to confirm through authenticated documents that the 19 alleged hijackers had boarded the four aircraft, the US government manifests its bad faith and justifies charges that it is lying to its population and to the international community about the events of 9/11.

3. By providing me with a deceptive reply regarding the passenger lists (see above), the FBI manifested its attempt to conceal their absence.

4. By ignoring the numerous and glaring contradictions regarding the identities of the alleged hijackers, the 9/11 Commission manifested its intent to maintain the official myth of 19 Muslim terrorists.

5. By refusing to allow interviews with personnel who were responsible for passengers boarding the four aircraft of 9/11,[1] the airlines manifested their intent to conceal evidence about the circumstances of the aircraft boarding.

The fact that the U.S. authorities—who can access all available facts—failed to prove, even on the preponderance of the evidence, that the 19 alleged hijackers boarded the respective aircraft and participated in the mass-murder of 9/11,

---

1   Media interviews were allowed with various airline and airport personnel, but not with those who boarded the passengers.

leaves only one reasonable conclusion to the ordinary citizen, namely that these 19 individuals did not board the respective aircraft and thus did not participate in the mass-murder.

Two objections can be raised against this conclusion:

1. It might be contented that the absence of publicly available evidence does not necessarily mean that the U.S. authorities do not possess it. They may, for reasons unknown to us, conceal that evidence from the public, as they often do. Although such objection is valid, it rests on two highly unlikely assumptions: (a) That the U.S. authorities might have a crucial interest in withholding from the world the most compelling evidence they possess to prove their own narrative on 9/11, even at the risk of perpetuating suspicion against themselves; and (b) that the U.S. authorities can be trusted to say the truth and refrain from deceiving the public. Those who present this objection bear the almost impossible burden of proving that these assumptions are warranted.

2. From the point of view of formal logic, it is admittedly true that the *absence of evidence* is not synonymous with the *evidence of absence*. If no one ever saw a white elephant, it does not necessarily mean that no white elephants exist. In practical life, this rule is rarely if ever used. For most decisions ordinary people adopt, they rely on the preponderance of the evidence. Even the standard of proof in criminal cases—"beyond reasonable doubt"—does not require 100% proof, as the aforementioned formal rule requires. There is no reason why ordinary citizens be required to adhere to a higher standard of proof than relied by criminal courts when judging suspects. Governments are certainly not the embodiment of honesty and morality. When a government acts overtly in a suspicious manner, such as by manipulating facts and grossly failing to prove its accusations in a case of mass-murder, it manifests guilty demeanor. The public is not only entitled to draw reasonable inference from such conduct, but would act irresponsibly by ignoring the implications arising from this suspicious conduct.

PART II. THE FOUR FLIGHTS

CHAPTER 3. NO IDENTIFICATION OF WRECKAGE

A central pillar of the official account on 9/11 is the alleged use of aircraft as weapons of mass destruction.[1] According to the official account, all deaths of 9/11 can be traced back to the crashing of these aircraft. The aircraft were thus the main tools of the mass-murder.

The federally registered aircraft reportedly used during Operation 9/11 were:

Aircraft with registration (tail) number N334AA is said to have flown as flight AA11 into the North Tower of the WTC in New York. Aircraft with registration number N612UA is said to have flown as flight UA175 into the South Tower of the WTC. Aircraft with registration number N644AA is said to have flown as flight AA77 into the Pentagon in Washington, D.C. Aircraft with registration number N591UA is said to have crashed as flight UA93 in Somerset County, Pennsylvania.

The present chapter examines a single question: How was the wreckage of the crashed aircraft identified and linked to specific airliners?

(1) The plotters intended to deceive air traffic controllers

Whether an aircraft crashes as a result of an accident or of a deliberate act, investigators are expected to *positively* identify the wreckage of the crashed aircraft[2]. Positive identification means a procedure that systematically and formally links debris found at the crash site to a specific aircraft. Why is such formal

---

1   US District Judge Leonie Brinkema instructed the jury in the Moussaoui trial that the term "weapons of mass destruction" includes airplanes flown into buildings. Source: Michael J. Sniffen, "Jury weighs wording of Moussaoui charges," *Boston Globe*, March 31, 2006, #1079

2   By *positive* identification I mean a determination by a human observer that item A belongs to item B.

identification essential? The answer may appear obvious, but will nevertheless be spelt out.

After reaching cruising altitude, a commercial aircraft ordinarily vanishes from sight. It can only be tracked on radar. When an aircraft crashes, the wreckage cannot be automatically attributed to a particular aircraft on the sole basis of what air traffic controllers could have observed on radar. The reason will be explained below.

Aircraft carry a device called transponder, which constantly emits the aircraft's identity, its coordinates and its altitude.(Final Report, 16) These data are captured on the radar of air traffic controllers who are thus able to track the flight of each aircraft, guide the pilots to follow specific routes and altitudes and thus prevent collisions. Turning off the transponder causes the aircraft's identity and altitude to disappear from so-called secondary radar, which is what air traffic controllers ordinarily use. Changing the transponder code causes the aircraft to assume a new identity, confusing thereby the controllers. The ability of pilots to change or hide the "identity" of an aircraft in flight must be taken into account by crash investigators, particularly when malfeasance or an enemy attack is suspected.

On September 11, 2001, the perpetrators, whoever they were, intended to deceive and confuse air traffic controllers. The transponder of flight AA11 was turned off at 8.21 a.m.[1] Between 8:45 and 8:48 a.m. the transponder of flight UA175 was turned off and then changed to code 3020 and very shortly thereafter to code 3321.[2] At 8:56 the transponder signal of flight AA77 was turned off when the aircraft was nearing the Kentucky border.[3] Sometime between 9:41 and 9:44 the transponder of flight UA93 was turned off.[4]

Shutting off transponders does not, however, make the aircraft completely invisible to air traffic controllers. They can change the configuration of their scopes to primary radar returns.(Final Report, 16) These are signals echoed from the aircraft's outer skin, as long as the aircraft is not hidden by mountains or flying too low. Primary returns provides the coordinates of an aircraft (its geographical location) but do not provide its identity and altitude.

Miles Kara, former staff member of the 9/11 Commission, set up his own webpage in which he discusses, *inter alia*, the problem of the transponders.[5] His analysis constitutes an attempt to explain the failure of US air force defenses

---

1   Ibid. p. 18 (Col. Robert Marr, head of NEADS claims the transponder was turned off some time after 8:30). However, according to the Final Report of the 9/11 Commission, the alleged hijackers had already taken over the control of the cockpit by 8:14 a.m. "or shortly thereafter" (p.2)
2   Summary of Air Traffic Hijack Events, September 11, 2001, *FAA*, #1028
3   Ibid.
4   Ibid.
5   Miles Kara, "The Ghosts of 9-11, the transponder story," *9-11 Revisited*, August 17, 2009, #918

on 9/11 by bad communications between various agencies, the chaotic situation on 9/11 and the "remarkable tactical achievement," of the Islamic hijackers, who apparently knew how "to exploit the transponders differently on each of the hijacked aircraft."

(2) To what aircraft did the wreckage belong?

Glen A. Stanish, a commercial airline pilot for various airlines and member of the American Line Pilots Association (ALPA), wrote on October 3, 2006, to ALPA a long letter in which he urged the Association to help "in the establishment and documentation of a more accurate account and correct historical record of September 11th." In his letter he mentioned how easy it is to identify parts of an aircraft from a crash site:

> I have been a proud member of the Air Line Pilots Association for almost 16 years ... [American Airlines Flight 77] was reported to be a Boeing 757, registration number N644AA, carrying 64 people, including the flight crew and five hijackers. This aircraft, with a 125-foot wingspan, was reported to have crashed into the Pentagon, leaving an entry hole no more than 16 feet wide.

> Following a cool-down of the resulting fire, this crash site would have been very easy to collect enough time-change equipment within 15 minutes to positively identify the aircraft registry. There was apparently some aerospace type of equipment found at the site but no attempt was made to produce serial numbers or to identify the specific parts found. Some of the equipment removed from the building was actually hidden from public view....With all the evidence readily available at the Pentagon crash site, any unbiased rational investigator could only conclude that a Boeing 757 DID NOT fly into the Pentagon as alleged.[1]

Flight numbers have no physical existence. They merely refer to a particular route scheduled to be flown at a particular time by a particular airline. The official killing tools on 9/11 were physical aircraft designated by their tail or registration numbers (sometimes also named call numbers or in the United States N-Numbers). They are usually displayed on the aircraft's fuselage or tail. In the United States, the Federal Aviation Administration (FAA) maintains a register of all licensed aircraft.[2]

In addition to the official registration number of an aircraft, manufacturers are also legally required to fix fireproof identification plates on aircraft and air-

---

1   Glen Stanish, Letter to the Air Line Pilots Association, October 3, 2006, #1080
2   Aircraft Registry of the Federal Aviation Administration (FAA): ‹registry.faa.gov/aircraftinquiry›

craft engines that contain their unique manufacturers' serial numbers.[1] It is also possible to derive the identity of an aircraft by the unique serial numbers of recoverable "time-change" parts, as explained below by Col. George Nelson, a FAA certified commercial pilot and former aircraft accident investigator:

> Following a certain number of flying hours or, in the case of landing gears, a certain number of takeoff-and-landing cycles, [certain] critical parts are required to be changed, overhauled or inspected by specialist mechanics. When these parts are installed, their serial numbers are married to the aircraft registration numbers in the aircraft records and the plans and scheduling section will notify maintenance specialists when the parts must be replaced. If the parts are not replaced within specified time or cycle limits, the airplane will normally be grounded until the maintenance action is completed. Most of these time-change parts, whether hydraulic flight surface actuators, pumps, landing gears, engines or engine components, are virtually indestructible. It would be impossible for an ordinary fire resulting from an airplane crash to destroy or obliterate all of those critical time-change parts or their serial numbers.[2]

It should be noted that investigators as well the 9/11 Commission have throughout, and for unexplained reasons, used the flight numbers rather than tail numbers to designate the tools of the crime. In order to prove that passengers who boarded onto aircraft designated by their flight numbers had died at the three crash sites (Ground Zero, the Pentagon and Shanksville, Pennsylvania), investigators would have to (a) determine the registration numbers of the aircraft onto which the passengers boarded; and (b) positively identify the wreckage at the crash sites as belonging to the aircraft onto which the passengers had boarded.

To understand the complexity of this exercise, one must remember that physical aircraft are continuously assigned to different flight numbers, even several times during a single day. Most ground personnel and even flight crew members do not need to know the registration (or tail) number of the aircraft they service. They usually designate their aircraft by the departing or arriving flight number. Someone within each airline, obviously, determines which physical aircraft will be assigned to a particular flight number, verifies that this assignment was accomplished and maintains records documenting the continuously changing locations of the airline's aircraft fleet.

Col. George Nelson, mentioned above, said that during his work as an aircraft accident investigator, he "never witnessed nor even heard of an aircraft loss, where the wreckage was accessible, that prevented investigators from finding

---

1   Federal Regulations, Title 14, Subpart B, (Identification of Aircraft and Related Products) Part 45, #1081

2   Col. George Nelson, USAF (ret.), "Aircraft Parts and the Precautionary Principle," Rense, April 23, 2005, #145

enough hard evidence to positively identify the make, model, and specific regis-tration number of the aircraft."[1]

(3) The failure to positively identify the wreckage

On May 28, 2008, I sent a FOIA application to the National Transportation Safety Board (NTSB), requesting "all documents regarding the identification of aircraft parts of the four aircraft that crashed on September 11, 2001." Melba D. Moye, FOIA Officer at the NTSB, answered shortly thereafter, that "the only re-cords that the Safety Board possesses that are within the scope of your request are photographs taken shortly after the crashes at the World Trade Center and the at the Pentagon, a Video Data Impact Speed Study report, and a Debris Tra-jectory Study report for United Airlines flight 175."[2] Yet, in a copy of a letter from Ronald S. Battocchi, General Counsel, NTSB, of April 23, 2002 to the US De-partment of Justice, attached to NTSB's response, Battocchi wrote that NTSB personnel "assisted the FBI and local authorities, on-scene and at the Fresh Kill landfill on Staten Island, locate and identify parts of the four aircraft involved."[3] No documentary evidence was apparently held by the NTSB about their partici-pation in these identification efforts.

Citizen investigator Aidan Monaghan requested in 2007 from the FBI under the Freedom of Information Act (FOIA) "documentation pertaining to any for-mally and positively identified debris" from the aircraft used in Operation 9/11.[4] In its first response of November 26, 2007, the FBI denied the request arguing that "these records in their entireties...are protected from disclosure" because their release "could reasonably be expected to interfere with enforcement pro-ceedings." This was actually a lie. For after Monaghan challenged in 2008 the FBI in court, Assistant US Attorney Patrick A. Rose admitted that the FBI did not at all possess such documentation. Here is how he explained this omission:

> Federal Defendant [the FBI] has determined that there are no responsive records [to the FOIA request]. The identities of the airplanes hijacked in the September 11 attacks was [sic] never in question, and, therefore, there were no records generated "revealing the process by which wreckage re-covered by defendant, from aircraft used during the terrorist attacks of September 11, 2001, was positively identified by defendant ... as belonging to said aircraft ..." (Amend Compl. Inj. Relief #15 at 1).[5]

1 Ibid.
2 NTSB letter to Mr. Davidsson, June 12, 2008, #920
3 Ibid.
4 Aidan Monaghan, "FBI Refuses To Confirm Identity of 9/11 Planes," *RINF News*, December 2, 2007, #1082
5 Aidan Monaghan, "F.B.I. Counsel: No Attempt Made By F.B.I. To Formally Indentify 9/11 Plane Wreckage Publically Known Information Suggests Otherwise," *Visibility911.com*, March 28, 2008, #1083

We note at first the convoluted language used to acknowledge that the FBI did not undertake a formal identification of the wreckage. By deconstructing this statement, its contrived nature can be revealed. Actually, this short statement contains several lies, as will be demonstrated henceforth.

The first lie—and possibly the least remarkable—is that airplanes were "hijacked in the September 11 attacks." That this claim is a lie follows from the fact that the US authorities (and particularly the FBI itself) did not prove that the 19 alleged hijackers had actually boarded the airliners used in the mass-murder (see chapter 2).

The second lie—or more accurately a deceptive formulation—is that the identities of the "hijacked" airplanes "was [sic] never in question." The statement may be understood in two ways, both of them deceptive.

According to the first interpretation, the FBI tried to imply that this statement was prompted by a FOIA request for records identifying the hijacked aircraft. The FBI would have simply believed that there is no difference between the identities of the hijacked aircraft and the identities of the wreckage and formulated its answer in accordance with its misunderstanding.

According to the second interpretation, the FBI tried to create the impression that it actually meant that the identities of the wreckage were not in question, but had formulated its answer negligently.

To believe that Counsel for the FBI would be negligent in formulating an answer to a court of law would, however, defy belief. It is safe to bet that language used in the FBI's statement to a court of law would be formulated with great care by legal counsel.

The third, and most outrageous, lie was to claim that the identities of the aircraft (hijacked or crashed) were "never in question." The evidence presented in chapter 14(A) demonstrates that air traffic controllers, the FAA and even the US military were so confused about the identities and the locations of suspect aircraft that up to 29 aircraft were at one time suspected to have been hijacked.

The failure to forensically identify the debris of the crashed aircraft—a relatively trivial procedure—could only be plausibly explained by the intent of the FBI to suppress their real identities.

Conclusions

The main findings of this chapter are:

- Exceptionally, no crash investigations were carried out by the National Transportation Safety Board (NTSB) regarding the four aircraft that allegedly crashed on September 11, 2001.

- The FBI, responsible for the investigation of 9/11, did not carry out a crash investigation of the four aircraft that allegedly crashed on September 11, 2001.

- The FBI did not formally identify the aircraft debris found at the three locations where aircraft allegedly crashed on September 11, 2001.

The above findings allow the conclusion that the US authorities have failed to formally identify the tools used to cause the deaths of approximately 3,000 people on September 11, 2001. These findings also mean that the passengers and crew of the four flights did probably not die at the officially designated crash sites.

We end this chapter by an excerpt from an article by Col. George Nelson, where he describes his own experience with the identification of crashed aircraft:

> In 1989 I graduated from the Aircraft Mishap Investigation Course at the Institute of Safety and Systems Management at the University of Southern California. In addition to my direct participation as an aircraft accident investigator, I reviewed countless aircraft accident investigation reports for thoroughness and comprehensive conclusions for the Inspector General, HQ Pacific Air Forces during the height of the Vietnam conflict.

> In all my years of direct and indirect participation, I never witnessed nor even heard of an aircraft loss, where the wreckage was accessible, that prevented investigators from finding enough hard evidence to positively identify the make, model, and specific registration number of the aircraft—and in most cases the precise cause of the accident...

> The government alleges that four wide-body airliners crashed on the morning of September 11 2001, resulting in the deaths of more than 3,000 human beings, yet not one piece of hard aircraft evidence has been produced in an attempt to positively identify any of the four aircraft.[1]

---

1   Col. George Nelson, Op. cit., #145

CHAPTER 4. IMPLAUSIBLE CRASH SITES

A central tenet of the official 9/11 narrative is that hijacked aircraft were flown into the Twin Towers of the WTC in New York and into the Pentagon, whereas the fourth aircraft crashed in Somerset County, Pa. While some investigators seriously doubt that any aircraft crashed on the Twin Towers and the Pentagon, I assume, absent compelling proof to the contrary, that some aircraft did crash at these locations. At issue here is not whether *some* aircraft crashed at these locations, but whether flights AA11, UA175, AA77 and UA93 or any large jetliners, crashed there. As will be shown below, there is no hard evidence[1] supporting that claim.

(1) The strange crash site at Ground Zero

The only official document containing photographs of debris from the aircraft that allegedly crashed on the Twin Towers of the WTC is FEMA's WTC Building Performance Study (BPAT).[2] It presents exactly one photograph for each of the crashed aircraft. One photo depicts an alleged "piece of Flight 11 landing gear" and one photo depicts an alleged "piece of Flight 175 fuselage." No known attempts were made by the FBI to forensically identify these parts.

The photographic evidence of aircraft debris from Ground Zero does not permit to determine the origin of the observed objects, the type of aircraft to which they belonged, the aircraft's identity and the exact circumstances that brought these objects to the location where they were photographed. It is inconceivable

---

1   By "hard evidence" I mean evidence that would be admissible, relevant and credible for the purposes of a criminal trial

2   World Trade Center Building Performance Study, FEMA, Chapter 2, #778

that these observed parts are all what remained from two Boeing 767-200 aircraft (flights AA11 and UA175), whose combined empty weight is 350,000 pounds.

"Piece of Flight 11 gear" (above)   "Piece of Flight 175 fuselage" (below)

The dearth of photographed aircraft debris strongly suggests that these few photographs did not depict debris from Boeing 767-200 aircraft that had crashed there.

According to the Final Report of the 9/11 Commission, the four "black boxes" of flights AA11 and UA175 were not found. This might appear understandable.

Yet Ted Lopatkiewicz, spokesman for the National Transportation Safety Board, said, "It's extremely rare that we don't get the recorders back. I can't recall another domestic case in which we did not recover the recorders."[1]

---

1   Brian Dakss, "Speed likely factor in WTC collapse," *CBS News*, 25, 2002, #1092

The claim by the FBI that the "black boxes" were not found stretches credulity because numerous hard computer disks were reportedly found in the rubble with information that could later be recovered.[1] In addition, the rubble was later sifted in order to look for far smaller objects, including human nails and teeth. In the period 1965–2001 only 8 cases are known world-wide of "black boxes" that could not be physically recovered.[2]

There is indeed some evidence that at least three of the four "black boxes" from the WTC had been found. The question remains: What motive could the authorities have for lying about these devices, other than their reluctance to acknowledge that what crashed in New York were not the Boeing 767s assigned to flights AA11 and UA175?

As of the spring of 2002, the remains of no passenger from flights AA11 and UA175 had been found at Ground Zero.[3]

(2) The strange crash site at the Pentagon

According to the official account, flight AA77, a Boeing 757, crashed on the Pentagon. An empty Boeing 757 weighs well over 100,000 pounds. Dave McCowan, quoted by David Ray Griffin, notes that the debris found within the Pentagon represent at most one percent of that weight, thus raising the question what happened to 99% of the plane.[4] Lee Evey, the Pentagon Renovation Manager, said on September 15, 2001, however, that "[t]here are other parts of the plane that are scattered about outside the building. None of these parts are very large, however. You don't see big pieces of the airplane sitting there extending up into the air. But there are many small pieces. And the few larger pieces there look like they are veins out of the aircraft engine. They're circular."[5]

On September 20, 2001, a press conference was held by Assistant Director of the FBI's Washington Field Office Van Harp with Chief Ed Flynn of the Arlington County Police Department and Major General James Jackson of the Military District of Washington.[6] Asked by journalists about the wreckage of the plane that reportedly crashed on the Pentagon, Harp answered, "Well, at the outset, I should have stated, I cannot get into the details of the investigation nor the so-called crime scene." To another similar question Harp answered, "All I can say is there has been some evidence already recovered with no more specificity." The

---

1   "Computer disk drives from WTC could yield clues," *CNN*, December 20, 2001, #1093
2   See Wikipedia: List of Unrecovered Flight Recorders, #1094
3   Eve Conant, Op. cit., #716
4   Ibid.
5   "DoD News Briefing on Pentagon Renovation," *US Department of Defense*, September 15, 2001, #849
6   FBI News Conference About the Pentagon Investigation, *The Washington Post*, September 20, 2001, #1035

reluctance of the FBI to provide even minimal information on the wreckage, even refusing to acknowledge the finding of the "black boxes," is duly noted.

At the Moussaoui trial, the following single photograph of bad quality was presented as evidence that an aircraft crashed on the Pentagon. This photograph is entitled "airplane parts in the Pentagon after Flight 77 crashed into the building"[1] Zacarias Moussaoui was induced to stipulate (to agree with) the "authenticity" of this photograph "without any further foundation."[2]

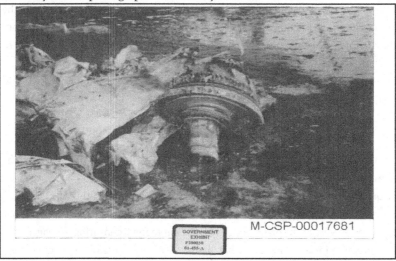

M-CSP-00017681

Another photograph, circulated on the Internet, purports to depict a fuselage piece from an American Airlines lying on the lawn outside the Pentagon. It is attributed to photographer Mark Faram. This photograph, presented below, has not been authenticated by the authorities as belonging to a specific aircraft and was not stipulated as evidence at the Moussaoui trial.

The evidence from the Pentagon crash site suggests, nevertheless, that an airborne object crashed at the Pentagon but does not permit to determine the type of object, its identity and the exact circumstances that led that object into the building.

Capt. Daniel Davis, former US Army Air Defense Officer and NORAD Tac Director, as well as founder and former CEO of Turbine Technology Services Corp. made the following statement:

> "As a former General Electric Turbine engineering specialist and manager and then CEO of a turbine engineering company, I can guarantee that none of the high-tech, high temperature alloy engines on any of the four planes that crashed on 9/11 would be completely destroyed, burned, shattered or melted in any crash or fire. Wrecked, yes, but not destroyed. Where are all

---

1   Moussaoui Prosecution Trial Exhibit No. P200030, #1165
2   Stipulations for Part II of the Penalty Phase, United States of America v. Zacarias Moussaoui, Criminal No. 01-455-A, Government Exhibit ST00004, United States District Court for the Eastern District of Virginia, Alexandria Division (undated), p. 10, #1134

those engines, particularly at the Pentagon? If jet powered aircraft crashed on 9/11, those engines, plus wings and tail assembly, would be there."[1]

Here is a photograph of a Boeing 757 engine. Each such aircraft carries two such monsters. Are we to believe that both vaporized at the Pentagon?

Barry and son Brian in front of a B-757 engine on the occasion of my [Petitt's] retirement flight, June 21, 1998 (Karlene Petitt)[2]

---

1   Daniel Davis, Statement to Patriots for 9/11 Truth, March 23, 2007, #850
2   Blog of Karlene Petitt: Flight to Success, #851

It is interesting to note that the contents of the cockpit voice recorder (CVR) from the object that crashed at the Pentagon were destroyed "by the intense heat it had been subjected to,"[1] while virtually all bodily remains of those who died there could be identified.

In spite of the inferno that was reported at the Pentagon, two pieces of a Virginia driver's license were allegedly recovered from the crash site, bearing the following readable information about one of the alleged hijackers:[2]

Name:	Majed M GH Moqed
Address:	5913 Leesburg Pike, Apartment #08
	Falls Church, Virginia 22041-2210
Customer Number:	A69-60-0405
Height: 5'7"	

Were these driver's licenses made out of steel?

The Pentagon is said to be surrounded by video cameras, but the Department of Defense has not been able (or willing) to produce a single credible video recording that would document the approaching and impacting airborne object. The single video sequence released after much prodding does not show anything resembling an aircraft.

Numerous questions remain unsettled regarding the nature of the event that occurred at the Pentagon on 9/11. It is not clear whether an aircraft, a missile or anything at all crashed on the Pentagon. If it was an aircraft, it is not clear what aircraft it was. And to crown all these questions, it is not even clear when the "crash" occurred: Reported crash times are distributed over no less than 25 minutes!

The New York Times reported in a September 12, 2001, article that Flight 77 "slammed into [the Pentagon] at "about 9:30,"[3] but in a second article in the *Times* that day, the impact was said to have occurred "at 9:40 a.m."[4] Then on September 15, in an article by Matthew Wald, "After the Attack: Sky Rules," *The New York Times* gave the time of the impact as 9:45 a.m.[5]

The *Washington Post* first reported (at 4:59 pm on 9/11) that the plane crashed at 9:20 a.m.[6] Next day the *Washington Post* wrote that the plane crashed at 9:37 a.m.[7]

---

1 MFR 04020027. May 13, 2004. Briefing by Dave Novak, Assistant US Attorney, FBI Special Agent and Ray Guidetti, NJ State Police to the staff of the 9/11 Commission

2 FBI 302-51296. September 16, 2001. Report of Driver's License finding in abandoned car

3 Don Van Natta and Lizette Alvarez, "A Highjacked Boeing 757 Slams Into the Pentagon, Halting the Government," *New York Times*, September 12, 2001, #558

4 Serge Schemann, "President Vows to Exact Punishment for 'Evil'," *New York Times*, September 12, 2001, #1095

5 Matthew L. Wald, "Pentagon Tracked Deadly Jet But Found No Way to Stop It," *New York Times*, September 15, 2001, #1096

6 Barbara Vobejda, "'Extensive Casualties' in Wake of Pentagon Attack," *The Washington Post*, September 11, 2001, 4:59 PM, #1097

7 "Timeline in Terrorist Attacks of Sept. 11, 2001," *The Washington Post*, September 12, 2001, #1098

According to an early CNN report a plane had struck the Pentagon at "about 9:20 a.m."[1] But then again, in the CNN Chronology of Terror, the strike is said to have occurred at 9:43 a.m.[2]

Here is an *excerpt* from a bewildering list of the crash times of Flight AA77 on the Pentagon, compiled by author Steven Welch:[3]

9:20 AM	The *Washington Post*, September 11, 2001 (see above)
9:20 AM	CNN interview, September 11, 2001 (see above)
~ 9:30 AM	The *New York Times*, September 12, 2001 (see above)
9:37 AM	The *Washington Post*, September 12, 2001 (see above)
9:40 AM	The *New York Times*, September 12, 2001 (see above)
9:40 AM	*San Antonio Express-News*, September 12, 2001[4]
9:43 AM	CNN timeline, September 12, 2001 (see above)
9:43 AM	*Daily Telegraph*, September 16, 2001[5]
9:45 AM	The *New York Times*, September 15, 2001 (see above) and *Boston Globe*, November 23, 2001[6]
~ 9:45 AM	The *Baltimore Sun*, September 12, 2001[7]

Won-Young Kim of the Doherty Earth Observatory of Columbia University and Gerald R. Baum of the Environmental Geology and Mineral Resources Program wrote that,

> Since the time of plane impact at the Pentagon had often been reported with large scatter, the United States Army contacted us to inquire whether we could obtain an accurate time of the Pentagon attack on September 11, 2001, based upon our seismic network. We analyzed seismic records from five stations in the northeastern United States, ranging from 63 to 350 km from the Pentagon. Despite detailed analysis of the data, we could not find a clear seismic signal. Even the closest station (= 62.8 km) at Soldier's Delight, Baltimore County, Maryland (SDMD) did not record the impact.[8]

---

1   "Eyewitness Discusses Pentagon Plane Crash," *CNN Breaking News*, September 11, 2001, 13:46 ET, #1099

2   "Chronology of terror," *CNN*, 12, 2001, #1100

3   Steven Welch, "When Did the Pentagon Get Attacked Exactly?," *StevenWarRan*, February 7, 2007, #1101

4   Gary Martin, "Lawmakers, tourists race to flee crash," *San Antonio Express-News*, September 12, 2001, #1102

5   Olga Craig, "At 8:46am, the world changed in a moment," *Daily Telegraph* (UK), September 16, 2001, #1103

6   Glen Johnson, "Probe reconstructs horror, calculated attacks on planes," *Boston Globe com*, November 23, 2001, #450

7   Tom Bowman, "Fire, chaos after attack on Pentagon," *The Baltimore Sun*, September 12, 2001, #1104

8   Won-Young Kim and Gerald R. Baum, "Seismic Observations during September 11, 2001, Terrorist Attack," Maryland Geological Survey (MGS), Undated, #1056

(3) The strange crash site at Somerset County, Pa.

(Source: website of the US Department of State)

(a) No visible aircraft wreckage

Many of those who rushed to the reported crash site of flight UA93 at Somerset County near Shanksville, were surprised to see no plane wreckage, nothing but a hole in the ground. Here are a series of observations from local people and journalists who arrived at the scene shortly after the crash:

- *Mark Stahl* of Somerset, a salesman, arrived at the site 15 minutes after the explosion. He told the *Tribune-Review* that he didn't realize a passenger jet had crashed until a firefighter told him. "It's unbelievable," he said.[1] To the CNN he said, "The plane is pretty much disintegrated. There's nothing left but scorched trees."[2] Yet, on September 12, 2001, the *Wall Street Journal* claimed that Mark had "snapped pictures of the downed plane [and] showed color photos of wreckage surrounded by a crater and flames."[3] No one apparently has ever seen these pictures.

- *Homer Barron*, a worker at Stoystown Auto Wreckers, told the *Pittsburgh Post-Gazette* that he and his coworker, Jeff Phillips, drove to the crash scene and found there a smoky hole in the ground: "It didn't look like a plane crash because there was nothing that looked like a plane," he

---

1   "Homes, neighbors rattled by crash," *Tribune-Review*, September 12, 2001, #915
2   "Hijacked passenger called 911 on cell phone," *CNN*, September 11, 2001, 11:35 PM, #752
3   Timothy Aeppel, Patricia Davis and Robert Guy Matthews, "A day of terror: United Flight 93's Pennsylvania crash site is being treated as crime scene by FBI," *Wall Street Journal*, September 12, 2001 (not anymore available online)

said. His colleague, however, said, "There was one part of a seat burning up there. That was something you could recognize."[1]

- *Scott Spangler*, a photographer with a local newspaper, was quoted in the book *Running Toward Danger: Stories Behind the Breaking News of 9/11*: "I didn't think I was in the right place. I was looking for a wing or a tail. There was nothing, just this pit.... I was looking for anything that said tail, wing, plane, metal. There was nothing."[2]

- *Frank Monaco* of the Pennsylvania State Police commented, "If you would go down there, it would look like a trash heap. There's nothing but tiny pieces of debris. It's just littered with small pieces."[3]

- *Jon Meyer*, a reporter with WJAC-TV, said, "I was able to get right up to the edge of the crater.... All I saw was a crater filled with small, charred plane parts. Nothing that would even tell you that it was the plane.... There were no suitcases, no recognizable plane parts, no body parts. The crater was about 30 to 35 feet deep."[4]

- *Ron Delano*, a local who rushed to the scene after hearing about the crash, said, "If they hadn't told us a plane had wrecked, you wouldn't have known. It looked like it hit and disintegrated."[5]

- *Gabrielle DeRose*, a news anchor with KDKA-TV, viewed the crash site from a hill overlooking it and said, "It was very disturbing to think all the remains just disintegrated.... There were no large pieces of airplane, no human remains, no baggage."[6]

- *Rick King*, a local assistant volunteer fire chief, who saw the crater at the crash site, said, "Never in my wildest dreams did I think half the plane was down there." King sent his men into the woods to search for the plane's fuselage, but they kept coming back, telling him, "Rick. There's nothing." (Longman, 216)

- *Wells Morrison*, a local FBI agent, told author Glenn Kashurba that after arriving at the crash site his first thought was, "Where is the plane?" because "what I saw was this honeycomb looking stuff, which I believe is insulation or something like that. I was not seeing anything that was distinguishable either as human remains or aircraft debris."(Longman, 216)

- *Faye Hahn*, an emergency medical technician (EMT) who arrived at the crash site, stated: "Several trees were burned badly and there were papers everywhere. We searched...I was told that there were 224 passen-

1   Bob Batz, Tom Gibb, Monica L. Haynes, Ernie Hoffman, Ginny Kopas, Cindi Lash and James O'Toole, "The crash in Somerset:: 'It dropped out of the clouds'," *Post-Gazette*, September 12, 2001, #613

2   Newseum, Cathy Trost and Alicia Shephard, *Running Toward Danger: Stories Behind the Breaking News of 9/11* (Rowman & Littlefield Publishers, 2002), p. 149

3   Bob Batz, et al, Op. cit., #613

4   Ibid. p. 148

5   Ibid.

6   Suzanne Huffman and Judith L. Sylvester, *Women Journalists at Ground Zero: Covering Crisis* (Rowman & Littlefield, 2002), p. 160-161

gers, but later found out that there were actually forty. I was stunned. There was nothing there."(McCall, 31-32)

- *Joe Little*, a 10News reporter, was working less than four miles from the crash site on the morning of 9/11 for an ABC/FOX affiliate. He said he and a photographer arrived on the crash scene within 30 minutes and were able to walk right up to the crater. He said there was nothing there other than a crater, some smoke and a few charred trees.[1] In a report he filed he wrote: "I still can't see a fire, let alone a plane"[2]

- *Nina Lensbouer*, the wife of a local former volunteer firefighter, told the *Pittsburgh Post-Gazette* that after seeing a mushroom flame rising, her first instinct was to run toward it, to try to help. "But I got there and there was nothing, nothing there but charcoal. Instantly, it was charcoal."[3]

- *Nick Tweardy* of Stonycreek Township, who came to help with the rescue effort, said "You couldn't see nothing. We couldn't tell what we were looking at. There's just a huge crater in the woods."[4]

- *Brad Reiman*, a young man from Berlin in Somerset County, said "the tail was a short distance from the rest of the wreckage. It looked like the plane hit once and flopped down into the woods." The largest piece of wreckage he could identify looked like a section of the plane's tail, he said.[5] No one else, apparently, saw this tail section.

On September 13, 2001, the *Pittsburgh Post-Gazette* reported that a self-piloting helicopter developed by Carnegie Mellon University's Robotics Institute was sent to Somerset County to photograph the scene. According to the *Post-Gazette* the 14-foot-long helicopter "can quickly produce a highly detailed, three-dimensional map of the impact crater and the surrounding spread of debris."[6] Chuck Torpe, director of the Robotics Institute was cited by the newspaper saying that the "aerial map can include objects as small as one or two inches in diameter." Pennsylvania Attorney General Mike Fisher said: "The aerial map may help identify key evidence faster than it might be found by physically canvassing the area." Where is that aerial map?

(b) The legend of the buried aircraft

The absence of visible debris led some reporters to conjecture that the plane did not disintegrate, but that the 155ft-long fuselage had completely vanished

---

1   Joe Little, "Reporter Witnesses Aftermath of Flight 93 Crash," *10News.com*, September 10, 2011, #1121

2   P.J. Bednarski, "For Pa. Crews, Biggest Story of Their Lives," *TVNewsCheck*, August 10, 2011, #1122

3   Bob Batz, et al, Op. cit., #613

4   Ibid.

5   Ibid.

6   Byron Spice, "Self-piloting copter from CMU aids in mapping Somerset crash site," *Post-Gazette*, 13, 2001, #506

into the spongy ground and was buried there, hidden from view. Thus Tom Gibb, of the *Post-Gazette*, speculated on October 15, 2001, that the "fuselage disintegrated in a crater that collapsed on itself."[1] This story reappeared in force a year after 9/11 and remained the official explanation for the lack of debris. Robb Frederick of *Tribune-Review* wrote on September 11, 2002, "The plane pitched, then rolled, belly up. It hit nose-first, like a lawn dart…digging more than 30 feet into the earth, which was spongy from the old mine work."[2] The Australian paper *The Age* wrote that the "rest of the 757 continued its downward passage, the sandy loam closing behind it like the door of a tomb."[3] Wes Allison of the *St. Petersburg Times* wrote on September 10, 2003, that "the site had been mined for coal, then refilled with dirt. It was still soft when Flight 93 crashed, and firefighters said the Boeing 757 tunneled right in. They had to dig 15 feet to find it."[4] Mary Jo Dangel of the *St. Anthony Messenger Online* explained in 2006 why the wreckage was not visible: "The ground had swallowed up much of the wreckage."[5] State police Maj. Frank Monaco from New Kensington told the *Post-Gazette* in 2006 that the plane had "burrowed into the soft, reclaimed earth of the former strip mine and crumpled like an accordion."[6]

According to WTAE-TV, Pittsburgh, of September 14, 2001, citing FBI spokeswoman Linda Vizi, the cockpit voice recorder (CVR) from flight UA93 was found "about 25 feet within the crater" at 8:25 p.m. of that day.[7] No independent observer was, however, present during the excavation. Blogger Killtown compiled an archive of reports in which it is claimed that most of Flight 93 had buried.[8] The reports include very few eyewitness reports that would verify that claim: They are either couched in passive language or attributed to unnamed sources. Killtown then makes a hugely perceptive observation:

> If the news reported when officials supposedly found the first black box after digging down in the ground and also reported they supposedly found part of one of the plane's engines also while digging, there is absolutely no logical reason for the news not to have reported right away that most of the 155ft-long, 60ton [sic] Boeing 757 was found. Contents of the plane that would have been found down in the ground along with the black boxes

1   Tom Gibb, "Newsmaker: Coroner's quiet unflappability helps him take charge of Somerset tragedy," *Post-Gazette*, Oct. 15, 2001, #1105

2   Robb Frederick, "The day that changed America," *Tribune-Review*, 11, 2002, #914

3   "On Hallowed Ground," *The Age* (Australia), September 9, 2002, #093

4   Wes Allison, "Small town shoulders a nation's grief," *St. Petersburg Times*, September 10, 2003, #1106

5   Mary Jo Dangel, "Sacred Ground in Pennsylvania," *American Catholic*, September 2006, #721

6   Michael Cowden, "Memories of Flight 93 crash still fresh at 5-year anniversary," *Post-Gazette*, 3, 2006 (reprinted in 2012), #766

7   Matthew P. Smith, "Flight 93 voice recorder found in Somerset County crash site," *Post-Gazette*, September 15, 2001, #996

8   Killtown, "Archive of reports that most of Flight 93 had buried," July 21, 2009, #1107

and engine that were reported would be: 44 passengers, their luggage, hundreds of passenger seats, 3 huge landing gears, 10 huge tires and rims, and possibly sections of the tail (since both black boxes located in the tail section supposedly burrowed far underground and there is no evidence of the tail section above ground), among tons and tons of other plane debris.

Blogger Dave captured well the extraordinary nature of this crash site:

> As we all know, September 11, 2001, was 'the day that everything changed.' Enormous office buildings, for example, suddenly and inexplicably acquired the ability to drop into their own footprints with no assistance from demolitions experts. Five-story masonry buildings suddenly acquired the extraordinary ability to swallow enormous airliners without leaving behind an appropriate entry hole or any trace of aircraft wreckage. And now we find, perhaps most amazingly of all, that the ground itself somehow also acquired the ability to swallow commercial aircraft. On that fateful day, and only on that day, a 100+ ton airplane measuring 155 feet long, 125 feet wide and 45 feet tall disappeared into a crater measuring, at most, "about 30 to 40 feet long, 15 to 20 feet wide and 18 feet deep."[1] Any skilled magician, I suppose, could make an airplane disappear into a building. But making an entire airplane disappear without a trace in an empty field? I have to admit that that is pretty impressive.[2]

Apart from Killtown's and Dave's cogent observations, is it physically possible that a Boeing 757 could disappear totally into the ground when crashing, at any speed whatsoever? A comparison with a similar aircraft crash, that of Helios Airways Flight 522, suggests an answer. That aircraft, a Boeing 737-300, crashed

1   Crews Begin Investigation Into Somerset County 757 Crash Officials Said Plane Targeted Camp David, The Pittsburgh Channel, October 11, 2001, #848
2   "September 11, 2001, Revisited," *The Center for Informed America*, Newsletter 86, November 4, 2006, #1108

on August 14, 2005, on a mountain in Greece, plunging to the ground from the altitude of 34,000 feet. Yet, the photograph from that crash site shows that a large part of the tail section remained recognizable. Nothing similar was shown from the crash site of flight UA93.

(c) The legend of aircraft parts hanging on trees

Two eyewitnesses—Eric Peterson[1] and Charles Sturtz[2]—told reporters on September 12, 2001, that they saw "pieces of clothing hanging from trees." An Associated Press release of September 29, 2001, told that the "bad weather this week might have shaken additional airplane parts out of the trees in a wooded area near the crash site."[3] A few weeks later the *Pittsburgh Post-Gazette* added that "high winds have dislodged additional airplane parts—seat cushions, wiring, carpet fragments and pieces of metal—from trees near the crash site." The paper quoted County Coroner Wallace Miller to the effect that "it's all aircraft parts, no human remains. We've collected them in 10 recycling bin-sized containers and eventually we'll turn them all over to United."[4]

In a 2009 *Newsweek* article, Miller told that during the recovery efforts at the crash site, he discovered a human tooth with silver filling embedded in a tree, which eventually "was matched to one of the passengers."[5] Lee Purbaugh told the *Daily American* that the "pine trees right next to the [crash] site were on fire from the explosion and the fire was also spreading through the woods."[6] Mark Stahl, who went to the site, confirmed to CNN that there was nothing there "but scorched trees."[7] Surprisingly, their testimonies were not corroborated by the FBI. There is no photographic evidence corroborating these stories. Additionally, it is difficult to reconcile the story of the plane vanishing into the ground, personal items hanging on trees and the absence of bodies and blood at the crash site.

(d) No bodies, no blood

Wally Miller, Somerset County's coroner, was also among the first to arrive at the crash site. He gave numerous interviews in which he expressed his

1 Jonathan D. Silver, "Outside tiny Shanksville, a fourth deadly stroke," *Post-Gazette*, September 12, 2001, #275

2 Bob Batz, et al, Op. cit., #613

3 Associated Press, "Searchers to return to Flight 93 crash site," *Post-Gazette*, September 29, 2001, #707

4 Don Hopey, "Another 14 victims of Flight 93 identified," *Post-Gazette*, October 27, 2001, #761

5 Eve Conant, Op. cit., #716

6 Sandra Lepley, "Sept. 11 Terror Touches Somerset County," *Daily American*, September 12, 2001 (updated in 2008), #1123

7 "Hijacked passenger called 911 on cell phone," CNN, 11, 2001, 11:35 PM, #752

surprise to see no bodies and no blood at the crash site. In one of the earliest interviews with the *Pittsburgh Post-Gazette*, he said, "It was as if the plane had stopped and let the passengers off before it crashed."[1] He repeated this comment in an interview with CNN on March 11, 2002.[2] He said he was stunned at how small the smoking crater looked, saying, "like someone took a scrap truck, dug a 10-foot ditch and dumped all this trash into it." Once he was able to absorb the scene, Miller said, "I stopped being coroner after about 20 minutes, because there were no bodies there."[3] A year after the events, he told the *Pittsburgh Tribune-Review*, "I have not, to this day, seen a single drop of blood [at the crash site]. Not a drop." To author David McCall he told, "I got to the actual crash site and could not believe what I saw...Usually you see much debris, wreckage, and much noise and commotion. This crash was different. There was no wreckage, no bodies, and no noise....It appeared as though there were no passengers or crew on this plane."(McCall, 86-87)

Somehow, approximately 600 lbs. of bodily remains were ultimately found at the crash site, where 44 people were supposed to have died. It was never revealed how many of these remains came from underground, where the alleged aircraft was buried. Of this amount only 200 lbs. could be linked to specific individuals.[4] This represents approximately 3.1 percent of the bodily weight of 44 people.[5] Yet not a drop of blood was sighted by eyewitnesses at the day of the crash. German criminal pathologist Prof. Wolfgang Eisenmenger says that he "cannot imagine such a consequence" from a plane crash.(Wisnewski, *Operation 9/11*, 231) In theory such total fragmentation might be conceivable had the plane crashed against solid rock, but in the case of UA93, the aircraft is said to have crashed onto soft ground, into which it allegedly entirely disappeared.

Investigators brought possible stab wounds and lacerations to the attention of FBI pathologists but the FBI responded that "the catastrophic nature of the crash and fragmentation" left the pathologists unable to draw conclusions, such as whether any of the people aboard were killed before the aircraft crashed and how they died.[6] Yet, determining the approximate time of death is most often possible days or even weeks after death. Forensic science provides a variety of solutions to determine the approximate time of death, by body temperature, skin color, and forensic entomology (the study of body decomposition, decay and in-

---

1   Tom Gibb, "Newsmaker...," Op. cit., #1105.
2   "Six Months After 9/11, It's a Changed World," *CNN*, March 11, 2002, #1109
3   Peter Perl, "Hallowed Ground," *Washington Post*, May 12, 2002, #500
4   "On Hallowed Ground," Op. cit., #093
5   Peter Perl, "Hallowed Ground," Op. cit., #500
6   Tom Gibb, "Flight 93 remains yield no evidence," *Post-Gazette*, December 20, 2001, #522 (cited in Gerhard Wisnewski, *Mythos 9/11 – Die Wahrheit auf der Spur* (Knaur Taschenbuch, 2004 – in German) p. 146-7

sect infestation)[1] The 200 lbs. of bodily remains were certainly sufficient material for such tests. Did the recovered human remains belong to individuals who had died long before and had been planted at the alleged crash site?

(e) The invisible recovery of the wreckage

Despite the apparent absence of wreckage from flight UA93 reported by witnesses, FBI agent Bill Crowley announced on September 24, 2001—merely 13 days after 9/11—that "95 percent of the plane was recovered...and the pieces of United Airlines Flight 93 that had been recovered were turned over Sunday to the airline..."[2] He said that the biggest piece recovered was a 6-by-7-foot piece of the fuselage skin, including four windows. The heaviest piece, he said, was part of an engine fan, weighing about 1,000 pounds. None of the eyewitnesses had mentioned having observed these objects at the crash site. With the exception of the two black boxes, all wreckage was reportedly passed on to United Airlines. Asked what United Airlines would do with the wreckage, an airline spokeswoman said, "I don't think a decision has been made...but we're not commenting."[3] According to Jeff Plantz, senior investigator of flight safety at United Airlines, eight of the dumpsters that "contain the wreckage of United Flight 93...are currently [May 31, 2002] in a hangar in Somerset, Pennsylvania. The wreckage is the property of United Airlines' insurance company."[4] In spite of the end of FBI's recovery work at the site, it remained surrounded by a chain-link fence. County coroner Wallace Miller warned: "If anybody is caught penetrating that perimeter and disregarding [the no-trespassing] signs, they will be prosecuted to the fullest extent of the law."[5]

Michael Renz of the German public television station ZDF tried to film the wreckage of the aircraft that crashed at Somerset County for a documentary. After asking for permission from United Airlines, he and his team were told that the insurance company had custody of the wreckage.[6] The insurance company said it could not provide any information: The responsible individual was in a meeting, then on a three-day business trip, then on an intercontinental trip that would take weeks. During this time he could not be reached by email or cellphone, "so we were told by the secretary of one of the largest airline-insurance companies in the United States."[7] After weeks and countless phone calls, finally a brief answer came: "We do not have the wreckage. The FBI in Washington is

1   Forensic Entomology Resources, #1091
2   "FBI finished with Pennsylvania crash site probe," *CNN*, September 24, 2001, #753
3   Tom Gibb, "FBI ends site work, says no bomb used," *Post-Gazette*, September 25, 2001, #509
4   FBI 302-116001. May 31, 2002. Communication from Jeff Plantz
5   Ibid.
6   Kerstin Decker, "Da ist was im Busch," *Tagesspiegel*, September 11, 2007, #534a
7   Ibid.

in charge." The FBI press officer refused an interview but said he would certainly give permission to film the wreckage, though not immediately. But alas! The FBI no longer had the wreckage. It had been returned to United Airlines. Back to square one! The producer returned to Germany without any evidence of the wreckage.[1] The producer described similar difficulties when he tried to obtain permission to film inside a Boeing flight simulator or when he approached New York officials to ask them about the fireproofing in the WTC. "But when we talk with officials off-the-record, many say a gag-order has been handed down from the top."[2]

In 2006, after the trial of Zacarias Moussaoui, the US Government released a set of photographs purporting to depict items found at the UA93 crash site.[3] These mostly low-quality photographs do not enable one to determine whether they relate to a Boeing 757, let alone whether they belonged to the aircraft designated as flight UA93. In addition, no chain-of-custody reports were attached to these photographs. It is, thus, not possible to confirm when, where and by whom these photographs were made.

(f) Extreme secrecy surrounding the crash site

State Police Lt. Col. Robert Hickes said that 280 state troopers were protecting the crash site.... Using horses and helicopters, state police have created a *double ring of security* around the area that spans *several miles*.[4]

John M. Eller, police chief in Brookhaven, PA, reported that approximately 600 troopers were utilized at the crash site in Shanksville, thereof 16 mounted troopers. To prevent unauthorized people from *seeing* the crash area, "inside and outside perimeters were established" and "checkpoints were established along... roadways" leading to the crash site. Initially, "the news media were staged in an area around the outer perimeter...The Major instructed that the news media be transported to the crash site in two buses. They were permitted to photograph the site for one half-hour and then return to the staging area."[5]

The FBI strictly prevented journalists and members of the public from photographing the crash site. As an example, a township supervisor from Blair County by the name of Terence Claar was physically subdued by state troopers for trying to sneak onto the crash site and was then hospitalized. He was the seventh

---

1   Ibid.
2   Barbara Möller, "War es eine Verschwörung?"[Was it a conspiracy?], *Hamburger Abendblatt*, 11, 2007 [in German], #534
3   Prosecution Trial Exhibits P200057-P200069 from the website of United States v. Zacarias Moussaoui, Criminal No. 01-455-A. ‹http://www.vaed.uscourts.gov/notablecases/mouss-aoui/exhibits/prosecution.html›
4   Acton and Gazarik, Op. cit., #386
5   John M. Eller, "United Flight 93 Revisited: Command and Control in Shanksville," *9-1-1 Magazine*, September 11, 2011 (originally published in the Sept./Oct. issue), #1110

person charged with trying to enter what was designated as a crime scene.[1] As a result of this secrecy, no photographs are available from the recovery of the aircraft's wreckage.

In the September/October 2002 issue of *9-1-1 Magazine*, a publication dealing with Managing Emergency Communications, John Eller, mentioned above, described some of the police efforts to control media coverage of operations at the Shanksville crash site:

> The outer perimeter, approximately five miles in length, was established along the edge of the tree line; the inner perimeter was inside the wooded area. Initially, the news media were staged in an area around the outer perimeter...The Major instructed that the news media be transported to the crash site in two busses. They were permitted to photograph the site for one half-hour and then return to the staging area. This allowed equal time for all news media on location. It also established a spirit of cooperation between law enforcement personnel and the media.[2]

Few photos exist of the operations at the site. Among those few is the following photograph showing a Penn State Police Mobile Command Post "during operation at the crash site of Flight 93 in Shanksville."

Paul Falavolito worked as a paramedic in Pittsburgh, PA, and following the events of 9/11 as part of an on-site medical support team for rescue workers and family members who traveled to the Shanksville crash site. Among his impressions:

---

1   Tom Gibb, "Blair supervisor seized at crash site," *Post-Gazette*, September 26, 2001, #1111
2   John M. Eller, Op. cit., #1110

Upon arrival at the site, we are greeted by a barrier of state police cars on a rural road in this town...At the checkpoint, we show our IDs and are allowed through. For the next two miles, I cannot believe my eyes. Down this country road, police cars and troopers are everywhere. Horseback troopers are patrolling the area...Checkpoints are everywhere...This is a scary feeling: I feel like I am in another country.[1]

According to the *Tribune-Review* (Pittsburgh), within hours after the crash, the authorities "cordoned off the area within a 4-mile radius of the crash site."[2] Later the FBI and state police confirmed that they had cordoned off a second area about six to eight miles away from the crater, where debris were found.[3]

German author Gerhard Wisnewski makes the cogent point that in accident cases, the police legitimately protects the dignity and privacy of victims, but usually allows journalists to observe from afar recovery operations.[4] Not so with regard to flight UA93. Shortly after the alleged crash, the entire zone was closed to journalists, who were herded to a location from which they could not, even with telephoto lenses, monitor the operations on the crash site.[5]

Apparently substantial efforts and expenses were spent to prevent reporters from actually seeing the alleged crash area, observing from afar the recovery work, take photographs of large items that had allegedly been found,[6] and monitor the excavation of the crater. Even the reported recovery of 95% of the aircraft by the FBI was not allowed to be photographed. Such secrecy could not be explained and indeed, was not explained, by the need to secure a crime scene against interference. The secrecy could, however, be explained by the need to hide the planting of evidence, such as that listed in the next sub-section.

(g) Were personal items planted at the crash site?

Eyewitnesses who came immediately to the alleged crash site, from where they heard an explosion and saw a cloud of smoke ascending, did not see anything there that reminded them of the wreckage of an aircraft. They saw no fuselage, no tail, no bodies, no blood. Yet the FBI claimed later to have found there an amazing collection of recognizable personal items that belonged to passengers, crew members and alleged hijackers.

---

1   Paul Falavolito, "United Flight 93 Crash Site, Shanksville," *EMS World*, September 8, 2011, #1112

2   "Scene of utter destruction," *Tribune-Review* (Pittsburgh), September 12, 2001, #757

3   "America under Attack," *CNN Breaking News*, September 13, 2001, #758

4   Wisnewski, *Mythos 9/11*, p. 150

5   Ibid.

6   Among large items allegedly found are a section of the engine, parts of the fuselage, the tail section, airline seats, and others. No photographic evidence of these findings has been released.

According to the FBI, the following items were recovered from the alleged crash site of flight UA 93 at Somerset County:

- Kingdom of Saudi Arabia ID card of alleged hijacker Ahmed Alnami (item Q1)

- Saudi Arabian Youth Hostels Association ID Card for same (item Q2)

- Three small color photographs, two strips of negatives and an enlarged photocopy of Kingdom of Saudi Arabia ID Card (items Q3)

- Handwritten letter with possible Arabic writing (item Q45)

- A "five page Arabic document [with] details regarding the strategy and preparation required to conduct a hijacking."[1]

- Personal effects belonging to passengers Christian Adams, Lorraine Bay, Todd Beamer, Alan Beaven, Mark Bingham, Deora Bodley, Sandra Bradshaw, Marion Britton, Thomas Burnett, Bill Cashman, Georgine Corrigan, Patricia Cushing, Donald Greene, Linda Gronlund, Richard Guadagno, Jason Dahl, Patrick Driscoll, Edward Felt, Jane Folger, Colleen Fraser, Andrew Garcia, Jeremy Glick, Louis Nacke, Nicole Miller, John Talignani and Leroy Homer.[2]

Another FBI document, released among the 9/11 Commission's papers in 2009, lists in addition the following knives or knife parts found at the UA93 crash site:[3]

Q17	Black knife handle (your item #2)
Q18	Silver colored blade and piece of black handle (your item #3)
Q44	Possible handmade knife (your item #20)
Q362	Pocket knife (Item 7, 1B26, Barcode E01991643)
Q363	Multi-purpose utility tool with knife blade exposed (Item 29, 1B286, Barcode E01991317)
Q377	Pocket knife (1B675, Barcode E01991305)
Q380	Open partial Leatherman tool (1B680, Barcode E01991344)
Q382	Green plastic handle for utility knife (1B682, Barcode E01991345)
Q522	Section of utility knife (1B726, Barcode E01991293)
Q524	Part of Leatherman multipurpose tool (1B732, Barcode E01991307)
Q640	Knife blade (1B1280)
Q641	Knife blade (1B1043)
Q642	Knife blade (1B1043)
Q1343	Possible knife blade (1B1340, Barcode E01991596)

---

1   FBI 265A-NY-280350-HQ-4809. The document is referred to in three FBI documents found among 9/11 Commission documents (stored at NARA), but has not been released.

2   FBI 302-83949. October 12, 2001. List of UA93 passengers for whom property was found

3   "Knives found at the UA Flight 93 crash site," 9/11 Commission documents, NARA, Team 7 Box 18, #565

For unexplained reasons, these FBI documents do not mention that a "business card in the name of Ziad Jarrah's uncle, Assem Jarrah, was recovered at the crash site of Flight 93 in Pennsylvania." In a Stipulation filed by the government in the trial of Zacarias Moussaoui,[1] it is even claimed that the:

> ...following handwriting appeared on the back of the partially torn card:
>
> Rajh Moham
> Billsteder Hauptstr, 14
> 22111 Hamburg
> Germany

The above FBI documents do not, either, mention CeeCee Lyles' driving license,[2] the passport of alleged hijacker Al Ghamdi,[3] alleged hijacker Alnami's Florida driver's license[4] and a visa page from alleged hijacker Ziad Jarrah's passport,[5] all of which were allegedly found at the crash site.

The *Pittsburgh Post-Gazette* of December 30, 2001, reported that many personal items were found at the Shanksville crash site, including jewelry, photos, credit cards, purses and their contents, shoes, a wallet and currency.[6] Craig Hendrix, a funeral coordinator and personal effects administrator with Douglass Air Disaster Funeral Coordinators, said to the paper: "We have some property for most passengers."[7] He said United Airlines' underwriter hired Douglass on September 12 (!) to handle not only funeral arrangements for the victims but also the return of personal effects.

Jerry and Beatrice Guadagno of Ewing, N.J., parents of Richard Guadagno, passenger aboard UA93, received Richard's credentials and his badge from the US Fish and Wildlife Service that were reportedly found at the crash site. Richard's sister Lori said of the credentials, which were returned in their wallet: "It was practically intact. It just looked like it wasn't damaged or hadn't gone through much of anything at all, which is so bizarre and ironic."[8]

---

1   Stipulation, Zacarias Moussaoui's trial, Exhibit ST00001, p. 85, #1166

2   A photograph of CeeCee Lyles' driver's license was allegedly found at the crash site in Somerset County, Pennsylvania and presented as Prosecution Exhibit No. P200069 at the Moussaoui trial

3   Moussaoui Prosecution Trial Exhibit No. PA00108, #1168

4   Moussaoui Prosecution Trial Exhibit No. PA00110, #1169

5   Moussaoui Prosecution Trial Exhibit No. PA00105.08, #1170

6   Steve Levin, "Flight 93 victims' effects to go back to families," *Post-Gazette*, 30, 2001, #566

7   Ibid.

8   Ibid.

Apart from some timid expressions of surprise by families who received intact personal effects—of which an example is provided above—few raised the question how these items could be found in good condition while their owners did not leave a visible trace.

Planting aircraft parts in order to fake a crash site was actually envis-aged by the US military as part of Operation Northwoods (discussed in chapter 6):

> It is possible to create an incident which will make it appear that Com-munist Cuban MIGs have destroyed a USAF aircraft over international waters in an unprovoked attack... (c) At precisely the same time that the aircraft was presumably shot down, a submarine or small surface craft would disburse F-101 parts, parachute, etc., at approximately 15 to 20 miles off the Cuban coast and depart. The pilots returning to Home-stead would have a true story as far as they knew. Search ships and aircraft could be dispatched and parts of aircraft found."[1]

This plan, seriously considered by the US military, demonstrates that planting incriminating evidence to fake an aircraft crash has been previously considered by public officials in support of what they regarded as overriding foreign policy objectives. The nature, number and condition of items found at the alleged crash site of flight UA93—as reported above—compounded by the revelations from the planned Operation Northwoods, support the view that the aforementioned personal items had been planted to fake the crash of flight UA93 after their owners had been murdered elsewhere.

(h) Debris were found up to eight miles from the official crash site

The following map summarizes the location of the most well-documented debris fields:[2]

- The primary crash site, centered at the impact crater
- The location of an engine: ~ 2000 feet away
- The Indian Lake marina, ~ 3 miles away
- The New Baltimore, ~ 8 miles away

1   Operation Northwoods. Memorandum for the Secretary of Defense, Justification for US Military Intervention in Cuba, March 13, 1962, signed by L.L. Lemnitzer, Chairman, Joint Chiefs, item 9, #765
2   "Rural Pennsylvania Crash Site of the Fourth Jet Commandeered on September 11th," *9-11 Research*, #1171

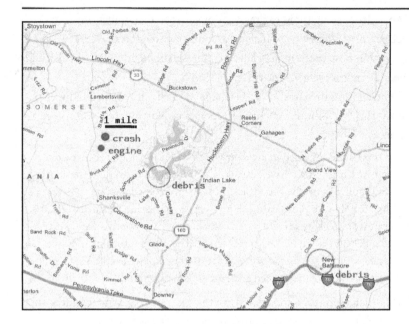

This analysis of the debris distribution suggests that an aircraft was shot down, and that it might have been flying west at the time.

On September 12, 2001, the *Pittsburgh Post-Gazette* reported that flight UA93, "fell from the sky near Shanksville at 10:06 a.m...., leaving a trail of debris five miles long."[1] Meanwhile leaders of Congress reportedly discussed "a possible shoot down of the aircraft."[2] Indeed, Glenn Cramer, a 911 supervisor at the Westmoreland County Emergency Operations Center reported that his center got a call on the morning of 9/11 at 9:58 "from a male passenger stating that he was locked in the bathroom of United Flight 93... [who] said he believed the plane was going down. He did hear some sort of explosion and saw white smoke coming from the plane, but he didn't know where. And then we lost contact with him."[3] It later transpired that the caller's name was Edward Felt.

According to the *Pittsburgh Post-Gazette* of September 13, 2001,

> Residents and workers at businesses outside Shanksville, Somerset County, reported discovering clothing, books, papers and what appeared to be human remains. Some residents said they collected bags-full of items to be turned over to investigators. Others reported what appeared to be crash debris floating in Indian Lake, nearly six miles from the immediate crash scene. Workers at Indian Lake Marina said that they saw a cloud of confet-

---

1   Jonathan D. Silver et al, "Day of Terror: Outside tiny Shanksville, a fourth deadly stroke," *Post-Gazette*, September 12, 2001(emphasis added), #275
2   Ibid.
3   Ibid.

ti-like debris descend on the lake and nearby farms minutes after hearing the explosion that signaled the crash at 10:06 a.m. Tuesday.[1]

In a report filed by the same journalists the next day, we read:

> On Wednesday morning, marina Service Manager John Fleegle found what he figured was a bone, washed up on one of the marina's concrete boat launches. "It was maybe five inches long. It put me in mind of maybe a rib bone," Fleegle said. "I called the state police. They contacted the FBI, and they picked it up."

> On the Lowery farm, it rained financial statements—enough that Lowery and wife Gerry had a handful in the three one-gallon plastic bags of debris they turned over to investigators.

> "They said they found unopened mail," Gerry Lowery said of the mix of state police and FBI searchers who walked almost shoulder-to-shoulder through their fields all day Wednesday and yesterday. "They found a picture, a snapshot of a baby. That just caused goose bumps for me."[2]

The *Tribune-Review* (Pittsburgh) wrote:

> [I]n nearby Indian Lake...residents reported hearing the doomed jetliner flying over at a low altitude before "falling apart on their homes." "People were calling in and reporting pieces of plane falling," a state trooper said. Jim Stop reported he had seen the hijacked Boeing 757 fly over him as he was fishing. He said he could see parts falling from the plane.[3]

Note that at least one eyewitness claimed to have been seen "parts falling from the plane," suggesting that the plane disintegrated in flight. Tom Spinelli, who was working at India Lake Marina, a mile and a half away from the alleged crash site, said that debris rained down on the lake:

> "It was mainly mail, bits of in-flight magazine and scraps of seat cloth. The authorities say it was blown here by the wind."[4]

CNN and the *Pittsburgh Post-Gazette* reported on September 13, 2001, that the police and the FBI "cordoned off" an area with plane debris, "about six to eight miles from the main crash site." In another news report, hours after the crash, teams of crime scene analysts from the FBI and Bureau of Alcohol, Tobacco and Firearms, plus state police, the Pennsylvania National Guard and state agencies..."cordoned off" the area within a 4-mile radius of the crash."[5]

Initially, the FBI "didn't want to speculate whether the debris was from the crash, or if the plane could have broken up in midair." Later, investigators said

---

1   Ibid. (emphasis added)
2   James O'Toole, Tom Gibb and Cindi Lash, "Flight data recorder may hold clues to suicide flight," *Post-Gazette*, September 14, 2001, #702
3   Acton and Gazarik, Op. cit., #386
4   Richard Wallace, "What did happen to flight 93?," *Daily Mirror*, September 12, 2002, #710
5   "Scene of utter destruction," *The Tribune-Review*, September 12, 2001, #757

that the debris was all "very light material, such as paper and thin nylon the wind would easily blow."[1] Ultimately, the secrecy surrounding the items collected from these various sites prevents a definite determination of what was found where. The suspicion remains in the minds of numerous inhabitants of the area that flight UA93 was shot down and disintegrated in mid-air. Even if an aircraft had been shot down there, there is no evidence it was flight UA93.

How did the 9/11 Commission address the issue of wide-spread plane debris in its Final Report? The Commission ignored it completely.

(i) The phantom engines

Among the sturdiest parts of an aircraft are its engines. A Boeing 757-200, the aircraft that allegedly crashed in Somerset County, carries two Pratt and Whitney engines Model 2000, or more accurately Model PW2037 (see photograph above). According to United Airlines, the Serial Numbers of these engines were 726610 and 726544.[2] Each of them weighs 3.3 tons and has a diameter of nearly 80 inches (2 meters).[3] In aircraft crashes such engines would typically incur damage, but won't vaporize, disintegrate or vanish. What happened to these engines?

On September 13, 2001, CNN announced that the biggest aircraft part found at the crash site "is an engine, an engine part, and most of the other pieces are probably no bigger than this particular notebook."[4] The following day, the *Tribune-Review* quoted State police Maj. Lyle Szupika, who said searchers had found one of the engines from the aircraft "at a considerable distance from the crash site, by a garden wall." He added: "It appears to be the whole engine."[5] On September 24, 2001, the story changed again. CNN said that according to FBI Agent William Crowley the heaviest piece from the aircraft found "was part of engine fan, weighing about 1,000 pounds."[6] A year later, *The Age* (Australia) wrote that a "section of the engine, weighing almost a ton, was found on the bed of a catchment pond, 200 metres downhill."[7]

Jim Svonavec, owner of Svonavec Inc., a coal company that owns 270 acres—including the impact site—told American Free Press (AFP) that the recovery

---

1   "Black box from Pennsylvania crash found," *CNN*, September 13, 2001, #725

2   9/11 Commission document, "UAL Jumpseat Fdr- Entire Contents- UA 175 and UA 93-Emails and Documents 562," Team 7, Box 18, #499

3   PW2000—Maintenance, Repair and Overhaul, *MTU Aero Engines*, #1087

4   Brian Cabell," CNN Breaking News," *CNN*, September 13, 2001, #1086

5   Richard Gazarik and Robin Acton, "Black Box Recovered: Authorities deny Flight 93 was shot down by F-16", Pittsburgh Tribune Review, September 14, 2001, #1172

6   "FBI finished with Pennsylvania crash site probe," *CNN*, September 24, 2001, #753

7   "On Hallowed Ground," Op. cit, #093

of the engine "at least 1,800 feet into the woods," was done solely by FBI agents using his equipment.[1]

Whichever of these above versions of the engine story is true, if any, the following facts should be retained from what is known: (a) There is no photographic evidence of this item; (b) No person actually testified to have seen this item; (c) The location where the item was found remains unsettled; (d) No mention is made why the other engine was not found; (e) The engine fan that was allegedly found, has not been confirmed as belonging to an engine bearing one of the above serial numbers; (f) No official document can be located which confirms that an engine, or part thereof, bearing one the aforementioned engine serial numbers, had been found. The story above may either be a legend or refers to the finding of an object resembling an engine or a fan but not belonging to the aircraft designated as flight UA93 (tail N591UA).

(j) No fuel contamination in the crash site

Assuming that a huge plane had crashed at this location and burrowed into the soil, one would expect substantial oil contamination in the soil into which the plane vanished. Yet according to Betsy Mallison, a spokeswoman of the Department of Environmental Protection, at least three test wells have been sunk to monitor groundwater, but no contamination has been discovered.[2]

(k) Concluding observations about the Somerset County crash site

The reported crash site at Somerset County and the events that occurred there on the morning of 9/11 remain an open mystery that the US authorities do not wish to reveal. Did an aircraft crash there? Was it shot down?[3] Was the crash site prepared in advance? Was a bomb detonated at the alleged crash site to fake a crash? Were body parts planted at the site? How did the local residents cope with the contradictions between their own sightings and the official account? These questions remain unsettled.

How did the 9/11 Commission address the testimonies regarding the absence of visible wreckage at the crash site of Flight 93 and the aforementioned testimonies? By simply ignoring them. This crash site is mentioned only a few times in the 9/11 Commission's Final Report and mainly to emphasize two points: That "no evidence of firearms or of their identifiable remains was found at the air-

1   Christopher Bollyn, "Three years after terror attacks, public still doubts 'official' story," *American Free Press*, 2004, #1089

2   Tom Gibb, "Latest Somerset Crash Site Findings May Yield Added IDs, *Post-Gazette*, October 3, 2001, #1088

3   Donald Rumsfeld is said to have misspoken when he, while addressing US combatants in Iraq in 2004, talked about the "people who [...] shot down the plane over Pennsylvania." *CNN*, December 24, 2004, #1090

craft's crash site"(Final Report, 13) and that "[t]he FBI collected 14 knives or portions of knives at the Flight 93 crash site."(Final Report, 457, n.82)

On September 14, 2001, the North American Aerospace Defense Command (NORAD) responded to "persistent rumors...that US military aircraft shot down United Airlines Flight 93 in Somerset County." An unnamed NORAD spokesperson said that "NORAD-allocated forces have not engaged with weapons any aircraft, including Flight 93."[1] This carefully worded statement limited the denial to "NORAD-allocated forces." Asked if there were any military aircraft flying in the vicinity of Flight 93 or activated in response to the hijacking of the plane, Capt. Adriane Craig, a NORAD spokeswoman, declined comment.[2]

The 9/11 Commission ignored these questions. None of the eyewitnesses from Shanksville, whose testimony might have undermined the official account, was invited to testify before the Commission. The Commission did not, either, demand from the FBI hard evidence that flight UA93 actually crashed at Shanksville, such as authenticated photographs of original aircraft parts and formal identification of aircraft parts by their serial numbers.

Conclusions

The main findings of this chapter are:

- Photographic evidence of aircraft wreckage from the three alleged crash sites is both sparse and inconclusive.

- At none of the three locations, designated as aircraft crash sites, did eyewitnesses observe wreckage that could plausibly account for Boeing 757 or 767 aircraft.

- The alleged crash site of flight UA93 extended over many miles.

- The FBI was unusually secretive about the UA93 crash site.

- No bodies or blood were sighted at the UA93 crash site but numerous paper documents belonging to UA93 passengers and crew members were found there, particularly after September 14, 2001

---

1   Jonathan D. Silver,"NORAD denies military shot down Flight 93," *Post-Gazette*, September 14, 2001, #764
2   Ibid.

Chapter 5. The Cockpit Voice Recorder Of Flight UA93

Every commercial aircraft carries two "black boxes," a Flight Data Recorder (FDR) and a Cockpit Voice Recorder (CVR). The CVR is an extremely sturdy device that stores sounds (including conversation) from the cockpit.

The only CVR found and deemed usable from the four 9/11 flights was said to be that from flight UA93. It was reportedly found at the alleged crash site of flight UA93 in Somerset County, PA, on September 14, 2001, "25 feet below ground in the crater" into which the aircraft had allegedly disappeared.[1] There are no known witnesses to the discovery of this device, reportedly found about 8:25 p.m.

According to official accounts, the CVR from Flight UA93 could only store the last 30 minutes of sounds from the cockpit. Ron Crotty, a spokesman for the avionics division of Honeywell, one of the largest manufacturers of cockpit voice records, told Pittsburgh *Post-Gazette*, however, that it was "pretty likely" that Flight 93 had a CVR that stored 120 minutes of information.[2] He also told the *Post-Gazette* that the "[black boxes] were brought [to Honeywell] by the FBI because the FBI had some difficulty retrieving the data. Our folks worked on it [sic] all weekend long." He added: "I don't know what was on there. None of our guys knows anything about the data. We just provide technical assistance. Our

1   Matthew P. Smith, "Flight 93 voice recorder found in Somerset County crash site," *Post-Gazette*, September 15, 2001, #996
2   Jonathan D. Silver, "Will black box reveal Flight 93's last moments?" *Post-Gazette*, September 14, 2001, #507

guys aren't trained in analyzing the data. They would not actually hear the data. They put it on some sort of medium. I'm not sure if it's some sort of tape or disc."[1]

It is interesting that the FBI brought the [black boxes] to Honeywell in order to "retriev[e] the data." According to Anna Cushman, a CVR analyst for the National Transportation Safety Board (NTSB), the "black box from the plane [which plowed into a field in Pennsylvania] came to NTSB [...] for the extraction of its data before being turned over to the FBI."[2] She did not mention that the NTSB had difficulty retrieving the data and had Honeywell carry out this task.

When Tom Flocco (or his aides) asked Michael Thompson, chief engineer in the CVR/FDR division of Allied Signal—Honeywell Corporation in Redmond, Washington—if he was the person in charge of flight data recovery in the 9/11 investigation, since Honeywell manufactured the data recorders in operation on all four Boeing jets allegedly involved in 9/11, he replied "I cannot answer that, under advice from legal counsel." When Flocco (or his aides) asked Thompson if he had ever seen or been involved in any recovery analysis of the 9/11 CVRs or FDRs, Thompson again stated, "That's a legal question, and on advice of counsel, I cannot answer any of those questions."[3]

No document could be found on the websites of the FBI and of the NTSB that would provide the Model and Serial Number of the CVR from Flight UA93. The absence of the CVR serial number is highly unusual.

According to Philly News of November 18, 2001, the FBI refused to release data from either of the critical "black boxes." Citing the ongoing war on terrorism, the FBI said it can't say when it will release the data—or indeed, if it ever will. Yet, earlier in November, flight AA587 crashed in New York and federal officials released detailed information about the cockpit recorder in less than 36 hours.[4]

Initially, "the FBI declined to play the tape [*sic*], saying it was too disturbing and it was evidence that might be used in criminal prosecutions related to the attacks."(Longman, 374) It also referred to the tradition of not revealing publicly the contents of the CVR from crashed aircraft. At behest of the families, the FBI lifted the traditional secrecy surrounding CVRs. On 18 April 2002, the FBI invited victims' families to listen to the CVR from Flight UA93. Department of Justice prosecutors "exhorted families not to describe the tapes' contents because they will be played as evidence in the terrorism conspiracy

1   Jonathan D. Silver, "FBI transcribing crash recording," *Post-Gazette*, September 20, 2001, #768

2   Ray Bert, "Hearing Voices, Transformations," *Worcester Polytechnic Institute's alumni magazine*, Spring 2002, #841

3   Tom Flocco, "Lawyers Seek Black-Box Data on Saudi Hijackers 9/11," November 27, 2002, #1029

4   William Bunch, "We know it crashed, but not why," *Philly News*, November 18, 2001, #623

trial of Zacarias Moussaoui."[1] FBI agents "asked the relatives to surrender all cell phones, palm pilots and pagers to prevent the recording of any of the day's proceedings."(Longman, 374) After the session, the family members left "under the escort of New Jersey state troopers and federal agents, who walked them to their cars and shielded them from reporters."[2] Without a transcript, listeners said they would have had difficulties to distinguish the spoken words.[3] Some said that tape raised more questions than it answered.[4] Reporter Stevenson Swanson of the *Chicago Tribune* said that "family members who spoke to reporters after listening to the contents were guarded in their remarks. But some, including [Deena] Burnett, indicated that they believed they recognized their relatives' voices on the tape."[5]

Deena Burnett described in her book *Fighting Back* the circumstances surrounding the playing of the CVR recording:

> We were led back into the main room where Mr. Novak addressed everyone. "There will be a transcript of the recording project on a large screen to make it easier to understand what you will be hearing," he said. He also told us there would be a timeline projected on the screen, so we could match the sounds to get a better idea of the scenario on the plane. (p. 201)

At one point she wrote, "I could hear one [hijacker] instructing the other on how to fly the plane.... One hijacker pilot was yelling at the second, telling him he was touching the wrong buttons. 'Get the pilot back up here to turn off these alarms,' he said."(p. 202) She does not indicate whether they talked in English, whether she understood Arabic or whether she relied on the transcript. The transcript, incidentally, does not mention anything about turning off these alarms. She wrote that she "heard" one of the hijackers say, "Should I finish it off?" and another hijacker said, "No, not yet," (p. 204) but according to the transcript of the CVR, these phrases were also said in Arabic.

The CVR recording was played towards the end of the Moussaoui trial at the specific request of the prosecution in order to emotionally impact the jury.[6] The day before, District Judge Leonie M. Brinkema overruled defense objections and allowed the prosecution to show the jury "some of the most grisly evidence

1 Phil Hirschkorn and David Mattingly, "Families say Flight 93 tapes prove heroism," *CNN*, April 19, 2002, #1030
2 Ibid.
3 Ibid. p. 376
4 Ibid.
5 Stevenson Swanson, "Flight 93 tape ends doubts for families," *Chicago Tribune*, April 19, 2002, #726
6 Government submission regarding relevance of cockpit voice recorders, in United States of America v. Zacarias Moussaoui, Criminal No. 01-455-A, US District Court for the Eastern District of Virginia (undated), #498

so far, including photos of badly burned bodies [from the Pentagon]."[1] All major newspapers in the United States reported about this "single most chilling piece of evidence"[2] to which jurors "listened raptly."[3] The trial judge agreed to have it played and then decided, upon the request of an unidentified family member, to reseal the recording after it served its manipulative purpose.[4]

When Tom Flocco asked lawyers for Ness-Motley's whether they had verified through an independent and expert source that the Flight 93 CVR transcription tape the FBI played for the families was complete, unaltered, authentic and was constructed from the actual raw data on the memory chip in the CVR, Michael Elsner, associate attorney at Ronald Motley, replied: "None of the lawyers have had access to the tapes, transcriptions, or the actual raw data in the recorders."[5]

The *Philadelphia Daily News* reported on 16 September 2002 that

> relatives of Flight 93 passengers who heard the cockpit tape April 18 at a Princeton hotel said government officials laid out a timetable for the crash in a briefing and in a transcript that accompanied the recording. Relatives later reported they heard sounds of an on-board struggle beginning at 9:58 a.m., but there was a final "rushing sound" at 10:03, and the tape fell silent.... Vaughn Hoglan, the uncle of passenger Mark Bingham, said by phone from California that near the end there are shouts of "pull up, pull up," but the end of the tape "is inferred—there's no impact."[6]

According to leading seismologists, referred to by the newspaper, flight UA93 crashed at 10:06. The same newspaper reported that the FBI and other agencies rejected repeated requests to explain the discrepancy in the crash time.

Jere Longman, who spoke with families who attended the session, wrote that near the end of tape they heard shouting, including "roll it," "pull it up" or "lift it up," or "turn up." A final rushing sound could be heard about three minutes after ten, "hinting at a possible hole somewhere in the fuselage."[7] Then the tape went silent. Longman's account would fit with the above news report.

A significant omission in the families' guarded observations should be mentioned here. According to the official account, the recording ended as the aircraft was on the way to crash. None of the family members mentioned, however, hear-

1   Timothy Dwyer, Jerry Markon and William Branigin, "Flight 93 Recording Played at Moussaoui Trial," *Washington Post*, April 12, 2006, #1005
2   Richard A. Serrano, "Jury Hears Cockpit Recording of Doomed Flight 93," *Los Angeles Times*, April 12, 2006, #1006
3   Neil A. Lewis, "Final Struggles on 9/11 Plane Fill Courtroom," *New York Times*, April 13, 2006, #1004
4   "Order to reseal the tape." April 10, 2006, *United States of America v Zacarias Moussaoui*, #1031
5   Tom Flocco, Op. cit., #1029
6   William Bunch, "Three-minute discrepancy in tape (CVR UA93)," *Philly News*, September 16, 2001, #927
7   Richard Wallace, "What did happen to flight 93?," *Mirror.co.uk*, September 12, 2001, #710

ing blood-curling screams or any other expressions of panic that would indicate that the passengers were expecting to die.

On July 23, 2004, CNN publicized a revised version, similar though not equivalent to that enclosed in the Final Report of the 9/11 Commission:[8]

> The passengers continued with their assault, trying to break through the cockpit door. At 10:02 a.m. and 23 seconds, a hijacker said, "Pull it down! Pull it down!" The airplane headed down; the control wheel was turned hard to the right. The airplane rolled onto its back, and one of the hijackers began shouting, "Allah is the greatest. Allah is the greatest."

The story has now completely changed:

- The 10:06 a.m. seismic event and the three missing minutes have disappeared from the later account. The impact of the plane now occurs at 10:03 a.m.

- We are told that hijackers were on the verge of being overwhelmed by passengers while the plane was apparently flying upside down.

- In the 2002 version a hijacker is claimed to have shouted "pull it up, pull it up," or something of that kind. Now the hijacker is said to have shouted "pull it down, pull it down."

- According to the new version one of the hijackers allegedly shouts: "Allah is the greatest. Allah is the greatest." No relative who listened to the recording in 2002, mentioned these religious calls.

If the aircraft was flying upside down and was on the verge of crashing, the CVR would have captured heart-wrenching screams. Listeners of the previous version did not mention any screaming at the end of the recording but only a "rushing sound" that has not been explained.

But it gets still better. In 2006 the story changed again. According to the *San Francisco Gate* of 13 April 2006:

> Three minutes after 10 a.m., passengers seem to be breaking through the cockpit door, fighting with the hijackers in a futile effort to take back the throttle. "Go! Go!" they encourage one another. "Move! Move!" But the terrorists have flipped the plane upside down. They spin it downward.... In its final plunge, the hijackers shout over and over in Arabic: "Allah is the greatest! Allah is the greatest!"

In this version not one but all of the hijackers are shouting in choir "Allah is the greatest! Allah is the greatest!"

We have thus three different versions of one and the same CVR. Logically, there can only one definite version of a CVR, not three. At least two of these ver-

---

8 Final Report of the 9/11 Commission, p. 14: "Jarrah stopped the violent maneuvers at about 10:01:00 and said 'Allah is the greatest! Allah is the greatest!' He then asked another hijacker in the cockpit, 'Is that it? I mean, shall we put it down?' to which the other replied, 'Yes, put it in it, and pull it down.'" Note, too, the editorial manipulation of the text enclosed in quotation marks.

sions, if not all three, are fake. It is, therefore, not surprising that the FBI has kept the CVR under seal.[1]

Beyond the discrepancies described above, there are good reasons to doubt also the authenticity of the *transcripts* that have been released to the public.

Here is the first page of the transcript from the CVR of flight UA93, as released to the Moussaoui Trial:[2]

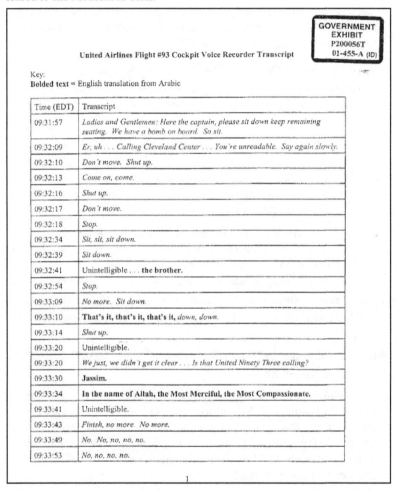

	GOVERNMENT EXHIBIT P200056T 01-455-A (ID)

United Airlines Flight #93 Cockpit Voice Recorder Transcript

Key:
Bolded text = English translation from Arabic

Time (EDT)	Transcript
09:31:57	*Ladies and Gentlemen: Here the captain, please sit down keep remaining seating. We have a bomb on board. So sit.*
09:32:09	*Er, uh . . . Calling Cleveland Center . . . You're unreadable. Say again slowly.*
09:32:10	*Don't move. Shut up.*
09:32:13	*Come on, come.*
09:32:16	*Shut up.*
09:32:17	*Don't move.*
09:32:18	*Stop.*
09:32:34	*Sit, sit, sit down.*
09:32:39	*Sit down.*
09:32:41	Unintelligible . . . **the brother.**
09:32:54	*Stop.*
09:33:09	*No more. Sit down.*
09:33:10	**That's it, that's it, that's it,** *down, down.*
09:33:14	*Shut up.*
09:33:20	Unintelligible.
09:33:20	*We just, we didn't get it clear . . . Is that United Ninety Three calling?*
09:33:30	**Jassim.**
09:33:34	**In the name of Allah, the Most Merciful, the Most Compassionate.**
09:33:41	Unintelligible.
09:33:43	*Finish, no more. No more.*
09:33:49	*No. No, no, no, no.*
09:33:53	*No, no. no. no.*

1

When we accidentally bump into another person's car and cause slight damage, the police are invited to come and make a detailed report that includes the exact location, the date and time of accident and the license numbers of the cars. Such reports are routinely made around the world.

1　Reuters News Service, "FBI refuses to release cockpit tape from hijacked flight," *Houston Chronicle*, 20 December 2001, #1032

2　Transcript of UA93 CVR released at the Moussaoui trial. Prosecution Exhibit P200056T, #285

In the above transcript—which was submitted to a criminal trial as a Government Exhibit—even the following basic identifying items are missing:

- The date of the event
- The time of the event
- The location of the event
- The tail number of the aircraft
- The serial number of the CVR
- The date on which the transcript was made from the CVR
- The name of the agency that produced the transcript
- The name(s) of the person(s) who transcribed the CVR
- The signature of the respective public officials responsible for the transcript

The lack of such identifying information would enable transcribers to disclaim responsibility, should it emerge that the transcript is a fraud.

According to the *Post-Gazette* of September 20, 2001, the FBI was already at the time "in the process of transcribing the contents of the cockpit voice recorder recovered...from the United Airlines plane that crashed in Somerset County." Yet, the transcript of the CVR that was sent to the 9/11 Commission and released after 2009 indicates that the transcript was made in March 1, 2002.

In an interview published in 2005, Anna Cushman of the NTSB describes how a CVR transcript is usually prepared. Once a CVR has been delivered to the NTSB, the analyst

> ...begins work immediately, day or night. Depending on how badly the unit has been damaged, [the analyst] may have to cut the box open to get at the tape or the memory chip. [The analyst] downloads the audio information and prepares a sound spectrum analysis and a transcript.... The transcript is prepared by a group, led by [the analyst], that includes representatives from the Federal Aviation Administration, the airline involved, the airplane and engine manufacturers, and the pilots union. The process can be tedious.[1]

An example of a authentic CVR analysis produced by the NTSB is Document DCA05MA003, Cockpit Voice Recorder—12, of January 27, 2005.[2] The first page names the members of the group that met on October 18, 2004, to analyze and transcribe the CVR, the aircraft type and tail number, the name of the airline and the flight number. The next pages list the name of the CVR manufacturer, its

---

1   Ray Bert, Hearing Voices, Transformations (Worcester Polytechnic Institute's alumni magazine), Spring 2002. #841

2   Anna Cushman, "Group Chairman's Factual Report," DCA05MA003 (analysis of Cockpit Voice Recorder, Flight 3701), NTSB, January 27, 2005, #1033

model and its serial number; a description of the audio recording and the sound quality of the four audio channels; timing and correlation and a summary description of audio events. Then follows a page explaining how audio quality is classified into five quality classes, a page with a legend explaining acronyms used throughout the transcript, and finally the transcript itself that includes the various ambient sounds and spoken text recorded by the CVR, with the exact time they were recorded and whenever possible the identity of the speaker. No such document was produced for the CVR from flight UA93.

A list of 29 transcripts from Cockpit Voice Recorders found at numerous aircraft crash sites around the world is posted on airdisaster.com.[1] They show what the transcript of flight UA93's CVR should have looked like and how ambient sounds are mentioned.

The only public document representing the CVR that was allegedly found at the Somerset County crash site is thus an undated and unsigned timeline of spoken phrases allegedly recorded on the CVR and typed on blank paper. Such an unauthenticated piece of paper, lacking attribution, has no probative value and is rightly suspected as a forgery. It may be retorted that the transcript was not meant to have a probative value, as its function was only to help listeners follow the audio version. But that transcript was officially released as the sole public representation of the CVR. It thus represents what the US government wishes the public to believe is recorded on the "authentic" CVR from flight UA93.

In 2007, CBS News reported that US District Judge Alvin K. Hellerstein ruled that jurors in cases filed by families of UA93 victims against the airlines, plane manufacturers, security agencies and the owners of airports, will not be allowed to listen to the entire recording from the CVR, only to "portions that the hijacked passengers may have heard."[2] Did the passengers hear anything from the cockpit? And if so, when? The idea behind playing that part of the recording was to convey to the jurors evidence of "substantial pain, suffering, terror and emotional distress" endured by the victims, as that could affect the amount of damages paid to the families.[3] Judge Hellerstein decided to reverse the traditional judicial procedure where liability is determined before damages are discussed in the hope that more cases might settle out of court, once families get a sense of how much money they are likely to get from a jury.[4] By this sleight-of-hand, Judge Hellerstein, with the acquiescence of defense lawyers, was able to prevent the contents of the CVR to be publicly scrutinized and the cases to advance to the merits phase, in which discovery procedures could reveal what really hap-

---

1   "List of voice CVR's transcripts," *AirDisaster.com*, #474
2   Associated Press, "Jury can hear part of flight 93 tape," *CBS News*, September 12, 2007, #720
3   Ibid.
4   Ibid.

pened on 9/11. Hellerstein, incidentally, did not hesitate to admit the manipulative purpose of his procedure, namely his efforts to induce claimants to forgo trial and take the money.

In 2009, NARA began releasing 9/11 documents. In one of the folders (Team 7 Box 17), a transcript from the CVR of UA93 is found which does mention cockpit sounds and is preceded by a page of explanations. It is dated as of 1 March 2002 and indicates a major review on 4 December 2003. No names of transcribers and translators are mentioned. The document is not, either, attributed to any particular agency.

The above facts strongly suggest that both the recordings of the CVR from flight UA93 played to the 9/11 families, to the 9/11 Commission and at the Moussaoui trial, as well as the transcripts of that CVR released to the public, were forgeries.

The transcripts of flight UA93's CVR constitute *prima facie* evidence of forgery.

Chapter 6. Aircraft Continued To Fly Past Crash Time

Chapter 3 provided evidence strongly suggesting that no commercial airliner had crashed at the known landmarks. In this chapter we provide circumstantial evidence that at least some of the 9/11 flights were doubled, meaning two or more aircraft flew under the same flight number in order to confuse air traffic control. In addition, we present positive evidence that at least flights UA175 and UA93 were still flying *after* their alleged crash times.

(1) Operation Northwoods

Operation Northwoods, proposed in 1962 by the Joint Chiefs of Staff and signed by Chairman Lyman Lemnitzer, was a secret plan for the US military to carry out real and simulated attacks in American cities and on US aircraft that would be blamed on Cuba in order to create a *casus belli* for a war against that country.[1] One part of the scenario was to have "selected passengers, all boarded under carefully prepared aliases" travel on a military aircraft painted to look like a civilian airliner. It was then to be claimed that the aircraft had been shot down by Cuba, justifying US attacks on that country. The heart of the operation involved switching the identities of aircraft in midair—without air traffic controllers noticing—to make it appear that a civilian aircraft had been shot. Here is the relevant excerpt from the Northwoods document:

> An aircraft at Eglin AFB would be painted and numbered as an exact duplicate for a civil registered aircraft belonging to a CIA proprietary organization in the Miami area. At a designated time the duplicate

---

1   "Operation Northwoods," Wikipedia

would be substituted for the actual civil aircraft and would be loaded with the selected passengers, all boarded under carefully prepared aliases. The actual registered aircraft would be converted to a drone. Take off times of the drone aircraft and the actual aircraft will be scheduled to allow a rendezvous south of Florida. From the rendezvous point the passenger-carrying aircraft will descend to minimum altitude and go directly into an auxiliary field at Eglin AFB where arrangements will have been made to evacuate the passengers and return the aircraft to its original status. The drone aircraft meanwhile will continue to fly the filed flight plan. When over Cuba the drone will begin transmitting on the international distress frequency a "MAY DAY" message stating he is under attack by Cuban MIG aircraft. The transmission will be interrupted by destruction of the aircraft which will be triggered by radio signal. This will allow ICAO radio in the Western Hemisphere to tell the US what has happened to the aircraft instead of the US trying to "sell" the incident.[1]

The "rendezvous point" mentioned in the Northwoods scenario is where the two aircraft would meet above each other (in order to merge into a single blip on the radar) and switch their transponder codes: Whereas the civilian aircraft would disappear from radar by "descend[ing] to minimum altitude," the military plane would, cruising under the changed transponder code, appear to air traffic controllers as the civilian aircraft continuing its flight.

The execution of Operation Northwoods, described by author James Bamford as perhaps "the most corrupt plan ever created by the US government," was ultimately rejected by President J.F. Kennedy. Although he then removed Admiral Lemnitzer from his position as Chairman of the Joint Chiefs of Staff, Lemnitzer became shortly thereafter the Supreme Allied Commander of NATO. The Northwoods document was published online in 2001 by the National Security Archive.[2]

(2) Evidence of doubles—Operation Northwoods 2.0?

A puzzling anomaly was discovered years ago by blogger *Woody Box* (or Ewing2001) regarding the gate number at Logan Airport (Boston) from which flight AA11 is said to have departed.[3] According to most media reports published in the days following 9/11, flight AA11 departed from gate number 26. Later reports put the departure of flight AA11 at gate 32, without explaining the reason for the change. American Airlines neither confirmed from which gate flight AA11 had departed nor commented on this discrepancy.

---

1   "Pentagon Proposed Pretexts for Cuba Invasion in 1962," *The National Security Archive*, 30, 2001, #1113
2   Ibid.
3   Woody Box (or Ewing2001), "Flight 11—The Twin Flight," #854

Were there two aircraft flying under the designation AA11 on that day, one departing from gate 26 (with passengers and crew) and another from gate 32 (without passengers)? Reported facts seem to support this hypothesis:

- Reporters from the German weekly *Der Spiegel* inquired at Logan Airport, Boston, about the departure of flight AA11. They found out that it had departed from gate number 26 and that boarding at that gate began at 7:35 a.m. Yet, according to the 9/11 Commission, boarding for flight AA11 began at 7:15 a.m. and took place at gate 32.

- According to Elizabeth D. Williams, an American Airlines employee at Logan, as reported by the FBI, a colleague of hers, Michael Woodward, "advised her that they needed to go to Gate 32 because two flight attendants had been stabbed. Upon arrival at the gate, [they] found an empty plane."[1]

- Williams' account appears congruent with what Wayne Kirk, a member of the cleaning crew, told FBI agents on September 12, 2001.[2] He said he found it "odd" that after the cleaning of the aircraft ended, only two crew members had arrived at the plane, whereas "usually, the entire crew is sitting around and talking when the cleaning crew finishes." Were the other crew members and passengers perhaps boarding at the other gate on a "double" flight?

- According to a Logan airport employee, "who asked not to be identified," flight AA11 left "on time from Gate 32 in Terminal B."[3] To prevent anyone from entering the terminal and interviewing personnel, the steel security gates to Terminal B were shut down at 10:00 a.m.[4] This departure gate and time was endorsed by the 9/11 Commission, whereas flight attendant Madeline Sweeney, scheduled on that flight, called home and told her husband that her flight would be "delayed,"[5] suggesting thereby that her flight did not leave gate 32 but gate 26. Her husband, interviewed by the FBI on September 20, 2001, said she called him "from the airplane," a fact he designated as "highly unusual." He, too, told the FBI agent that Madeline's plane left later than scheduled. Yet, according to a confidential report provided to the 9/11 Commission, flight AA11 pushed back from the gate at 7:40, five minutes earlier than scheduled.[6]

- Richard Ross, a passenger scheduled on flight AA11, called his wife before leaving, telling her that his plane "was leaving a bit late." Michael Woodward, who on 9/11 received a call from flight attendant Madeline Sweeney on flight AA11, confirmed to the staff of the 9/11 Commission in 2004 that the flight was "late departing," although he did not remember why.

---

1   FBI 302-28828. September 13, 2001. Interview with Elizabeth D. Williams

2   FBI 302-11476. September 12, 2001. Interview with Kirk Wayne

3   Stephen Kurkjian and Raphael Lewis, "Two flights from Logan are hijacked," *Boston Globe*, September 11, 2001, #154

4   Ibid.

5   Gail Sheehy, "Stewardess ID's hijackers early, transcripts show," *New York Observer*, February 16, 2004, #638

6   Information provided by the American Airlines Systems Operation Control (SOC) to the 9/11 Commission regarding flight AA11. 9/11 Commission's document in Team 7 Box 20, Timelines 9-11 2 of 2 Fdr- AA SOCC Log- Redacted Version.pdf, #317

- According to Tom Kinton, Aviation Director for Massport (Logan Airport), who was interviewed in 2003 by staff members of the 9/11 Commission, flight AA11 left not from gate 32 or 26 but from gate...31.[1]

Some evidence suggests that flights UA175 and UA93 were also doubled: According to the RITA database of the Department of Transportation,[2] flight UA175 took off from Logan Airport, Boston, at 8:23 a.m. (wheels-off-time), whereas according to the 9/11 Commission, the aircraft had already left Logan at 8:14 a.m.(Final Report, 7) (see illustration below).

Detailed Statistics
Departures

Airport: Boston-Cambridge-Quincy, MA-NH - Logan International (BOS)
Airline: United Airlines (UA)
Month(s): September
Day(s): 11
Year(s): 2001

NOTE: A complete listing of airline and airport abbreviations is available. Times are reported in local time using a 24 hour clock. Airlines began reporting tarmac times for cancelled and diverted flights in October 2008. Tarmac times for cancelled or diverted flights operated prior to Oct. 1, 2008 are not available. Cause of delay data is available on this database beginning with flights operated in October 2008. For cause of delay data from June 2003, when cause of delay data was first reported, see BTS Causes of Delay or the On-Time Performance database For an explanation of the Cause of Delay reporting, see Understanding the Reporting of Causes of Flight Delays and Cancellations. All Cause of Delay (in minutes) are referring to the Arrival Delay.

Excel | CSV

Carrier Code	Date (MM/DD/YYYY)	Flight Number	Tail Number	Destination Airport	Scheduled Departure Time	Actual Departure Time	Wheels-off Time
UA	09/11/2001	0051	UNKNOWN	LAX	12:55	00:00	00:00
UA	09/11/2001	0159	UNKNOWN	SFO	12:55	00:00	00:00
UA	09/11/2001	0161	UNKNOW	SFO	09:00	00:00	00:00
UA	09/11/2001	0163	N526UA	SFO	07:00	06:57	07:20
UA	09/11/2001	0167	UNKNOW	SFO	10:45	00:00	00:00
UA	09/11/2001	0169	UNKNOW	LAX	17:35	00:00	00:00
UA	09/11/2001	0171	UNKNOW	SFO	17:40	00:00	00:00
UA	09/11/2001	0173	UNKNOW	SFO	19:40	00:00	00:00
UA	09/11/2001	0175	N612UA	LAX	08:00	07:58	08:23
UA	09/11/2001	0177	UNKNOW	LAX	18:55	00:00	00:00
UA	09/11/2001	0199	UNKNOW	IAD	10:45	00:00	00:00

Take-off time of flight UA175 on 9/11 from Logan Airport according to official database RITA

---

1   MFR 03007050. August 15, 2003. Site visit and briefing at Logan International Airport
2   RITA (Research and Innovative Technology Administration), Bureau of Transportation Statistics, Detailed Statistics, Departures

Detailed Statistics
Departures

Airport: New York-New Jersey-Long Island, NY-NJ-PA - Newark Liberty International (EWR)
Airline: United Airlines (UA)
Month(s): September
Day(s): 11
Year(s): 2001

NOTE: A complete listing of airline and airport abbreviations is available. Times are reported in local time using a 24-hour clock. Airlines began reporting tarmac times for cancelled and diverted flights in October 2008. Tarmac times for cancelled or diverted flights operated prior to Oct. 1, 2008 are not available. Cause of delay data is available on this database beginning with flights operated in October 2008. For cause of delay data from June 2003, when cause of delay data was first reported, see BTS Causes of Delay or the On-Time Performance database For an explanation of the Cause of Delay reporting, see Understanding the Reporting of Causes of Flight Delays and Cancellations. All Cause of Delay (in minutes) are referring to the Arrival Delay.

Excel | CSV

Carrier Code	Date (MM/DD YYYY)	Flight Number	Tail Number	Destination Airport	Scheduled Departure Time	Actual Departure Time	Wheels-off Time
UA	09/11/2001	0031	UNKNOWN	DEN	11:30	00:00	00:00
UA	09/11/2001	0075	UNKNOWN	SFO	14:30	00:00	00:00
UA	09/11/2001	0077	UNKNOWN	SFO	19:20	00:00	00:00
UA	09/11/2001	0079	UNKNOWN	SFO	17:30	00:00	00:00
UA	09/11/2001	0081	N520UA	SFO	07:00	06:56	07:13
UA	09/11/2001	0083	N402UA	LAX	07:00	06:54	07:20
UA	09/11/2001	0085	UNKNOW	LAX	12:20	00:00	00:00
UA	09/11/2001	0087	UNKNOW	LAX	18:00	00:00	00:00
UA	09/11/2001	0089	UNKNOW	LAX	15:20	00:00	00:00
UA	09/11/2001	0091	UNKNOW	SFO	09:20	00:00	00:00
UA	09/11/2001	0093	N591UA	SFO	08:00	08:01	08:28
UA	09/11/2001	0419	UNKNOW	DEN	17:05	00:00	00:00

Take-off time of flight UA93 on 9/11 from Newark International according to official database RITA.

Woody Box has also publicized interesting facts supporting the hypothesis of a "double" flight UA175.[1] He discovered that an aircraft given a similar flight number, UA177, was scheduled to depart Boston at 6:55 a.m. for Los Angeles. Marcus Arroyo (a regional manager) reported at 9:25 a.m. that several aircraft, including flight AA77, UA175 and UA177 had been hijacked. Note the similarity of the numbers. *Woody Box's* hypothesis is that the plane tracked by United Air-

1   Woody Box, "The mysterious United 177 from Boston," November 30, 2009, #917

lines as flight 175 was tracked by the FAA as flight UA177. That United Airlines and the FAA tracked each a different plane, both believing it to be flight UA175, is strengthened by the following facts:

At 8:41, the pilots of UA175 report to air traffic controllers that they heard a "suspicious transmission" from another aircraft on their departure from Logan Airport (Boston). Yet this information is not, unusually, passed on to personnel at the United Airlines Systems Operations Control (SOC) center. Rich Miles, the manager there, will later tell the 9/11 Commission that, "though he normally received relevant information about United flights from FAA air traffic control, on September 11, 2001, he did not recall receiving information about any air traffic control communications with or from Flight 175, including the 8:41 a.m. report"(Staff Report, 20). None of the other senior UAL officials at the SOC on this morning are told of that communication. These officials said "they never received any communication from the FAA or the air traffic control system advising United to contact its aircraft about the hijackings."[1]

Evidence for a "double" flight UA93 has also surfaced. The RITA database indicates that flight UA93 took off from Newark International Airport at 8:28 a.m., whereas according to the 9/11 Commission, it left only at 8:42 a.m.[2] (See illustration below.) The entries for flights AA11 and AA77 in the RITA database manifest other surprising features, as illustrated below and discussed thereafter.

We note that American Airlines provided to RITA the *scheduled departure time* of flights AA11 and AA77 but neither the aircraft tail number and actual departure time. The entries for these two flights on the RITA database have, incidentally, been manipulated: For the first two years after 9/11, no entry for these two flights appeared on the RITA database, but after this fact was discovered and publicized on the internet, entries for these flights suddenly appeared. Please note that the tail numbers for flights AA11 and AA77, which reportedly took off on 9/11, are missing, whereas these data are included for other aircraft which also took off at similar times on that day.

Responding to my question regarding the puzzling entries for flights AA11 and AA77, Robert M. Kern II, Attorney at the US Department of Transportation explained on June 16, 2008 that "information regarding AA flights 11 and 77 are not in BTS's data system because the airline did not provide information concerning those flights." In a follow-up letter to Robert M. Kern,[3] I pointed out that that "records regarding flights AA11 and AA77 for September 9, 10, 12, 13 and 14, 2001, were present in the BTS database in 2002/3.

---

1   Ibid.
2   Ibid. p. 10
3   Letter from Elias Davidsson to Robert M. Kern , Department of Transportation (RITA), June 27, 2008 and response, #922

Detailed Statistics
Departures

Airport: Boston-Cambridge-Quincy, MA-NH - Logan International (BOS)
Airline: American Airlines (AA)
Month(s): September
Day(s): 11
Year(s): 2001

Excel | CSV

NOTE: A complete listing of airline and airport abbreviations is available. Times are reported in local time using a 24 hour clock.
Airlines began reporting tarmac times for cancelled and diverted flights in October 2008. Tarmac times for cancelled or diverted flights operated prior to Oct. 1,
2008 are not available. Cause of delay data is available on this database beginning with flights operated in October 2008. For cause of delay data from June
2003, when cause of delay data was first reported, see BTS Causes of Delay or the On-Time Performance database For an explanation of the Cause of Delay
reporting, see Understanding the Reporting of Causes of Flight Delays and Cancellations.
All Cause of Delay (in minutes) are referring to the Arrival Delay.

Carrier Code	Date (MM/DD /YYYY)	Flight Number	Tail Number	Destination Airport	Scheduled Departure Time	Actual Departure Time	Wheels-off Time
AA	09/11/2001	0011	UNKNOW	LAX	07:45	00:00	00:00
AA	09/11/2001	0145	UNKNOW	SJC	11:00	00:00	00:00
AA	09/11/2001	0153	N232AA	ORD	08:30	08:29	08:41
AA	09/11/2001	0163	UNKNOW	LAX	15:30	00:00	00:00
AA	09/11/2001	0181	UNKNOW	LAX	11:00	00:00	00:00
AA	09/11/2001	0189	N3BMAA	SEA	08:45	08:43	08:56

111

Detailed Statistics
Departures

Airport: Washington-Arlington-Alexandria, DC-VA-MD-WV - Dulles International (IAD)
Airline: American Airlines (AA)
Month(s): September
Day(s): 11
Year(s): 2001

NOTE: A complete listing of airline and airport abbreviations is available. Times are reported in local time using a 24 hour clock. Airlines began reporting tarmac times for cancelled and diverted flights in October 2008. Tarmac times for cancelled or diverted flights operated prior to Oct. 1, 2008 are not available. Cause of delay data is available on this database beginning with flights operated in October 2008. For cause of delay data from June 2003, when cause of delay data was first reported, see BTS Causes of Delay or the On-Time Performance database For an explanation of the Cause of Delay reporting, see Understanding the Reporting of Causes of Flight Delays and Cancellations. All Cause of Delay (in minutes) are referring to the Arrival Delay.

Excel | CSV

Carrier Code	Date (MM/DD YYYY)	Flight Number	Tail Number	Destination Airport	Scheduled Departure Time	Actual Departure Time	Wheels-off Time
AA	09/11/2001	0075	UNKNOW	LAX	18:00	00:00	00:00
AA	09/11/2001	0077	UNKNOW	LAX	08:10	00:00	00:00
AA	09/11/2001	0135	UNKNOW	LAX	11:15	00:00	00:00
AA	09/11/2001	0143	UNKNOW	LAX	15:00	00:00	00:00
AA	09/11/2001	0371	UNKNOW	DFW	16:10	00:00	00:00
AA	09/11/2001	0397	UNKNOW	DFW	12:55	00:00	00:00
AA	09/11/2001	0510	UNKNOW	DFW	17:51	00:00	00:00
AA	09/11/2001	0573	UNKNOW	DFW	09:23	00:00	00:00
AA	09/11/2001	0599	N871AA	DFW	07:56	07:49	07:59
AA	09/11/2001	0771	N3BFAA	SJU	07:00	06:57	07:10

The presence of these records meant that American Airlines had forwarded to the BTS in advance of these dates the schedule for those flights and should also have included the scheduled departure time for September 11, 2001."[1] In that same letter, I pointed out that records for flights AA11 and AA77 suddenly appeared in the BTS (now RITA) database sometime in 2004. Others have equally noted this

---

1   David West, "Interview with Gerard Holmgren," June 27, 2005, #923; see also Peter Meyer, "Evidence that Flights AA11 and AA77 Did Not Exist on September 11, 2001," #856

addition.[1] I asked for the reason for this belated addition. On November 18, 2004, I discovered that the departure time on these records had been updated from 00:00 to the official departure time of these flights. What was the reason for this belated amendment? The letter and the underlying documentation shows that BTS (RITA) made various changes to the records of flights AA11 and AA77 (9/11) that beg for an explanation. No explanation was given.

(3) Flight UA93 flew past crash time [2]

(a) No evidence of Boeing 767 wreckage

The absence of visible wreckage, the failure of the authorities to prove the source and identity of whatever was found at the alleged crash site, the lack of photographic and video evidence of recovery operations and the secrecy surrounding the site and the recovery, have been covered in detail in chapters 3 and 4.

(b) ACARS

Edward Ballinger was on September 11, 2001, the flight dispatcher in command for all 16 United Airlines' East Coast to West Coast flights, including flights UA175 and UA93.[3] A document from the 9/11 Commission released in 2009 contains the log of so-called ACARS messages sent on the morning of 9/11 by Ballinger to numerous United Airlines aircraft, warning the pilots of cockpit intrusion.[4]

ACARS, the acronym for Aircraft Communications Addressing and Reporting System, is a digital datalink system for transmission of short, relatively simple messages between aircraft and *ground stations* via radio or satellite.[5] A network of VHF ground radio stations ensure that aircraft can communicate with ground end systems in real-time. VHF communication is line-of-sight and provides communication with ground-based transceivers (often referred to as Remote Ground Stations or RGSs). The typical range is dependent on altitude, with a maximal 200-mile transmission range common at high altitudes. Remote ground stations (RGS) are located throughout the United States.

---

1   On September 30, 2004, a person named Bruce Miller wrote on the forum *democraticunderground.com*: "I discovered that more than three years after [9/11], somebody has inserted AA11 and AA77 into the BTS records for 9/11/01. They were not there as of two weeks ago. I am kicking myself for not having the foresight to have run off copies of not only Sept. 11, but also 9/12, 13, 14 as well since the two AA flights were still shown as scheduled for those days." #925

2   I am indebted to blogger Woody Box ("United Airlines tracked a different Flight 93 than the FAA"), September 23, 2009, for this incredible discovery. #1119

3   MFR 04020009. April 14, 2004. Interview of Ed Ballinger.

4   Ballinger's ACARS log. 9/11 Commission records. Team 7 Box 13 UAL ACARS-2, #1173

5   "ACARS." *Wikipedia*

Sending an ACARS message can be done in two ways: "either as a bell that chimes to let the flight deck know they have an electronic message on the screen or as a hard message that automatically prints at a console in between the pilot and first officer's seats."[1]

Michael J. Winter, an official of United Airlines, was interviewed by the FBI on January 28, 2002. He explained that ACARS

uses radio ground stations (RGS) at various locations throughout the United States for communication. The messages from the aircraft utilize the RGS in a downlink operating system. A central router determines the strongest signal received from the aircraft and routes the signal/message to UAL flight dispatch.[2]

Michael J. Winter then commented upon the various ACARS messages sent from and to the aircraft designated as flight UA93 and indicated which radio ground stations were selected by the central router to communicate with the aircraft.

The ACARS log provides, among other information, the following relevant items:

- Sending time (day-of-month and exact universal time[3])
- Aircraft registration number
- Three-letter code of the radio ground station (RGS)
- Flight number
- Departure and destination airports (three-letter codes)
- Text of message
- Name of sender
- Reception time in aircraft (month-and-day and universal time)

Ballinger stated that "the ACARS messages have two times listed: the time sent and the time received." He also stated that "once he sends the message it is delivered to the addressed aircraft through ARINC immediately. He is not aware of any delay in the aircraft receiving the message after he sends it."[4] The reception time allows the sender to ascertain that the message had been duly received by the devices aboard the aircraft.

The three-letter RGS code allows the approximate reconstruction of where the aircraft was located at the time the message was transmitted. As can be ascertained from the aforementioned log, ACARS messages were transmitted by

---

1   MFR 04020009. April 14, 2004. Interview with Ed Ballinger
2   FBI 302-111892. January 28, 2002. Interview with Michael J. Winter at UAL World Headquaters.
3   More commonly known as "GMT" (Greenwich Mean Time). To find the US EST time, subtract four hours.
4   MFR 04020009. April 14, 2004. Interview with Ed Ballinger

Ed Ballinger to aircraft N591UA (which was assigned to Flight UA93) via the following radio ground stations (RGS) at the following times[1]:

Time of ACARS message:	Transmitted to the aircraft via the radio ground station at:
9:21	PIT (Pittsburgh)
9:31	CAK (Canton/Akron)
9:40	CLE (Cleveland)
9:46	TOL (Toledo)
9:50	TOL (Toledo)
9:51	FWA (Fort Wayne, IN)
10:10	CMI (Willard Airport, Champaign, IL)

Michael Winter confirmed that ACARS messages were transmitted to flight UA93 in the above sequence via the aforementioned ground stations.[2] David Knerr, Manager, Dispatch Automation at United Airlines, attended the interview.

The above timeline indicates that the last successful ACARS transmission to flight UA93 occurred at 10:10 via the remote ground station CMI located at Willard Airport near Champaign (IL), that is, seven minutes after that aircraft had allegedly crashed near Shanksville, PA, nearly 500 miles away!

(c) Testimony of Col. Robert Barr

Col. Robert Marr told the 9/11 Commission Staff in 2003 that "his focus [on 9/11] was on [flight] UAL93, which was circling over Chicago."[3] Col. Marr did not specify when exactly the flight circled "over Chicago." His statement, however, provided independent confirmation that flight UA93 was noticed in the vicinity of Chicago. It could have been flying towards Chicago from a point triggering a link to the ground station at Fort Wayne, triggering on the way a link to the ground station in Champaign. This testimony undermines the official flight path of UA93.

(d) Phone call retransmissions

A further document independently confirms that Flight UA93 was proceeding westwards towards Indiana and did not crash at Somerset County. This document lists the Radio Base Stations (RBS) which transmitted phone calls from Flight UA93 to ground recipients. That document was comprised of a set of 28 pages forwarded by the Department of Justice to the 9/11 Commission "that describe cell phone and air phone calls placed by passengers and crew aboard flights American Airlines Flight No. 11, American Airlines Flight No. 77, United Airlines Flight No. 175, and United Airlines Flight No. 93 on September 11, 2001."[4]

---

1   Ballinger's ACARS log. Op. cit., #1173
2   FBI 302-111892. January 28, 2002. Interview with Michael J. Winter
3   MFR 03012970. October 27, 2003. Interview with Robert Marr
4   9/11 Commission documents, NARA, Team 7, Box 13 Flight 11 Calls Folder—Response from DOJ to Doc Req 14 Calls, #779

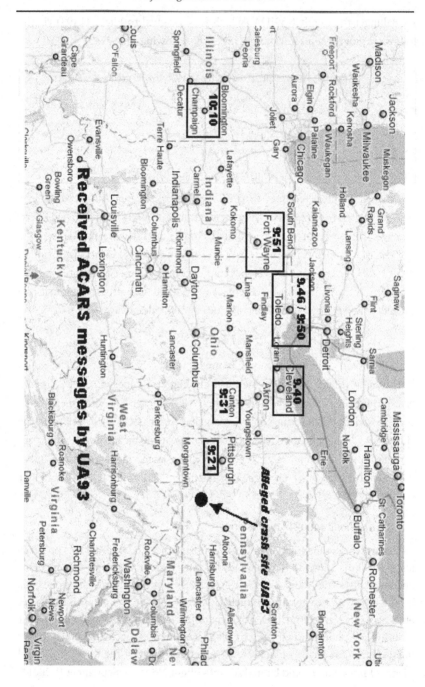

The list of phone calls from Flight UA93 found in this document includes the codes of the Radio Base Stations (RBS) through which these calls were transmitted. The calls are listed in chronological order, beginning with a call by Thomas

Burnett made at 8:30:32 (Indiana Standard Time), i.e. at 9:30:32 (EST). That call was transmitted by a Radio Base Station (RBS) at Fort Wayne (Indiana), while subsequent calls were transmitted by Radio Base Stations at Belleville (IL) and Columbus (IL). The software of the network operating the RBS's determines on the base of the aircraft's heading and other parameters the ground station that would establish the connection and allow the longest connect time with that particular station before handing the call to the next station.[1]

This information is corroborated in a document of the 9/11 Commission released by the National Archives. According to a 9/11 Commission Memorandum For the Record, "[t]wo [phone] calls [from UA93] occurred when the plane was in the Central Time Zone."[2] The Central Time Zone begins nearly 400 miles from the westernmost point that flight UA93 had reached according to the official flight path. Champaign is in fact located within the Central Time Zone.

We have thus three official and independent sources indicating that the aircraft designated as Flight UA93 and carrying passengers, was last located at 10:10 (EST) in the vicinity of, or heading towards, Champaign (IL). On the base of this information, it is possible to trace the approximate flight path of the real flight UA93: It passed near Pittsburgh at 9:21, near Akron (Ohio) at 9:31, slightly changed direction to North-West, flying south past Elyria (Ohio) as if it were heading to Toledo, then veered again slightly southwards as if flying to Lima (Ohio) but heading towards Fort Wayne, which it passed around 9:51 and vanished somewhere near Champaign (IL) at 10:10.

If any aircraft crashed at Somerset County (PA), it was certainly not flight UA93. The official legend of UA93 is thereby null and void.

(e) Two differing take-off times

Similarly to flight UA175, flight UA93 had also two take-off times, as shown in a previous section. The existence of two take-off times suggests that two flights designated as UA93 took off from Newark and served different purposes.

(4) Flight UA175 flew past crash time

(a) ACARS messages

According to the official account (the 9/11 Commission), flight UA175 crashed on the South Tower of the WTC at 9:03. Four minutes before the alleged crash time of UA175, Jerry Tsen sent the following ACARS message to flight UA175 (tail number N612UA): "I heard of a reported incident aboard your acft.

---

1   Explanation provided to me by a credible telecommunications expert
2   MFR 04020027. May 13, 2004. Briefing by Dave Novak, Assistant US Attorney, FBI Special Agent and Ray Guidetti, NJ State Police to the staff of the 9/11 Commission

Plz verify all is normal..." The message was routed to the aircraft via ground station MDT (Harrisburg International Airport, also known as Middleton), located approximately 170 miles from New York City.

Four minutes later, at 9:03, when UA175 was supposed to have crashed on the South Tower, Edward Ballinger sent another ACARS message to Flight 175, inquiring "How is the ride. Anything dispatch can do for you." That message was also routed via MDT.

ACARS messages are routed by the RGS that prompts the strongest signal from the aircraft. Numerous ground stations nearer to New York City would have routed these messages, had the aircraft been nearing the city. There is no apparent reason why these ACARS messages were routed to the aircraft via MDT, unless that ground station was the nearest one to the aircraft.

Ballinger stated that he received no response from to his message of 9:03.[1] This does not mean, however, that the message was not transmitted to and received by the aircraft. Ballinger stated that "the ACARS messages have two times listed: the time sent and the time received" and that "once he sends the message it is delivered to the addressed aircraft through ARINC immediately."[2]

At 9:23 a.m. Ballinger transmitted a "cockpit intrusion" ACARS message (identical to the previous one) to several flights, including UA175. That message was routed to the aircraft via ground station PIT (Pittsburgh International Airport). PIT is located approximately 350 miles from New York City. The signal received from the aircraft by the PIT ground station (as part of the "handshake" protocol) was thus stronger than that received by MDT (Harrisburg). It follows that the aircraft, after passing near Harrisburg, continued westwards and was located in the vicinity of Pittsburgh at 9:23. Hence, it did not crash on the South Tower of the WTC.

A detailed and easy-to-follow analysis of the ACARS messages sent to flight UA175 was posted on the website of Pilots for 9/11 Truth.[3]

It is surprising that at the time the FBI interviewed Edward Ballinger—in January 2002—the FBI agent apparently failed to request from him the ACARS log. Ballinger said in that interview that 20 minutes after the crash on the South Tower of the WTC (attributed to flight UA175), he still was not aware that flight UA175 had been hijacked. It appears from that interview, from a media interview and from an interview with the staff of the 9/11 Commission,[4] that for some reason Ballinger was kept in the dark about the aircraft for which he was respon-

---

1   MFR 04020009. April 14, 2004. Interview with Ed Ballinger
2   Ibid.
3   "ACARS confirmed – 9/11 aircraft airborne long after crash," Pilots for 9/11 Truth, #1116
4   MFR 04020009. April 14, 2004. Interview with Ed Ballinger

sible. He was forced to retire from United Airlines on October 31, 2001, and was put on total disability by a psychiatrist of the Social Security Administration.[1]

(b) RITA

According to the RITA database of the Department of Transportation, flight UA175 took off from Logan airport, Boston, at 8:23 a.m. (wheels-off time) whereas according to the 9/11 Commission, the aircraft pushed back from the gate at 7:58 and took off at 8:14 a.m.(Final Report, 7)

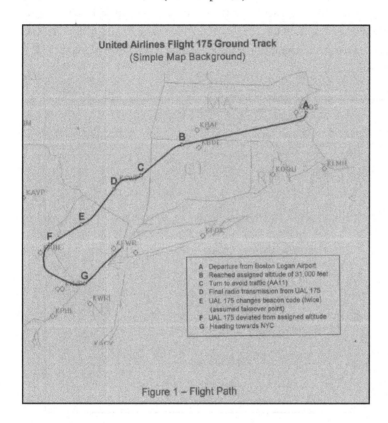

United Airlines Flight 175 Ground Track
(Simple Map Background)

A Departure from Boston Logan Airport
B Reached assigned altitude of 31,000 feet
C Turn to avoid traffic (AA11)
D Final radio transmission from UAL 175
E UAL 175 changes beacon code (twice)
   (assumed takeover point)
F UAL 175 deviated from assigned altitude
G Heading towards NYC

Figure 1 – Flight Path

(c) A Boeing 767 cannot fly at 774 mph

According to the NTSB flight path study of flight UA175[2] a radical change of flight path occurred between 8:51 and 8:56, essentially a 180i turn; and the aircraft descended from 25,000 feet at 8:58 to 1,000 feet at 9:03 (crash time), with the last 8,000 feet descended in one minute[3] (see the following two diagrams).

---

1   Jon Davis, "Suburban Flight Dispatcher to recount worst day," *Daily Herald (Illinois)*, April 14, 2004, #1117

2   "Flight Path Study, UA175," *NTSB*, February 19, 2002, p. 3, #128

3   Ibid. p. 4

The last 60 miles of the flight were thus flown in approximately 4'40" minutes, putting the average speed for this segment at 774 mph., which is above Mach 1.[1]

Setting aside the fact that a Boeing 767-200 is not able to fly at such speed without compromising its structural integrity, we note that none of the phone callers from flight UA175 (see chapter 8) mentioned the radical turn made between 8:51 and 8:56 and the steep descent of the aircraft. Peter Hanson and Brian Sweeney talked to their families when their aircraft was supposedly descending at almost 6,000 feet per minute (or 100 feet per second) without mentioning the descent (see following diagram showing the estimated altitude of flight UA175 along the time axis).

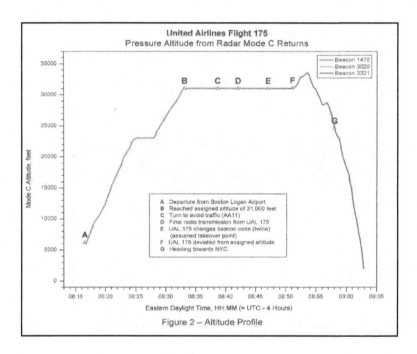

Figure 2 – Altitude Profile

1   Factfinder General, USAF 84 RADES Data for UA175 Indicates Mach 1 Speed? *Pilots for 9/11 Truth*, September 21, 2007, #1118

PART III. THE PHONE CALLS

INTRODUCTION TO PART III

In preceding chapters it was demonstrated that there exists no evidence that the 19 individuals named by the FBI as the "hijackers" actually boarded the four 9/11 flights, and that the FBI failed to identify the debris of the aircraft that allegedly crashed at the known landmarks. The question, therefore, arises what to make of the numerous phone calls from passengers and crew, in which they reported hijackings.

Let it be emphasized here that the official account of 9/11 is mainly based on the phone calls. It is the callers who told people on the ground that their aircraft was being hijacked. The official account of four hijacked aircraft was based on what invisible callers said over the telephone

Among the questions pursued herein are: What exactly did callers say about the hijackings? Did they report what they saw with their own eyes? Did they describe the hijackers? Did they explain how the hijackers managed to enter the cockpits? Did they see weapons? Did they witness stabbings? Did they express fear? Did they mention the location of the aircraft? Were the callers' reports consistent among themselves? Is there any basis for doubting the testimonies of the phone callers?

Deprived of the opportunity to examine material evidence and observe the body language of passengers and crew members who allegedly witnessed the crime, the only means to assess the credibility of the phone calls, is to analyze statements made by the recipients of these calls, available transcripts and recordings, and the wider circumstances surrounding the calls. Statement analy-

sis, incidentally, is widely used in criminal investigations. The main goal of statement analysis is to determine the truth or falsity of a person's statements.

At the trial of Zacarias Moussaoui, the US Government produced a document from the FBI that listed all the phone calls reportedly made from hijacked
planes on 9/11, including the names of callers and recipients, the time of the calls,
their durations and the seat number in the airplane from where the call was
made.[1] The information released by the FBI regarding calls made from American
Airlines aircraft, was not confirmed by the airline. Christopher R. Christensen,
counsel for American Airlines, stated that by 2004 the company did not have
"any records for telephone calls made from the GTE phones on flights 11 and 77."[2]

Zacarias Moussaoui was induced to stipulate to "the authenticity of the underlying documents that support the admission of [Exhibits P200018, P200019,
P200054 and P200055] without any further foundation,"[3] that is to relieve the
government from proving the authenticity of the documents listing the phone
calls from the aircraft. The Moussaoui phone call evidence rested thus "on its
own authority."[4]

Although I cannot vouch for the authenticity, reliability and comprehensive-
ness of the the released FBI compilation, it will be used here as a baseline reference. For ease of consultation throughout this chapter, the FBI compilation is
listed below by flight number.

Chapters 7 to 10 that follow comprise a detailed examination of each of the
phone calls. They constitute the basic reference material from which conclusions
are drawn. Reading systematically through these chapters can be tedious. Readers might, therefore, wish to jump directly to chapter 11, where the findings from
chapters 7 to 10 are categorized and where the main conclusions from the phone
calls are stated. Should the need arise, readers can always check the detailed
analysis in order to evaluate the conclusions.

	Caller	Flight	Call placed from seat	Time of call	Call duration in seconds	Call to
1	Ong, Betty	AA11	Rear (unspecified)	8:18:47	1,620	(800) 433-7300*[1] American Airlines
2	Sweeney, Madeline	AA11	Unspecified	8:22.24	0	(617) 634-XXXX American Airlines

---

1   Detailed Account of Telephone Calls from September 11th Flights, 911 Research. Based on
    Moussaoui Prosecution Trial Exhibit P200055, made easier to read on ‹http://911research.
    wtc7.net/planes/evidence/calldetail.html›
2   Email from Christopher R. Christensen, American Airlines counsel, to John Raidt, the 9/11
    Commission, of January 20, 2004, #331
3   Moussaoui's Trial: Stipulations for Part II. Op. cit. p. 8-9, #1134
4   Rowland Morgan, *Voices: 40 phone calls changed the world that day*, ebook (2000), p. 12

	Caller	Flight	Call placed from seat	Time of call	Call duration in seconds	Call to
3	Sweeney, Madeline	AA11	Unspecified	8:24:00	0	(617) 634-XXXX American Airlines
4	Sweeney, Madeline	AA11	Unspecified	8:25:20	107	(617) 634-XXXX American Airlines
5	Sweeney, Madeline	AA11	Unspecified	8:29:25	43	(617) 634-XXXX American Airlines
6	Sweeney, Madeline	AA11	Unspecified	8:32.39	793	(617) 634-XXXX American Airlines
7	Sweeney, Brian	UA175	Row 31AB	8:58:45	27	(508) 362-XXXX (Residence)
8	Sweeney, Brian	UA175	Row 31AB	9:00:02	60	(508) 885-XXXX (Parents)
9	Bailey, Gamet	UA175	Row 32 CDE	8:52:07	22	(781) 334-XXXX
10	Bailey, Gamet	UA175	Row 32 CDE	8:54:14	No connection	(781) 334-XXXX
11	Bailey, Gamet	UA175	Row 32 CDE	8:57:39	25	(781) 334-XXXX
12	Bailey, Gamet	UA175	Row 32 CDE	8:58:57	9	(781) 334-XXXX
13	Hanson, Family	UA175	Row 30 CDE	8:52:00	99	(203) 261-XXXX C. Lee Hanson
14	Hanson, Family	UA175	Row 30 CDE	9:00:03	192	(203) 261-XXXX C. Lee Hanson
15	Flight attendant (not identified)	UA175	Rows 31 CDE and FG	8:52:01	75	(650) 634-XXXX United Airlines
16	Flight attendant (not identified)	UA175	Rows 31 CDE and FG	8:56:19	31	(650) 634-XXXX United Airlines
17	Flight attendant (not identified)	UA175	Rows 31 CDE and FG	8:57:28	No connect.	(650) 634-XXXX United Airlines
18	May, Renee	AA77	Unspecified	9:11:24	0	(702) 252-XXXX Parents
19	May, Renee	AA77	Unspecified	9:12:18	158	(702) 252-XXXX Parents
20	Olson, Barbara	AA77	Seat 3E	9:18:58	0	(202) 514-XXXX Dep. of Justice

	Caller	Flight	Call placed from seat	Time of call	Call duration in seconds	Call to
21	Unknown caller	AA77	Unspecified	9:15:34	102	Unknown number
22	Unknown caller	AA77	Unspecified	9:20:15	274	Unknown number
23	Unknown caller	AA77	Unspecified	9:25:48	159	Unknown number
24	Unknown caller	AA77	Unspecified	9:30:56	260	Unknown number
25	Beamer, Todd	UA93	Row 32 DEF	9:42:44	0	(800) 225-XXXX AT&T
26	Beamer, Todd	UA93	Row 32 DEF	9:43:48	0	(609) 860-XXXX Residence
27	Beamer, Todd	UA93	Row 32 DEF	9:43:48	3,925	(200) 200-XXXX GTE operator
28	Bingham, Mark	UA93	Row 25 DEF	9:36:10	5	(408) 741-XXXX (Vaughn Hoglan)
29	Bingham, Mark	UA93	Row 25 DEF	9:37:03	166	(408) 741-XXXX Vaughn Hoglan
30	Bingham, Mark	UA93	Row 25 DEF	9:41:20	0	(408) 741-XXXX Vaughn Hoglan
31	Bingham, Mark	UA93	Row 25 DEF	9:41:53	3	(408) 741-XXXX Misdial
32	Bradshaw, Sandra	UA93	Row 33 DEF	9:35:40	353	Speed Dial Fix United Airlines
33	Bradshaw, Sandra	UA93	Row 33 DEF	9:49:30	0	(336) 282-XXXX Residence
34	Bradshaw, Sandra	UA93	Row 33 DEF	9:50:04	470	(336) 282-XXXX Residence
35	Britton, Marion	UA93	Row 33 ABC	9:49:12	232	(718) 805-XXXX Fred Fiumano
36	Burnett, Thomas	UA93	Row 24 ABC & Row 25 ABC	9:30:32	28	(925)735-XXXX Residence
37	Burnett, Thomas	UA93	Row 24 ABC & Row 25 ABC	9:37:53	62	(925)735-XXXX Residence
38	Burnett, Thomas	UA93	Row 24 ABC & Row 25 ABC	9:44:23	54	(925)735-XXXX Residence
39	DeLuca, Joseph	UA93	Row 26 DEF	9:42:13	14	(908) 688-XXXX Parents
40	DeLuca, Joseph	UA93	Row 26 DEF	9:43:03	130	(908) 688-XXXX Parents
41	Felt, Edward	UA93	From toilet (Cell phone call)	9:58:00	?	Westmoreland 911
42	Glick, Jeremy	UA93	Row 27 DEF	9:37:41	7,565 (line left open)	(518) 734-XXXX Joanne Makely

	Caller	Flight	Call placed from seat	Time of call	Call duration in seconds	Call to
43	Grandcolas, Lauren	UA93	Row 23 DEF	9:39:21	46	(415) 454-XXXX Residence
44	Grandcolas, Lauren	UA93	Row 23 DEF	9:40:42	0	(415) 454-XXXX Kris Kor / Global
45	Grandcolas, Lauren	UA93	Row 23 DEF	9:41:34	4	(415) 454-XXXX Residence
46	Grandcolas, Lauren	UA93	Row 23 DEF	9:42:03	2 / 3 / 3	(415) 454-XXXX Residence
47	Grandcolas, Lauren	UA93	Row 23 DEF	9:43:24	0	(973) 665-XXXX Vaughn C. Lohec
48	Grandcolas, Lauren	UA93	Row 23 DEF	9:43:44	7	(973) 665-XXXX V. Nadel
49	Gronlund, Linda	UA93	Row 26 DEF	9:46:05	71	(603) 673-XXXX Elsa Strong
50	Lyles, CeeCee	UA93	Row 32 ABC	9:47:57	56	(941) 274-XXXX Residence
51	Lyles, CeeCee	UA93	Cell phone call	9:58:00	?	(941) 274-XXXX Residence
52	Martinez, Waleska	UA93	Row 34 ABC	9:45:37	0	(212) 509-XXXX Dratel Group
53	Wainio, Honor	UA93	Row 33 ABC	9:53:43	269	(414) 788-XXXX Parents
54	Flight attendant (unidentified)	UA93	Row 33 ABC	9:35:56	4	Speed Dial Fix United Airlines
55	Flight attendant (unidentified)	UA93	Row 34 ABC	9:31:14	2	Speed Dial Fix United Airlines
56	Flight attendant (unidentified)	UA93	Row 34 ABC	9:32:29	95	Speed Dial Fix United Airlines
57	Flight attendant (unidentified)	UA93	Row 34 ABC	9:35:48	4	Speed Dial Fix United Airline

All times are given in Eastern Standard Time unless otherwise indicated.

Chapter 7. Phone Calls From Flight AA11

A Boeing 767 aircraft assigned to flight AA11 is said to have crashed into the North Tower of the WTC at 8:46 a.m. EST on September 11, 2001. The figure on the next page shows the seating arrangement of that flight, as reproduced in a document produced in evidence in the Moussaoui trial. The arrangement can help in assessing the feasibility of the alleged hijacking. It may be referred to in the following sections.

(1) Betty Ong's Phone Call

Introduction

According to the FBI, Betty Ong, a flight attendant aboard flight AA11, made a telephone call from that flight to American Airlines Southeastern Reservation Office (SERO) in Cary, North Carolina, after the aircraft was hijacked on September 11, 2001, at around 08:14 (Final Report, 5). It has not been determined why Ong called the Reservation Office to report the incidents aboard the aircraft.

Betty Ong's phone call was the first communication that signaled a crisis aboard one of the flights on the morning of 9/11. According to the FBI, Ong's call started at 08:18:47 and lasted exactly 1620 seconds, thus ending at 08:45:47.[1] According to the 9/11 Commission, Ong's call started "about five minutes after the hijacking began"(Final Report, 5) and ended at 08:44, when "[Nydia] Gonzalez reported losing phone contact with Ong."

---

1   Information from Moussaoui's trial on Betty Ong's phone call, #1174

American Airlines Flight #11

BOEING 767

SEAT PASSENGER

AA AmericanAirlines

ZONE A - FIRST 9 SEATS
ZONE B - BUSINESS 30 SEATS
ZONE C - ECONOMY 119 SEATS

SEAT	PASSENGER
10B	Al Suqami, Satam
34C	Allison, Anna
8G	Alomari, Abdul
2A	Alshehri, Wail
2B	Alshehri, Waleed
8A	Angell, David
8B	Angell, Lynn Edwards
25C	Aoyama, Selma
26C	Aranson, Myra
8D	Atta, Mohamed
25C	Barbuto, Christine
11D	Berg, Carolyn
26G	Booms, Kelly
9A	Bouchard, Carol
33H	Casey, Neilie
3B	Cosey, Nellie
2H	Coombs, Jeffrey
3J	Creamer, Tara

SEAT	PASSENGER
27J	Cucchello, Thelma
10J	Curnan, Patrick
25J	Dale, Brian
27H	DiMeglio, David
23B	DiTullio, Donald
1J	Dominguez, Alberto
7A	Farley-Hackel, Paige
31G	—
2J	Filipov, Alexander
22H	Flyzik, Carol
3H	Flyzik, Carol
21J	—
25H	Friedman, Paul
20B	Fyfe, Karleton
9H	Gay, Peter
28	George, Linda
31J	Gordenstein, Lisa
11A	Green, Andrew
32J	Hashem, Peter
20A	Hayes, Robert
9J	—

SEAT	PASSENGER
10A	Hennessy, Jr., Edward
24J	Holes, John
27H	Holland, Cora
22A	Humber, Jr., John N.
31A	Iskandar, Waleed
30J	Jenkins, John
31G	Jones, Charles
3A	Kaplan, Robin
22H	Keating, Barbara
19B	Kovalkin, David
20B	Lanoque, Judith C.
26J	Lasden, Natalie Janis
22A	Lee, Daniel
31J	Lewin, Daniel
9B	Low, Sara
32J	Mackay, Susan
	Martin, Karen
	McGuinness, Jr., Thomas

SEAT	PASSENGER
11B	Mello, Christopher
11H	Mladenik, Jeffrey
22B	Montoya, Carlos
29H	Morabito, Laura
24B	Nainan, Mildred
28B	Neira, Laurie
3A	Newell, Renee
25B	Nicosia, Kathleen
34J	Norton, Jacqueline
27B	Norton, Robert
27C	—
3C	Ong, Betty
31B	Orth, Jane
29J	Pecorelli, Thomas
19A	Perkins, Berinthia
3J	Puopolo, Sonia
2H	Retik, David
	Roger, Jean

SEAT	PASSENGER
11G	Rosenzweig, Philip
2J	Ross, Richard
28B	Sachs, Jessica
35G	Salle, Rahma
26B	Smith, Heather
25B	Snyder, Dianne
25B	Stone, Douglas
34J	Suarez, Xavier
35C	Sweeney, Madeline
30A	Theodoridis, Michael
30B	Trentini, James
23J	Trentini, Mary Barbara
36J	Valdes, Antonio Montoya
10H	Vamsikrishna, Pendyala
37G	Waldie, Kenneth
24H	Wendus, John
24A	Williams, Candace
29A	Zarba, Jr., Christopher

Legend:
- American Airlines Flight 11
- American Airlines Flight 77
- United Airlines Flight 93
- United Airlines Flight 175
- 11 Crew
- Passenger
- 5 Hijacker

The aircraft from which the call is said to have originated, designated as flight AA11, is said to have impacted the North Tower of the WTC at exactly 8:46:40. Ong's call thus terminated one or two minutes before the alleged impact. According to an FBI document from its Dallas office dated September 12, 2001, Nydia Gonzalez, an American Airlines employee, stated "that she was on the phone with Ong for approximately five more minutes after the recording ended," i.e., beyond the crash time.[1] The persons who initially talked to Betty

---

1   FBI DL 2719. September 12, 2001 (from Dallas to SIOC).

Ong were Vanessa Minter, Winston Sadler and Nydia Gonzalez, all of them employees of American Airlines at SERO, Raleigh, North Carolina. All three were subsequently interviewed by the FBI.[1]

A significantly different time for Betty Ong's call was given by Vanessa Minter in her testimony to the FBI on September 12, 2001. She said that the call was received at approximately 7:59 a.m. and that the caller's first words had been, "I think we're being hijacked."[2] In an interview with ABC Local on September 10, 2002, Minter placed the call at "minutes after 8 a.m."[3] Her testimony differs significantly from the official account, as represented by the timeline of the 9/11 Commission. According to reporter Jennifer Julian, who interviewed Minter, American Airlines gave Minter another assignment: "They didn't want me to talk about it," she said. Vanessa Minter was then laid off by American Airlines. Asked by ABC about her dismissal, the airline "wouldn't comment specifically on Vanessa's layoff."[4]

According to the FBI, only about four minutes of Ong's call were recorded. This recording was played for the first time publicly in an open hearing of the 9/11 Commission on January 27, 2004.[5] A recording and a transcript of that recording purporting to represent the recording played to the 9/11 Commission were later released and are posted on various internet sites. Shortly before the 4-minute recording ended, Nydia Gonzalez used a second telephone to relay to Craig Marquis, manager on duty at the AA operations center in Fort Worth, Texas, what Ong was telling her. That relayed conversation (between Gonzalez and Marquis) was recorded and lasted about 24 minutes. Of these 24 minutes, the 9/11 Commission extracted approximately four minutes that were publicly played at the aforementioned hearing. The rest was never played in public but a printed transcription in two parts of Nydia Gonzalez's call to Craig Marquis was released.[6]

(a) Two versions of Betty Ong's phone call

Version A. The first transcript of Betty Ong's phone call is enclosed in FBI document 265A-NY-280350-302-3005 of September 11, 2001.[7] The cover page

---

1   FBI CE-1018. September 12, 2001. Interview with Nydia E. Gonzalez; FBI 265D-NY-280350-CE (no serial number visible, Bates 000000447). September 12, 2001. FBI CE-1022, September 12, 2001, Interview with Winston Courtney Sadler

2   FBI CE-1020, Lead Numbers DL-257 and CE-66. September 12, 2001. FBI Interview with Vanessa Minter

3   Jennifer Julian, "One of the last calls" (interview with Vanessa Minter), *ABC Local*, September 11, 2002, (file on p. 25), #719

4   Ibid.

5   "9/11 commission hears flight attendant's phone call," CNN, January 27, 2004, #057

6   Transcripts of 9/11 phone calls, 9/11 Commission documents, Team 7, Box 13, #634

7   FBI 302-3005. September 11, 2001. This document is included in 9/11 Commission documents, NARA. Team 7, Box 17, FBI-302s-of-Interest-Flight-11-Fdr-Entire-Contents, #692 (p. 1-8)

---

contains the following explanation: "*This is a taped telephone conversation between Flight Attendant Betty Ong of AA and American Airlines Southeast Reservation Center, Winston [Sadler] and Vanessa [Minter]. She [Ong] was on Flight 11 of American Airlines. Today's date is September 11, 2001.*" The pages that follow are composed of three distinct sections:

1. The first section of the document is a transcription of a telephone conversation between Nydia Gonzalez, who describes herself as "the Operations Specialist on duty at the time" at American Airlines, SERO, Raleigh, North Carolina, and Larry Wansley, Managing Director, Corporate Security, American Airlines at Dallas Headquarters. This conversation took place on September 11, 2001, at 12:28 p.m. Central Time, i.e. shortly after the deadly events. In that section, Gonzalez relates to Wansley that she and her colleagues had received a phone call from a flight attendant on one of the "hijacked" airliners, recorded a part of the call and offered to play that recording over the telephone to Wansley. Nydia then plays that recording over the phone to Larry Wansley.

2. The second section of the document represents a transcription of the recording that Nydia Gonzalez had played to Larry Wansley over the phone.

3. The third section of the document represents a transcription of the conversation between Gonzalez and Wansley, resumed after she ended playing for him Ong's call. In that section, Gonzalez related to Wansley from memory what Betty Ong told her after the recording of their conversation had ended. In addition to repeating facts Ong had already mentioned in the recorded section, Gonzalez told Wansley that Ong advised about the fatal stabbing of Daniel Lord [sic], the "erratic" behavior of the aircraft and the relocation of first class passengers to coach class. Wansley asked her whether Betty Ong had used a cell phone, to which Gonzalez answered that she did not know, as it was not determined.

Three facts should be mentioned here:

• The recorded part of Ong's call was a conversation she, Winston Sadler and Vanessa Minter had with Ong. Nydia Gonzalez only entered that conversation towards the end but according to what she said to Wansley, she listened in on the call in its entirety.

• Gonzalez does not mention to Wansley that she relayed the balance of Ong's call to Craig Marquis.

• Wansley specifically asked Nydia Gonzalez: "The conversation lasted another five or ten minutes but that's all the recording we have?" to which she answered: "Right."

It is possible that Gonzalez did not know that her relayed conversation with Marquis was recorded or did not think that she had to mention this fact to Wansley. On the other hand, one has to wonder how Wansley came to ask whether the conversation between Gonzalez and Ong had continued for "another five or ten minutes." Gonzalez acknowledged this fact, which was corroborated in an FBI document of September 11, 2001: "Gonzalez states that she was on the phone with Ong for approximately five more minutes after the recording ended."[1]

However, according to later reports, Gonzalez talked to Ong for almost 24 minutes, i.e., from the time she entered the conversation until one or two minutes before the aircraft allegedly crashed. This is far more than the "five to ten minutes" mentioned in this conversation.

According to the FBI, David Divan of American Airlines' Corporate Security in Dallas, Texas, made a copy of the recording made by Wansley in the presence of an FBI Special Agent, and then provided the agent with that copy.[2] At Cary, North Carolina, Larry David Yarbrough, described in an FBI document as a field service consultant for Rockwell Electronic Commerce (REC), "routed" the original Ong call—which according to Troy Wreggelsworth, described by the FBI as a Systems Analyst for SERO was in a "Rockwell proprietary software format"—to a "stand-alone computer connected to the phone system so it would be safe from any computer crashes."[3] Whether any of these details are relevant to the investigation, cannot be ascertained at this point.

Version B. The second version of Ong's phone call (or more accurately of its first four minutes) is included in FBI document 265A-NY-280350-CE-1024, dated September 12, 2001.[4] The document is composed of a cover section and of a transcript of the recorded part of Betty Ong's phone call played at a hearing of the 9/11 Commission in January 2004.[5]

The cover section explains that this is a "re-recorded transcription obtained from American Airlines by [FBI] Special Agent [redacted] on Tuesday, September 11, 2001. The material is being re-recorded from a CD-ROM onto an Analog Audio Tape for transcription purposes. Flight Attendant: Ong; AA Agent: Winston Sadler; Operations OP Agent: Nydia E. Gonzalez." The transcription is said to have been made on September 12, 2001. In this version, the name of Vanessa Minter, who participated in the conversation with Betty Ong, is not mentioned. The recording given to the FBI was a copy of the telephonic recording made by Wansley and referred to above, the quality of which is said to be "poor."[6]

---

1 FBI 302-6545. September 11, 2001. Interview with David Divan
2 Ibid.
3 FBI Leads DL-267 and CE-66. September 11, 2001. Bates 000000442-3. Cary, CE-1017
4 FBI CE-1024. This document is included in 9/11 Commission documents, NARA. Team 7, Box 17, FBI-302s-of-Interest-Flight-11-Fdr-Entire-Contents, #692 (p.10-13)
5 Ibid.
6 FBI DL-2719. September 12, 2001 from Dallas to SIOC

The recording provided to the FBI should normally have been the equivalent to that played by Nydia Gonzalez to Larry Wansley, as described above. As the comparison below shows, Versions A and B *differ significantly*. The first obvious difference is that the statements do not appear in the same sequence in both versions. A more thorough comparison reveals, however, that some statements differ widely or are omitted in one or the other version.

Table 1 below lists the statements made in both versions in the chronological order in which they appear in the respective documents. This presentation permits the reader to realize the significant difference between these two transcripts.

TABLE 1. The Two Versions Side by Side

ONG Telephone Call Version A FBI 265A-NY-280350-302-3005 of Sept.11, 2001	ONG Telephone Call Version B FBI 265A-NY-280350-CE-1024 of Sept. 12, 2001
1. ONG: Uh, This is ah ONG. We can't breathe Uh. He's got mace or something	0:00 ONG: Number 3 in the back, ah, the cockpit is not answering, somebody stabbed in business class and ah, I think there is mace that we can't breathe, I don't know, I think we're getting hijacked.
2. Winston: Can you describe the person that you said went into the flight deck or Uh?	0:10 AA Agent (male voice): Which flight are you on?
3. ONG: I'm, I'm sitting in the back coming back from business. Can you hold on for one second, he's coming back.	0:12 ONG: Flight 12
4. Unintelligible noise in background.	0:13 AA Agent (female voice): And what seat are yon in? Ma'am are you there?
5. ONG: On, on number one. He stood upstairs UI. Ah, nobody knows what he's going to do. UI Ah, I'm UI in his UI right now. UI Ah, we can't get to the cockpit, the door won't open. Hello?	0:18 ONG: Yes
6. Winston: Can you UI information relative to ah, you know, force, force that. Uhm, at this point? What operation, what flight are we talking about, Flight 12?	0:22 AA Agent (male): What, what, what seat are you in? 0:27 AA Agent (female): Ma'am what seat are you in?
7. ONG: Right now? Okay. We're on Flight 11 right now. Flight 11.	0:29 ONG: We're in flight, we just left Boston. We're up in the air.
8. Winston: Flight 11. Okay.	0:32 AA Agent (female): I know, what
9. ONG: UI we are working on.	0:33 ONG: We are suppose (sic) to go to LA and the cockpit is not answering their phone
10. Winston: Yeah.	0:36 AA Agent (female): Okay, but what seat are you sitting in? What's the number of your seat?
11. ONG: One of the flight attendants UI has been stabbed.	0:39 ONG: Okay, I'm in my jumpseat right now.

ONG TELEPHONE CALL VERSION A FBI 265A-NY-280350-302-3005 of Sept.11, 2001	ONG TELEPHONE CALL VERSION B FBI 265A-NY-280350-CE-1024 of Sept. 12, 2001
12. Vanessa: Can anybody get up to the cockpit? Can anybody get up to the cockpit?	0:41 AA Agent (female): Okay [strange that it took four attempts to get the reply.]
13. ONG: We can't even get a manager to the cockpit. We don't know what's going on up there.	0:42 ONG: At 3R
14. Winston: UI keep the door closed and	0:43 AA Agent (male): Okay, you're the flight attendant? 0:50 I'm sorry, did you say you're the flight attendant?
15. ONG: Okay.	0:54 ONG: Hello?
16. Winston: UI Did you seen the girl who got stabbed?	AA Agent: Can't
17. ONG: I think the guys are up there. They might have gone, they are on their way up there or, or something. Nobody can call the cockpit to see if we can get inside. Hey, is anybody still there?	ONG: Hello
18. Winston: Yes, I'm still here.	0:56 AA Agent (male): What, what is your name?
19. ONG: Okay. I'm staying on the line as well.	0:56 ONG: You'll have to speak up. I can't hear you.
20. Winston: Okay.	0:59 AA Agent (male): Sure, what is your name?
21. Vanessa: UI, who is calling reservations? Is it a flight attendant, or who? UI	1:00 ONG: Okay, my name is BETTY ONG, I'm number 3 on Flight 11
22. Winston: We need for UI call.	1:05 AA Agent (male): Okay
23. ONG: I'm number three. I'm number three on this flight. UI on this flight and UI Flight 11 UI. Have you guys called anyone else? You know, ah somebody's calling medical and we can't get them.	1:08 ONG: And the cockpit is not answering their phone. And there is somebody stabbed in business class, and there is, we can't breathe in business class, so somebody's got mace or something.
24. *Unidentified male*: UI is anybody there? Is anybody there?	1:18 AA Agent (male): Can you describe the person that you said, someone is in is business class.
25. Winston: What, what seat are you in? What seat are you in?	1:21 ONG: Ah, ah, I'm sitting in the back, somebody is coming back from business. If you can [hold] on for one second.
26. ONG: We've just left Boston and we're up in the air. We're suppose (sic) to go to LA and UI.	AA Agent: Certainly
27. Winston: But what seat? What's the number of your seat?	1:31 ONG (in background): They want to know who's..[alternative: Does anyone know who stabbed who? Do you know?] 1:33 I don't know but Karen and Bobbie got stabbed
28. ONG: Okay. I'm in the jump seat right now. 3R	Lots of talking with other individuals at this point

ONG TELEPHONE CALL VERSION A FBI 265A-NY-280350-302-3005 of Sept.11, 2001	ONG TELEPHONE CALL VERSION B FBI 265A-NY-280350-CE-1024 of Sept. 12, 2001
	1:38 ONG: Our number 1 got stabbed. A person is stabbed, nobody knows who stabbed who and we, we can't even get up to business class right now, cause nobody can breathe. Ah, our number 1 is stabbed right now.
29. Winston: Okay, are you the flight attendant? I'm sorry, did you say your're the flight attendant?	
30. ONG: Hello?	AA Agent (male): Okay
31. Winston: Hello, what is your name?	1:55 ONG: Our number 5, our first class passengers are, our first class, our galley flight attendant and our purser has been stabbed. And we can't get into the cockpit, the door won't open. 2:11 Hello?
32. ONG: Uhm, you'll have to speak up. I can't hear you.	2:12 AA Agent (male): Yeah, I'm taking it down, all the information, we're also ah, you know of course recording this, ah, at this point.
33. Winston: What is your name?	2:21 OP Agent (Nydia Gonzalez): This is operations, what flight number we talking about?
34. ONG: Okay, my name is Betty Ong. I'm number three on Flight 11	2:24 AA Agent (male): Flight 12
35. Winston: Okay	2:25 OP Agent (female): Flight 12, okay
36. ONG: The cockpit is not answering their calls and there's somebody back in business class and there, we can't breathe in business class. Somebody's got mace or something.	2:27 ONG: We're on flight 11 right now. This is flight 11
37. Winston: Can you describe the person that you said, someone is flying business class?	2:29 AA Agent (male): It is flight 11, I'm sorry Nydia
38. ONG: I'm, I'm sitting in the back, he's coming back from business. If you can hold on for one second, he's coming back.	2:31 ONG: Boston to Los Angeles
39. Unintelligible in background	2:31 AA Agent: Yes
40. ONG: Our, our number one who UI stabbed. Or, something stabbed. Ah, nobody knows who stabbed who and we can't even get up to business class because nobody can breathe. Our number one in UI stabbed right now. In number five. The first class passenger that, ah first ah class galley flight attendant and our passenger is stabbed. We can't get to the cockpit, the door won't open. Hello?	2:36 ONG: Our number 1 has been stabbed and our 5 has been stabbed. 2:44 (in the background) Can anybody get up to the cockpit? Can anybody get up to the cockpit? 2:49 We can't even get into the cockpit. We don't know who's up there.
41. Winston: Yeah, we're getting all the information. We're also, you know, of course, recording this. Uhm, at this point?	2:56 AA Agent (male): Well if they were shrewd, they would keep the door closed, and
42. Vanessa: This is operations. What flight number are we talking about?	3:00 ONG: I'm sorry?
43. Winston: Flight 12	3:01 AA Agent (male): Would they not maintain a sterile cockpit?

ONG Telephone Call Version A FBI 265A-NY-280350-302-3005 of Sept.11, 2001	ONG Telephone Call Version B FBI 265A-NY-280350-CE-1024 of Sept. 12, 2001
44. Vanessa: Flight 12, Okay.	3:05 ONG: I think the guys are up there, they might have gone or jammed their way up there or something, nobody can call the cockpit, we can't even get inside. 3:26 Is anybody still there?
45. ONG: Okay, we are Flight 11 right now. This is flight 11.	3:28 AA Agent (male): Yes, we'll still here.
46. Winston: This is flight 11, okay.	3:29 ONG: Okay, I'm staying on the line as well
47. ONG: Boston to Los Angeles	3:32 AA Agent: Okay
48. Winston: Yeah	3:34 OP Agent (Nydia Gonzalez): Hi, who is calling reservations? Is this one of the flight attendants or who, who are you, hon?
49. ONG: And the one that has been stabbed and our flight attendant has been stabbed.	3:42 AA Agent (male): She gave her name as BETTY ONG
50. Vanessa: Can anybody get up to the cockpit? Can anybody get up to the cockpit?	3:44 OP Agent (Gonzalez): Betty
51. ONG: We can't even get into the cockpit. We don't know who's up there.	3:45 ONG: I'm number 3, I'm number 3 on this flight
52. Winston: UI keep the door closed and	3:47 OP Agent (Gonzalez): You're the number 3 on the flight?
53. ONG: I'm Sorry?	3:48 ONG: Yes
54. Winston: Can they not see the girls get upset?	3:50 OP Agent (Gonzalez): And this is flight 11, from where to where?
55. ONG: I think the guys are up there. They might have gone or they are on their way up there or, or something. Somebody can call the cockpit. We can't even get inside. Is anybody still there?	3:51 ONG: Flight 11
56. Winston: Yes, we're still here.	3:52 OP Agent (Gonzalez): Have you guys called anyone else?
57. ONG: Okay, I'll stay on the line as well.	3:55 ONG: No. Somebody is calling medical and we can't get
58. Winston: Okay	End of tape
59. Vanessa: UI who is calling reservations? Is it a flight attendant or who?	
60. Winston: I believe her name is BETTY ONG	
61. Vanessa: BETTY	
62. ONG: I'm number three. I'm number three on this flight. UI on this flight.	
63. Winston: Yeah.	
64. ONG: I'm flight 11	
65. Vanessa: From where to where? Have you guys called anyone else?	
66. ONG: No, we're just calling medical and we can't get	
Recording concluded	

Anyone listening to Ong's phone call (available on the internet) will immediately notice that the recording does not correspond to Version A above. By displaying these two versions side by side, the reader will realize that there exist two significantly different official versions of Ong's phone call, one transcribed on September 11, 2001, and one transcribed a day later. It is important to note that Version A remains practically unknown. It is Version B that became the "official version" of this phone call.

In order to test whether Version A represents merely an erroneous transcription, we resequenced in Table 2 the phrases of Version A so as to achieve the highest number of matches with those of Version B. This attempt left many unexplained mismatches.

TABLE 2. Aligning Version A to fit Version B

ONG Telephone Call Version A	ONG Telephone Call Version B
FBI 265A-NY-280350-302-3005 of Sept.11, 2001	FBI 265A-NY-280350-CE-1024 of Sept. 12, 2001
A1 ONG: Uh, This is ah ONG. We can't breathe Uh. He's got mace or something	(no corresponding entry)
A2 Winston: Can you describe **the person that you said went into the flight deck** or Uh?	(no corresponding entry)
A3 ONG: I'm, I'm sitting in the back coming back from business. Can you hold on for one second, **he's coming back**.	(no corresponding entry)
A4 *Unintelligible noise in background.*	(no corresponding entry)
A5 ONG: On, on number one. **He stood upstairs UI. Ah, nobody knows what he's going to do.** UI Ah, I'm UI in **his** UI right now. UI Ah, we can't get to the cockpit, the door won't open. Hello?	(no corresponding entry)
A6 Winston: Can you UI **information relative to ah, you know, force, force** that. Uhm, at this point? What **operation, what flight are we talking about, Flight 12?**	(no corresponding entry)

ONG Telephone Call Version A	ONG Telephone Call Version B
A7 ONG: **Right now? Okay.** We're on Flight 11 right now. Flight 11	(no corresponding entry)
A9 ONG: UI **we are working on.**	(no corresponding entry)
A10 Winston: Yeah.	(no corresponding entry)
A11 ONG: One of the flight attendants UI has been stabbed.	(no corresponding entry)
(no corresponding entry)	B1 0:00 ONG: Number 3 in the back, ah, the cockpit is not answering, somebody stabbed in business class and ah, I think there is mace that we can't breathe, I don't know, **I think we're getting hijacked.**
(no corresponding entry)	B2 0:10 AA Agent (male voice): Which flight are you on?
(no corresponding entry)	B3 0:12 ONG: **Flight 12**
A25 Winston: What, what seat are you in? What seat are you in?	B4 0:13 AA Agent (female voice): And what seat are you in? Ma'am are you there? B5 0:18 ONG: Yes B6 0:22 AA Agent (male): What, what, what seat are you in? 0:27 AA Agent (female): Ma'am what seat are you in?
A26 ONG: We've just left Boston and we're up in the air.	B7 0:29 ONG: We're in flight, we just left Boston. We're up in the air.
(no corresponding entry)	B8 0:32 AA Agent (female): **I know, what**
A26 ONG: We're suppose (sic) to go to LA and UI.	B9 0:33 ONG: We are suppose (sic) to go to LA and the cockpit is not answering their phone
A27 **Winston:** But what seat? What's the number of your seat?	B10 0:36 AA Agent (**female**): Okay, but what seat are you sitting in? What's the number of your seat?
A28 ONG: Okay. I'm in the jump seat right now.	B11 0:39 ONG: Okay, I'm in my jump seat right now.

ONG Telephone Call Version A	ONG Telephone Call Version B
no corresponding entry)	B12 0:41 AA Agent (female): Okay.
A28 ONG: 3R	B13 0:42 ONG: At 3R
A29 Winston: Okay, are you the flight attendant? I'm sorry, did you say your're the flight attendant?	B14 0:43 AA Agent (male): Okay, you're the flight attendant? 0:50 I'm sorry, did you say you're the flight attendant?
A30 ONG: Hello?	B15 0:54 ONG: Hello?
(no corresponding entry)	B16 AA Agent: Can't
(no corresponding entry)	B17 ONG: Hello
A16 Winston: UI **Did you seen the girl who got stabbed?**	(no corresponding entry)
A17 ONG: **I think the guys are up there. They might have gone, they are on their way up there or, or something.** Nobody can call the cockpit to see if we can get inside. Hey, is anybody still there	(no corresponding entry)
A31 Winston: Hello, what is your name?	B18 0:56 AA Agent (male): What, what is your name?
A32 ONG: Uhm, you'll have to speak up. I can't hear you.	B19 0:56 ONG: You'll have to speak up. I can't hear you.
A33 Winston: What is your name?	B20 0:59 AA Agent (male): Sure, what is your name?
A34 ONG: Okay, my name is Betty Ong. I'm number three on Flight 11	B21 1:00 ONG: Okay, my name is BETTY ONG, I'm number 3 on Flight 11
A35 Winston: Okay	B22 1:05 AA Agent (male): Okay
A36 ONG: The cockpit is not answering **their calls** and there's somebody back in business class and there, we can't breathe in business class. Somebody's got mace or something.	B23 1:08 ONG: And the cockpit is not answering **their phone**. And there is somebody stabbed in business class, and there is, we can't breathe in business class, so somebody's got mace or something.
A37 Winston: Can you describe the person that you said, someone is flying business class?	B24 1:18 AA Agent (male): Can you describe the person that you said, someone is in is business class.

ONG Telephone Call Version A	ONG Telephone Call Version B
A38 ONG: I'm, I'm sitting in the back, **he´s coming back from business. If you can hold on for one second, he's coming back.**	B25 1:21 ONG: Ah, ah, I'm sitting in the back, **somebody** is coming back from business. If you can [hold] on for one second.
(no corresponding entry)	B26 AA Agent: Certainly
(no corresponding entry)	B27 1:31 ONG (in background): **They want to know who's**..[alternative: Does anyone know who stabbed who? Do you know?] 1:33 **I don't know but Karen and Bobbie got stabbed**
A39 *Unintelligible noise in background.*	B28 Lots of talking with other individuals at this point
A40 ONG: Our, our number one who UI stabbed. Or, something stabbed. Ah, nobody knows who stabbed who and we can't even get up to business class because nobody can breathe. Our number one in UI stabbed right now. In number five. The first class passenger that, ah first ah class galley flight attendant and our passenger is stabbed. We can't get to the cockpit, the door won't open. Hello?	B29 1:38 ONG: Our number one got stabbed. A person is stabbed, nobody knows who stabbed who and we, we can't even get up to business class right now, cause nobody can breathe. Ah, our number one is stabbed right now. B30 AA Agent (male): Okay. B31 1:55 ONG: Our number 5, our first class passengers are, our first class, our galley flight attendant and our purser has been stabbed. And we can't get into the cockpit, the door won't open. 2:11 Hello?
A41 Winston: Yeah, we're getting all the information. We're also, you know, of course, recording this. Uhm, at this point?	B32 2:12 AA Agent (male): Yeah, I'm taking it down, all the information, we're also ah, you know of course recording this, ah, at this point.
A42 Vanessa: This is operations. What flight number are we talking about?	B33 2:21 OP Agent (Nydia Gonzalez): This is operations, what flight number we talking about?
A43 Winston: Flight 12	B34 2:24 AA Agent (male): Flight 12
A44 Vanessa: Flight 12, Okay.	B35 2:25 OP Agent (female): Flight 12, okay
A45 ONG: Okay, we are Flight 11 right now. This is flight 11.	B36 2:27 ONG: We're on flight 11 right now. This is flight 11

ONG Telephone Call Version A	ONG Telephone Call Version B
A46 Winston: This is flight 11, okay.	B37 2:29 AA Agent (male): It is flight 11, I'm sorry Nydia
A47 ONG: Boston to Los Angeles	B38 2:31 ONG: Boston to Los Angeles
A48 Winston: Yeah	B39 2:31 AA Agent: Yes
A49-51 ONG: And the one that has been stabbed and our flight attendant has been stabbed. Vanessa: Can anybody get up to the cockpit? Can anybody get up to the cockpit? ONG: We can't even get into the cockpit. We don't know who's up there.	B40 2:36 ONG: Our number 1 has been stabbed and our 5 has been stabbed. 2:44 (in the background) Can anybody get up to the cockpit? Can anybody get up to the cockpit? 2:49 We can't even get into the cockpit. We don't know who's up there.
A52 Winston: UI keep the door closed and	B41 2:56 AA Agent (male): Well if they were shrewd, they would keep the door closed, and
A53 ONG: I'm sorry?	B42 3:00 ONG: I'm sorry?
A54 Winston: **Can they not see the girls get upset?**	B43 3:01 AA Agent (male): **Would they not maintain a sterile cockpit?**
A55 ONG: I think the guys are up there. They might have gone or they are on their way up there or, or something. Somebody can call the cockpit. We can't even get inside. Is anybody still there?	B44 3:05 ONG: I think the guys are up there, they might have gone or jammed their way up there or something, nobody can call the cockpit, we can't even get inside. 3:26 Is anybody still there?
A56 Winston: Yes, we're still here.	B45 3:28 AA Agent (male): Yes, we'll still here.
A57 ONG: Okay, I'll stay on the line as well.	B46 3:29 ONG: Okay, I'm staying on the line as well
A58 Winston: Okay	B47 3:32 AA Agent: Okay
A59 **Vanessa**: UI who is calling reservations? Is it a flight attendant or who?	B48 3:34 OP Agent (**Nydia Gonzalez**): Hi, who is calling reservations? Is this one of the flight attendants or who, who are you, hon?
A60 Winston: **I believe** her name is BETTY ONG	B49 3:42 AA Agent (male): **She gave** her name as BETTY ONG

ONG Telephone Call Version A	ONG Telephone Call Version B
A61 Vanessa: BETTY	B50 3:44 OP Agent (Gonzalez): Betty
A62 ONG: I'm number three. I'm number three on this flight. UI on this flight.	B51 3:45 ONG: I'm number 3, I'm number 3 on this flight
	B52 3:47 OP Agent (Gonzalez): **You're the number 3 on the flight?**
A63 **Winston**: Yeah.	B53 3:48 ONG: Yes
A65 **Vanessa**: From where to where?	B54 3:50 OP Agent (**Gonzalez**): And this is flight 11, from where to where?
A64 ONG: I'm flight 11	B55 3:51 ONG: Flight 11
A65 **Vanessa**: Have you guys called anyone else?	B56 3:52 OP Agent (**Gonzalez**): Have you guys called anyone else?
A66 ONG: No, **we're** just calling medical and we can't get	B57 3:55 ONG: No. **Somebody** is calling medical and we can't get
Recording concluded	End of tape

Analysis of the differences between the two versions

Let us begin by visually comparing the two versions of the transcripts as presented in Table 2. We first notice that statements A1-A12 (the first twelve statements in Version A) do not appear in the start of Version B. Some of these statements appear later in Version B, starting with statement B23, but not with the exact *wording of Version A*. Let us, to start with, assume that due to some technical hitch the sequence of the statements was mixed up when transcribing Version A. Yet, in spite of reordering the statements, we find significant differences between the versions.

Sentences that do not appear in Version B (and not in the recording) but appear in Version A are:

- "went into the flight deck or Uh?" (A2)
- "He stood upstairs" (A5)
- "Nobody knows what he's going to do" (A5)
- "information relative to ah, you know, force, force that Uhm at this point? (A6)
- "What operation...we are talking about?" (A6)

- "we are working on." (A9)

- "Did you seen [*sic*] the girl who got stabbed?" (A16)

- "Can they not see the girls get upset?" (A54)

- In A6 Sadler asks Ong "Can you [unintelligible] information relative to ah, you know, force, force that. Uhm, at this point?" This strange question remains unanswered and does not appear in Version B. Sadler then asks "What operation, what flight, are we talking about"? The word "operation" does not appear in Version B.

- In A9 Ong says "We are working on," a phrase that does not make much sense in the context. It is absent from Version B.

- In A16 Sadler asks "Did you seen [*sic*] the girl who was stabbed?" This question is not mentioned in Version B. By eliminating this question, the lack of answer could be concealed. In fact Ong never said that she actually saw anyone stabbed, notwithstanding her statement "our number one is stabbed right now." In A40 (and B29) she says, "nobody knows who stabbed who" and never describes the aggressor.

- In A24, an unidentified male enters the conversation. In Version B no such intruding remark is found.

Sentences that do not exist in Version A but only in Version B are:

- B1: "I think we're getting hijacked." This is the *single mention* made by Ong that a "hijacking" might have taken place. Yet, surprisingly, it is not mentioned in Version A.

- B27 "(...) Karen and Bobbie got stabbed."

- A further significant difference is the modification of all third person references in Version A ("he") to "somebody" or the outright elimination of the respective sentence. This may be explained by the wish to obfuscate the fact that Ong may have described that person prior to the start of the recording.

- A1 ("He's got mace or something") is eliminated in Version B

- A3 ("He's coming back") is eliminated in Version B

- A5 ("He stood upstairs") is eliminated in Version B

- A5 ("Ah, nobody knows what he's going to do") is eliminated in Version B

- A38 ("He's coming back from Business [class]") is changed to "Somebody is coming back from Business [class]."

Who was the person Ong was talking about?

Clues of fraud

After listing all significant differences between the versions, we turn to examine whether these differences could be accounted for by faulty transcription.

An FBI document from September 12, 2001, refers to the poor quality of the recording made by Wansley and tasks an FBI lead to obtain the original recording.[1] I therefore listened repeatedly to the recording of Betty Ong's call while following the left column of Table 2. The only discrepancy mentioned above that could plausibly be attributed to an unclear recording or faulty transcription was the replacement of "he" with the word "somebody."

Version A does not mention the term *hijacker* or *hijacking*. One might conjecture that for some unexplained mistake the first statements in the recording were not transcribed onto Version A. Assuming that this had been the case, it would nevertheless remain surprising that Ong did not subsequently use the "h" word (for hijackers) when referring to the alleged attackers. Was this sentence added fraudulently to Version B of the recording?

Some changes from Version A to Version B appear to have been intended to obfuscate the fact that Betty Ong did not personally see what she was reporting. By deleting Sadler's question whether Ong had actually seen the person being stabbed (A16), evidence was suppressed that she never answered this question.

The deletion of the sentence "What operation... are we talking about?" (statement A6) from Version 2 is highly significant. In that particular case, it was Sadler, whose voice was consistently clear and crisp, who uttered this sentence. It is therefore not possible to attribute its deletion to the low quality of the recording. The word "operation" suggests that Sadler was aware of an "operation" taking place. What "operation"? Significantly, Sadler immediately corrected himself as if he was aware that he blurted something he should not say: "What operation, what flight are we talking about. Flight 12?" The word "operation" does not appear in Version 2.

(b) Clues that Betty Ong was not describing real events

Clues within Betty Ong's phone call

Parsing Ong's account, we note that most of it is couched in *passive* language, i.e., not in the language of direct observation. Indeed, she even acknowledges (statement B25) that someone else is relaying to her information about what is happening in the front of the aircraft. This is further reinforced in Vanessa Minter's interview with the FBI conducted on September 12, 2001.[2] In that interview Minter said "that she thought Ong was relaying information that was being provided to her. She did not believe Ong could actually see what was going on."[3] The

1   Ibid.
1   FBI CE-1020, Lead Numbers DL-257 and CE-66. September 12, 2001. FBI Interview with Vanessa Minter
2   Ibid.

same impression was gleaned by Winston Sadler and Ray Scott, who listened to Ong. In his testimony to the FBI, Sadler said that "[d]uring the entire conversation, Ong seemed to be talking to someone else in the background and retrieving information..."[1] In Scott's testimony to the FBI he said that it "appeared to [him] that [Ong] was getting her information from another individual and relaying it to the Reservation Office."[2]

Considering the indirect nature of Ong's reporting, we further note that she does not apparently attempt to obtain more details from her informants about the identities of the attackers and the actual events. Is this lack of curiosity consistent with the conduct of a competent flight attendant in the case of a real hijacking? She seems content to repeat again and again the same phrases. Within the short recorded segment of her call she repeats six times that the cockpit does not answer or appears locked (statements B1, B9, B23, B31, B40, B44); seven times that stabbings take place (statements B1, B23, B25, B27, B29, B31, B40); and three times that "mace or something" causes breathing difficulties in business class (statements B1, B23, B29). When repeating these statements, she does not add additional details. The transcript of Nydia Gonzalez's conversation with Craig Marquis, approximately 24 minutes long, in which she relays Ong's continuing report, includes little additional information: (a) that the aircraft is at one point flying erratically and then stabilizing; (b) that it is apparently descending; (c) and that all passengers from first class were moved to coach, omitting to explain when this happened and who ordered them to do so.

It is also surprising that Ong, instead of attempting to help her colleagues against the attackers, remains on the phone talking *calmly* with ground personnel for 27 minutes while failing to provide some of the most basic information about the events.

A further indication that suggests the absence of a real attack is that most passengers are said unaware of what was going on. In his testimony to the FBI, Winston Sadler who talked with Ong, said that she "did not believe that the coach passengers were aware of the hijacking."[3] Listeners to Ong's phone call will also note that her voice is devoid of fear or panic and the absence of background yelling, crying, or praying that would be expected if people were stabbed or murdered on the plane.

As relayed by Nydia Gonzalez to Craig Marquis, Ong reported that a passenger by the name of Daniel Lewin had been fatally wounded by a person bearing an Arab name. By that time, however, passengers should have been fully aware of stabbings, because, according to Ong, two flight attendants had already been

---

3 FBI CE-1022. September 12, 2001. Interview with Winston Sadler

4 FBI 302-1013. September 12, 2001. Interview with Ray Cornell Scott

1 FBI 302-1022. September 12, 2001. Interview with Winston Sadler

stabbed. Daniel Lewin, incidentally, was identified by the Israeli newspaper *Ha'aretz* September 17, 2001, as "a former member of the Israel Defense Force Sayeret Matkal, a top-secret counter-terrorist unit, whose Unit 269 specializes in counter-terrorism activities outside Israel."[1] According to Brad Rephen, a New York lawyer and a childhood friend of Lewin, "with his training, [Lewin] would have killed [his attackers] with his bare hands." He added: "I can tell you, their knives would not have stopped him. He would have taken their knives or their box cutters and used them against them...He knows how to fight with knives."[2]

It is inconceivable that three sequential stabbings could have taken place in the aircraft without the awareness of the passengers. Yet, this is what Ong reported.

Conflicting testimonies by Craig Marquis

As mentioned above, Nydia Gonzalez contacted Craig Marquis shortly after joining the conversation with Betty Ong. Craig Marquis, who was interviewed on September 11, 2001, at his place of employment at American Airlines, Fort Worth, Texas, said to the interviewing FBI agent that Ong's call "was transferred to central dispatch in Fort Worth, Texas"[3], that is to his location. After the call was *transferred* to him, "Marquis first confirmed that Ong was an AA flight attendant."[4] That he did so, was also reported in *Wall Street Journal* on October 15, 2001:

> Calm and quick-thinking, [Mr. Marquis] told others in the operations center of the call he'd just received from a woman who identified herself as Betty Ong, an attendant aboard Flight 11.(...) Fearing a hoax, he called up her personnel record and asked her to verify her employee number and nickname. She did. This was real.[5]

In his FBI interview, Craig Marquis additionally mentioned that in the background,

> [he] could hear the flight attendant shrieking and gasping for air.[6]

Marquis talked about "his telephone conversation with Ong," implying that he talked directly with her.

2   "UPI hears, Insider notes from United Press International," *UPI*, March 6, 2002, #883. See also interview with Lewin's childhood friend Yehuda Schwartzberg, in Paul Sperry, "Friends think flight 11 Israeli was 'executed'," *WorldNetDaily*, March 1, 2002, #1085

3   Paul Sperry, "Lewin: Flight 11's unsung hero?," *WorldNetDaily*, March 27, 2002, #1084

4   FBI 302-30391. September 11, 2001. Interview with Craig Marquis

5   Ibid.

1   Scott McCartney and Susan Carey, "Airlines watched and worked in horror as hijackings unfolded," *Wall Street Journal*, October 15, 2001, #740

2   FBI 302-30391. September 11, 2001. Interview with Craig Marquis

All of Marquis' phone calls appear to have been recorded.[1] A transcript of the conversation between Nydia Gonzalez and Craig Marquis was released[2] but not an audio recording of the conversation.[3] On October 11, 2012, the FBI informed me that my FOIA request for the recordings of Gonzalez' phone calls made on September 11, 2001, was denied.[4] This includes, evidently, phone calls for which transcripts had been released.

On November 19, 2003, Craig Marquis was interviewed by Lisa Sullivan and Bill Johnstone, staffers of the 9/11 Commission.[5] In that interview Marquis contradicted what he told the FBI on September 11, 2001, namely that Ong's call had been transferred to him. The staffers wrote in their report of that interview:

> Marquis wanted [Ong's] call to be transferred to him, but Ms. Gonzalez was unable to do so...Marquis recalled that the conversation with Gonzalez was "tough" because he was unable to hear Ong directly.

In her multiple testimonies, Nydia Gonzalez did not mention that Marquis had asked her to transfer the call to him, or that she was unable to do so. Why did Marquis contradict himself?

Puzzling comments made by Craig Marquis and others

Transcripts of phone calls in which Craig Marquis participated on the morning of 9/11 were released in 2009 along with numerous documents of the 9/11 Commission. The transcripts provide evidence that some information emanating from flight AA11 was suppressed.

"This is between you and me"

- In a phone call to Peggy Houck, Craig Marquis said: "[D]on't spread this around. This is between you and me right now. Okay?"[6]

- In the conversation between Marquis and Nydia Gonzalez, he said: "I don't want this spread all over this office right now" and "This is just between you and me right now. Okay?"

- In a conversation between Nancy Wyatt of Boston Flight Service and Ray Howland, she said: "And what do you want us to do as far as just

3   Transcripts of 9/11 Telephone Calls, Private and Confidential, Sensitive Security Information, AA Kean Comm 006327-8. Undated. #634

4   Transcript of conversation between Nydia Gonzalez and Craig Marquis, 9/11 Commission records, Team 7, Box 13, #634

5   Part 1: File AACTRMGR1_825A_0 (20:50 minutes)
     Part 2: File AACTRMGR1_825A_1(3:51 minutes)

6   Letter signed by David M. Hardy, Section Chief, FBI, Washington, D.C., October 11, 2012, re. FOIPA Request No. 1189587-0m #1175

7   MFR 04017189. November 19, 2003. Interview with Craig Marquis, Craig Parfitt, Joe Bertapelle, Mike Mulcahy, by 9/11 Commission staffers

1   Transcript of phone call between Craig Marquis and Peggy Houck, 9/11 Commission documents. NARA. Team 7 Box 13 documents, #634

keeping our mouths shut and not..." to which Howland responded: "That's basically it." She was also overheard to say: "Evelyn, don't mention this to anyone. Me, you, Beth, just the five of us. Okay?"

Here is how Erik Larson explained this secrecy:

> It seems at least as plausible, if not more, that this indicates [Peggy Houck and Craig Marquis] realized the seriousness and sensitivity of the matter, and wanted to keep rumors and panic from spreading while they worked to get the situation under control. It could also mean they felt it was important to manage perceptions regarding AAL's responsibility; clearly, those in management would have recognized the hijacking was a major liability issue for AAL. The 2004 news of this seeming 'cover up' (cited by Griffin) contributed to negative perceptions about AAL, and infuriated family members, some of whom were suing AAL. Prior to the tape's release, it would have been obvious to AAL management that it could make AAL look bad, thus there would be no incentive for AAL to fabricate these statements, and no incentive for the government to do so either, as it had bailed out the airlines and was working to shield them from liability.[1]

Another explanation will be discussed in chapter 14.

Delay in "locking out" the flight

To "lock out" a flight means to prevent access to the system, including to the flight manifests, by anyone without special clearance. Craig Marquis did not rush to "lock out" flight AA11, as one would have expected. He clearly did not initially believe that what Ong was reporting was a real event. It was already 8:45 a.m. when he finally said: "We contacted air traffic control, they are gonna handle this as a confirmed hijacking."[2] It was only at that time that he changed his mind. According to Vanessa Minter's testimony to the FBI, however, the information about flight AA11 was still accessible in the system after the reported crash of the flight, because she heard an unidentified person instruct someone to "block it."[3] However, in 2004, Craig Marquis claimed in an interview with staffers of the 9/11 Commission that he had already begun, at 8:38 a.m., to institute lock-out procedures for fight AA11.[4]

Marquis's apparent delay in locking out the flight, as suggested by Vanessa Minter, would have been a serious mistake on his part, had he believed that Ong was reporting a real event.

---

2   Erik Larson, "Critique of David Ray Griffin's 9/11 Fake Calls Theory," February 2011, *9/11 Blogger.com*, #1038

3   Transcript of phone call between Craig Marquis and Nydia Gonzalez. Included in 9/11 Commission documents. NARA. Team 7 Box 13 documents, #634. At minute 20:19

1   FBI interview with Vanessa Minter. Op. cit. p. 4

2   MFR 04017189. November 19, 2003. Interview with Craig Marquis, Craig Parfitt, Joe Bertapelle, Mike Mulcahy, by 9/11 Commission staffers

Analysis of Betty Ong's voice

According to Craig Marquis, who initially claimed to have talked to Betty Ong, as reported by the *Wall Street Journal*, she was "screaming" and "hysterical with fear."[1] Those who listen to the four released minutes of Ong's phone call will immediately be struck by the absence of concern, let alone fear, in the inflections of her voice, while she was reporting an attempted murder of her colleague a few feet away. She "could not have sounded much calmer on the morning of Sept. 11, 2001."[2] An Associated Press report wrote that Ong's calm and professional demeanor was "beyond reason."[3] Even if one assumes that Betty Ong did not directly witness the stabbings in the aircraft, but was only relaying information from somebody else, her voice would under normal circumstances betray her anxiety or fright when she said that her colleague was *being* stabbed (statement B30). The lack of any such anxiety in her voice suggests that she was not reporting an actual attack on her colleague.

On the other hand, in Gonzalez's call to Marquis, Gonzalez is quoted saying to Ong: "Betty you need to calm down honey" (minute 3:10), "You're doing a great job, just just stay calm" (minute 6:00), "What's going on Betty? Relax, honey. Betty. Betty. Okay, just take it easy" (minute 17:56), "Relax hun. Relax, you'll be okay" (minute 18:40). Note that these statements appear on a transcript of which no recording has been released. If corroborated by the original recording, it would indicate that Ong *did* express signs of anxiety or dread as the call proceeded. Yet in her testimony before the 9/11 Commission, Gonzalez did not repeat these words. She described Ong's call in the following terms:

> In a very calm, professional and poised demeanor, Betty Ong relayed to us detailed information of the events unfolding on Flight 11... Several media accounts of what occurred on Flight 11 claimed that Betty was 'hysterical with fear," "shrieking" and "gasping for air." I am here to tell this Commission that those accounts are wrong.[4]

Another telltale sign supporting the hypothesis that Ong was not reporting real events are the audible hesitations in Ong's narrative, which suggest that she was reading from script or mechanically relaying information, rather than describing what she actually experienced or saw. This is particularly apparent in statements B23 and B31.

3   Scott McCartney and Susan Carey, "American, United Watched and Worked in Horror as Sept. 11 Hijackings Unfolded," *The Wall Street Journal*, October 15, 2001. #740

4   Philip Shenon, "A calm voice as disaster unfolded in the sky," *New York Times*, January 28, 2004, #635

5   Ibid.

1   Statement of Nydia Gonzalez to the 9/11 Commission, January 27, 2004, #648

Content analysis of Betty Ong's call

The content analysis is based on both the transcript of Ong's call (Version B) and that of Gonzalez's call to Craig Marquis.

- When asked to describe the attackers (minute 3:06 into Gonzalez's call to Marquis) Ong did not answer. In her long conversation she never described the hijackers. She merely talks about two "guys."

- Ong does not mention the *radical* change of course by the plane that according to the official account occurred at 8:26:30.[1] This omission suggests that either the plane did not change course or that she was not calling from the plane. As a veteran flight attendant on that particular route she would have immediately noticed a radical change of course. Vanessa Minter, Winston Sadler and Ray Scott specifically mentioned in their testimonies to the FBI that Ong had not mentioned the location of the aircraft.

- Gonzalez reported that the passengers in "coach [are] not aware of what's going on" (minute 3:10 into her call to Marquis) and "[i]t seems like the passengers in coach might not be aware of what's going on right now" (minute 7:00 into Gonzalez's call to Marquis). Yet Ong previously said "we cannot breathe" because of "mace or something" (statements B1 and B23). If the statements about "mace or something" were true, numerous passengers would by that time have difficulties in breathing and thus be aware of a major crisis in the aircraft. Ong said that two flight attendants were stabbed and a passenger was reported dying after he was "fatally stabbed" (minute 12:33 into Gonzalez's call to Marquis). Are we to believe that this could occur without the attacked person(s) fighting back or anyone sitting nearby yelling, or alerting passengers?

- Ong repeatedly surmises that "the guys" or "two guys" are in the cockpit and that the cockpit does not answer (statements B44 and minutes 3:06. 4:21+, 7:30, 17:30 and 19:20 into Gonzalez's call to Marquis). She does not report, however, when and how they broke into the cockpit. And she apparently is not curious to find out.

- Around minute 7.00 Gonzalez relates to Marquis (from Ong) that the men who are in the cockpit with the pilots "were sitting in 2A and 2B." Later, at minute 14:00 Nydia says "[a]pparently one of the passengers that's in the cockpit...was Tom Al Zukani [sic] and he was in 10B not 9A and B as they previously stated." Yet no one had previously mentioned seats 9A and B. According to this count, Ong referred to two, or at most three, attackers, all of whom would be in the cockpit "with the pilots." According to the seating plan of flight AA11, Mohamed Atta, the alleged pilot, had seat 8D.[2] No caller mentioned him entering the cockpit and his seat was not mentioned by Betty Ong. By Ong's account, no hijacker was left in the cabin to guard the passengers.

---

2 "Flight Path Study, AA11," *NTSB*, February 19, 2002, p. 2, #127
1 Summary of Penttbom Investigation, Department of Justice, FBI, February 29, 2004, #1776

- Ong says that all business and first class passengers had been moved to coach because of the difficulty of breathing. The evacuation of first class passengers is mentioned by Gonzalez at minute 16:00. This would mean that they should have known a crisis was occurring, could describe the hijackers and must have witnessed the cockpit entry. Yet nothing of that was reported by Ong.

- When Gonzalez asks (shortly after minute 7:00 into her call to Marquis) whether the "men that are in the cockpit with the pilots were...from first class," Ong responds immediately that "they were sitting in 2A and B," as if Ong had been prepared to answer this particular question. Note that Ong sat in the rear of the aircraft. She relied, therefore, on what others told her. But, as will be seen later, the seat numbers provided by Ong did not match those provided by her colleague Sweeney, nor did these numbers match with the seat numbers mentioned by the 9/11 Commission.

- At minute 17:00 Gonzalez asks Ong "Betty, we don't have an idea as to who the other person might be in the cockpit with the pilots. You did mention there was...you did mention there was two guys in the cockpit with the pilots, correct? Okay. Do we know who the second passenger might be?" Ong does not reply to that question but instead gets nervous. Gonzalez tells her immediately thereafter: "What's going on Betty? Relax, honey. Betty, Betty. Okay, just take it easy."

(2) Madeline Sweeney's calls

According to the FBI, Madeline Sweeney, a flight attendant aboard flight AA11, made five telephone calls to American Airlines at Logan, the first two of which were unsuccessful, followed by three successful phone calls[1]:

8:22   0 seconds
8:24   0 seconds
8:25   107 seconds
8:29   43 seconds
8:32   793 seconds

The recipients of the calls, however, mentioned only two calls: The first was received by Evelyn Nunez (either at 8:25 or at 8:29) and the second (at 8:32) by either Jim Sayer or Michael Woodward or both. Neither the FBI nor the 9/11 Commission explained this discrepancy. Was there one more call made by Sweeney, the existence of which is suppressed or were the reports by the recipients inaccurate?

(a) Sources

Recordings and transcripts of Sweeney's call(s) are not (publicly) available. Larry Wansley, Director of Security with American Airlines in Dallas, Texas, ad-

---

2   See "Overview of the phone calls from the four flights" above.

vised the FBI on September 20, 2001, that he "is not aware of anyone at AA releasing a transcript of a telephone call involving AA flight attendant Sweeney."[1] Note that Wansley did not affirm that there was no transcript, only that he wasn't aware that such a transcript had been "released." For that reason, we can only evaluate released reports that purport to reflect testimonies of those who have received Sweeney's calls, i.e. third-hand evidence. These reports must, therefore, be treated with the requisite circumspection.

The following three persons are said to have talked to Madeline Sweeney:

1. Evelyn Nunez, interviewed by the FBI on September 11, 2001[2]

2. James W. Sayer, interviewed by the FBI on September 11, 2001[3]

3. Michael Woodward, interviewed on September 11, 2001, by a State Trooper and by the FBI[4], on September 13, 2001, by the FBI[5] and some ten (10) more times by the FBI, CIA and the State Department! Woodward was also later interviewed by the staff of the 9/11 Commission.

According to an interview with Elizabeth Williams, conducted by Robert M. Irwin, Mass. State Police on September 13, 2001, she "was on the phone with Systems Operation Control (SOC) [in Dallas, Texas and] repeating the information [Michael] Woodward was calling out to her." She stated that Woodward had asked Sweeney, "What's wrong? What's wrong?" Williams explained that Woodward looked up from the phone and told everyone the phone line had died.[6]

According to the *New York Observer*[7] and Michael Woodward (when he was interviewed by the staff of the 9/11 Commission in 2004), he called Nancy Wyatt, the supervisor of pursers at Logan Airport. Holding telephones in both hands, Woodward repeated to Wyatt everything that Sweeney was saying to him. Wyatt in turn simultaneously transmitted his account to the airline's Fort Worth, Texas, headquarters. The conversation between Wyatt and managers at headquarters *was* recorded.[8]

It is not clear whether Williams and Wyatt were talking about the same relayed phone call, or whether each of them was relaying to another recipient.

1   FBI 302-21991. September 20, 2001. Communication from Larry Wansley
2   FBI 302-9787. September 11, 2001. Interview with Evelyn Nunez
3   FBI 302-14510. September 11, 2001. Interview with James W. Sayer
4   FBI 302-57614. September 11, 2001. Interview with Michael Woodward
5   FBI 302-28820. September 13, 2001. Interview with Michael Woodward
6   FBI 302-28828. September 13, 2001. Interview with Elizabeth Williams
7   Gail Sheehy, "9/11 tapes reveal ground personnel muffled attacks," *New York Observer*, June 20, 2004, #207
8   Nancy Wyatt (BOS flight service) to Ray Howland. Transcript of conversation. NARA. 9/11 Commission documentation Team 7, Box 13, #646

(b) What did the recipients of Sweeney's calls report?

Evelyn Nunez mentioned to her FBI interviewers on September 11, 2001[1] the following details:

- She received a call "after 8:30" from a flight attendant who did not give her name
- The flight attendant said that Flight 12 [*sic*] at Gate 32 had two flight attendants stabbed
- The flight attendant said that a passenger in row 9 had their [*sic*] throat cut by a passenger in seat 10B
- The flight attendant said that the "hijackers" announced they had a bomb
- The flight attendant was talking fast and then got disconnected
- A second call was made by the flight attendant and was answered by Jim Sayer

Trooper Joseph Masterson, Suffolk County, interviewed *Michael Woodward* on September 11, 2001,[2] and documented the following observations by Woodward:

- Flight 11 left gate 30/31 [*sic*] at approximately 7:45 a.m.
- The first phone call from Sweeney was taken by "Evi"[Nunez]
- Shortly thereafter, "Evi" handed the phone to Woodward
- Two flight attendants had been stabbed *in the neck*
- A business class passenger had *his throat cut* and was "dying"
- Flight attendants treated that passenger with oxygen
- Three men of *Middle Eastern descent* had "hijacked" the plane
- The three men were "in the cockpit" and "in control of the plane"
- One of them spoke very good English, another poor/no English. Unsure about third.
- Their seat numbers were 9C, 9G and 10B.
- The men had "a bomb with yellow wires"
- Passengers in business/first class knew of the hijacking but those in coach did not.
- Woodward stated it sounded calm on the flight and there was no significant background noise
- Betty Ong was on the phone with an unknown subject.

---

1   FBI 302-9787. September 11, 2001. Interview with Evelyn Nunez
2   FBI BS-1951 in Team 7 Box 13 DOJ Doc Req 35-13 Packet 6 Fdr. Bates 482, September 11, 2001. #1777

- Sweeney then appeared to grow more excited, stating "we are in rapid descent" and that she could "see water." The call went "dead" at that point.

Michael Woodward told his FBI interviewers on September 11, 2001, the following:

- He recognized the voice of Madeline Sweeney. They were friends.

- Sweeney said the flight had been hijacked.

- Sweeney said two flight attendants had been stabbed (Karen and Bobbi)

- Sweeney said a business class passenger was stabbed

- Sweeney said a doctor and nurse were caring for him

- Sweeney said three hijackers had gained access to the cockpit

- Sweeney said the crew could not gain access or communicate with the pilots or the cockpit

- Sweeney said the hijackers were sitting in seats 10B, 9C and 9G or 9D and 9G.

- Sweeney said the hijackers looked like "Middle Eastern males"

- Sweeney said one of the hijackers spoke good English and another spoke poor English.

- Sweeney said later in the call that the plane was flying low over the water, then said 'Oh my God' and the call was terminated.

- Sweeney also mentioned that flight attendant Betty Ong was sitting in the last row of coach, talking on the Airfone

- As the conversation continued, Sweeney said the gentleman in business class is not going to make it because his throat was slashed and he's bleeding severely.

Michael Woodward was interviewed again by the FBI on September 13, 2001, and revealed the following new details:

- Woodward said he boarded the airliner assigned to flight AA11 *before it departed from Logan* to check that everything was OK. He said he talked to several flight attendants before they left. He did not mention at which gate number the airliner was.

James W. Sayer told to his FBI interviewers on September 11, 2001, the following:

- He said he is an American Airlines flight attendant but was "currently" assigned as a staffing assistant to Kelly Cox, the AA base flight service manager.

- He said that when he entered the office on the morning of 9/11, he heard Evelyn Nunez state that "two flight attendants had been stabbed on Flight 11 at Gate 32." Nunez [then] called Elizabeth Williams and

Michael Woodward to tell them what happened. Sayer said that Williams and Woodward went down to gate 32 and discovered there was no plane.... Nunez then checked the AA computer for flight information, and called someone on the telephone. While Nunez was on the telephone, another telephone rang which Sayer said he had answered.

- Sayer said that a female flight attendant calling from flight AA11 was on the phone.

- The flight attendant said that two other flight attendants were stabbed and a man in business class had been stabbed in the throat.

- The flight attendant said a doctor and nurse on the plane were caring for the injured man.

- The flight attendant said two people who said they had a bomb, had gone to the cockpit. She observed two boxes connected with red and yellow wire.

- The flight attendant said these two people had mace and pepper spray and she could detect an odor in the cabin.

- The flight attendant said they were in the air over New York City.

- She also said the hijackers were sitting in seats 10B, 9C and 9G.

- Sayer then turned over the telephone to Mike Woodward who also spoke to the flight attendant.

- Sayer added that he took some notes while he was talking to the flight attendant, signed and dated these notes and turned them over to the investigating agent.

According to Elizabeth Williams, Jim Sayer answered the phone "as [she] and Woodward entered the room" and Sayer "advised everyone that he was speaking with the same flight attendant Nunez had spoken with. Woodward then took the phone from Sayer and began conversing with the flight attendant."

Williams' testimony implies that Sweeney's call arrived as they were entering the room and that Sayer only exchanged one or two sentences with Sweeney, after which Woodward took over the conversation. In that case it is surprising that Sayer succeeded in obtaining all the above information.

Michael Woodward did not apparently mention to the FBI Jim Sayer's conversation with Sweeney, suggesting that he was not aware that Sayer had engaged in any substantive conversation with her. On the other hand, Nunez did not mention Woodward's conversation with Sweeney. She merely mentioned that Jim Sayer took the second call. Sayer's handwritten notes have not been released.

Michael Woodward told 9/11 Commission's staffers on January 25, 2004, that he saw several of the crew members board the plane and he talked to several of them, but he did not remember *why* the flight was late departing.[1]

He also confirmed that he went with Elizabeth Williams to gate 32 after Evelyn Nunez received a call from a flight attendant saying that someone was hurt on Flight 12 at that gate. After going there, they found *nothing amiss*. He said it then dawned on him that flight 12 comes in at night and has not yet left Los Angeles. He and Williams then returned to the office. As he went back to the office, another call had come in and Jim Sayer said that it was Amy Sweeney, a flight attendant aboard Flight 11. She was calling again on a cell phone. Woodward took the call over from Jim Sayer. Woodward added that Sayer, in his position, was not trained to handle emergency calls.[2]

Here is what Woodward reported from Sweeney's call to the staffers of the 9/11 Commission in 2004:[3]

- Sweeney's speech was "normal, very matter-of-fact, and official."
- She was in the back of the plane sitting next to Betty Ong.
- The plane had been hijacked.
- A man in first class had his throat slashed.
- Two flight attendants had been stabbed, they were Karen Martin and Bobby Arestegui.
- They couldn't contact the cockpit.
- There's a bomb in the cockpit.
- A doctor had been paged.
- The hijackers' seats were 10B, 9D and 9G.
- The hijackers had gained entry to the cockpit.
- The hijackers were Middle Eastern.
- One of the hijackers spoke very little English and one spoke excellent English.
- The people in coach were under the impression that there was a routine medical emergency in First Class.
- Jeff Collman, Sara Low and Diane Snyder (other flight attendants on flight 11) were running around doing things like getting medical supplies while Ong and Sweeney were reporting the events.
- Sweeney said, "Something is wrong. We are in a rapid descent." The plane was "all over the place."

---

1   MFR 04017171. January 25, 2004. Interview with Michael Woodward
2   Ibid.
3   Ibid.

• The passenger in business class was bleeding severely.

Woodward asked Sweeney to look out the window to see if she could determine where they were. Sweeney said,

"We are flying low. We are flying very, very low. We are flying way too low." And seconds later she said, "Oh my God we are way too low" and then the phone call ended.

Woodward believes the phone call lasted a total of eight or nine minutes. Sweeney didn't say anything about a gun, mace, pepper spray or box cutters. She only mentioned the stabbings and the bomb in the cockpit.

Considering that Woodward was interviewed more than two years after the events, one has to admire his ability to recall all the above details.

(c) The dubious quote

In the document containing Michael Woodward's FBI interview from September 13, 2001, (see above), the following paragraph is enclosed within quotation marks and purports to represent exactly what Madeline Sweeney had said:

"The flight has been hijacked. This flight is Flight 11 from Boston to LA. The plane is a 767. I am in the back with Betty Ong AA Flight Attendant. A man in business class has had his throat slashed and is presumably dead. #1 flight attendant has been stabbed and #5 flight attendant has been stabbed. There is a bomb in the cockpit. I can't make contact with the cockpit, can you do it? We have paged for a doctor or nurse for the flight attendants. The coach passengers don't know what's happening. BOBBI is not on oxygen and KAREN is. BOBBI is on the floor behind the cockpit. The hijackers are of Middle Eastern descent. One spoke good English and one didn't. It is a rapid descent. Something is wrong. I don't think the captain is in control. I see water. I see buildings. We're very, very low. Oh, my God."[1]

By examining other testimonies, it emerges that the above quoted paragraph represents a compilation of various phrases uttered over the entire duration of the call. It does not, therefore, represents a verbatim transcription of what Sweeney said and constitutes, therefore, a deliberate misrepresentation.

This paragraph also includes statements that do not accord with other testimonies:

• The bomb is said to be "in the cockpit"

• Bobbi is "on the floor behind the cockpit"

• The plane is said to be a [Boeing] 767 (a statement not mentioned in the September 11, 2001, interview)

---

1   FBI 302-28820. September 13, 2001. Interview with Michael Woodward

- Sweeney is said to have urged Woodward to contact the cockpit ("I can't make contact with the cockpit, can you do it?"). This was not mentioned in the September 11 interview.

- In the September 11 interview, Woodward related from Sweeney that a doctor and nurse were taking care of the wounded passenger. In the quoted paragraph, the passenger is not yet cared for ("we have paged for a doctor and nurse"). In his interview, it was the flight attendants—and not a doctor and nurse—who treated the wounded passenger.

- In the quoted paragraph the number of hijackers and their seat numbers are not mentioned. If the quoted paragraph was based on Woodward's notes, it is surprising that this information is missing.

FBI agents conducted additional interviews with Jane Allen, Elizabeth Williams and Michael Sweeney [Madeline's husband]) regarding Madeline's phone calls, but what these persons told about her call are what they learned from Michael Woodward. Reports of Michael Woodward's other interviews by the FBI, the CIA and the State Department have not been released.[1]

(d) Nancy Wyatt's call to Ray Howland (SOC), September 11, 2001

As mentioned above, Nancy Wyatt relayed Michael Woodward's part of the conversation with Madeline Sweeney in real-time to Ray Howland at American Airlines' Systems Operation Control (SOC), in Dallas, Texas.[2] This relayed call was recorded. Michael Sweeney, Madeline's husband, told reporter Gail Sheehy in 2004, "I was shocked that I'm finding out, almost three years later, there was a tape with information given by my wife that was very crucial to the happenings of 9/11. Suddenly it miraculously appears and falls into the hands of the F.B.I.? Why and how and for what reason was it suppressed?"[3] Below are details from Sweeney's call based on what Wyatt relayed to Ray Howland:

- It looks like "he's Middle Eastern" (*note the singular*—E.D.)

- He speaks no English. He was in [seat] 10B (The sentence suggests that Wyatt told Howland previously that "he" had slashed a passenger)

- 9D and G speaks no...speaks no English.

- The plane is in a rapid descent.

- The flight attendants don't know what's going on in the cockpit.

- It looks like there is severe bleeding (*repeated twice*). There is a slashed throat.

- Michael Woodward is heard in the background: Karen Martin's been stabbed...And this is a business class passenger whose throat...

---

1 Ibid.
2 Nancy Wyatt, Op. cit., #646
3 Gail Sheehy, "9/11 tapes...," Op. cit., #207

- Two flight attendants have been stabbed, Barbara Orestegui [*sic*] and Karen Martin

- It looks like he's got things written here. That the two flight attendants are okay.

- The hijackers are in the cockpit.

The facts transmitted by Wyatt to Howland corroborate for the most part those told by Woodward in interviews. The slight differences can be attributed to the difficulty in relaying such a conversation in real-time.

The transcript reveals that Ray Howland wanted to conceal information, including from Madeline Sweeney herself. He thus said to Nancy Wyatt, "We're trying to get in contact with the cockpit [of AA11]," yet "we don't really want to tell her that," to which Nancy Wyatt agrees ("Okay. Don't. Okay, okay. Got it").[1]

About two minutes later Ray Howland tells Nancy Wyatt, "it looks like it's going to JFK" but adds immediately thereafter, "We...I mean, we don't really want to give a whole lot of information to that flight. Okay?," to which Nancy Wyatt again agrees ("Okay, we're not. We're not giving them that information to that flight."). Later in the transcript, Nancy Wyatt asks Evelyn [probably Evi Nunez]: "don't mention this to anyone. Me, you, Beth [Elizabeth Williams?], just the five of us. Okay?" to which Ray Howland agrees ("Yup. Absolutely"). Later, just before minute 8:00 Nancy Wyatt asks Ray Howland, "And what do you want us to do as far as just keeping our mouths shut and not...," to which Howland responds, "That's basically it."[2]

Similar statements were made by Craig Marquis to whom Peggy Houck reported the call by Betty Ong. Marquis advises Houck at minute 0:35, "Don't spread this around. This is between you and me right now. Okay?" to which Houck agrees.[3] He also made similar comments to Nydia Gonzalez.

A possible explanation for the secrecy imposed by Ray Howland and Craig Marquis will be provided in chapter 14.

(e) Anomalies

- According to Nunez, the caller (who for some reason did not identify herself), said that flight 12 at gate 32 had two flight attendants stabbed. On the basis of this message Woodward and Williams went to gate 32, where they found no plane, an empty plane or nothing amiss (depending on the testimonies). Why did Sweeney mention flight 12? Why did Sweeney mention gate 32, as the location of the stabbings?

---

1   Nancy Wyatt, Op. cit, #646
2   Ibid.
3   Craig Marquis to Peggy Houck. Transcript of conversation. NARA. 9/11 Commission documentation Team 7, Box 13, #634

- Woodward was not only repeatedly interviewed by the FBI but also by the CIA and the State Department. What prompted the CIA and the State Department to interview him in particular?

- Sayer said he took the second call from Sweeney and talked for a substantial time with her. This fact is surprisingly not mentioned by Woodward. Yet Sayer's long communication with Sweeney was not mentioned in the media, while Woodward has been widely cited.

- Sayer reported details which neither Nunez nor Woodward reported. According to him Sweeney had observed "two boxes connected with red and yellow wire." This was not reported—at least not in such detail—by Nunez and Woodward. He also said that the "hijackers had mace and pepper spray" and that the caller "could detect the odor in the cabin." Why did Sweeney fail to mention the mace and the odor when talking to Nunez and Woodward, if this had been the case? Sayer cited Sweeney saying the plane was "in the air over New York City," something no others apparently heard her say. Yet, by the time Woodward took over the call from Sayer, flight AA11 was not supposed to have reached New York City. He said he took some notes, which he signed, dated and turned over to the interviewing agent. These notes have not released. Did they include the above details? In his 2004 interview with the 9/11 Commission's staff, Woodward said that Sayer hadn't be trained to handle emergency calls. What did he intend to suggest by this statement?

- The quoted paragraph in Woodward's September 13, 2001, interview is surprising, because FBI 302 forms do not ordinarily include such quoted paragraphs. What was the source, purpose and rationale for such a quotation?

- Sweeney does not mention when and how the "hijackers" entered the cockpit. How did she determine their seat numbers?

- Sweeney does not mention the radical change of course of the aircraft.

- Sweeney does not report what the English-speaking "hijacker" had said.

- According to Nunez and Woodward, Sweeney did not mention mace or pepper-spray.

- The FBI claims Sweeney called three times, but only two calls are publicly known to have been received. Was there a third, suppressed, call?

- While Sweeney reported stabbings, none of the call's recipients mentioned hearing anyone yelling in the background.

- While Sweeney mentions flying "very low" and seeing water and buildings, no passengers are heard in the background shrieking in fear. Was the aircraft perhaps landing somewhere?

(3) Conflicting Reports Of Ong And Sweeney

Some of the differences between Ong's and Sweeney's accounts may be attributed to the assumed fact that Ong was sitting at the back of the airliner while Sweeney was said to move about and would have been partly in proximity to the alleged hijackers. This might explain the difference in seat numbers of the "hijackers" given by Ong and Sweeney, the fact that Sweeney gave a summary description of the "hijackers" ("Middle Eastern males"), that she reported about their English language skills, and that she saw something resembling a bomb in their hands.

Other differences, however, cannot be attributed to their presumed locations within the aircraft.

- Ong complains repeatedly of mace and of difficulties in breathing. Yet, Sweeney—who is apparently moving between the front and the rear of the aircraft—does not mention mace or pepper-spray. This suggests that Ong reported a non-existing situation.

- Ong states (via Nydia Gonzalez) that the passengers from first class had been moved to coach, in part because of the difficulties in breathing. Sweeney does not mention such move. She would certainly have done so, had this occurred.

- Sweeney mentioned (via Sayer and Woodward) that a doctor and nurse were treating a slashed passenger. Yet, according to Ong (via Nydia Gonzalez) there was no doctor on board.

- Ong mentions repeatedly that the plane flies "erratically." This is not mentioned by Sweeney. Sweeney, on the other hand, emphasizes that the aircraft is descending rapidly, whereas Ong only "thinks" it is descending, suggesting that this is not so obvious.

- Sweeney mentions the seat numbers of the alleged hijackers as 10B, 9D and 9G, whereas Ong mentions seat numbers 10B, 2A and 2B. Both of them mention the presence of no more than three "hijackers" on board, yet according to the official tally they were five.

(a) Further anomalies

In addition to the conflicting reports, the testimonies of both Ong and Sweeney contain anomalies that undermine the credibility of their account:

- Neither Ong nor Sweeney explain or even suggest how the alleged hijackers broke into the cockpit. Even if they did not personally witness their entry into the cockpit, their entry must have been at least witnessed by first class passengers sitting in proximity. The following seven passengers in first class had the cockpit in their line of sight (See Seating Diagram): Carol Bouchard (3B), Carol Flyzik (3H), Laura Morabito (2D), Renee Newell (3A), David Retik (2H), Sonia Puopolo (3J), and Richard Ross (2J). Yet none of these passengers apparently told the flight attendants how the "hijackers," who allegedly wielded knives and a bomb, broke into the cockpit. We furthermore note that Ong and Sweeney did not appear curious about the manner by which the cockpit was allegedly broken into.

- Both Ong and Sweeney emphasized that coach passengers were unaware of the hijacking. Yet both reported that two flight attendants had been stabbed and a passenger in seat 9B, later identified as Daniel Lewin, had been murdered by a passenger from seat 10B. A person slashed with a knife does not die instantaneously. The victim's reactions and his heavy bleeding would have drawn the attention of all proximate passengers, such as those sitting in seat numbers 9A (Edmund Glazer), 11D (Carolyn Beug) and 11B (Christopher Mello) (See Seating Diagram). If not actually attempting to jump the attacker, these passengers would have immediately alerted the crew and their fellow passengers to the act of violence they had observed and urged people to neutralize the attacker. Yet, there is no evidence of any passengers trying to neutralize the attacker of Daniel Lewin or spreading the information around. This alleged unawareness of the coach passengers is furthermore puzzling in the light of Ong's repeated claims that mace or pepper-spray had made breathing difficult, even to her, sitting at the rear of the aircraft. The lack of awareness by passengers of a major crisis aboard the plane suggests that no such crisis took place..

- Sweeney claims that one of the hijackers spoke English well (or very well) and another spoke English badly or spoke no English. It follows from her statement that the hijacker who spoke English well (or very well), had said something intelligible that she had understood. Yet, in her reports to Nunez, Sayer and Woodward, she did not mention anything that this hijacker had said. This omission is surprising, for flight attendants are specifically instructed to report hijackers' statements. Had she heard a "hijacker" say something, she would certainly have reported what he said. As we assume that Sweeney was a trained and conscientious flight attendant, this omission suggests that the hijackers said nothing, that the person who said something was no hijacker, or that the story of these hijackers was bogus.

- Listeners to Ong's and Sweeney's calls expressed their admiration for the professional calm displayed by these flight attendants while reporting these dreadful events. Keeping calm in a crisis situation is certainly admirable, but even professionals cannot hide their anxiety in the presence of *existential* threats, such as murders being committed in close proximity to them. It is one thing to report the heart failure of a passenger and another to report that one's colleague is *being* murdered a few feet away. Presuming that Ong and Sweeney possessed human empathy, as is typical of flight attendants, their sober reporting suggests that no one was actually stabbed or murdered aboard the airplane.

- According to the official account, Ong's telephone call lasted 27 minutes. She sat all that time talking on the phone while colleagues and passengers were allegedly being murdered. It defies belief that a competent flight attendant would sit calmly and chat away in such circumstances.

Such a person would be rushing to the help of the victims and try to calm frightened passengers. Presuming that Ong was a responsible, dedicated flight attendant and a loyal colleague, the only conclusion from her puzzling conduct is that she was not reporting real events.

• Neither Ong nor Sweeney mentioned the radical course change by the aircraft, reported in the official flight path of AA11, yet they knew the route by heart. They would have immediately noticed a radical change of course, had it occurred. The fact that they did not mention it suggests either that the aircraft did not make this turn, but continued according to its flight plan, or that they were not calling from an aircraft.

(4) Concluding observations about the AA11 calls

Only two persons are known to have made phone calls "from flight AA11": Betty Ong and Madeline (Amy) Sweeney, both of them veteran flight attendants. In addition, air traffic controllers said they heard radio communications they attributed to the alleged suicide-pilot on flight AA11, that is, Mohamed Atta. These communications were not, however, forensically traced to a particular location. They could have emanated from anywhere.

CHAPTER 8. FLIGHT UA175 CALLS

A Boeing 767 aircraft assigned to flight UA175 is said to have crashed on the South Tower of the WTC at 9:03 a.m. A diagram of the seating arrangement of that flight is shown on the following page, as reproduced in an Exhibit to the Moussaoui trial. The arrangement can help in assessing the feasibility of the alleged hijacking. It may be referred to in the following sections.

(1) Peter Burton Hanson's Calls

Peter Hanson, his wife Sue Kim, and their 2-year-old daughter, Christine Lee, traveled together on Flight UA175.

According to the FBI, Peter Hanson made two telephone calls from the aircraft to his parents:[1]

At 8:52	99 seconds
At 9:00	192 seconds

(a) FBI Document NH-3718 of September 11, 2001. Interview with James R. Candee

According to Captain James Candee of the Easton Police Department, Lee Hanson—Peter Hanson's father—called the Easton Police Department at approximately 8:55 a.m. on September 11, 2001, and advised that his son had called him from flight UA175.[2] Captain Candee indicated that "he would secure the tape of the Hanson 911 call and copy it onto a separated cassette tape."[3] This was probably the first call made by Lee Hanson after he received a call from his son Peter. The recording of this call was not released.

---

1   Overview of phone calls: Introduction to Part III of this book
2   FBI NH-3718. September 11, 2001. Interview with James R. Candee
3   Ibid.

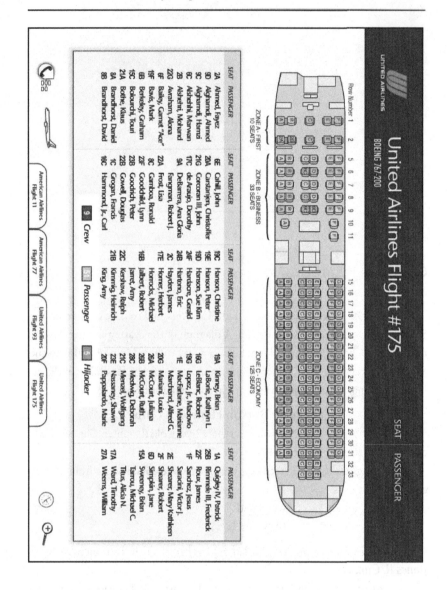

(b) FBI Document TP 18 issued on September 12, 2001

On September 11, 2001, at 12:02 p.m. an unidentified person called the Kennedy Space Center (NASA) in Florida to report that Eunice and Lee Hanson (Peter's parents) had received a cell phone call from their son aboard flight UA175. According to the report about this call to NASA, Peter had advised his parents that he was aboard a hijacked plane from Boston and *had heard the hijackers talking about 8 planes that were hijacked.*[1]

---

1   FBI TP 18 (Tampa Office). September 12, 2001 (Case ID 265D-TP-280350)

(c) FBI Document 265D-HQ-1348101, (Ser 354), issued on September 12, 2001

Shortly thereafter, at 12:30 p.m., a person by the name of Jack Signor, working with Security Office, Kennedy Space Center, spoke with Mr. [Lee] Hanson (Peter's father), who confirmed that he had received a phone call from his son Peter, advising his father from an airplane that he "overheard hijackers talking about eight (8) planes being hijacked."[1] For the record, let it be noted that the document which contained this particular detail was issued by FBI headquarters in Washington on September 12, 2001.

(d) FBI Document TP 201, issued on September 13, 2001

On September 13, 2001, FBI Tampa (Florida) drafted a Lead sheet, requesting FBI New Haven at Trumbull (Conn.) to interview Peter Hanson's parents for further information, if available, about what Peter had overheard the hijackers say. The reason given for this request was that "parents of a victim on one of the hijacked planes...advised his parents by cellphone that he heard the hijackers say eight planes were being hijacked."[2]

Surprisingly, this particular detail relayed by Peter to his father and confirmed by him to the FBI, was not mentioned anywhere after that. Yet, such information was relevant for several reasons. It would be reasonable to ask how Peter could "overhear" such a conversation if the "hijackers" were talking in their own language, Arabic. Was Peter fluent in Arabic? If he did not understand Arabic, how did he know what they were talking about? If, however, the "hijackers" were talking among themselves in English, did they intend passengers to overhear this remark and transmit it, and if so, for what purpose? Would that be wise from their perspective? Apparently, US authorities did not relish to have such questions asked. This detail was thoroughly suppressed thereafter.

(e) FBI Document IN 32838, undated (SKH:skh)

In addition to the telephone call between Lee Hanson and the Easton Police Department on September 11, he was interviewed twice by FBI Special Agents on that very day. The first interview was conducted by telephone. No record of this interview was released. After that interview, the agent himself was interviewed by another FBI special agent. That second special agent and another unidentified agent went to interview Lee Hanson and his family in person. After talking with Lee Hanson and other family members present at the Hanson residence, the second special agent informed the first special agent that he (the second)

---

1   FBI HQ-1348101, (Ser 354) issued on September 12, 2001, by FBI HQ to Tampa FBI
2   FBI TP 201. September 13, 2001

would write the FD-302 on the interview, and that there was no need for the first agent to write an FD-302 concerning the initial telephone interview.[1] We note that certain early statements by Peter Hanson's father, such as that regarding the "hijackers" mentioning eight hijacked planes, did not appear in any subsequent FBI document.

(f) FBI Document 302 9269 of September 11, 2001. Interview with Lee Hanson

The second interview with Lee Hanson constitutes what could be designated as the "official" FBI interview with Peter Hanson's father.[2] This document includes a verbatim paragraph, set in quotes, that purports to represent what Peter had told his father:

> I think they've taken over the cockpit...and attendant has been stabbed... and someone else up front may have been killed. The plane is making strange moves. Call United Airlines...Tell them it's Flight 175, Boston to LA.

Lee Hanson told the FBI that his son "was talking in a low tone, but not whispering. He believed his son was calling from his cellular telephone."[3] In a later media report, Lee Hanson was cited as saying that his son's voice "was soft, not too nervous."[4] Such serenity is surprising, to say the least, considering that he told his father that the aircraft in which his entire family was sitting had been taken over by ruthless murderers!

Rowland Morgan, author of the e-book "Voices" on the telephone calls, made the following comment on Lee Hanson's conduct:

> Lee Hanson...apparently was capable of immediately giving a lucid account to his local police headquarters, taking less than seven minutes to convince them that the first hijacking in 15 years had just been reported in a personal call made from a cell phone on an aircraft six miles high. We know that his alarming and unexpected report took only a few minutes, because Hanson Sr. was quickly off the line and ready to receive a second call. (Morgan, Voices, 166)

Within a matter of minutes, Lee Hanson said he received a second telephone call from his son. In that call his son reportedly said:

> It's getting bad, Dad...A stewardess was stabbed...they seem to have knives and mace...They said they have a bomb...It's getting very bad on the plane... passengers are throwing up and getting sick...the plane is making jerky movements...I don't think the pilot is flying the plane...I think we're going

---

1   FBI IN 32838. undated (SKH:skh)
2   FBI 302-9269. September 11, 2001. Interview with Lee Hanson.
3   Ibid.
4   Richard A. Serrano, "Moussaoui Jury Hears the Panic From 9/11," *Los Angeles Times*, April 11, 2006, #997

down...I think they intend to go to Chicago or someplace and fly into a building.[1]

Rowland Morgan made the interesting observation that this report. . .

was translated into direct speech, complete with telegraphic hyphenation of the sort pioneered by "spontaneous bop prosody" author Jack Kerouac... It is hard to imagine a more action-packed three minute telephone call, culminating in a ghastly fatality, replayed on television almost instantly in all its flaming horror, and again innumerable times thereafter (Morgan, *Voices*, 167).

The following facts relayed to Lee Hanson, which appear in other FBI documents based on interviews with Lee, were, however omitted from the "official" Hanson interview:

- That Peter had just *seen* a stewardess being shot.[2] In another version Peter allegedly said that a stewardess had just been shot *in the head*.[3]

- That the plane was still on the ground when Peter called.[4]

- That Peter overheard the hijackers mention 8 hijacked planes.[5]

On June 20, 2002, Lee Hanson was again interviewed by an unnamed FBI Special Agent. At that occasion Assistant US Attorney David Novak and an unnamed official of the Port Authority attended.[6] It is not possible to glean from the report of that FBI interview why Hanson was again interviewed and why the aforementioned officials attended the interview. Lee Hanson told them extensively about the life of his son and finished by recounting once again their conversations from 9/11. In that account Lee Hanson mentioned most facts he had previously told the FBI[7] but there were a few significant differences, mentioned below.

When interviewed on September 11, 2001, by the FBI, Lee Hanson reportedly said that he heard the noise of a woman screaming in the background. In the June 20, 2002 interview, he said he "could not hear any background noise" and mentioned no screaming.

In the interview of September 11, 2001, Lee Hanson said his son had advised that the "hijackers" said to have a bomb. In the 2002 interview, he did not mention the bomb. He did not either mention the three details listed above.

---

1   FBI 302-9269. September 11, 2001. Interview with Lee Hanson

2   FBI CG 35. September 11, 2001, at 10:20 a.m. FBI Chicago

3   FBI AT-15449 (FBI Atlanta). September 12, 2001, 7:55 a.m.

4   Ibid.

5   FBI TP 18; Ser 354; TP 201.

6   FBI 265A-NY-280350 (unnumbered). June 20, 2002 (Boston, Mass.). Interview with Lee Hanson

7   FBI 302-9269. September 11, 2001. Interview with Lee Hanson.

According to both interviews—those of September 11, 2001, and of June 2002—Peter reportedly referred to the hijacking and the stabbings in passive language (the plane "was being" hijacked, a flight attendant "had been stabbed"), without describing those who carried out the "hijacking" and the "stabbing" or without indicating how many they were. From the way the testimony was narrated by his father, it appears that Peter did not personally see any of these acts. He did not either describe how the "hijackers" entered the cockpit. He merely said, "I think [the hijackers] have taken over the cockpit" and "I don't think the pilot is flying the plane," but did not offer any evidence in support for these statements. He said he "thought" that they were going down but at the same time "thought" that the [hijackers] "intend[ed] to go to Chicago or some place and fly into a building." The aircraft was not scheduled to fly to Chicago and at the time of the call, Peter Hanson could not have known that an aircraft had flown into the North Tower of the WTC. Who were the "hijackers" who suggested to him that they intended to "fly into a building"?

(2) Brian Sweeney's Phone Calls

According to the FBI, Brian Sweeney made two telephone calls to his family:[1]

- At 8:58:45 27 seconds, to his wife Julie

- At 9:00:02 60 seconds, to his mother Louise

As Brian's wife did not answer the phone, he left a message on her answering machine. According to the FBI, who listened later to the message, he only said that the plane had been hijacked but did not leave any information about the alleged hijackers or about what he was experiencing. His wife claimed later that he used his cell phone for this call.[2] The recording left on her answering machine was not released. The transcript of Brian Sweeney's call to his wife Julie, was published in a court document in 2011. According to this transcript he said, "Hey, Jules [sic]. It's Brian. Listen, I'm on an airplane that's been hijacked. If things don't go well, and it's not looking good, I want you to know that I absolutely love you. I want you to do good, go have good times—the same to my parents and everybody—and I just totally love you, and I'll see you when you get there. Bye, Babe, I'll call you."[3]

Brian then called his mother, Louise. She was interviewed by the FBI on September 11, 2001. She told the interviewing agent that she asked Brian whether he knew their location and he said he believed "that the plane was flying some-

---

1   Overview of phone calls: Introduction to Part III of this book
2   FBI 302-46325. September 11, 2001. Interview with Julie Sweeney
3   The Bavis family's memorandum of law in opposition to defendants' motion for summary judgment, In Re September 11 litigation, *Bavis v. United Air Lines, Inc. et al*, CV 7154, United States District Court, Southern District of New York, September 16, 2011, #1133

where over Ohio." This observation was remarkable because it would indicate that Brian had not noticed the aircraft's alleged radical change of route and the dramatic descent of the aircraft towards New York City at that very moment.

She also said to the interviewing agent, that she asked him who the "hijackers" were, to which he reportedly answered "I don't know who they are."[1] Yet in 2004, she told a reporter, that the "hijackers" were Middle Eastern.[2] According to his mother, Brian mentioned that the "passengers were thinking of storming the cockpit" but ended saying "they are coming back," omitting to say who "they" were and from where they were coming back.[3] Peter Hanson and flight attendant Fangman, who called from the same aircraft,[4] did not mention in their calls any plan to "storm the cockpit." Was Brian the only person on board aware of such a plan?

Brian did not mention having seen knives, mace or a bomb in the hands of the alleged hijackers, or any violent action committed by them. His mother mentioned in a later interview with the FBI that "there were no loud noises or commotion in the background. Brian was *speaking in quiet tones*."[5] Brian did not mention the sinister actions reported by Peter Hanson from the same flight.

Brian Sweeney was a former fighter jet pilot who served in the Gulf War. His mother said he was a "natural leader." His class fellow mates at Pensacola had, according to her, two "call signs" for Brian: "Moose," because he was big and was from New England, and "Preacher" because he was always trying to inspire others to do their best and keep everyone in line.[6] She said he would not have hesitated to organize a counter-attack on attackers, if the need had arisen.

(3) Garnet "Ace" Bailey's phone calls

According to a 9/11 Commission Staff Report, Garnet "Ace" Bailey, who was a passenger on UA175, tried four times to call his wife Katherine, on both her business and home phone lines.(Staff Report, 21) According to the FBI, three of his attempts lasted 22, 25 and 9 seconds.[7]

Apparently somebody at his home answered the first three calls. His wife, however, claimed she did not recall any such calls. She said in an interview with a reporter in 2007 that the family "had no idea that Dad was on that plane. I had

---

1 FBI 302-46330. September 11, 2001. Interview with Louise Sweeney.
2 Corky Siemaszko, "Passengers battle WTC hijack," *New York Daily News*, March 9, 2004, #998
3 Ibid.
4 See next sub-section, "A call by an unidentified flight attendant"
5 FBI 302-[redacted], March 24, 2004. Interview with Louise Sweeney. #1778
6 Ibid.
7 Overview of phone calls: Introduction to Part III of this book

no thought he was in harm's way because his plane was headed for Los Angeles."[1] Author Rowland Morgan, mentioned earlier, observed that in the wake of the 9/11 events, no public mention of Bailey's calls could be found. (Morgan, *Voices*, 178) Did Garnet Bailey talk to someone at all? And if so, with whom? The FBI, meanwhile, did not explain why three connected phone calls by Bailey from a hijacked plane have been listed on the Prosecution's Exhibit in Moussaoui's trial.

(4) A phone call by an unidentified flight attendant

According to the FBI, two successful telephone calls were made from Flight UA175 on the morning of 9/11 to SAMC, a United Airlines maintenance center in San Francisco.[2]

>   At 8:52:01 (EST)   75 seconds
>   At 8:56:19 (EST)   31 seconds

According to a letter from United Airlines to Assistant US Attorney David J. Novak of July 31, 2002,[3] the airline "learned from GTE-Airfone that *three* calls were made from flight UA175 on September 11, 2001, to SAMC Fix controller desk," at 8:52 (75 seconds), 8:56 (31 seconds) and 8:57 (267 seconds), the last and longest call surprisingly making no connection.

In the aforementioned letter United Airlines emphasized that the information from GTE-Airfone is inconsistent with the controller's recollection: "The controller who took the [...] call from flight 175 (Mr. Policastro) reported only one call/one conversation with the flight.... Any statements made by [a UAL employee] to the FBI about a second call, may have been the result of confusing flight 93 and 175 calls."[4]

It is not clear, however, which of the above two calls listed by the FBI was attributed to flight UA175. Further, no explanation was provided how the phone company could confuse a call made from flight UA175 with one made from flight UA93.

The call from flight UA175 was taken by Marc R. Policastro at approximately 5:55 a.m. (Pacific time), or 8:55 a.m. (EST).[5] Policastro was interviewed by the FBI on September 11, 2001.(Staff Report, n. 168) The 302 form of his interview was not released. However, a hand-written note he wrote about the call was released to NARA. It states:

---

1   Doug Krikorian, "Ace Bailey's legacy lives on," *Press-Telegram* (Longbeach, Calif.), October 9, 2007, #738

2   Overview of phone calls: Introduction to Part III of this book

3   Letter from United Airlines to Assistant US Attorney David J. Novak, July 31, 2002. In NARA 9/11 Commission documents. Team 7, Box 13. Flight 175 Calls Folder. #803

4   Ibid.

5   Handwritten statement by Marc Policastro of SAMC, on phone call from UA175, Sept.11, 2001. In NARA 9/11 Commission documents. Team 7 Box 12. Flight 93 Calls —Gen. Folder 9-11-01, #886

> I was working the StarFix desk, at 0555 on 9-11-01 I received a call from a flight attendant claiming he was on Flt 175 from Boston to LAX. He informed me that the flight was in the process of being hijacked. He also stated that one flight attendant had been stabbed and both pilots had been killed. He stated his name, but hung up before I could ask to hear it again. I then told my shift manager everything I had just heard, and he took over.[6]

On November 21, 2003, Policastro was interviewed by staffers of the 9/11 Commission.[7] In this interview, *attended by three airline lawyers*, Policastro said he:

> was working the night shift from 9:00 p.m. to 6:00 a.m. (Pacific Time)... He was getting ready to leave at about 5:55 a.m., when he received a call. Per standard practice, he immediately asked for the flight number. The man on the phone told him it was on UAL 175. [Policastro] assumed it was a flight attendant because Star-Fix calls are always made by the attendants.

Policastro did not immediately recall the name but when the list of male flight attendants from Flight 175 was read to him, he thought it was probably Robert Fangman.

According to Policastro,

> the caller told him the plane had been hijacked, both pilots had been murdered and a flight attendant had been stabbed. Furthermore, he believed that the hijackers were flying the plane. Policastro was reluctant to believe him because the caller was calm and there was no background noise. There was no mention of guns or bombs or any type of weapon (such as box-cutters). After about two minutes, the caller said he had to go but did not indicate why. The call then terminated.

An unidentified employee at the same location, later identified as Andrew Lubkemann, who began working at SAMC merely two weeks before 9/11, was interviewed by staff members of the 9/11 Commission and described Policastro's conversation with the flight attendant from flight UA175.[8] The same three United Airlines lawyers who attended Policastro's interview, also attended this interview.

Lubkemann's description of Policastro's conversation differed slightly from that provided by Policastro. Lubkemann said: "Policastro just listened to the caller and *didn't say anything*. Then he took his headset off and said, "That flight was hijacked." Lubkemann said he asked Policastro if it was a joke but Policastro said, "No, it's for real." The two of them then walked over to the desk of the supervisor and spoke to the manager on duty. The impression gained by Lubkemann was that the call received by Policastro from the flight attendant on flight

---

6   Handwritten statement by Marc Policastro of SAMC, Op. cit., #886

7   MFR 04017221. November 21, 2003. Interview with Marc Policastro at Star Fix

8   MFR 04017218. November 21, 2003. Interview with unidentified operator at Star Fix

UAL 175 "was very short. He was not able to really say anything to *her*. It was like good morning and then he was taking the headset off."[1]

Lubkemann told the staff members of the 9/11 Commission that his notes where he wrote down the flight and aircraft number ended up in the trash somewhere and that he *hasn't spoken to anyone about this since 9/11*. He also mentioned that after a later call, this time from flight UA93, "United management personnel separated him and Policastro from the other staff members until the crisis was over and told them not to speak to anyone."[2]

- Why was the name of Andrew Lubkemann from the Star-Fix initially redacted by the FBI and the 9/11 Commission's staff?

- Why were three lawyers from United Airlines present at Lubkemann's and Policastro's interviews?

- Why was Lubkemann told "not to speak to anyone"?

- Is it conceivable that a new employee would throw away notes from such a momentous day without consulting his superior?

- Lubkemann said that "he hasn't spoken to anyone about *this* since 9/11." Was he warned not to speak about "this" in the future?

(5) Concluding observations on UA175 calls

Phone calls from three individuals "on flight UA175"—Peter Hanson, Brian Sweeney and an unidentified flight attendant—were received at the ground. None of the callers described the hijackers or told how many hijackers they were. None of them described how the alleged hijackers broke into the cockpit. Those who mentioned hijacking and stabbings did so in passive language, suggesting that they did not personally observe the action. The only mention of mace was made by Peter Hanson, though it was not a definite statement. Four details initially mentioned by Lee Hanson (shooting a stewardess, the hijackers talking about 8 hijacked planes, hearing a scream in the background, and that the plane was still on the ground when the call was made), did not appear in later interviews with him and were not mentioned by the other callers.

Three indices suggest that some of the details mentioned by the callers were suppressed either by United Airlines and/or by the FBI and that efforts were pursued to silence witnesses: (a) The unresolved contradiction between FBI's claim that two phone calls were made to StarFix from the aircraft and United Airlines' definite rejection of this claim. (b) The suppression of a particular StarFix employee's identity and attempts to silence him. (c) The omission of a set of details initially reported by Lee Hanson from later official records.

---

1   Ibid. Emphasis added
2   Ibid.

Chapter 9. Flight AA77 Calls

Flight AA77 is said to have crashed on the Pentagon at 9:37 a.m.[1] The seating arrangement of that flight, as reproduced in an Exhibit to the Moussaoui trial, is shown on the next page. The arrangement can help in assessing the feasibility of the alleged hijacking. It may be referred to at various places in the following sections.

(1) Renee May's Phone Calls

According to the FBI, Renee May, a flight attendant aboard flight AA77, made two telephone calls to her parents, only one of which was successful, namely at 9:12, lasting 158 seconds.[2]

On September 11, 2001, an unnamed FBI Special Agent was assigned a lead from the WFO Command Center to contact Ron May, Renee's father, in relation to his daughter, Renee.[3] At approximately 5:30 p.m. (Pacific time) or 8:30 p.m. (EST) the Special Agent contacted Renee's father Ronald May, who, according to the FBI document, provided the following information: At exactly 6:13 a.m. (Pacific Time) or 9:13 a.m. [EST], his wife Nancy May received a call from their daughter Renee using, what they believed, her *cellular* phone. Renee stated she was on flight AA77 and that the flight "had been hijacked by six hijackers." Renee further said that the hijackers put "us" in the back of the airplane, without specifying what she meant by "us." The Special Agent then spoke directly with

1 This crash time is subject to dispute but this dispute does not affect the subject of the present section
2 Overview of phone calls: Introduction to Part III of this book
3 FBI 302-86447. September 11, 2001. Interview with Ronald May

Nancy May, who confirmed what her husband had said. Nancy added that Renee "sounded as though she was very calm during the conversation." She also said that Renee had given her contact phone numbers at American Airlines and asked her to contact them. She also said she "could hear several other people in the background of the conversation attempting to give contact numbers to her daughter." That was all that Nancy May was able to report to the Special Agent. After talking to Renee, the May family immediately called the contact numbers given by her.

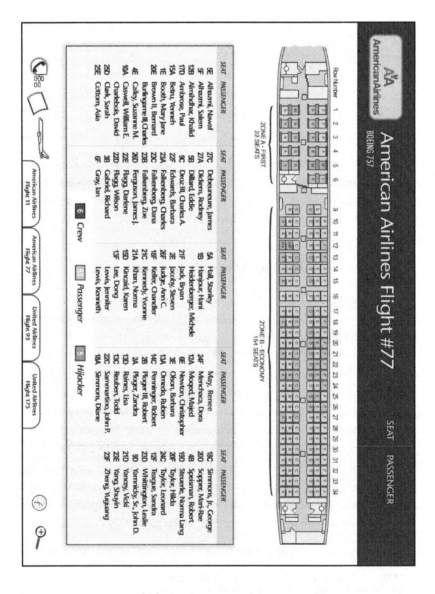

Source: Memorandum For the Record (MFR), DOJ briefing to 9/11 Commission's staff, May 20, 2004

COMMISSION SENSITIVE
~~LAW ENFORCEMENT SENSITIVE~~

[LES] Airfone Calls (all Times Eastern AM):

TIME	CALLER	NUMBER CALLED	RECIPIENT	LENGTH OF CALL
9:11:24	Renee May		Parents	No Connection
9:12:18	Renee May		Parents	158 seconds
9:15:34	Unknown	Operator	Unknown	102 seconds
9:18:58	Barbara Olson	202-514-2201	Ted Olson Office	No Connection
9:20:15	Unknown	Unknown	Unknown	274 seconds
9:25:48	Unknown	Unknown	Unknown	159 seconds
9:30:56	Unknown	Unknown	Unknown	260 seconds

9/11 First
Responder/Family
Privacy

On September 12, 2001, an unnamed FBI special agent and an unnamed FBI chaplain interviewed again Ronald and Nancy May, Renee's parents.[1] Nancy May confirmed to the FBI that she received on the morning of 9/11 at approximately 9:13 a.m. (EST), a phone call from her daughter, Renee. Following the conversation, Nancy and Ron immediately contacted *Patty Carson* at American Airlines to relay the information. The September 12, 2001, interview essentially confirmed what was already gleaned from the parents the previous day.

On June 5, 2002, Ronald and Nancy May were again interviewed by one or more unnamed FBI officials at their residence. At that time, Assistant US Attorney Robert Spencer also attended the interview.[2] It is not apparent why the interview took place nine months after 9/11 and why Robert Spencer attended the interview. Renee's parents confirmed what they had originally told the FBI regarding her phone call. They neither retracted nor added anything. They mainly provided information about Renee's life.

(2) Barbara Olson's Call(s)

According to the FBI, Barbara Olson, a passenger aboard that flight, made one *unsuccessful* telephone call with an Airfone to her husband at 9:18:58. The FBI lists four additional, successful, phone calls allegedly made from flight AA77 by an unknown caller to an unknown number, but attributes these four calls to Barbara Olson:[3]

(a) FBI document 302 22171. Interview with Mercy Lorenzo, September 11, 2001

Mercy Lorenzo contacted the FBI to report an emergency call while at duty at AT&T. A female passenger had called from an Airfone. The passenger requested to be connected to her husband, a *sergeant* residing in Washington.

The passenger advised the plane was *currently* being hijacked. The hijackers, armed with *guns* and knives, were ordering the passengers to move to the back of the plane. The passenger wanted to know how to let the pilots know what was happening. It did not appear as if the pilots were aware of the situation.

According to John Raidt of the 9/11 Commission's staff, the call to Lorenzo was "probably" made by Barbara Olson, asking the AT&T operator to connect her to her husband ("probably Ted Olson").[4] In Raidt's paper he recommends to

---

1   FBI 302-39718. September 12, 2001. Interview with Ronald and Nancy May
2   FBI 265A-NY-28030 (unnumbered). June 5, 2002, Yerington, Nevada. Interview with Nancy May and Roland May, #321, p. 73
3   Overview of phone calls: Introduction to Part III of this book
4   John Raidt, "Phone calls from aircraft hijacked on 9/11 as per Concordance." April 8, 2004. In 9/11 Commission document. Team 7, Box 21. MFR-IV Notes Fdr 4-8-04. #750, p. 7

find out if Lorenzo is certain the caller said "gun" and "sergeant." Nothing has transpired about any such inquiry.

Lorenzo was interviewed twice by the FBI, but only one 302 form was released. FBI 302 form, Serial 4082, which is referred to in John Raidt's aforementioned paper, is still suppressed.

(b) FBI document 302 22170. Interview with Teresa Gonzalez, September 11, 2001

Teresa Gonzalez, an operator for AT&T Services, was interviewed by the FBI regarding an emergency phone call received by AT&T in the morning of 9/11. She advised that her colleague, Mercy Lorenzo (see above), received a call from a female passenger on flight AA77 requesting to be transferred to telephone number (202) 514 2201. That number, she said, is that of her husband's number, a "sergeant" residing in Washington, D.C. A quick examination of the website of the Office of the Solicitor General at the Department of Justice revealed a similar number, (202) 514 2203[1], suggesting that the female caller was indeed trying to reach her husband's office, Ted Olson. In view of the contents and timing of this reported call, it is plausible that the designation of the caller's husband as a "sergeant" was a misunderstanding and that the caller was Barbara Olson. It remains unsettled whether this call was actually transferred, as requested, and if so, whether it was one of the calls referred to by Ted Olson, or a call that has not been mentioned publicly. From the interviews of both Gonzalez and Lorenzo it appears that resolving these questions is not particularly significant in determining whether Barbara Olson reported real events.

(c) FBI document 302 30777. Interview with Theodore ("Ted") Olson, September 11, 2001

According to Ted Olson, Barbara Olson was on the phone at approximately 9:00 a.m. (he said he did not look at his watch). He said he spoke with her about one minute. Barbara told him that her plane had been hijacked. She said they had knives and box cutters. He asked if they knew she was on the phone and she replied they didn't. Barbara told him they put the passengers in the back of the plane. Her call was then *cut off* (emphasis added).

Shortly thereafter, Ted was buzzed again and told that Barbara was on the phone. She was put through to him. Barbara said the pilot had announced that the plane had been hijacked. She asked her husband what she should tell the captain to do. Ted asked her for her location. She said they were over homes and asked someone else in the plane who told her they were traveling North East.

---

1   See Website of the Office of the Solicitor General of the Department of Justice

Ted told his wife that two planes had been hijacked and had crashed on the WTC. Barbara did not seem panicked, he said. This second call was then also cut off.

Barbara did not describe the hijackers. She referred to them only as "they." She did not mention any stabbing or slashing. Ted doesn't know if the calls were made from Barbara's cell phone or from an Airfone. She always had her cell phone with her, he said.

(d) FBI document 302 32633. Interview with Helen Voss, September 11, 2001

Helen Voss, Ted Olson's secretary, was contacted telephonically at her residence. Early on that morning Barbara Olson called her husband's office twice to speak with him. Lori Keyton was the secretary who took both of these calls. Voss *believes* both calls were collect calls.

Voss said that Lori Keyton called to her to relay to Ted Olson that his wife was on the phone. Keyton said that Barbara was in panic. Voss heard Ted say "hijacked." Ted Olson came out of his office and said, "they have knives and they are making them go to the back of the plane."

(e) FBI document [unreadable serial number]. Interview with Lori Keyton, September 11, 2001

Lori Keyton, a secretary at the Department of Justice, was contacted telephonically at her residence by the FBI. She said that at approximately 9:00 a.m. she received a series of approximately *six to eight* collect telephone calls. Each of the calls was an automatic collect call. There was a recording advising of the collect call and requesting she hold for an operator. A short time later another recording stated that all operators were busy, please hang up and try your call later.

Keyton then received a collect call from a live operator. The operator advised that there was an emergency collect call from Barbara Olson for Ted Olson. Keyton advised that she would accept the call. Barbara was put through and sounded *hysterical*. Barbara said, "Can you tell Ted." Keyton cut her off and said, "I'll put him on the line."

There was a second telephone call a few to five minutes later [*sic*]. This time Barbara was on the line when she answered. She called direct. It was not a collect call. Barbara said, "It's Barbara." Keyton said, "he's on the phone with the command center, I'll put you through."

Keyton advised that there is no caller identification feature on the phone she was using. Keyton didn't know if Barbara was calling from an Airfone or from her cell phone.

(f) Interview with Theodore Olson on CNN Larry King Live, September 14, 2001

Larry King conducted on his show of September 14, 2001, a lengthy interview with Theodore Olson regarding his wife's phone call.[1] Olson said he was not certain about the exact time of his wife's calls, but put her first call between 9:15 and 9:30. He added, "Someone would have to reconstruct the time for me." He confirmed that he had two conversations with his wife, that his first call lasted one to two minutes and was then cut off. He said his second call lasted two or three or four minutes. He essentially confirmed what he had said to the FBI on September 11, 2001, as related above.

Asked whether Barbara sounded terrified, anxious, nervous, scared, Olson answered, "No, she didn't. She sounded very, very calm...In retrospect, enormously, remarkably, incredibly calm." His answer contradicted what Lori Keyton, his secretary, told the FBI.

Asked whether he heard other noises on the plane, Olson answered, "No, I did not." He said he asked her which direction the plane was going. "[Barbara] paused—there was a pause there. I think she must have asked someone else. She said I think it's going northeast."

Asked how the second conversation ended, Olson said,

> We are—we suguéd back and forth between expressions of feeling for one another and this effort to exchange information. And then the phone went dead. I don't know whether it just got cut off again, because the signals from cell phones coming from airplanes don't work that well, or whether that was the impact with the Pentagon.

Assuming that this second call was made around 9:20, it was certainly not cut off as a result of a crash (which occurred after 9:30). As to his speculative statement about cell phones, Olson could not determine the nature and location of the phone from which his wife had called.

Asked whether Barbara had described the hijackers, he answered in the negative. His answer was, however, couched in a way that might suggest he was not revealing everything: "No, she not. And I—we just didn't, that didn't come up." His interviewer immediately changed the focus of the interview.

(g) Fox News, September 14, 2001

On September 14, 2001, Ted Olson was interviewed by Brit Hume of Fox News. In this interview Olson essentially confirmed the facts he had initially told

---

1 Larry King Live, "Recovering from tragedy," *CNN*, Sept. 14, 2001. Interview. with Ted Olson. #744

his FBI interviewers. One new fact appeared in that interview: He said that she told him the plane "had been hijacked shortly after takeoff."[1]

(h) Theodore Olson's lecture at the Federalist Society

The lecture did not concentrate on the phone calls, but on the person of Barbara Olson and on the need for the United States to combat the evil scourge of terrorism.[2] It provided primarily a glimpse into the ideological world of Ted and Barbara Olson:

> Barbara died...not only because she was an American, but as one more American who refused to surrender to the monstrous evil into whose eyes she and her fellow countrymen stared during those last hideous moments.

> While the terrorists of September 11 invoke the name of Islam, that is simply a mask for their hate, envy and despicable ambitions...They are tyrants, and so they hate democracy. They are bigots and religious zealots who persecute Christians and Jews and Hindus and Buddhists and women. So they must hate America because America stands for tolerance and freedom and respect for all races, all religions, and all peoples, regardless of their sex, color, national origin or accent. They are despots who will not permit children to go to school...These terrorists can succeed only through corruption, cruelty and brutality...And these terrorists can enslave the people they wish to subjugate only by keeping them poor and destitute.

> As a very brassy and gusty intern, [Barbara] managed to be the only employee of the government of the United States willing, feisty and fearless enough to personally serve the papers on the PLO mission to the United Nations in New York announcing that it was being expelled from this country—because they were terrorists. How Barbara loved to tell that story to her friends at Cardozo!

(i) Briefing by US Attorney David Novak and his team to 9/11 Commission's staff, May 20, 2004

Novak and his team insisted that all calls from AA77 had been made via the onboard Airfone system. They also indicated that the cockpit voice recorder (CVR) for AA77 was found, but that its contents were destroyed by the intense heat it had been subjected to. They said the identities of the callers had been derived from interviews of the recipients except for one call made at 9:12:18 a.m. which left a credit card trail. These interviews led the briefers to the conclusion that "all of these unknown calls" listed by the FBI, were "from Barbara Olson to her husband Ted's office."[3]

---

1   "Interview with Ted Olson," *Fox News*, September 14, 2001, #287

2   Theodore Olson, "Barbara K. Olson Memorial Lecture," November 16, 2001, #664

3   MFR (unnumbered). May 20, 2004. Department of Justice briefing on cell and phone calls from AA77 to the staff of the 9/11 Commission, in Team 7 Box 12 Flight 93 Calls - General

(j) Final Report of the 9/11 Commission

Under footnote 57 to Chapter 1 of the Final Report, the 9/11 Commission tells the public that the "records available for the phone calls from American 77 do not allow for a determination of which of four 'connected calls to unknown numbers' represent the two between Barbara Olson and her husband's office." The Commission did somehow fail to explain how apart from these four calls, every other call could be accurately traced.

(k) Analysis

- Barbara Olson, like other callers, said they "were" hijacked. She did neither describe the actions representing the "hijacking" nor the "hijackers." She referred to them only as "they."

- She said "they" had knives and box cutters. She did not say that she saw any such items herself and did not report any violent action committed with knives or box cutters.

- She said "they" put the passengers in the back of the plane. Yet she neither quoted what they said nor mentioned their presumably foreign accent.

- She said the pilot announced that the plane had been hijacked. This implies that at the time of her second call, 9:20 a.m. or later, the cockpit had not yet been overtaken by hijackers. The legitimate pilot was, therefore, still in control and knew about the hijacking. Yet, he did not report it to air traffic control and to the airline. This statement, in addition, contradicts significantly the official account, according to which the hijacking of flight AA77 began between 8:51 a.m. and 8:54 a.m., almost half an hour earlier.[1] Renee May, incidentally, did not mention such an announcement by the pilot.

- Ted Olson said Barbara was very calm, even "incredibly calm." Indeed, she did not mention any violent action aboard the aircraft.

- Barbara Olson did not mention that the "hijackers" broke into the cockpit.

- There was no apparent follow-up to the initial report by Lorenzo of guns on the aircraft.

- No definite conclusion can be made from the above source documents regarding the type of phone used by Barbara. According to research conducted by Prof. David R. Griffin and others, it appears that airfones were not anymore available on Boeing 757s on 9/11.[2] On the other hand, at the time Barbara Olson's phone calls were made (9:15 and 9:20) the

---

Fdr - 5-20-04. # p. 2, #1779

1   In Final Report of the 9/11 Commission ["the hijackings began between 8:51 and 8:54" (p. 8) and at "8:54, the aircraft deviated from its assigned course." (p. 9)]

2   David Ray Griffin, "Barbara Olson's Alleged Call from AA77," *Information Clearing House* (ICH), May 7, 2007, #1000

aircraft was reportedly flying at 25,000 feet.[1] This would have precluded the use of cell phones. If Prof. Griffin's research is conclusive and if one assumes that Ted Olson's account is credible, it follows that her phone calls were made with cell phones from low altitude or from ground level.

(3) Concluding observations on AA77 calls

Renee May and Barbara Olson's reported phone calls give rise to serious doubts about the official hijacking account. Only the most glaring anomalies will be cited below:

- Barbara Olson reported that the pilot had announced that the aircraft had been hijacked, thereby contradicting significantly the official timeline of the hijacking and everything that ensues from that timeline, including the flight path of the aircraft. It might be argued that the person she believed was the pilot had been the suicide-pilot, Hani Hanjour. However, Hanjour spoke very badly English. She would have immediately noted that fact. Renee May did not, however, mention having heard any such announcement. This suggests that Barbara Olson was reporting a bogus fact.

- Renee May's call at 9:12 and Barbara Olson's calls, starting at 9:15 were made approximately 20 minutes after the "likely take-over" of the aircraft by hijackers, which according to the 9/11 Commission occurred between 8:51 and 8:54.(Final Report, 33) This time gap of 20 minutes is nowhere accounted for. What did the alleged hijackers do in that time that looked like a hijacking operation?

- The FBI was allegedly unable to trace four phone calls made from flight AA77, yet attributed those to Barbara Olson, contradicting thereby Ted Olson's testimonies. In that case, either the FBI produced forged data or Ted Olson was lying.

---

1   "Flight Path Study, AA77," NTSB, 19, 2002. p. 4, #129

Chapter 10. Flight UA93 Calls

A Boeing 757 aircraft assigned to flight UA93 is said to have crashed at Somerset County, PA, on September 11, 2001, at 10:03 a.m. The seating arrangement of that flight, as reproduced in an Exhibit to the Moussaoui trial, is shown on the next page. The arrangement can help in assessing the feasibility of the alleged hijacking. It may be referred to in the following sections.

(1) Todd Beamer's Call

Probably none of the phone calls of 9/11 was as widely reported as that of Todd Beamer, a passenger on flight UA93, who spoke with Lisa Jefferson, a GTE operator.

Blogger *John Doe II* sums up succinctly his research of this call as follows:

> There is basically not a single sentence of the call that is not in dispute. Worse, many details stand in strong conflict with other phone calls, and/or the official story. And some simply make no sense at all. Even the famous last words, "Let's Roll" are in dispute.[1]

In this section, we will independently test *John Doe*'s conclusions.

According to the FBI overview of calls, Todd Beamer attempted to make one unsuccessful call to AT&T at 9:42; a minute later—on 9:43:48—an unsuccessful call to his residence; and on the same second, a call to a GTE operator, that according to the FBI lasted over an hour (3,925 seconds).[2] It was never explained how he could have initiated two phone calls on the very same second.

---

1 John Doe II, "Deconstructing Todd Beamer's Call," July 18, 2005, #681
2 Overview of phone calls: Introduction to Part III of this book

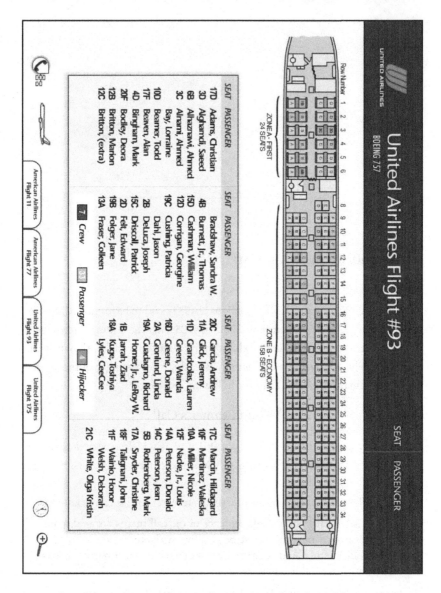

United Airlines Flight #93

ZONE A - FIRST 24 SEATS

SEAT	PASSENGER
1D	Adams, Christian
3D	Alghamdi, Saeed
6B	Alhaznawi, Ahmed
3C	Alnami, Ahmed
	Bay, Lorraine
10D	Beamer, Todd
1F	Beaven, Alan
4D	Bingham, Mark
20F	Bodley, Deora
12B	Britton, Marion
12C	Britton, (extra)

SEAT	PASSENGER
4B	Bradshaw, Sandra W.
15D	Burnett, Jr., Thomas
15D	Cashman, William
12D	Corrigan, Georgine
18C	Cushing, Patricia
2B	Dahl, Jason
	DeLuca, Joseph
15C	Driscoll, Patrick
2D	Felt, Edward
19B	Folger, Jane
13A	Fraser, Colleen

SEAT	PASSENGER
20C	Garcia, Andrew
11A	Glick, Jeremy
11D	Grandcolas, Lauren
1D	Green, Wanda
18D	Greene, Donald
2A	Gronlund, Linda
19A	Guadagno, Richard
	Homer, Jr., LeRoy W.
1B	Jarrah, Ziad
18A	Kuge, Toshiya
	Lyles, CeeCee

SEAT	PASSENGER
17C	Marcin, Hildegard
10F	Martinez, Waleska
10A	Miller, Nicole
12F	Nacke, Jr., Louis
14A	Peterson, Donald
14C	Peterson, Jean
5B	Rothenberg, Mark
17A	Snyder, Christine
18F	Talignani, John
11F	Wainio, Honor
	Welsh, Deborah
21C	White, Olga Kristin

ZONE B - ECONOMY 158 SEATS

7 Crew | Passenger | 4 Hijacker

Only two persons were apparently interviewed on September 11, 2001, regarding Beamer's call: *Lisa Jefferson* (twice) and *Robert Combs* (once).

It was, however, *Phyllis Johnson*, who initially took the call from Todd Beamer. Yet the earliest *known* FBI interview with her was conducted in June 2002. It is, however, implausible that the FBI forgot to interview her on September 11, 2001, suggesting that her initial interview remains, for whatever reasons, classified.

(a) FBI document 302 95682. Interview with Robert W. Combs, September 11, 2001

On September 11, 2001, at approximately 9:45 a.m., an unnamed FBI Special Agent of the Chicago Office (initials BGM), wrote that he received a telephone call from Robert W. Combs, Director of Technical Operations for GTE Airfone, Oak Brook, IL. Combs advised he was relaying information from GTE Airfone employee Lisa Jefferson who was "currently talking to a passenger on UAL Flight 93." Combs then relayed in real-time to the FBI the following information from Jefferson, who was talking with Todd Beamer aboard Flight UA93:

- The passenger's name was Todd Beamer.

- His flight was hijacked by three Arab individuals.

- Two of the hijackers had knives and the third had a bomb strapped to him.

- Beamer was apparently sitting next to a flight attendant, who was relaying information to him.

- Beamer stated that the hijacker [with the bomb] seemed to be aware of the fact that he was on the telephone, but that they [*sic*] did not seem to care.

At 10:03 a. m. (EST), Combs advised that "he believes the telephone call had been disconnected." At 10:11 a. m. (EST), he advised "the call had not been disconnected, and that the phone might be in the seat pocket." At approximately 10:15 a. m. (EST) Combs advised "he was putting Jefferson on the phone, and that a patch of Beamer's phone call to the FBI Special Agent was ready."

Then something puzzling occurred. Instead of patching Beamer as he announced, a party line call ensued, in which Captain John Noonan of the New York State Police advised that "he was on the phone with whom he believed was the mother-in-law of UA93 passenger Jeremy Glick." Captain Noonan advised Jeremy's mother-in-law "was relaying to information her husband was currently obtaining from [Jeremy] Glick." Among those on the "party line" were Phyllis Johnson and Marshall Starkman, a Verizon Wireless employee.

Apparently the conversation with Todd Beamer continued thereafter. According to the FBI report, Jefferson then asked Beamer the location and number of passengers on flight UA93, a question he answered. Captain Noonan then advised that "some screams were heard from Glick's phone and then things became quiet." Beamer was no longer heard from, but Jefferson reported no noise other than what appeared to be background noise.

At 10:36 a.m. (EST), both Captain Noonan and Jefferson stated they lost their respective phone calls.

(b) FBI document 302 107853, Sept. 11, 2001. Interview with Robert W. Combs

Robert W. Combs provided later on September 11, 2001, the following information to an unnamed FBI agent:

> Beamer's call came first to Phyllis Johnson who turned over the call to her supervisor, Lisa Jefferson. Both took notes of their conversations. During one of the Beamer conversations [*plural* – E.D.], Jefferson performed a "print screen" to document Beamer's credit card number. In this interview, Combs did not provide any information on the contents of the call, which he had relayed in the morning, probably because the FBI already had all that information.

(c) FBI document 302 95630, Sept. 11, 2001. Interview with Lisa Jefferson

Lisa Jefferson was a GTE Airfone Customer Service Representative. At approximately 1:00 p.m., before leaving work for home, she was interviewed telephonically by three FBI agents. They asked her "scores of questions." Evidence of this interview emerged for the first time in a book she published in 2006.[1] No 302 form of this particular interview has been released. Jefferson did not elaborate upon the contents of this interview.

Jefferson was interviewed again telephonically on September 11, 2001, by Chicago Special Agent Christopher W. Hockman,[2] when she was at her residence. She told him that at approximately 9:45 a.m. she had received a phone call from a man who identified himself as Todd Beamer and was a passenger on flight UA93. Beamer said to her "that the airplane was *about* to be hijacked" by three individuals—whom he did not describe—two of whom wielded knives, and one that had a bomb strapped to his waist with a red belt (emphasis added). They "were *preparing* to take control of the flight," said Jefferson (emphasis added).

Jefferson estimated that she spoke to Todd Beamer for seven minutes before the "two hijackers armed with knives *entered* the cockpit, securing the door behind them." (emphasis added). The third hijacker with the bomb—so she reported—"remained in the main cabin with the passengers after closing the privacy curtain between the First Class and Economy Class." This information is highly significant, for if Jefferson faithfully reported what Beamer had said, this meant that the cockpit was only breached after 9:50, whereas according the official account the aircraft had been taken over by "hijackers" before 9:30.

---

1   Lisa Jefferson & Felicia Middlebrooks, *Called* (Chicago, Northfield Publishing, 2006), p. 61-62

2   The source for the name of the agent is FBI OUT-3255, May 17, 2002, from Counterterrorism PENTTBOM to FBI Chicago ("request to arrange interview with Lisa Jefferson")

Jefferson said she continued her conversation with Beamer for another eight minutes. During this time she said she could hear screams, prayers, exclamations, and talk of subduing the hijackers. At approximately 10:00 a.m., Beamer said to Jefferson the passengers were about to attack the hijackers.

Jefferson's last exchange with Beamer, in which he asked Jefferson to call his pregnant wife, Lisa, occurred at 10:00 a.m. Next, Jefferson heard *another* passenger give what she believed to be the "go-ahead" to make their move. After that point, she heard nothing. She said she kept the connection open for another twenty minutes without hearing anything, at which time she disconnected the call. This would have put the end of the call at approximately 10:20, whereas the FBI, basing itself on telephone company records, said the call lasted 3,925 seconds, ending at approximately 10:49.

(d) FBI document 302 41407. Interview with Lisa Beamer, September 22, 2001

Lisa Beamer, Todd's wife, told to an unidentified FBI interviewer, that on 9/11 "her phone rang a few times around 10:00 a.m. but when she picked it up there was no connection. She believes Mr. Beamer may have tried to get in touch with her."[1] According to the FBI, however, Todd Beamer's made only one unsuccessful attempt to call home and that was at 9:43.

Lisa Beamer did not speak with her husband during the events of 9/11. In a later interview with Newsweek she said she wonders why her husband, a man strongly attached to his cell phone did not call her from the plane as many others did.[2]

Lisa Beamer was not told about her husband's phone call with Lisa Jefferson until the evening of September 14, 2001, when Nick Leonard, a United Airlines official, called her. He read to her over the phone a synopsis of Jefferson's conversation with her husband and gave her Lisa Jefferson's phone number. Mrs. Beamer called Lisa Jefferson on September 15, 2001, and taped their conversation. The transcript of their conversation was released.[3]

Lisa Beamer said to the FBI interviewer that Jefferson had told her she "stayed on the phone until she learned that Flight #93 had crashed."[4] This is also what Lisa Jefferson later wrote in her book (see below). Yet, this statement contradicts Jefferson's initial statement to the FBI interviewer, as reported above, and the duration of the call, as reported in the FBI Overview of phone calls.

1   FBI NK-41407. September 22, 2001. Interview with Lisa Beamer
2   Karen Breslau, Eleanor Clift and Evan Thomas, "The Real Story of Flight 93," Newsweek, December 3, 2001, #754
3   9/11 Commission's document. Team 7, Box 12, Flight 93 Calls—Todd Beamer, 9-15-01 FBI 302 Transcript, September 15, 2001, #124
4   Ibid.

(e) FBI document 302 115861, June 5, 2002. Interview with Phyllis Johnson

Phyllis Jo Johnson, a Verizon Airfone Customer Service Representative, was interviewed at her place of employment with Verizon on June 5, 2002. It is probable that she was interviewed on September 11, 2001, or shortly thereafter, because she initially took Beamer's call. But the FBI did not release any evidence of such an interview.

As a part of her normal duties, Johnson answered a phone call at approximately 8:40 a.m. Central time (9:40 EST), on September 11, 2001. Her computer screen indicated that this call originated aboard a United Airlines flight. The caller identified himself as Todd Beamer. He said that his flight "was being hijacked." He said he *saw* two people with knives and stated further that "we think we saw someone entering the cockpit." Beamer remained "very calm and courteous" while conveying this information. Johnson recalled particularly the absence of the usual background sounds created by the activity and conversations of other passengers.

After providing the flight number and its destination, *Beamer asked if he could be connected to his wife.* After Phyllis talked to Beamer, Lisa Jefferson took over the call. Johnson believes the total period of time she spent either speaking with Beamer or conferring with Jefferson to be less than ten minutes. She estimates having placed Beamer on hold three times during her period of the call. She does not recall hearing him describe the hijackers.

(f) Transcript of call by Nick Leonard, United Airlines, to unknown person, September 14, 2001

On September 14, 2001, Nick Leonard of United Airlines called an unnamed *male* and informed him about Todd Beamer's phone call with Lisa Jefferson. He then read to him over the phone the following letter and a so-called Synopsis of the call, formulated as if written by Lisa Jefferson:[1]

> September fourteenth, two thousand one U-A-L flight Ninety-three Incident Information. The attached information includes text recollection of Miss Lisa Jefferson, Supervisor, Customer Service, G-T-E Air Phone concerning a call that was routed to the Care Center from U-A-L Aircraft Ninety-three. This information in it's raw form may be disturbing and should be handled carefully. G-T-E Air Phone is deferring to United Airlines expert knowledge in this area to decide how and when this information should be passed on to Mister Beamer's family. In the brief time Lisa spoke to Mister Beamer he made a request that she contact his wife directly

---

1 Transcript of call by Nick Leonard, United Airlines, to unidentified male, September 14, 2001, 9/11 Commission document, Team 7, Box 12, Flight 93 Calls- Todd Beamer Fdr- 9-15-01 FBI 302 Transcript- UAL SAC Nick Leonard re Jefferson-Beamer Call, #124

and tell her that he, Todd, loves her. Miss Jefferson would prefer to speak to the United Airlines Support Representative directly regarding the details of this very personal conversation. Contact information for Miss Jefferson is provided. So the second page has her information. I'll skip down to the uh actual transcripts.

[Synopsis of Todd Beamer's call]

This page is dated September eleven, two thousand one. Eight forty-five a.m. Call came into station number fifteen. PHYLLIS received the initial call. When PHYLLIS realized that it was a real hijacking situation, I took over the call. I spoke to TODD BEAMER from Cranbury, New Jersey, flight number ninety-three, seven five seven UNITED from Newark, New Jersey, leaving at eight a.m. to San Francisco, arriving at eleven fourteen a.m. San Francisco time. TODD told me that there were three people, nationality unknown, on the flight hijacking the plane. Two with knives, and one with a bomb strapped around his waist with a red belt. The plane consisted of twenty-seven passengers on the front (telephone ringing in background) and ten in the back, with five flight attendants. I asked him if there were any children on the plane. TODD responded, not that he could see. From what TODD could see two people were hurt, not sure if they were dead or alive. The hijackers went into the cockpit and locked the door. They were flying the plane and turned the plane around. He thought they might have been flying north. Some of the passengers on the plane had decided to jump on the hijacker with the bomb and try to get him down. The last thing TODD said to me was to call his wife for him and to pray for him. At this point TODD started reciting the Lord's Prayer. Then someone said let's roll. The call was still connected but there was nothing but silence. The call ended at nine a.m. That's the end of the letter.

[Continuation of Nick Leonard's phone call]

UM (Unknown male): Great. You can appreciate it.

NL (Nick Leonard): Well, sometimes I can't either (chuckle).

T. JM (Unidentified): (Chuckle). Well it's calls like this that we uh, that are very refreshing and we, we appreciate it.

NL: I'm glad I could uh...

UM: We all kind of knew that that was Todd, so we're glad to get uh, uh, ya know...

NL: Yea.

UM: ...confirmation and that he would have taken action, so.

NL: Todd sounds like a great guy.

UM: Oh he was the best friend you could ask for. Nick thank you very much for your help.

NL: Thank you.

UM: And we'll talk to ya.

NL: Take care.

UM: Bye bye.

Was this the text that was faxed to Lisa Beamer on September 14? Who drafted the Synopsis? Who was Todd Beamer's male friend to whom Leonard was reading this text over the phone and when did this conversation take place? Who was the third person mentioned above as T.JM.? What was so "refreshing" about the "call"? Who are the "we" mentioned by T. JM?

In her book, "Called," Lisa Jefferson diplomatically avoids stating who wrote the Synopsis. Instead she writes:

> A letter was quickly fashioned and sent by fax to United Airlines grief counselors, who were already working with Lisa Beamer. The letter informed Mrs. Beamer, that I, Lisa Jefferson, had a message for her from her husband, whenever she felt ready to talk. The letter included contact information for my home and work. The grief counselors delivered the letter to Lisa Beamer (Jefferson, 78).... Lisa Beamer explained [later] that she had received the faxed letter late Friday evening (Jefferson, 81).

(g) Transcript of phone call between Lisa Jefferson and Lisa Beamer, September 15, 2001[1]

According to Lisa Beamer, Lisa Jefferson called her on Saturday, September 15, 2001, at, 10:00 a.m. Mrs. Beamer said that she had already received the aforementioned synopsis late last evening. She asked Jefferson whether she herself had written up the summary, to which Jefferson answered with a noncommittal "yes." Asked by Mrs. Beamer in what emotional state her husband had been, Jefferson emphasized that he was "calm, very calm. You wouldn't of thought it was a real call [...] because he was, um, he wasn't nervous at all. He was speaking in a normal tone of voice, he never got upset, not one time." She also said to Mrs. Beamer that "they" asked everyone to sit down on the flight and that Todd had gotten the information "from the flight attendant that was sitting next to him." Jefferson said that according to Todd two of the guys "had went [sic] into the cockpit, taken the pilot and the co-pilot out and locked the door."

Then Jefferson added: "[H]e asked me what did they want, is it ransom that they want or what, and um, I told him we really don't know at this point..." Jefferson told Mrs. Beamer that she recited the Lord Prayer's with Todd "top to bottom," and that Todd had "asked Jesus to help him."

---

1 Transcript of phone call between Lisa Jefferson and Lisa Beamer, September 15, 2001, 9/11 Commission documents, Team 7, Box 12, Flight 93 Calls- Todd Beamer Fdr- 9-15-01 FBI 302 Transcript- UAL SAC Nick Leonard re Jefferson-Beamer Call, #124

About the plan to attack the alleged hijackers, Jefferson said: "He told me that they were about to jump the guy, that's the term that he had used [...] The guy that had the bomb." Apparently Todd only mentioned one "guy" left in the cabin.

Before ending their conversation Lisa Beamer asked Jefferson "Lisa, would it be okay if we had a member of the press contact you?" Upon Jefferson's positive reply, Lisa Beamer added, "Alright, I will uh, I will follow up on that then.... We're gonna try to get this information out today; ... we'll get people in touch with you if we need that." Lisa Beamer, who had just lost her husband, was already busy promoting in the name of some group ("we") the UA93 story and had clearly good media connections.

(h) FBI Lead Control Number NK-5381[1]

On September 29, 2001, Verizon Wireless provided FBI with the following list of calls made on September 11, 2001, with a cellular phone belonging to Todd Beamer (with the exception of one "incoming call" that occurred on 10:43 a.m. EST):

Time	Place	Number Called	Minutes
0627	San Carlos, CA		1:00
0628	San Carlos, CA		2:00
0630	San Carlos, CA		2:00
0633	San Carlos, CA		2:00
0649	Santa Ana, CA		4:00
0743	Incoming Call		21:00
1107	Woodbridge, NJ		1:00
1245	Woodbridge, NJ		1:00
1248	Woodbridge, NJ		1:00
1337	Woodbridge, NJ		1:00
1422	Woodbridge, NJ		1:00
1443	Woodbridge, NJ		1:00
1451	Woodbridge, NJ		1:00
1530	Woodbridge, NJ		1:00
1532	Woodbridge, NJ		1:00
1548	Woodbridge, NJ		1:00
1602	Woodbridge, NJ		1:00
1605	Woodbridge, NJ	9/11 Personal Privacy	1:00
1613	Woodbridge, NJ		1:00
1618	Woodbridge, NJ		1:00
1654	Woodbridge, NJ		1:00
1737	Woodbridge, NJ		1:00
1905	Woodbridge, NJ		1:00
1956	Woodbridge, NJ		1:00
2058	Woodbridge, NJ		1:00

---

1   FBI Lead Control Number NK 5381 in 9/11 Commission's documents, Team 7, Box 12

No explanation has been given to the fact that Beamer's cell phone was used to make multiple short calls after the crash of the flight and received a 21-minute call at 10:43 (EST). (Please add 3 hours to the times to obtain EST.)

(i) MFR 04020031. *Briefing by Lisa Jefferson to John Raidt of the 9/11 Commission Staff, May 11, 2004*

In her telephone briefing to John Raidt of the 9/11 Commission's staff Lisa Jefferson essentially confirmed what she had already told to the FBI and in media interviews. Yet, a few details mentioned and reported by John Raidt might be significant:

Jefferson said Todd Beamer told her that the "hijackers" had ordered everyone to sit down. He also reportedly told her that "two people were lying on the floor bleeding." Jefferson added that she "heard the flight attendant [who was sitting near Beamer] say to Mr. Beamer that the two on the ground were the pilot and co-pilot."

Jefferson told Raidt that she and Beamer recited together the 23rd Psalm, which is part of the Lord's Prayer, and then heard him say to someone near him: "Are you ready? Okay. Let's roll." That was the last she heard from him, she said.

Jefferson said to Raidt that she then held the phone for 15 minutes, calling his name now and then, but did not hear anything. Others in her office, she said, heard the news reports that the plane had crashed. The call was then terminated.

(j) *Pittsburgh Post-Gazette, September 22, 2001*[1]

In a telephone interview with the newspaper, Lisa Jefferson said, "I felt like the time that Todd and I had together, we had bonded. It's like I lost a good friend." She said that Todd Beamer told her about his family and asked her to pray with him. This sentimental interview with Lisa Jefferson gave birth to Todd Beamer's heroic cult. We will, therefore, cite that part of the interview in full:

Beamer regained his composure. "Lisa," he said.

"I said, 'Yes?' And he said, "That's my wife's name," Jefferson said.

That's my name, too, Todd."

"Oh, my God," Beamer said.

He asked Jefferson to call his wife. If he didn't survive, he wanted Jefferson to give his wife a message, that he loved her and the family. He asked Jefferson to recite the Lord's Prayer.

"And he did that, start to finish," Jefferson said.

---

1   Jim McKinnon, "13-minute call bonds her forever with hero," *Pittsburgh Post-Gazette*, September 22, 2001, #644

The plane ride got more bumpy, and Beamer raised his voice again.

"Lisa! Lisa!"

"I'm still here, Todd," she said. "I'll be here as long as you're here."

This conversation is not mentioned in the FBI interview from September 11, 2001, and in the Synopsis delivered to Mrs. Beamer. Combs—who related the conversation to the FBI—did neither mention this dialogue nor Beamer's common prayer with Jefferson.

(k) Lisa Jefferson and Felicia Middlebrooks, Called, Northfield Publishing (2006)

In 2006, Lisa Jefferson published a short book entitled *Called*, assisted by Felicia Middlebrooks, a known American radio news broadcaster. Her book focuses on Todd Beamer's call.

In her book, Jefferson repeated what she initially told the FBI, namely that three people had hijacked the plane and two of them had taken over the cockpit. As her call was relayed by Robert Combs, the FBI was on the line and had Combs ask her to find out, through Beamer, about the nationality of the hijackers. Jefferson writes that she "never got a chance to ask that question, because the caller was providing a steady stream of other vital information." She explained: "I didn't want to carelessly cut him off, break his focus, and possibly make him nervous"(Jefferson, 35).

In addition to what she had initially told the FBI, she wrote that "*they* ordered everyone to sit down".(Jefferson, 35) This must therefore have happened before *they* entered the cockpit, because thereafter only one of them was left in First Class, to "guard the passengers," allegedly standing there with a bomb. That fits with what Jefferson told Mrs. Beamer in their conversation on September 15, 2001, (see above), when she said Todd had mentioned a plan to rush "the guy" (in singular). Continuing along these lines, she wrote: "The flight attendants were standing. The hijackers ordered them to sit, and one just happened to sit next to me. That's how I'm getting my information."(Jefferson, 36) Jefferson thus confirmed that Beamer relayed information from someone else. She repeated these statements in an interview with Beliefnet, probably in 2008: "There was a flight attendant that sat next to Todd that gave us all the information that we needed...I could hear everything she was saying because she was speaking loud enough for me to hear her through the phone...So whatever he couldn't answer, she was able to answer."[1] Surprisingly, Jefferson did not ask to talk directly to the flight attendant.

---

1   Wendy Schuman, interview with Lisa Jefferson," *beliefnet*, undated (probably 2008), #678

Jefferson wrote she offered Todd to patch his call through to his wife but Todd had allegedly answered,

> No, no. I don't want to upset her unnecessarily. She's expecting our third child in January, and if I don't have to upset her with any bad news, then I'd rather not (Jefferson, 48).

Here, Jefferson contradicts Phyllis Johnson's testimony to the FBI, according to which Todd had specifically asked whether his call could be connected to his wife. According to the FBI phone call overview, Todd initially attempted to reach his wife (see beginning of this section).

Jefferson wrote in her book that she held the phone line open until the crash of flight UA93 was reported in the news.

> I constantly called Todd's name... No response. This went on for what seemed like hours.... Then came the news: United Airlines Flight 93 had just crashed in Pennsylvania. "Lisa," one of my colleagues said gently. "Lisa, release the phone line. That was Todd's plane." One of the engineers had been tracing the call from the moment Todd phoned for help (Jefferson, 54).

According to her account, Lisa Jefferson was informed of the plane's crash by an unidentified "engineer" who had traced Todd Beamer's call. Who was this mysterious "engineer" who knew before anyone else that UA93 had crashed?

Jefferson did not, however, release the phone. She continued:

> "Todd, Todd! Can you hear me? Are you there, Todd?"

> "Lisa, release the phone line now."

> "No, no, just wait a minute," I said. "Someone might still be there!" Still I sat, in the midst of a crowded room and a deafening silence. Then the tears began to flow....

> "Lisa, the radio station just reported it. Flight 93 is down. Please, Lisa, you can release the phone line now," said a male colleague who was visibly shaken. I knew it was over (Jefferson, 55).

The problem is that the first news of the alleged crash of UA93 only emerged at 11:23, over an hour after the plane's alleged crash.

Concluding observations

(1) Todd Beamer said to Jefferson that he was relaying information from a flight attendant who sat beside him. This means that he did not report direct observations. It is odd that Jefferson did not ask to talk directly to that flight attendant, who was the source of the information.

(2) Todd Beamer did not, according to Jefferson, mention any violent action aboard the aircraft, such as stabbing or the use of mace. He did not either mention hearing calls for help that would have suggested a violent action.

(3) Todd Beamer did not report how the "guys" managed to enter the cockpit, meaning that he neither observed their entry nor was informed about their entry by the flight attendant who sat next to him.

(4) Lisa Jefferson emphatically denies in her book that Todd Beamer had provided any description of the "guys." She wrote that she "never got a chance to ask that question, because the caller was providing a steady stream of other vital information." She explained: "I didn't want to carelessly cut him off, break his focus, and possibly make him nervous."(Jefferson, 35) This explanation is not compelling. There must have been another reason for Jefferson not to ask "that question" and for Todd to refrain from describing the "guys." That reason will become apparent in chapter 14.

(5) According to Lisa Jefferson, Todd Beamer refused to be connected to his wife because "I don't want to unsettle her unnecessarily." This claim is contradicted by the testimony of Phyllis Johnson, who initially took Beamer's call. Phyllis stated to the FBI that Todd Beamer specifically asked to be connected to his wife. Who was telling the truth?

(6) According to Lisa Jefferson, she recited over the telephone with Todd Beamer the Lord's Prayer. If Jefferson's account is true, it means that Todd Beamer did not consider his circumstances particularly threatening and urgent. Ordinary persons facing an existential and imminent threat do not usually sit and engage in prayers with a stranger over the telephone.

(7) Jefferson did not mention hearing any impact sound at the end of the conversation that would suggest that the plane had crashed, though the phone line remained open for twenty minutes or longer. Later she expressed her surprise about this fact, saying: "I never heard a crash—it just went silent because—I can't explain it. We didn't lose a connection because there's a different sound that you use. It's a squealing sound when you lose a connection. I never lost connection, but it just went silent."[1]

(8) Jefferson mentioned in her book that Todd Beamer's composure and calm puzzled her: Todd's "voice was devoid of any stress. In fact, he sounded so tranquil it made me begin to doubt the authenticity and urgency of his call."(Jefferson, 33)

(9) Jefferson, who worked for many years as a supervisor at GTE Airfone, said she "had not had a chance to press the switch in [her] office that initiates the taping" of the conversation with Todd Beamer.(Jefferson, 36) It is inconceivable that she "had not a chance" to press the switch. Did she forget to press the

---

1   Ibid.

switch? Did someone tell her not to record the conversation? Did she record the conversation but was told to suppress that fact?

(10) It is noteworthy that Jefferson did not name in her interviews and in her book Phyllis Johnson, the operator who initially took the call from Todd Beamer, and Robert W. Combs, who relayed her call to the FBI. Phyllis' identity was kept virtually secret until 2009, when the documents of the 9/11 Commission were re-leased. As mentioned above, the first known FBI interview with Phyllis Johnson took place nine months after 9/11. The secrecy surrounding that person calls for an explanation. Did Phyllis, perhaps, know facts that might have undermined Jefferson's testimonies? And why has no media interview been conducted with Robert W. Combs, who played a key role in monitoring the calls of both Todd Beamer and Jeremy Glick and relayed crucial information to the FBI?

In her book, Jefferson claimed that she took the call from an unnamed operator because she was "clearly traumatized" and sat there, "completely frozen."(Jefferson, 29) Is there evidence for Jefferson's description?

In her FBI interview (reviewed above), Phyllis Johnson advised that Todd Beamer was "very calm and courteous" while conveying information, that she did not hear "the usual background sounds created by the activity and conversa-tions of other passengers," and estimates that she placed Beamer on hold three times during her period of the call (during which she probably tried to find out whether his call could be patched to his wife, as he had requested from her). She did not mention to the FBI having been shocked or traumatized by the call and did not explain why Lisa Jefferson took over the call. According to Robert W. Combs, Phyllis Johnson's alleged trauma did not prevent her from participating in the party line call from Capt. Noonan, where information from another UA93 call was relayed.[1] Was there another, undisclosed, reason for Jefferson to have taken the call from Phyllis Johnson and for suppressing the fact that Phyllis ini-tially took Todd Beamer's call?

(11) Lisa Jefferson changed with time certain details in her account, suggest-ing that she either invented new details or that some "higher-ups" asked her to add these details in order to strengthen the official legend:

According to her book "Called," published in 2006, Todd Beamer said in a calm voice, "There are two people lying on the floor in First Class. I think they' re hurt [...] I can't tell if they're dead or alive. The flight attendant next to me says it's the pilot and co-pilot"(Jefferson, 29) .

According to the staff of the 9/11 Commission, which interviewed Jef-ferson in 2004, she told them she "heard the *flight attendant* say to Mr. Beam-er that the two on the ground were the pilot and co-pilot." Here it was not

---

1   FBI 302-95682. September 11, 2001. Interview with Robert W. Combs

Beamer who related this fact but Jefferson who overheard this comment. According to the transcript of Jefferson's conversation with Lisa Beamer of September 15, 2001, she did not mention anyone hurt, let alone lying on the floor, only that "the guys went into cockpit, took the pilot and co-pilot out and locked the door." In the written Synopsis of Beamer's phone call, faxed to Mrs. Beamer on September 14, 2001, "from what Todd could see, two people were hurt, not sure if they were dead or alive." Here no pilot or co-pilot is mentioned and no one is reported lying on the floor. According to the FBI interview with Jefferson from September 11, 2001, no mention is made of any hurt person, or anyone lying on the floor. According to that interview, the "guys" had not even entered the cockpit when Todd Beamer's call started.

According to her book *Called* and to what she told Mrs. Beamer on September 15, 2001, Jefferson and Todd Beamer recited "together" the Lord's Prayer over the phone. This prayer is not at all mentioned in the interview with Jefferson with the 9/11 Commission staff and in her FBI interview of September 11, 2001. According to the Synopsis of September 14, 2001, Todd Beamer recited the prayer alone.

According to the 9/11 Commission, Jefferson attributed to Todd Beamer the motto "Let's roll," allegedly his last words. In her book *Called* she used a stylistic device to imply the same without stating it explicitly: "[Todd] then apparently turned away from the phone. 'Are you ready?' I couldn't hear the other person's response. 'Okay, let's roll!'"(Jefferson, 53) In Jefferson's conversation with Lisa Beamer on September 15, 2001, Jefferson used a different set of words for same: "Last I heard he said you ready, we're gonna roll." According to the Synopsis of September 14, 2001, the words were not uttered by Beamer. Rather: "Someone said let's roll." According to the FBI interview of September 11, 2001, "another passenger gave the *go ahead*." No mention is made here of the words "let's roll."

The transformation of the reported message from September 11, 2001, to later versions is significant because "let's roll" became a catchphrase used widely in the United States after 9/11 as a battle-cry. It became especially known and popular after being used by President George W. Bush in a speech to AmeriCorps volunteers and during his 2002 State of the Union Address.[1] In early 2002, United States Air Force Chief of Staff Gen. John P. Jumper ordered that one airplane in each USAF squadron and all USAF demonstration planes would bear an image of an eagle on an American flag with the words "Let's Roll" and "Spirit of 9-11," to remain until the first anniversary of the attack. It was also used by Lisa Beamer in a 2003 book titled Let's Roll: Ordinary People, Extraordinary Courage.[2] Was a decision made some time after 9/11 by "higher-ups" to "upgrade" Jefferson's account in order to build-up the cult of the UA93 heroic passengers?

---

1   Wikipedia "Let's Roll"
2   Ibid.

In her book Jefferson wrote," [Todd] raised his voice a bit. Then I heard raw panic. 'Oh my God, we're going down! We're going down! Jesus help us!' My body chilled as I heard Todd's cries. I was shaking on the inside...In my spirit, I cried out and prayed for God's help." By such words the author intended to convey the sinister nature of Beamer's statement.

Yet when she talked to Lisa Jefferson on September 15, 2001, she did not think these words meant anything sinister. After telling Mrs. Beamer about Todd's call, she remembered to add: "And he just said oh, S-H-I-T, real loud. That's the only thing he had said ya know, because they had turned the plane around. And it was more like they didn't know how to control the plane and he just felt, he said, we're goin' down, we're goin' down, oh we're coming back up, oh they turned it around, I think we're going back north. Then he said at this point I don't know where we're going, but I think we're going back north." Here no mention is made of God or of Jesus. "Going down" is immediately followed by "coming back up," implying that Todd Beamer was only reporting erratic flying.

Neither the Synopsis of September 14, 2001, nor the FBI interview of September 11, 2001, mention Beamer's alleged claim that the aircraft was "going down." These words seem to be belated additions made by Jefferson to dramatize Todd Beamer's account.

(12) According to the transcript of Jefferson's conversation with Lisa Beamer on September 15, 2001, Jefferson "knew" that Todd was sitting in the back of the plane. She did not explain how she *knew*. Nowhere does she report Beamer telling her this fact. According to the seating arrangement, Todd Beamer was assigned seat 10D. His presence in the back of the plane is not reported in the FBI interview with Jefferson, in the Synopsis of September 15, 2001, and in the report of the 9/11 Commission staff.

(13) According to the transcript of Jefferson's conversation with Lisa Beamer and to the report of the 9/11 Commission staff, Todd (as related by Jefferson) said that passengers and crew were told to sit down. This order was not mentioned in the FBI interview of September 11, 2001, and the Synopsis of September 14, 2001. The strange aspect of this allegation is that Todd apparently did not mention the foreign accent of those who gave this order (officially they were Arabs), nor what they actually said. The abstract nature of this "order" suggests that either Beamer was reporting a bogus order or the "guys" were no Arabs.

(14) It should be noted that the FBI did not interview GTE personnel in person, only by telephone, including Lisa Jefferson. No explanation is provided for this fact, particularly in the light of the importance of Todd Beamer's call for the official account.

(15) A question that has not been answered until today is whether a complete or partial recording exists of Todd Beamer's call. According to Lisa Jeffer-

son, Todd Beamer's call was traced by an unidentified "engineer" of GTE Airfone, (Jefferson, 54) suggesting that the call was recorded. One can also assume that information relayed by Robert W. Combs to the FBI would have been recorded by the FBI. A presumption exists, therefore, for the existence of such a recording.

(16) One of the statements that reveal the bogus nature of Todd Beamer's account, is found in the summary of Jefferson's FBI interview from September 11, 2001. According to that interview, Beamer said to Jefferson "that the airplane was *about* to be hijacked" by three individuals who "were *preparing* to take control of the flight" (emphasis added). Jefferson estimated that she spoke to Todd Beamer for seven minutes *before* the "two hijackers armed with knives *entered* the cockpit, securing the door behind them" (emphasis added). As Beamer's call only started at 9:45 (EST), it means that the cockpit was only breached after 9:50, whereas according the official account the aircraft was taken over by "hijackers" before 9:30. These facts, reported by Lisa Jefferson on the very day of 9/11 and documented in the FBI 302 form, disappeared from later testimonies by Lisa Jefferson, suggesting that someone, somewhere, noticed the toxic nature of these statements and ordered their suppression.

(17) According to FBI document 302 95682, based on what Robert W. Combs advised to a Special Agent on September 11, 2001, Jeremy Glick and Todd Beamer were reporting from flight UA93 after 10:15 a.m. (EST). According to that document, phone contact with Glick and Beamer was lost at 10:36 (EST), that is, half an hour after the official crash of flight UA93 at Somerset County, Pa. If one lends credibility to Robert W. Combs' account, as reported by the FBI, it means that Todd Beamer and Jeremy Glick did not call from an aircraft that crashed on 10:03 at Somerset County, Pa. It means either that they were not passengers on flight UA93 or that flight UA93 was still in the air after its official crash time, as demonstrated in chapter 6. In that case, the reports from the aircraft would have to be presumed as bogus and the official account of 9/11, thus, a monumental lie.

In this context, it might be useful to note that Robert W. Combs was no ordinary employee at GTE Airfone, but the Director of Technical Operations. He later became Director of Operations and finally the President of Verizon Airfone. He was also responsible, together with Mark Rugg, in compiling spreadsheets of all phone calls from flights UA175 and UA93 for the FBI.

(2) Mark Bingham's Calls

According to the FBI, Mark Bingham, a passenger, made 4 telephone calls from Airfone located in Row 23 DEF, only one of which was successful, namely at 9:37, lasting 166 seconds. [1]

---

1   Overview of phone calls: Introduction to Part III of this book

At 9:36:10	5 seconds to Vaughn Hoglan
At 9:37:03	166 seconds to Vaughn Hoglan
At 9:41:20	0 second (misdial)
At 9:41:53	3 seconds to Vaughn Hoglan

(a) FBI document 302 63761. Interview with Alice Hoglan. September 11, 2001

Carol Phipps, a family friend of Mark Bingham's mother, Alice Hoglan, answered the phone at about 9:35 but no one was on the line. A few minutes later the phone rang again. The caller, a male, stated, "Get Alice or Kathy quickly." Kathy Hoglan took the phone. As she ran to answer the phone, she looked at the clock. The time was 6:44 (EDT) or 9:44 (EST). Hoglan recognized the caller's voice as that of her nephew, Mark Bingham. Bingham stated, "This is Mark. I want to let you guys know that I love you, in case I don't see you again. I'm on UA Flight 93. It's being hijacked." Hoglan said, "We love you too. Let me get your mom." Alice, Mark's mother, who was staying with her sister-in-law Kathy, came and picked up the phone. Mark stated the following: "Hello mom, this is Mark Bingham. I'm flying from Newark to San Francisco. I'm calling from the Airfone. The plane has been taken over by three guys. They say they have a bomb." Hoglan asked: "Who are these guys?" Mark answered, "Yes. It's true..." The phone went dead in the middle of the sentence. Alice Hoglan advised that the entire time Bingham was on the telephone was no more than three minutes.

(b) FBI document 302 31805. Interview with [redacted]. September 17, 2001

According to the [redacted], a successful call from Mark Bingham was made at 9:44. It was answered by a family friend (Carol Phipps). Mark told Phipps that he needed to speak to Alice or Kathy [Hoglan] and that it was an emergency.

[Redacted] ran down the hall to [redacted] bedroom and knocked on the door...When [redacted] answered the phone, the caller was Bingham. Bingham said [to redacted], "this is Mark. I just want to tell you I'm on a plane and it's being hijacked." [Redacted] then got a piece of paper and asked Bingham what flight he was on. Bingham replied "United Flight 93." [Redacted] told Bingham to stay on the telephone and that she was going to get [redacted]. As [redacted] proceeded down the hall, she was met [by redacted who] heard the telephone ring and exited her bedroom.

It is probable that [redacted] was Kathy Hoglan, Alice Hoglan's sister.

(c) FBI document 302 8422. Interview with [probably Alice Hoglan].

September 17, 2001

Alice Hoglan essentially repeated what she told the FBI on September 11, 2001. She described in greater detail his answer to her question about the identities of the "hijackers."

Alice said she asked Mark, "Who are they, Mark?" She said Bingham was distracted and did not answer. Hoglan was not sure if Mark had heard the question. There was an interruption for approximately five seconds. Bingham then stated to his mother, "You've got to believe me. It's true." His mother responded and asked again: "I do believe you, Mark. Who are they"? There was another approximate five-second pause, similar to the first, wherein his mother heard activity and voices in the background. People were murmuring. There were no screams. Alice got the impression that Mark was distracted because someone was speaking to him. Then the phone went dead.

If there were "hijackers" on board, it is surprising that Bingham had no clue who they were and was not even able (or willing) to describe them, because he was sitting in row 4, very close to the cockpit.

Alice said that her account of the conversation was nearly verbatim. Throughout the entire call Mark sounded calm, controlled, matter-of-fact, and focused. She called immediately 911 and was patched through to the FBI.

When interviewed on CNN Live Event/Special on September 12, 2001, Alice Hoglan quoted her son in the following manner:

> I'm on a flight from Newark to San Francisco and there are three guys have to taken [sic] over the plane and they say they have a bomb. And I said, Mark, who are they? I said, Mark, I love you too. And I said, who are these guys?—and then he seemed to be pulled away from the phone for a minute [and never answered this question].[1]

(d) Discussion

Some observers find it puzzling—or even suspicious—that Mark Bingham should have introduced himself to his mother with his full name. And indeed, his mother said, chuckling, to national networks that when he called, he introduced himself not as Mark, but as Mark Bingham.[2] This is cited by some observers as evidence that this call was made by an impersonator. However, it is possible that Mark did so by sheer habit. He actually talked first to Carol Phipps, then to his mother's sister-in-law, and then to his mother. Were he an impersonator, he would hardly have known that his mother was staying with his aunt and distinguish the voice of his aunt from that of his mother.

---

1   "America Under Attack: World Leaders Express Horror, Outrage," CNN, September 12, 2001, #746

2   See, for example, interview by ABC News with Alice Hoglan, September 12, 2001, 5:55 p.m.

We note, however, that he avoided answering his mother's repeated ques-tion *Who are they?* This avoidance is significant, for if they had been Arab or Mus-lim, he most probably would have mentioned this fact. His repeated avoidance suggests that "someone" prevented him from answering this question. We note, also, that he did not mention any violent action aboard the aircraft.

(3) Sandy Bradshaw's Calls

According to the FBI, Sandra Bradshaw, a flight attendant aboard flight UA93, made 3 telephone calls from an Airfone located in Row 33 DEF, two of which were successful.[1]

At 9:35:40	353 seconds to UAL StarFix (SAMC)
At 9:49:30	0 seconds
At 9:50:04	470 seconds to Residence

(a) FBI Document 302 1888. Interview with Richard Belme (SAMC). September 11, 2001

According to Richard Belme, interviewed on September 11, 2001, by the FBI, a flight attendant from flight UA93 (later identified as Sandra Bradshaw), called his center, located at United Airlines, San Francisco International Airport, at ap-proximately 6:40 a.m. (Pacific Time), or 9:40 a.m. (EST). The call was received by [redacted] who "was on the phone with the attendant for only a couple of minutes." Belme provided a hand-written statement to the interviewing agents, as follows:

> I was called over to the STARFIX Desk at approximately 0640 PST. STAR-FIX informed me a flight attendant was on the line from Flight 93 and it was being hi-jacked. I took over the call and the flight attendant reported two men with knives are onboard. One man in the flight station and one man at first class. One man attacked a flight attendant but no passengers or crew were hurt. I asked the condition of the aircraft, she said a few small dives but OK. Then I lost contact.

(b) MFR (unnumbered). Interview with Richard Belme (SAMC). November 21, 2003

Richard Belme, Manager of United Airlines SAMC in San Francisco, was interviewed telephonically by staffers of the 9/11 Commission. Monitoring the conference call were three UAL lawyers.

Belme said he arrived to work at 6:00 a.m. (Pacific time). According to Belme, when he arrived, an employee named Policastro said, "something like 175

---

1   Overview of phone calls: Introduction to Part III of this book

was hijacked, the crew was killed, and they [the hijackers] have taken over the airplane."

Months prior to that, disgruntled mechanics had prank-called the SAMC, Belme said. Initially, Belme thought that this might be another prank call. Belme said that given the way Policastro looked, he immediately told him to make a written statement of what occurred.

At some point after that, Belme became aware that the Star-Fix people "over there" had received another strange call from a flight attendant and were in the process of trying to transfer the call to a manager. Belme immediately took the call and talked to a UAL 93 female flight attendant, later identified as Sandra Bradshaw. She was, according to Belme, "shockingly calm." He was not sure of the time of the call, but his notes indicated 6:40 a.m.

Bradshaw told Belme on the phone that two hijackers were in first class at the curtain. They had attacked and killed a flight attendant. She said they did not harm any passengers. She said there were two more hijackers behind the curtain in first class. (His notes indicated she had reported a total of three hijackers.) There was some dead air during the course of the call. Belme didn't ask about what weapons they used. She was in the back of the plane. Right after speaking to Belme, she called her husband.

Bradshaw did not describe the hijackers. She did not mention anything about passengers moved to the back of the plane. She told Belme the hijackers announced they had a bomb on the plane. There was no indication of a struggle.

Belme said he took one set of notes when he talked to her. He made another set of notes after the fact. He turned one set over to the FBI and he can't find the set he kept (It was not clear which set was the contemporaneous record). He sent United lawyers everything he had by Fed Ex. FBI said his call with the flight attendant from UAL 93 took place at 6:30 a.m. pacific time. He thinks it was rather 6:40 a.m.

To the best of Belme's knowledge, Policastro, Belme and [redacted] were the only people in the SAMC office to talk to someone on board a hijacked flight.

The only other point Belme wanted to emphasize was that the flight attendant he spoke to was very cool and calm; she was extremely impressive.

(c) FBI Document 302 95686. Interview with Philip G. Bradshaw. September 11, 2001

This is what Sandra's husband, Philip, reported to the FBI:

Sandra (Sandy) Bradshaw was working First Class. She called her husband shortly before 10:00 a.m. and asked him if he had seen what happened today. He told her that two planes had crashed into the WTC. Sandra told him that her plane had been hijacked by three men with dark skin, and she said "they almost looked Islamic." She said that one of the hijackers was seated in first class and added that she actually looked at him. He was "a little short guy." *The other hijackers were seated in the back of the plane,* she said. Sandra said she only saw the hijackers carrying knives as weapons. All three of the hijackers put red headbands on their heads as they were hijacking the plane. Additionally, Sandra did not know the location of the plane but she thought that the plane might be around the Mississippi River because they had just passed over a river.

Sandra stated the hijackers went up to the front of the plane and all passengers and flight attendants were in the rear of the plane. Sandra told her husband that she counted about 27 people in the back of the plane with her. The pilots were not in the back. Sandra did not say anything about what the hijackers said nor the language spoken during the hijacking. Further, Sandra did not say if the hijackers went into the cockpit of the plane. Sandra "was permitted to use the phone and speak freely." She therefore opined that the hijackers were not closely watching the passengers. Additionally, Sandra told her husband that the passengers were getting hot water out of the galley and were going to rush the hijackers. At the end of the call she told her husband that everyone was running up to first class and she hung up the telephone.

(d) FBI document 302 526, September 12, 2001

Another interviewer spoke with Philip G. Bradshaw, a day later.

In that interview Philip said Sandra had informed him that three hijackers were on the airplane, *all were sitting at the front of the plane* and possessed knives. Sandra was able to observe one of the hijackers who was sitting at the back of first class. She observed this individual from behind and described him as being a little guy with light dark skin, who looked Islamic. Philip stated he took his wife's description of red bands to mean red bandanas. Sandra's view was reportedly obstructed by the first class curtain, which prevented her from clearly seeing all the hijackers. Sandra informed her husband the passengers at the back of the plane were discussing how to overpower the three hijackers.

Philip believes Sandra was calling him from a GTE telephone, the connection was not good, and he could thus not hear any background conversations or noise. Mostly, he heard air noise. He estimated the call from Sandra lasted five to ten minutes and included discussions between them about their family. During the conversation, Sandra also mentioned the plane had turned back and they were currently located over a big river. Following his conversation with his wife, Philip immediately called United Airlines in Newark and informed them about his conversation.

(e) Discussion

- In his written note to the FBI on September 11, 2001, Belme advised that Bradshaw had told him one man had "attacked" a flight attendant. To the 9/11 Commission staff he later told that the attackers had been two and that they had "attacked and killed" a flight attendant. While we do not know about the reason of this discrepancy, it is no wonder Belme found Sandra Bradshaw "shockingly calm" when relating the stabbing and possibly the killing of a colleague.

- In his written note to the FBI, Belme indicated that Bradshaw counted two hijackers. In his interview with the staff of the 9/11 Commission Bradshaw is said to have reported four hijackers, two "at the curtain" and two "behind the curtain" of First Class. What prompted Belme to change his testimony?

- In her call Bradshaw to her husband, Sandra Bradshaw did not mention having seen or experienced any violent action aboard the aircraft nor cockpit entry. Such omission is surprising in the light of Belme's account. More surprising still is her apparent lack of curiosity to find out who is in the cockpit and how it was broken into. Such lack of curiosity suggests that she was not reporting real events.

- According to the first FBI interview with Sandra's husband, she called him at 9:50 a.m. (EST) after calling the SAMC, and stated that one "hijacker" was sitting in First Class while the "others" were sitting in the "back of the plane." According to the second FBI interview, "all three" hijackers were sitting in First Class, indicating that the cockpit had not yet been broken into. This story conflicts head-on with the official account, as well as with other testimonies, according to which the cockpit had been broken into at 9:28 a.m. Sandra's testimony suggests that she was not reporting real events.

(4) Marion Britton's Phone Call

According to the FBI Overview of calls, Marion Britton, passenger aboard flight UA93, made one phone call at 9:49:12, lasting 232 seconds. She called her friend Fred Fiumano.

(a) FBI Document Serial 302 25306 . Interview with Fred Fiumano. September 17, 2001

According to Fred Fiumano, Marion Britton called him at approximately 9:30 am or 9:45 a.m. (according to the FBI she called at 9:49). Britton said her plane was hijacked and told Fiumano to take down phone number (410) 788-1343. Fiumano told her not to worry because they would probably just take her to some other country. Britton said the hijackers had cut two passengers' throats. Fiumano told her that two planes had crashed on the WTC and Britton said she knew. Britton said they were turning and going to crash. Fiumano said he heard a lot of screaming and then the phone went dead.[1]

When he tried to call back the phone number she gave him, he got a message to the effect that the phone was not in service.[2] Because the number she gave him was different than her cell phone number, he assumed she had borrowed a cell phone from another passenger.[3] In her nearly four-minute conversation, Britton did not describe the hijackers, how many they were, how they were armed, where they currently were on the plane, who was currently flying the plane, where the plane's destination was, or what other passengers on the plane were doing.

(b) FBI Document PG-961, September 22, 2001

Britton's [redacted] advised that Britton's [redacted] received a cellular telephone call from Britton during the hijacking. Britton reportedly told him that two people's throats had been slit and the plane will crash in 20 seconds.

(c) Jere Longman's account

In his book about flight UA93, Jere Longman emphasizes two further points: First, that Britton made her call with a borrowed cell phone; and second, that she was crying when she talked to her friend Fred:

> Marion Britton was on the line, frantic...Marion was crying...Her cell phone was not working. She gave him the number of another passenger (Longman, 228).

(d) Discussion

What makes Britton's call different from practically all other calls, is that she is not described as calm but as frantic and crying. It is impossible for anyone to ascertain whether her fright and crying were genuine or acted. The contrast with other callers is remarkable.

Other noteworthy elements in Britton's call are: (a) The likelihood that Britton used a cell phone, a fact contradicted by the FBI; (b) Britton's report that "the hijackers had cut two passengers' throats," while omitting to describe the "hijackers," their number and any actual actions they had undertaken. This omission is puzzling in the light of her call's duration; (c) Her claim that the "hijackers had cut two passengers' throats" conflicts with the absence of any reference to violent actions in the calls of Beamer, Bingham and others.

---

1   FBI 302-25306. September 17, 2001. Interview with Fred Fiumano, boyfriend of Marion Britton
2   Ibid.
3   Ibid.

According to Neil A. Lewis of *The New York Times* who attended the trial of Zacarias Moussaoui, Britton's call was played to the jurors in the trial.[1] *The New York Times* actually quotes some phrases from that call. FBI documents, released to the 9/11 Commission, do not mention the existence of this recording. No other media source corroborates Lewis' account.

(5) Thomas Burnett's Phone Calls

According to the FBI, Thomas Burnett, passenger aboard flight UA93, made three telephone calls to his wife, Deena:[2]

At 9:30:32	28 seconds
At 9:37:53	62 seconds
At 9:44:23	54 seconds

According to Tom's wife, Deena, her husband made *four* telephone calls to her and their times do not coincide with those provided by the FBI (Burnett, pp. 61, 63, 65, 66):

At 9:27
At 9:34
At 9:45
At 9:54

Deena emphasizes that she wrote down the exact times of her husband's calls. Even if one concedes that her clock could have been three minutes too late, the two latter calls would not fit the FBI account. It is logically impossible that both accounts are true. Who was lying?

(a) FBI Document 302 535. Interview with Deena Burnett. September 11, 2001

Deena Burnett was interviewed at her home by an FBI agent on September, 11, 2001. According to the agent, she received "three to five cellular phone calls" from her husband, starting at approximately 6:30 a.m. (Pacific time), i.e. 9:30 a.m. (EST).

She said she received the second call approximately 10 minutes later. In that call, her husband asked her if she had heard about any other (hijacked) planes. She told him about the plane crashes on the WTC. Deena told the interviewer that during that call, her husband mentioned that the "hijackers were talking about flying the plane into the ground."

Approximately five minutes later, Deena said she received another cell phone call from her husband. She said she was able to determine that he was using the

---

1   Neils A. Lewis, "Final Struggles on 9/11 Plane Fill Courtroom," *The New York Times*, April 13, 2006, #1004

2   Overview of phone calls: Introduction to Part III of this book

cell phone because the caller ID was showing. One of the calls from her husband did not show on her screen because she was on the line with another call. Thomas advised that one passenger had been knifed and was dead. He told her that "they" were in the cockpit. Thomas stated he did not think "they" had a bomb because he did not see a bomb, only knives. Thomas then told his wife "we are turning toward the World Trade Center, no we are turning away." Then he told his wife "I have to go" and hung up.

During his fourth and last call he told her "a group of us are getting ready to do something," and he may not speak to her again, whatever he meant by that.

Deena advised to her interviewer that her husband did not describe the hijackers. She never noted any background noise other than one would normally expect on an airplane.

According to Deena's book (Burnett, 74), she was interviewed by several FBI agents, *one after the other* (a fact not mentioned in the 302 form):

> After 30 minutes or so of questioning, the [FBI] agent seemed satisfied and went outside. Then the second agent began asking questions. The exact same ones. When he was finished, the third agent chimed in and started going over the same questions again. Each time, they assured me that they didn't think I was lying. They just wanted to make sure I wasn't forgetting anything.

Why was the FBI repeatedly asking Deena the same questions? Was someone attempting to catch her in contradictions? Was the FBI attempting to make her change her story regarding the cell-phone or the times of the calls? Why was the repeated questioning not mentioned in the 302 form?

(b) MFR 04020024. Interview with Deena Burnett by 9/11 Commission staff[1]

On April 26, 2004, Deena Burnett was interviewed by John Raidt and Lisa Sullivan, members of the 9/11 Commission Staff. In that interview Deena confirmed to have spoken four times to Tom, her husband. She claimed that he said, "I think one of [the hijackers] has a gun."

She said that he did *not* mention the number of hijackers. Deena said she *believes* that the hijackers held a woman (possibly a flight attendant) at knife point. Deena then elaborated upon the individual calls:

Call 1: Deena *believes* he called from first class. She believes this because there were many sounds she could hear in the background, as he narrated to her what was going on. She also thinks this was the one call he placed to her from his cell phone, because she recognized the number on the caller ID.

---

1   MFR 04020024. April 26, 2004. Interview with Deena Burnett

Call 2: She believes he told her the hijackers had entered the cockpit. He was further back in the plane for the call, and for the other calls that followed.

Call 3: He was looking out of the window to describe to her where they were located. She thought he was moving around the cabin.

Call 4: She did not provide any specific information from this call.

Surprisingly, Burnett's calls made from his cell phone did not show on the invoice, nor did the one he reportedly placed to his secretary before take-off nor those he placed to Deena.

Deena said she turned the notes she had written down about her conversations with Tom into a typed transcript and gave it to the FBI. These notes have not been released.

(c) Transcript of Tom's calls to Deena, posted on the website of the Tom Burnett Foundation[1]

6:27 a.m.(pacific time) First cell phone call from Tom to Deena

Deena: Hello.

Tom: Deena.

Deena: Tom, are you O.K.?

Tom: No, I'm not. I'm on an airplane that has been hijacked.

Deena: Hijacked?

Tom: Yes, they just knifed a guy.

Deena: A passenger?

Tom: Yes.

Deena: Where are you? Are you in the air?

Tom: Yes, yes, just listen. Our airplane has been hijacked. It's United Flight 93 from Newark to San Francisco. We are in the air. The hijackers have already knifed a guy, one of them has a gun, they are telling us there is a bomb on board, please call the authorities. He hung up.

6:34 The phone rang in on call waiting, Tom's second cell phone call.

Deena: Hello.

Tom: They're in the cockpit. The guy they knifed is dead.

Deena: He's dead?

Tom: Yes. I tried to help him, but I couldn't get a pulse.

---

1   Tom Burnett Foundation. Also #653

Deena: Tom, they are hijacking planes all up and down the east coast. They are taking them and hitting designated targets. They've already hit both towers of the World Trade Center.

Tom: They're talking about crashing this plane. (a pause) Oh my God. It's a suicide mission...(he then tells people sitting around him)

Deena: Who are you talking to?

Tom: My seat mate. Do you know which airline is involved?

Deena: No, they don't know if they're commercial airlines or not. The news reporters are speculating cargo planes, private planes and commercial. No one knows.

Tom: How many planes are there?

Deena: They're not sure, at least three. Maybe more.

Tom: O.K. ... O.K. ... Do you know who is involved?

Deena: No.

Tom: We're turning back toward New York. We're going back to the World Trade Center. No, wait, we're turning back the other way. We're going south.

Deena: What do you see?

Tom: Just a minute, I'm looking. I don't see anything, we're over a rural area. It's just fields. I've gotta go.

He hung up.

6:45 a.m. Third cell phone call from Tom to Deena

Tom: Deena.

Deena: Tom, you're O.K. (I thought at this point he had just survived the Pentagon plane crash).

Tom: No, I'm not.

Deena: They just hit the Pentagon.

Tom: (tells people sitting around him, "They just hit the Pentagon.")

Tom: O.K....O.K. What else can you tell me?

Deena: They think five airplanes have been hijacked. One is still on the ground. They believe all of them are commercial planes. I haven't heard them say which airline, but all of them have originated on the east coast.

Tom: Do you know who is involved?

Deena: No.

Tom: What is the probability of their having a bomb on board? I don't think they have one. I think they're just telling us that for crowd control.

Deena: A plane can survive a bomb if it's in the right place.

Tom: Did you call the authorities?

Deena: Yes, they didn't know anything about your plane.

Tom: They're talking about crashing this plane into the ground. We have to do something. I'm putting a plan together.

Deena: Who's helping you?

Tom: Different people. Several people. There's a group of us. Don't worry. I'll call you back.

6:54 a.m. Fourth cell phone call from Tom to Deena

Deena: Tom?

Tom: Hi. Anything new?

Deena: No.

Tom: Where are the kids?

Deena: They're fine. They're sitting at the table having breakfast. They're asking to talk to you.

Tom: Tell them I'll talk to them later.

Deena: I called your parents. They know your plane has been hijacked.

Tom: Oh...you shouldn't have worried them. How are they doing?

Deena: They're O.K. Mary and Martha are with them.

Tom: Good. (a long quiet pause) We're waiting until we're over a rural area. We're going to take back the airplane.

Deena: No! Sit down, be still, be quiet, and don't draw attention to yourself! (The exact words taught to me by Delta Airlines Flight Attendant Training).

Tom: Deena! If they're going to crash this plane into the ground, we're going to have to do something!

Deena: What about the authorities?

Tom: We can't wait for the authorities. I don't know what they could do anyway. It's up to us. I think we can do it.

Deena: What do you want me to do?

Tom: Pray, Deena, just pray.

Deena: (after a long pause) I love you.

Tom: Don't worry, we're going to do something.

He hung up.

Some facts reported to the FBI on 9/11 to have been mentioned by Tom in the third call were later posted under call nr. 2: On September 11, 2001, Deena told the FBI that Tom only reported in his third call the death of a passenger who was previously knifed. On the website this information is reported in the second call, implying a faster death. In addition, in the second call, as reported on the website, Tom is said to have tried to help him, but couldn't get a pulse. Surprisingly, no mention is made of any attempt to find a doctor or nurse on board.

On September 11, 2001, Deena told the FBI that the presence of the "hijackers" in the cockpit was only reported in the third call whereas on the website, this information is shifted to the second call.

(d) The Telegraph (UK), September 14, 2001

In an interview with The Telegraph on September 14, 2001, Deena Burnett confirmed that her husband made four cellphone calls to her on 9/11. Deena said she believes that, "after she told her husband about the WTC attacks, he and the other passengers decided to turn the tables on their hijackers."[1]

(e) The San Francisco Chronicle, April 21, 2002

According to the San Francisco Chronicle, a police officer came to Deena's house already "on the morning of the crash" to bring her bad news.[2]

Deena Burnett told the Chronicle that she received four cellphone calls from her husband, scribbled down notes and later made a transcript that she always carries with her. Thomas also said to her that one of the hijackers has a gun. He asked her to call the authorities.[3]

According to Deena, Thomas had already mentioned at 9:45 a.m. a plan he was putting together with others to overcome the hijackers, because "they're talking about crashing this plane into the ground."[4] Yet, he did not report what the "hijackers" actually said or what accent they had. Furthermore, it is inconceivable that the "hijackers"—assuming they were Arabs—would discuss their

---

1   Bill Fenton, "Hijacked passengers 'go down fighting'," *The Telegraph* (UK), September 14, 2001, #637

2   Susan Sward , "The voice of the survivors: Flight 93, fight to hear tape transformed her life," *San Francisco Chronicle*, April 21, 2002, #302

3   Ibid.

4   Ibid.

plan in English and do so within ear-reach of passengers. The "hijackers" certainly had no interest in prompting a counter-attack.

(f) Books

In her book *Never Forget, An Oral History of September 11, 2001*, Mrs. Burnett reiterates that her husband used a cell phone: "I looked at the phone and I saw on the caller ID that it was Tom's cell phone"[1] (p. 192). She also reiterates that he mentioned a gun.[2] According to her, she told him in that occasion about the crashes on the WTC. She said he hadn't known about it yet, reacted with, "Oh, my God, it's a suicide mission," and started asking questions: "Who's involved? Was it a commercial airplane? What airline was it? Do you know how many airplanes are involved? And he was relaying my answers to people sitting around him. Then he told me he had to go and he hung up."

According to Deena, Tom asked in his fourth call "Is there anything new?" Deena wrote that Tom was "very quiet this time, very calm. He had been very calm and collected through the other conversations, but he was very solemn in this conversation, and I couldn't hear anything in the background. I could hear the roar of the engines and I could tell that he was sitting in a seat and very still and not walking around like he had been." He then said, "We're waiting until we're over a rural area. We're going to take back the airplane."

According to Deena, a policeman showed up around the third or fourth phone call to sit with her. By the time Tom's fourth phone call came, firemen had shown up on the front lawn.

(g) Analysis

- In her first interview by the FBI, Deena did not apparently mention that Tom reported a gun on board. Yet this is what Deena insisted he mentioned in his first call, as posted on the website of the Thomas Burnett Foundation and in Deena's book. How can that discrepancy be explained? If Tom was saying the truth, why did the FBI deny it? Was FBI implying that Deena was lying?

- Tom's first *cell phone* call was made on 9:27, when the aircraft was—according to the official timeline—flying at 35,000 feet. As this was technically impossible, there are two explanations for this anomaly: One is that Deena Burnett was lying about having seen his cellphone number on the ID indicator; another is that the official timeline on flight UA93 is a fraud.

---

1   Mitchell Fink and Lois Mathias, *Never Forget, An Oral History of September 11, 2001* (Harpers Collins, 2002), p. 192
2   Ibid.

- According to the officially released transcript of the Cockpit Voice Recorder (CVR) from flight UA93, one "hijacker" (or two) entered the cockpit at 9:28 a.m. and struggled with the pilot. Yet Tom Burnett does not report this fact in spite of having been seated in First Class at 4B, that is in proximity of the cockpit.

- Tom Burnett fails to describe the alleged hijackers and even to mention how many they are. In view of the fact that he called four times, this omission is incongruous.

- At one point Tom is quoted as saying "They're talking about crashing this plane." At that time, two of the alleged hijackers are already said to be in the cockpit. As most callers mentioned only three hijackers in all, this leaves just one "hijacker" outside the cockpit. So, who is Tom referring to as "they," who allegedly talk about crashing the plane? Why should "they" announce their murderous plans to the passengers, if by doing so they would actually encourage passengers to rise up?

- According to the transcript of the CVR, the hijacker-pilot says on 9:39, that "they're going back to the airport." How does that statement fit with their alleged announcement that they intend to crash the plane?

- Other passengers mentioned that the "hijackers" closed the curtain of First Class. Tom in his four calls does not mention this information.

- A few times Tom mentions that "they" announce this or that. "They" certainly did not speak as a choir, but had one of their representatives make the announcement. Yet he used the plural ("they"), while omitting to report what "they" actually said and "their" allegedly Arab accent. Such omissions are surprising.

- Tom Burnett does not mention that the "hijackers" put on red bandanas on their heads, as some other callers mentioned. Didn't he notice this glaring fact, or was this just one of the numerous bogus facts reported from the aircraft?

- Tom Burnett mentions in his first call, which started at 9:27 (according to his wife) that one "guy" had already been knifed. In other words, deadly violence allegedly erupted on that aircraft before 9:30. It must be remembered that according to the official account, the cockpit was then already controlled by the "hijackers," leaving only a single "hijacker" to guard 35 odd passengers. Yet we are asked to believe that no efforts were undertaken for another half an hour by the passengers to overpower a single "hijacker."

- Tom Burnett claims in his second call that he "tried to help" the "guy they knifed," who meanwhile had died. He said that he "couldn't get a pulse." But why did none of the flight attendants seek the assistance of the three medical emergency technicians on the plane (Lauren Grandcolas [Longman, 179], Linda Gronlund [Longman, 221] and Jean Peterson [Longman, 18-19]), if someone was really stabbed? Neither Grandcolas nor Gronlund mentioned in their phone calls having been asked to, or having volunteered, to assist the wounded. Is that plausible?

While the above contradictions and anomalies are certainly significant, one particular fact in Deena's testimony sticks out: her absolute certainty that her husband used his cell phone to call her. She consistently maintained that she saw the number of his cell phone on her telephone receiver and knew, therefore, that the caller was her husband. This particular fact has huge implications.

In 2001, it was nearly impossible to make cellphone calls from airliners flying at cruising altitudes. This fact has been acknowledged by professionals, demonstrated by controlled experiments and verified by numerous travelers, who tried without success to make phone calls from cruising altitude. The higher the altitude and the faster the plane, the less likely a cellphone call would succeed. Even Tom Burnett's wife Deena, a former flight attendant, expressed surprise that he was able to call her from the aircraft with his cell phone: "I didn't understand how he could be calling me on his cell phone from the air"(Burnett, 61). But she did not apparently pursue this anomaly any further.

Alexa Graf, AT&T spokesperson, told Wireless Review that cell phone systems were not designed for calls from high altitudes. She suggested shortly after 9/11 that it was almost a "fluke" that the [9/11] calls reached their destinations: "On land, we have antenna sectors that point in three directions—say north, southwest, and southeast," she explained. "Those signals are radiating across the land, and those signals do go up, too, due to leakage." From high altitudes, the call quality is not very good, and most callers will experience drops.[1]

Marco Thompson, President of the San Diego Telecom Council, commented: "Cell phones are not designed to work on a plane. Although they do." The rough rule is that when the plane is slow and over a city, the phone will work up to 10,000 feet or so. "Also, it depends on how fast the plane is moving and its proximity to antennas," Thompson says. "At 30,000 feet, it may work momentarily while near a cell site, but it's chancy and the connection won't last." Also, the hand-off process from cell site to cell site is more difficult. It is created for a maximum speed of 60 mph to 100 mph. "They are not built for 400 mph airplanes."[2]

Toby Seay, Vice President of national field operations for AT&T Wireless, said in 2001 that the technological limits to using a cell phone aboard a plane include the signal strength, potential signal inhibitors and "free space loss" as the signal gradually loses strength.... Performance is usually compromised in calls from above because cell site antennas are configured to pick signals horizontally and not from overhead. The biggest problem with a phone signal sent from the air is that it can reach several different cell sites simultaneously. The signal can interfere with callers already using that frequency, and because there is no way for one cell site to hand off calls to another that is not adjacent to it, signals can

---

1   Betsy Harter, "Final Contact, Connected Planets," *Connected Planet*, November 1, 2001, #893
2   "San Diego Scene," *San Diego Metro*, October 2001, #781

become scrambled in the process. That's why wireless calls from jetliners don't last long, says Kathryn Condello, vice president of industry operations for CTIA. The network keeps dropping the calls, even if they are re-established later.[1]

In a series of controlled experiments conducted by Prof. A. K. Dewdney in 2003 over London (Ontario, Canada), an area "supplied with some 35 cell sites distributed over an area of about 25 square miles," he established a "distinct trend of decreasing cell phone functionality with altitude."[2] Using a variety of cell phones, he found that "the chance of a typical cell phone call from cruising altitude making it to ground and engaging a cell site there is less than one in a hundred." Already at 8,000 feet, only 8 percent of calls were successful. To my knowledge, Prof. Dewdney's findings were not scientifically challenged by anyone.

If it was virtually impossible in 2001 to make sustainable cell phone calls from aircraft flying at cruising altitudes—such as above 30,000 feet—four questions arise in relation with Mrs. Burnett's statement:

1. Was Mrs. Burnett a reliable witness?

2. Is there a possibility that Mrs. Burnett erroneously believed that her husband called her with a cell phone?

3. Is it plausible that Mrs. Burnett deliberately lied about her husband using a cell phone?

4. From what altitude were Tom Burnett's calls made?

Was Mrs. Burnett a reliable witness?

I found no evidence that Mrs. Burnett was an unreliable or untruthful witness. All publicly available evidence suggests that Mrs. Burnett has been (and is) a meticulous, well-organized person. When he called, she rushed to note the exact times of his calls and made notes of what he said. She immediately contacted the authorities. Her statements regarding her husband's calls and other facts have remained consistent over the years.

Is it probable that Mrs. Burnett was mistaken?

While some recipients of calls from Flight UA93 said they "believed" the caller had used a cell phone, Mrs. Burnett relied on what she actually saw with her own eyes in more than one call. She said "she recognized the [phone] number on the caller ID" on her receiver as that of her husband. She did not waver on this point: She consistently maintained that Tom called her with his cell phone. She made this statement in her FBI interview, in media interviews, in an interview

1   Brad Smith, "Making Calls From The Air," *Wireless Week*, September 24, 2001, #1001

2   A.K. Dewdney, "Project Achilles Parts One, Two and Three," January 23, 2003, #630

with staff of the 9/11 Commission, on the website of the Tom Burnett Foundation and in a book she authored. There is no basis for suspecting that she was repeatedly mistaken in her observation (Tom called four times).

Is it plausible that Mrs. Burnett deliberately lied?

Mrs. Burnett did not have a motive for lying to the FBI and the public about this matter. On the contrary: by emphasizing that her husband called her with a cell phone, she placed herself in contradiction to the FBI. She did not contradict the FBI out of spite or because she suspected official malfeasance. In fact she never disputed the official account of 9/11. She even took pride in being regarded by President Bush as the wife of a national hero.(Burnett, 152-3) The fact that she stuck to her account—in spite of knowing that it conflicts with that of the government—strengthens the reliability of her statement.

From what altitude were Tom Burnett's calls made?

If one accepts that Tom Burnett's calls (or some of them) to his wife on the morning of 9/11 were made with a cell phone, could they have been made from a cruising passenger jet?

The National Transportation Safety Board (NTSB) issued an Altitude Profile for Flight UA93 which indicates the altitude at which that aircraft was believed to be flying at various times (see below).

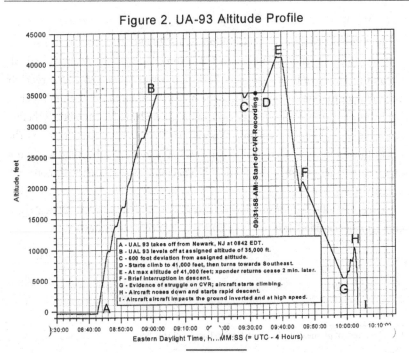

Figure 2. UA-93 Altitude Profile

A - UAL 93 takes off from Newark, NJ at 0842 EDT.
B - UAL 93 levels off at assigned altitude of 35,000 ft.
C - 600 foot deviation from assigned altitude.
D - Starts climb to 41,000 feet, then turns towards Southeast.
E - At max altitude of 41,000 feet; xponder returns cease 2 min. later.
F - Brief interruption in descent.
G - Evidence of struggle on CVR; aircraft starts climbing.
H - Aircraft noses down and starts rapid descent.
I - Aircraft aircraft impacts the ground inverted and at high speed.

Eastern Daylight Time, h:MM:SS (= UTC - 4 Hours)

Tom Burnett's *first* call was made at 9:27 (according to Deena) or at 9:30:32 (according to the FBI). At these times Flight UA93 was flying—according to the NTSB document—at 35,000 feet. The likelihood of a successful cell phone call from that altitude is less than one percent. Tom's *last* phone call was made at 9:54 (according to Deena) or at 9:44 (according to the FBI). At 9:54 Flight UA93 would have been flying at approximately 10,000 feet. According to the FBI's time, the aircraft would have been flying at 28,000 feet. In either case, a successful, let alone a sustainable cell phone call, would have been very unlikely from these altitudes.

In addition to the discrepancy in the times of the calls, the FBI claimed that Tom made only three calls home, whereas Deena consistently maintained that he called her four times and provided specific information for each call, including the exact timings.

If Mrs. Burnett was telling the truth, the FBI must have been presenting falsified evidence. There is, actually, no escape from that conclusion.

(6) Joseph Deluca's Phone Calls

According to the FBI, Joseph DeLuca, a passenger aboard flight UA93, made three telephone calls from an Airfone located in Row 26 DEF. [1]

At 9:42:13   14 seconds to parents

At 9:43:03   130 seconds to parents

At 9:48:48   0 seconds to Atwell Haines

Joseph DeLuca and Linda Gronlund (seats 2B and 2D respectively) sat between alleged hijackers Ziad Jarrah (1B), Ahmed Alnami (3C) and Saeed Alghamdi (3D). There is no evidence that DeLuca was "relocated to the rear." It is significant that he did not describe the hijackers and indicate their number.

According to author Longman, DeLuca phoned his father "shortly before ten." The only thing known from this call is: "Dad, there are terrorists on the plane. I love you very much" (Longman, 227). It is inconceivable that he did not offer any further information, taking into account that his second phone call lasted 130 seconds.

Exceptionally, and for no known reason, FBI interviews with DeLuca's parents remain classified. It is not even known when these interviews took place.

---

1   Overview of phone calls: Introduction to Part III of this book.

(7) Edward Felt's Phone Call

According to the FBI, Edward Felt, a passenger aboard flight UA93, made a telephone call from that flight to the Westmoreland County 911 Emergency Center at 9:58 a.m., the duration of which is given by the FBI as undetermined.[1]

(a) Initial FBI interviews of John W. Shaw on September 11, 2001

John W. Shaw, a Telecommunications Officer for Westmoreland County 911 (Emergency) Center at Greensburg (PA), was interviewed by the FBI on September 11, 2001, not less than *three* times.[2] As the times of the interviews are not mentioned, it is not possible to ascertain which was the first, the second and the third interview, nor why he was interviewed three times. All three interviews were conducted by telephone. The interviews were documented on 302 forms. FBI serial 302 38710 was dictated and transcribed on September 11, 2001; serial 302 107608 was dictated and transcribed on September 13, 2001; and serial 302 3725 was dictated and transcribed on September 17, 2001.

According to FBI document 302 107608, Shaw said he answered at approximately 9:58 a.m. an incoming call and heard a male caller state in an excited voice that he needed help: "There is a hijacking on a plane." Shaw said the caller said he was locked in the restroom of the aircraft. Shaw said the caller's name was Ed and believed his last name was "Wart." Ed said this was flight 93, a 757 type aircraft and there were *not* a lot of passengers on board. Ed also provided his cell phone number as 732-241-6909. Shaw explained that the call was intermittent: he lost contact with Ed on several occasions. While the call was in progress, Shaw summoned his co-workers for assistance.

According to FBI document 302 3725, Shaw said he answered an incoming call on the 1103 line and spoke with a male caller who identified himself as Ed Wart (phonetic), who gave him a cellular telephone number. The caller was said "extremely hysterical," stated that he needed help and that he was on board flight UA93. The caller repeated several times that a hijacking was in progress and that he attempted to find out where the aircraft was. Shaw asked the caller how many people were on the plane. Shaw said that the caller answered, "There were *lots* of individuals on the plane." He said he was hiding in the bathroom (he did not indicate whether it was in the rear or the front of the aircraft) and was apologetic because he apparently knew that reception on the cell phone call was bad and that Shaw had trouble hearing him. He repeatedly said, "Hijack, hijack, hijack" but did not provide any description of the hijackers or their number. He

---

1   Final Report of the 9/11 Commission, p. 5. In FBI documents, including interviews with John W. Shaw and Glenn W. Cramer, the duration of the call is, however, consistently given as 3-4 minutes.

2   FBI 302-10760, 302-38710, and 302-3725. September 11, 2001. Interviews of John W. Shaw

gave no indication of bombs or guns aboard the flight. During the estimated *three to four* minutes conversation he had with this caller, he heard no explosions or gunfire in the background, nor any background conversations.[1] According to FBI document 302 38710 the call lasted *less than five minutes.* Shaw confirmed that Glenn Cramer, his supervisor, monitored the conversation.

According to the transcript of the call (below), the caller said that the plane "was pretty empty." Note the unexplained past tense used in the transcript and the difference between "pretty empty" and what Shaw told the FBI.

Surprisingly, in *Among the Heroes,* Jere Longman, wrote that the conversation lasted merely seventy seconds before the call disconnected (Longman, 275).

(b) FBI Serial 17823. Interview with Glenn W. Cramer. September 12, 2001

Glenn W. Cramer, John W. Shaw's supervisor, was interviewed by the FBI on September 12, 2001.[2] Cramer said that on 9/11 at approximately 9:58 a.m. John Shaw answered a call that came in on Line 1103 (which is a line at the Emergency Center for incoming cell phone calls). Cramer's attention was directed to the call when he heard Shaw state, "You are what hijacked?" At that point in time, Cramer immediately picked up on another phone at the Center referred to as a "spy phone" at which time he heard a male caller who identified himself as ED WART and who said he called from his cell phone Nr. 732-241-6909. This individual "was talking in a low-tone voice, yet in listening to him his voice was one filled with terror." The caller advised "hysterically" that he was locked in the bathroom of [flight] UA93, a 757 jet with *lots* of passengers, which was en route to San Francisco from Newark. He heard the caller repeat several times to Shaw that the aircraft was being hijacked, that *he believed the aircraft was going down, and that some sort of explosion had occurred aboard the aircraft.* The male caller also stated that there was *white smoke somewhere on the plane.*

During the conversation between the male caller and John Shaw, the male caller did not indicate whether he was located in the front or rear bathroom of the aircraft nor describe the hijackers. Yet he sat very close to them (seat 2D). The caller made no statements regarding any weapons that the hijackers had in their possession and made no statement regarding any bombs other than the fact that "some sort of explosion occurred aboard the aircraft." Cramer said that the call "contained static but the phone call itself was constant in that he Cramer

---

1 It is surprising that he should at all mention having NOT heard explosions or gunfire in the background. There would have been no reason for such a comment unless he was specifically asked about such an occurrence by the interviewing agent. As FBI documents do not indicate what questions are asked by agents, it is impossible to know whether he volunteered this information and if so, why.

2 FBI 302-17823. September 12, 2001. Interview with Glenn W. Cramer

could hear it as it transpired." This last statement contradicted John Shaw's account about the quality of the reception.

Based on what he heard, Cramer immediately got off the phone and advised the other supervisor present at the time, Ed Milliron, of the facts. Other individuals located in the Emergency 911 Center were instructed to notify the FAA and the FBI. Cramer said he notified Richard Madison, Director of Westmoreland County 911 of what was transpiring.

Cramer advised that at approximately the same time as the cell phone call was received, the Westmoreland County 911 Center received a telephone call from an individual identified as Walter Astonisen, who resides at Acme, Mt. Pleasant Township (Pennsylvania). Astonisen advised that he had observed a large plane heading in a northeast direction and that the plane was banking left and right. Based on where Astonisen said he was located, and the path of flight indicated by him, Somerset County 911 Center was notified of such, and that an aircraft might be going down.

The alleged mention of an explosion in Ed Felt's phone call was reported by major media. Glenn Cramer was cited by media to the effect that the caller from the plane "heard some sort of an explosion and saw white smoke coming from the plane, and we lost contact with him."[1]

(c) Transcript of Edward Felt's phone call

(as reproduced in attachment to FBI 302 4889 of Sept. 11, 2001, released by NARA as part of the 9/11 Commission documents: Team 7, Box 12, 93 Calls EdFelt)

Caller:	"Hijacking in pro —"
911:	"Excuse me? Hey somebody's reporting a—"
Caller:	"Hijacking in progress."
911:	"Sir I'm losing you, where are you at?"
Caller:	"United flight 93"
911:	"Wait a minute, wait, United—night flight—United flight. United flight 93."
Caller:	"Hijacking in progress!"
911:	"Okay, where you at up? Where are you at up?"
Caller:	"I'm in the bathroom, United flight 93."

---

1   "Jet crashes near Somerset; passenger reported hijacking in phone call," *Post-Gazette*, September 11, 2001, #727; Ed Hayward et al, "Attack on America: Suspects ID's in terror strikes," *Boston Globe*, September 12, 2001 (3d edition), #162

911:	"Okay, where are you at?"
Caller:	"I don't know."
911:	"Where are you at?"
Caller:	"I don't know where the plane is."
911:	"Where did you take off at?"
Caller:	"Newark to San Francisco."
911:	"Newark to San Francisco."
Caller:	"United flight 93."
911:	"I got it, okay stay on the phone with me sir."
Caller:	"I'm trying to...UI at the bathroom. I don't know what's going on."
911:	"Hey somebody get the FAA, Newark to San Francisco and they got a highjacking in progress. Okay, yeah. Dude, get somebody from the airport on the line. This is a highjacking in progress. Are you still there sir?"
Caller:	"Yes I am."
911:	"What's your name sir?"
Caller:	"EDWARD FELT."
911:	"EDWARD FELT? What's your phone number sir?"
Caller:	"Seven, three, two 732."
911:	"Go ahead."
Caller:	"Two, four, one 241."
911:	"Go ahead."
Caller:	"Six, nine, seven, four 6974."
911:	"How big of a plane sir?"
Caller:	"It's like a seven-fifty-seven 757."
911:	"This is a seven-fifty-seven 757. Hey we need. It's a seven-fifty-seven 757. Sir, sir?"
Caller:	"Yes."
911:	"Okay, how many people's on the plane?"
Caller:	"It was—it was pretty empty, maybe UI."

911:         "Can you still hear me sir, sir, sir can you still hear me? It's over UI. There's a plane...said the plane's going down. It's over Mt. Pleasant Township somewhere. Sir? It's going down. You better make an announcement on UI. It's over Mt. Pleasant somewhere. Hello?

Call terminated.

(d) Analysis

The following analysis relies partly on an analysis of anomalies surrounding Felt's phone call unearthed by blogger *John Doe II*.[1]

John Doe II reveals that Shaw was interviewed *three* times by the FBI on September 11, 2001[2] and again on March 25, 2002.[3] According to FBI 302 3725, a tape recording of the call received from ED WART (ph.) "was turned over" to Special Agent Gregory Kerpchar of the Pennsylvania Attorney General's Office, AntiTerrorism Task Force on September 11, 2001, "at approximately 12:14 p.m." There is no mention in the 302 forms of any FBI official going to the Westmoreland County 911 Center in Greensburg (PA) to get hold of the tape recording. It was not indicated who brought the tape to SA Kerpchar.

A brief examination reveals the following discrepancies between the transcript and the interviews:

- According to the transcript, Edward Felt does not mention an explosion and white smoke, as reported by Glenn Cramer.

- According to the transcript, Felt claims that the plane "was pretty empty," whereas both Cramer and Shaw in one his interviews maintained that Felt said there were "lots of individuals on the plane."

- Shaw said that Felt had been "apologetic because he apparently knew that reception on the cell phone call was bad." There is no mention of any such apologetics by Felt in the transcript.

- Both Shaw and Cramer were unable to hear correctly the caller's name, whereas the transcriber apparently had no difficulty to hear the correct name of Edward Felt.

- Both Shaw and Cramer said that Felt gave his telephone number as 732-241-6909, whereas on the transcript the number is given as 732-241-6974.

According to author Jere Longman, Ed Felt said at one point, "We're going down, we're going down."(Longman, 275) Yet, this statement is not mentioned in the transcript. The transcript is neither identified by a document number nor

1   John Doe II, "Edward Felt's phone call," May 16, 2005, #1002
2   FBI 302-3725, 302-38710 and 302-107608. September 11, 2001. Interviews with John W. Shaw
3   Source: FBI Newark from Pittsburgh Squad 4/JTTF to Counterterrorism, New York, March 26, 2002. Bates 344. PG 3585, #1780

by the name of the transcriber and does not provide a timeline for the conversation. It represents, therefore, an unauthenticated and possibly forged document.

On March 20, 2002, Assistant United States Attorney David Novak and FBI Special Agent Gregory Kerpchar met with John W. Shaw at his place of employment and had him listen for the first time to a copy of the recorded telephone call from Edward Felt while reviewing the transcript. Upon the conclusion of the tape recording, Shaw reportedly stated that "both the tape recording and the transcript were accurate."[1] Was he presented with the above transcript? It appears that the FBI still remained anxious regarding this tape; for in a communication from FBI Newark to FBI New York two days later, the contents of which are for the most part redacted, the following sentence is found: "Under no circumstances is Newark to provide [the family of] Felt with a copy of the recording or a copy of the transcript."[2] What was the FBI fearing?

After obtaining from Felt's attorney a non-disclosure agreement signed by Sandra Felt, FBI officials visited her at her residence on March 26, 2002 and allowed her and members of her immediate family to listen *in their presence* to "a 911 telephone call made by Edward Felt from United flight 93 on September 11, 2001."[3] This was the first time, since 9/11, she and her family were allowed to hear the recording, on which her husband reported the hijacking.

Glenn Cramer, who initially reported to have heard Felt mention an explosion and white smoke, was interviewed again by the FBI on April 10, 2002, two weeks after Sandra Felt was allowed to hear the tape. He confirmed what he told the FBI on September 12, 2001. He did not retract his initial testimony (about an explosion and white smoke) and added a significant fact: He was not given an opportunity to listen to the recording of Felt's call which was played to Felt's family (and before that to his colleague Shaw). There is no evidence that he was told why he was not allowed to hear that recording.[4]

Shortly thereafter, the *Pittsburgh Post-Gazette* informed its readers that Felt's family was among those invited by the FBI to listen to the recording of the cockpit voice recorder (CVR) from flight UA93. Before they joined the other relatives, Sandra Felt, Ed's wife, Ed's brother, Gordon, and his mother, Shirley,

> were led to a small conference room...where they were joined by two FBI agents and a victim-assistance counselor. Sitting around a polished wood table, the agents handed each of the Felts a typed transcript of [Ed Felt's] 911 call, and then played it....[H]e spoke in a quivering voice saying, 'We are being hijacked. We are being hijacked.' He went on to describe an "explo-

---

1   FBI PG 3585. March 26, 2002. Interview with Daniel Stevens and John W. Shaw
2   FBI OUT-2526. March 3, 2002. FBI New York to FBI Newark, #1780, p. 113
3   FBI OUT-2675. September 28, 2002. FBI Newark, Franklin Township Squad 1. #1780 p. 118
4   FBI 302-110116. April 10, 2002. Interview with Glenn W. Cramer

sion" that he heard, and then white smoke on the plane from an undetermined location. Then the line went dead.[1]

According to Jere Longman, Sandra Felt, like John Shaw, denied that Ed had mentioned an explosion or a puff of smoke aboard the plane.(Longman, 369) Who was telling the truth? Was Felt's family perhaps presented with another version of Edward's call, one that included a mention of an "explosion" and of "white smoke"?

From a communication issued later by FBI Counterterrorism and addressed to the FBI Newark office,[2] we glean that Felt's family apparently wanted to listen once more to the tape. Was the Felt family suspicious of some irregularity regarding the tape? The document includes the following warning: "Although Sandra Felt has signed a non-disclosure letter, the possibility exists of negative media reporting.... The Newark Division is requested, with Sandra Felt's permission, to stay with the family while the tape is played." What sort of negative media reporting did the FBI fear? Why was it imperative for FBI agents to stay with the family while the tape was played (for the third time)?

From the foregoing accounts, it appears that the FBI possessed two versions of Ed Felt's call, one mentioning an explosion and white smoke and another without.

Apart from the numerous discrepancies cited above, which ought to have prompted questions by the 9/11 Commission and the media, it should be evident that Edward Felt did not report any real hijackings: While repeating—mantra-like—"Hijacking in progress," he did not offer any concrete facts to support this claim, let alone any indications that he personally observed any acts that amounted to a hijacking.

(8) Jeremy Glick's Phone Call

According to the FBI, Jeremy Glick, a passenger aboard flight UA93, made one call to his mother-in-law Joanne Makely and his wife Lyzbeth, from an Airfone located in Row 27 DEF at 9:37:41 lasting 7565 seconds (the line was kept open).[3]

(a) FBI document 302 6390. Interview with Elizabeth Glick.

---

1   Steve Levin, "A wife describes pain of hearing 911 call from Flight 93," *Post-Gazette*, April 21, 2002, #199
2   FBI VS-238. September 12, 2003. From Counterterrorism (PENTTBOM) to FBI Newark. #1780. p. 142-3
3   Overview of phone calls: Introduction to Part III of this book

September 11, 2001

Elizabeth Glick is Jeremy Glick's wife. She was interviewed by an FBI agent in the evening of September 11, 2001.

Elizabeth, or Lyzbeth, stated that she received an approximately 20-minute long telephone call from her husband from the airplane prior to the crash. In the course of his call, he told her:

- His flight from Newark to San Francisco detoured in Cincinnati, Ohio

- Three dark complexion Arab males wearing red bands took over the cockpit of the airplane. The three Arabs did not speak English

- There was no communication from the cockpit

- At least one of the Arab males held a knife in one hand

- Another Arab male had what appeared to be a bomb in his hand

- The 30 or 40 passengers on board were forced to the back of the airplane

- At least one other passenger's wife also spoke with a hijack victim

- A decision had been made to resist the terrorist and take back the airplane.

- At times Jeremy reportedly sounded confused when she informed him of "other terrorist attacks" staged on September 11, 2001

(b) FBI document 302 11721. Interview with Richard Makely. September 12, 2001

Richard Makely is the father-in-law of Jeremy Glick. He was interviewed by the FBI at his residence in the presence of his wife, JoAnne Makely, on September 12, 2001.

Richard Makely said that he took over the call from Lyzbeth (Jeremy's wife) in the morning of 9/11. When he got the receiver from her, he "only heard silence on the telephone, then three, four, or five minutes went by, and there were high pitched screaming noises coming over the telephone, that sounded like they were coming from a distance from the airplane telephone [sic]." Makely described the noises as "sounding similar to the screams coming from individuals riding a roller coaster." Several minutes of silence ensued. Then Makely heard a series of high pitched screaming sounds again, followed by a noise which he described as "wind sounds." The "wind sounds" were followed by noises that sounded as though the Airfone was hitting a hard surface several times or banging around. Then silence again ensued. During the screaming and other sounds that Makely heard, a telephone operator from Horizon broke into the telephone call and relayed the information to police officials. Makely was sure that the operator was from Horizon, not Verizon, and that there was a tape recording of the conversation.

Makely and the telephone operator stayed on the telephone for approximately 1½ hours, that is until approximately 10:45 a.m., but never heard any further noises on the line. The call was then terminated.

(c) FBI document 302 11722. Interview with Elizabeth Glick. September 12, 2001

This was the second FBI interview with Mrs. Glick, conducted at the residence of her parents. Present during the interview was a New York State Police Investigator and Elizabeth's parents, JoAnne and Richard Makely.

During his call from the aircraft, Jeremy initially spoke to his mother-in-law and immediately asked to talk with his wife. After giving the receiver to Lyzbeth, JoAnne contacted "911" via her cellular phone. Jeremy told his wife that his flight (93) had been hijacked by three "Iranian-looking" males, with dark skin and bandanas *ethnic type* as opposed to *hippie type* on their heads. One of the males stated that he was in possession of a bomb in a red box and one was armed with a knife. Jeremy advised that they were over land, although it felt as if they were circling instead of flying straight towards California. Jeremy advised Lyzbeth that the hijackers had herded the passengers into the rear of the plane and told them that if they did not crash into the WTC, they were going to blow-up the plane. One of the hijackers then told the passengers to call their loved ones. The three hijackers then entered the cockpit of the plane. Jeremy told his wife that he was unsure if the hijackers were going to crash or blow-up the plane.

The entire call lasted approximately fifteen to twenty minutes. Lyzbeth could not hear any unusual sounds in the background of the call and the connection was extremely clear, "as if he was calling from the next room." Jeremy was "extremely calm, but sounded very concerned and confused." Jeremy advised that the Captain had not made any announcements and that the people were scared because they did not know what was happening.

Jeremy advised Lyzbeth that the other passengers had contacted their wives and husbands and asked if it were true that people were crashing planes into the WTC.... Jeremy advised Lyzbeth that he and four other male passengers were contemplating to "rush" the hijackers and asked Lyzbeth if that was okay with her. Lyzbeth told Jeremy that she did not know if that was okay and asked Jeremy if any of the hijackers had guns, to which Jeremy replied they did not.... Jeremy told Lyzbeth that he loved her and asked her not to hang-up the telephone.

(d) MFR 04020025. Interview with Lyzbeth Glick by 9/11 Commission staffers. April 22, 2004[1]

On September 12, 2001, Lyzbeth Glick told the FBI that according to her husband the hijackers said that if they did not crash into the WTC, they were going to blow-up the plane. In the present interview with 9/11 Commission staffers, 30 months later, she denied her previous statement. She now claimed Jeremy only said that they threatened to blow-up the plane but did not mention any target. She also said that her husband did not tell her the hijackers had "urged" the passengers to call loved ones, only that they did not seem to care that passengers were on the phone.

(e) Pittsburgh Post-Gazette, September 13, 2001[2]

According to the *Post-Gazette*, Jeremy Glick used a "cell phone" in his call. This fact is contradicted by the FBI, which claims the call was made with an Airfone (see above). It is unknown on what base the *Post-Gazette* made this assertion. In that article, the authors claim that the "terrorists" had ordered "the pilots, flight attendants and passengers" to the rear of the plane. According to Mrs. Glick, her husband did not mention the pilots among those ordered to move to the rear of the plane.

According to the *Post-Gazette*, the FBI "monitored the last 20 minutes of the call and are studying a tape and transcript." If this report is correct, there should be, somewhere, a suppressed recording of this call.

(f) MSNBC, September 3, 2002

Lyz Glick: "I was a little bit, I think, surprised by the aura of what was going on on the plane. I was surprised by how calm it seemed in the background. I didn't hear any screaming. I didn't hear any noises. I didn't hear any commotion."[3]

(g) Concluding observations:

- The 9/11 Commission does not refer to the transcript of Makely's call or to a recording of Glick's call.

- Most media reports mention that Glick used a cell phone but this is denied by the FBI. What was the source of these media reports?

- Glick did not mention any act of violence committed on the plane.

---

1   MFR 04020025. April 22, 2004. Interview with Lyzbeth Glick

2   Charles Lane and John Mintz, "Calls tell of heroics on board flight 93," *Post-Gazette*, September 13, 2001, #703

3   "A story of heroism that inspired Americans in their darkest hours," MSNBC, September 3, 2002, #728

- Glick did not mention the presence of a "guarding hijacker." All of the "hijackers," according to him, were "in the cockpit," leaving the passengers by themselves.

- Glick repeatedly mentioned announcements by the "hijackers," but did not tell in what language they spoke, what accent they had, and what exactly they said. If they were Arabs, he would certainly have mentioned their accent or their difficulties in expressing themselves. In the first FBI interview, the "hijackers" were said to speak no English at all. In subsequent interviews, they are said to make various announcements. Did they learn English between the interviews?

- According to Jeremy (Lyz Glick's interview of September 12, 2001) the "hijackers" entered the cockpit a few minutes after his call started, that is after 9:40 a.m. According to the official account the cockpit was overtaken by the "hijackers" at 9:28 a.m. This discrepancy cannot be reconciled except by either dismissing Glick's reporting or the official timeline of flight UA93 as untrue.

(9) Lauren Grandcolas' Phone Calls

According to the FBI, Lauren Grandcolas, a passenger on flight UA93, made the following 6 telephone calls from an Airfone located in Row 23 DEF: [1]

At 9:39:21 Call to her residence lasting 46 seconds

At 9:40:42 Call to her residence lasting 9 seconds

At 9:41:34 Call to her residence lasting 4 seconds

At 9:42:03 Call to her residence lasting 2 seconds

At 9:42:25 Call to her residence lasting 3 seconds

At 9:42:45 Call to her residence lasting 3 seconds

(a) FBI document 302 638. Interview with Jack Grandcolas. September 11, 2001

Jack Grandcolas, Lauren's husband, said to the FBI interviewer that his wife called him twice during the morning of 9/11 and left messages on the answering machine. Jack said that he would play the messages for the agents. However, the messages were so personal in their substance, that he was extremely concerned about his own and his in-laws' privacy and did not want the recordings to be made public. He nevertheless proceeded and played both recordings.

According to Mr. Grandcolas, the first message was left by Lauren at approximately 4:30 a.m. Pacific Time (7:30 EST), that is prior to the boarding of UA93, while the second message was left at approximately 6:00 a.m. Pacific Time (9:00

---

1   Overview of phone calls: Introduction to Part III of this book

EST). In the agent's words: Lauren's second message indicated that there were *problems* on the flight but she reassured him that everything was alright. Her voice was very calm and there were no audible background noises. Lauren told Jack numerous times in the message that she loved him. Lauren also told Jack to advise her family that she loved them. In her second message there was no mention of a hijacking, any descriptive information about the hijackers or weapons used.

(b) FBI document IN 131 of September 14, 2001

On September 14, 2001, the FBI called Grandcolas' residence in order to speak again with Jack Grandcolas. Jim Grandcolas, Jack's brother, answered the phone and told the FBI that his brother, Jack, was "so emotional about the recent loss of his wife, [that] he did not want to speak to the FBI."

Shortly thereafter, the FBI special agent received a telephone call from Larry Catuzzi, Lauren's father. He said the message left by Lauren was so personal they did not want the FBI to record the message because it could possibly be released to the public if the case went to trial.

The special agent then reminded Catuzzi that a San Francisco Chronicle article published on September 12, 2001, had already cited Jack Grandcolas about the following message:

"We have been hijacked, they are being kind. I love you"

Catuzzi responded that the press had been pestering them and they had even to call the police. Therefore, Catuzzi had written a press release which Jack had read to the press on September 12. Catuzzi stated that in his press release Lauren was *not* cited as saying "we have been hijacked." Lauren did actually not mention anything about a hijacking in her message, Catuzzi said. The same message was publicized ten days later by the *Post-Gazette*: "We have been hijacked" [Grancolas] told her husband Jack. "They are being kind. I love you."[1] Who was telling the truth?

(c) FBI document OUT-2969, April 24, 2002

On April 24, 2002, FBI Counterterrorism sent a *request* to FBI San Francisco to obtain a copy of the digital answering machine messages left by Lauren Grandcolas on 9/11 and the AT&T bill for her cellular telephone.

In justifying the request, FBI Counterterrorism advised that:

a review of the GTE Airfone record for UA93 on 9/11 revealed five telephone calls [that] were placed from GTE Airfone to telephone number [redacted], which is the Grandcolas residence telephone and one call was placed to

---

1   Sharon Cohen, "A September morning, four flights, a collision course with tragedy," *Associated Press*, September 12, 2001, #694

number (415) [redacted], which is subscribed to by Global Workplace, San Rafael, CA. Global Workplace is believed to be the home-based business of Jack Grandcolas....

(d) MSNBC, September 2002

In a September 2002 interview with MSNBC, Jack Grandcolas confirmed that Lauren sounded very calm: "She might have been calling from a supermarket."[1]

(e) Discussion

According to the overview of phone calls from the aircraft, presented at the Moussaoui trial (as mentioned above), six (6)—not five—phone calls were attributed to Lauren Grandcolas, only two of which were probably long enough to leave a message. It is noteworthy, too, that on April 2002, as reflected in the aforementioned FBI document, Lauren's calls were still considered by the FBI to have been possibly made with a cell phone. Yet, on September 18, 2001, the FBI had already received from GTE a detailed list of all calls made from UA93. Why was the FBI on 2002 still equivocating?

Lauren Grandcolas did not report a hijacking and did not describe any violent acts on the plane. By stating that "they are being kind," as cited above, she must have mentioned to him to whom the word "they" refers. That "they" were kind and did not appear threatening is corroborated by Lauren's calm voice, reported by her husband. Her message thus contradicts completely the sinister impression other calls flight UA93 were supposed to leave with listeners.

A further anomaly is the listing by the FBI of six phone calls allegedly made by Lauren from the aircraft. Yet none of these calls was made at 9:00 a.m. (EST), the time at which her message was left on the answering machine. That call, however, was not mentioned by the FBI on its listing. In her phone message, allegedly left at approximately 9:00 a.m., i.e. half an hour *before* the alleged hijacking began, Lauren reportedly mentioned "problems" on the plane. What problems aboard the airplane prompted her to call home? As the 46-second message left by Lauren on the answering machine remains suppressed, the public is prevented from knowing who were these "kind" people to whom Lauren referred and what "problems" occurred aboard flight UA93 before the "hijacking" began.

(10) Linda Gronlund's Phone Call

According to the FBI, Linda Gronlund, a passenger aboard flight UA93, made one telephone call from an Airfone at 9:46:05, lasting 71 seconds.[2]

---

1 "A story of heroism...," Op. cit., #728
2 Overview of phone calls: Introduction to Part III of this book

(a) FBI document 302 4080. Interview with Elsa Strong. September 11, 2001

On September 11, 2001, Elsa Strong was interviewed in her home by an unidentified FBI agent around 7:30 p.m. regarding her sister, Linda Gronlund.

Elsa Strong advised that her sister Linda was aboard flight UA93. She said she was aware that Linda was flying on that aircraft. She talked to her sister prior to take-off. Linda told Elsa she had her cell phone with her, but that it had a low charge and could be reached through the cell phone of her boyfriend Joseph DeLucca, who was accompanying her on the flight.

Elsa said she had been away from home during the earlier part of the morning and returned at approximately 10:30-10:45 a.m. At that time, she checked her telephone answering machine. The first message was from her mother asking if she had heard anything about the events in New York. The second recorded message was from her sister aboard UA93.

The recorded message from her sister, Linda, which was stamped at 9:51 a.m., lasted less than one minute (Note that according to the FBI, the call was made at 9:46:05 and lasted slightly over one minute). According to the message the aircraft was being hijacked by terrorists and that they had a bomb. Linda further expressed the feeling that they were about to die. The rest of the message was of a personal nature, relating how much she loves them and where they could find her personal papers in a safe at her home and indicated the combination to the safe. She then quickly ended the call.

Elsa Strong then furnished the interviewing agent with a micro-cassette from their answering machine. She advised that she and her husband, Tom, had listened twice to the tape, and that even though the tape was three years old and used daily, it was in good condition. The agent then checked the current time on the answering machine and noted that it was approximately three minutes fast, showing 7:50 p.m. compared to 7:47 p.m. on his watch.

(b) FBI document 302 4082. Interview with Elsa Strong. September 11, 2001

A second report covering the *same* interview with Elsa Strong was compiled by an unidentified "writer" (as distinct from "special agent"). In that report the "writer" stated that he/she contacted Elsa Strong telephonically at approximately 6:45 p.m. on September 11, 2001. During that conversation Elsa Strong provided the "writer" brief information about her sister's call and advised that she would make the recorded message on the cassette tape available to the FBI. At approximately 7:30 p.m. the "writer" interviewed Strong in reference to this matter—probably at Strong's residence—and "received [*sic*] the cassette tape recording from her answering machine. This tape was then transported by the writer directly to the FBI Office in Boston, Mass., and turned it over to Assistant Special Agent in Charge James D. Burkett at approximately 9:20 p.m."

(c) FBI document 302 25851. Interview with Elsa Strong. September 14, 2001

On September 14, 2001, Elsa Strong was again interviewed—at that time telephonically—by an FBI agent. She gave the agent detailed personal information about her sister Linda . She told the agent that she had spoken to another FBI agent [unidentified] from the Boston Office on the day of the crash. That agent had come to Strong's residence and taken the cassette tape from her answering machine. Otherwise, she confirmed what she had told the FBI on 9/11.

(d) MFR 04020023. Conference call by 9/11 Commission staffers with Elsa Strong. April 22, 2004[1]

Elsa Strong said that she did not talk to her sister on UA93. What she knew was based on a message she found on her answering machine. She said the information provided to the FBI by Dicki and Robert Macy was partly incorrect. She said she did NOT tell Dicki Macy that Gronlund had stated "the terrorists repeated that they were all to be killed and that the pilot had redirected the plane. The terrorists told them that the plane was going to the White House." Ms. Strong stated that no such information was provided by Ms. Gronlund. What was on the tape is all the information that was communicated. A transcript of Linda's message was later released (see below).

(e) RFBI 04020619. Transcript of Linda Gronlund's message left on Elsa Strong's answering machine

Elsa, it's Lynn.

Um.

I have only a minute. I'm on United 93 and it's been hijacked, uh, by terrorists who say they have a bomb. Apparently, they, uh, flown a couple of planes into the World Trade Center already and it looks like they're going to take this one down as well.

Mostly, I just wanted to say I love you..and...I'm going to miss you...and... and

Please give my love to Mom and Dad, and

(sigh)

Mostly, I just love you and I just wanted to tell you that,

I don't know if I'm going to get the chance to tell you that again or not.

(sigh)

Um...

(unintelligible)

All my stuff is in the safe. The uh, the safe is in my closet in my bedroom. The combination is: you push C for clear and then 0-9-1-3 and then, uh, and then it should...and maybe pound and then it should unlock.

(sigh)

I love you and I hope that I can talk to you soon.

Bye.

(f) Discussion

Joseph DeLuca and Linda Gronlund had seats 2B and 2D. They thus were supposed to sit between three "hijackers." Yet, it is surprising that Gronlund does not make any attempt to describe them, let alone any violent acts they committed or weapons that they might have held. She reported that they "say they have a bomb," yet does not mention their supposedly foreign accent or their words. She does not either mention the number of "hijackers." The term "hijacking" in her message thus remains an abstraction not supported by actual observations.

The absence of any concrete observation by Linda Gronlund suggests that she was not reporting actual events. It defies credulity that a person experiencing a real and immediate threat would fail to relate what actually happens and instead engage in a personal, intimate, talk, as reflected in the above transcription.

(11) CeeCee Lyles' Phone Calls

According to the FBI, CeeCee Lyles, a flight attendant on flight UA93, made two telephone calls from flight UA93: [1]

At 9:47:57 an Airfone call from Row 32 ABC lasting 56 seconds.

At 9:58:99 a cell phone call with undetermined duration.

---

1 Overview of phone calls: Introduction to Part III of this book

(a) Call 1

The first call, made from an Airfone on 9:47:57, was recorded on her husband Lorne's answering machine and later released to the public. It can be listened to on the internet.[1] Here is a transcript of this short message:

> Hi Baby. You have to listen to me carefully. I'm on the plane that's being hi-jacked. I'm on the plane. I'm calling from the plane. I want to tell you I love you. Please tell my children that I love them very much, and...I'm so sorry, babe. Um...I don't know what to say. There's three guys. They've hijacked the plane. I'm trying to be calm. We're turned around and I've heard that there's planes that's been, been flown into the World Trade Center. I hope to be able to [with a sobbing voice] see your face again, baby. I love you. Goodbye.

Keen listeners say they are able to discern in the background, at the end of CeeCee's call, someone whispering to her, "You did great!"[2] This has led to speculation regarding the nature of this remark, implying that she put up an act and was commended for it. I have not been able to distinguish this sentence on the recording.

(b) Call 2

On September 12, 2001, an unidentified FBI agent interviewed CeeCee Lyles' husband Lorne[3].

Lorne told the agent that he received a call from CeeCee at 9:58 a.m. made on her cell phone. He was in a deep sleep at the time when the phone woke him up. He said he saw CeeCee's cell phone number on the caller ID. He related the conversation as follows:

> LL: Hey Baby. How you doing?
>
> CCL: Babe, my plane is being hijacked, my plane is being hijacked.
>
> CCL: Babe, they are forcing their way into the cockpit.
>
> CCL: They forced their way into the cockpit.

Lorne commented that the she spoke in the past tense, indicating that the hijackers had already made their way into the cockpit. He recalled the following statements:

> CCL: Babe, I called to tell you I love you, tell the kids that I love them.

---

1   The audio version of CeeCee Lyles call was extracted from Exhibit P200055 of the Moussaoui Trial. This Exhibit is no more available on the original site. The recording of CeeCee Lyles's call is widely posted on Youtube.

2   Paul Zarembka, "Critique of David Ray Griffin regarding Calls from 9-11 Planes," *ITHP (International Human Press)*, October 14, 2011, #1003

3   FBI TP-0026 (later designated as FBI TP-419). September 12, 2001.

CCL: Oh Lord, it feels like the plane is going down.

Thereafter, Lorne heard screaming in the background and the phone went dead. He did not hear anyone giving commands.

(c) FBI documents 302 96092 and 302 108562

These two documents, included in a 9/11 Commission staff folder dedicated to CeeCee Lyles, are completely redacted.[1] It is not known why.

(d) Discussion

It should be noted that CeeCee Lyles does not mention any violent action, statements made by the "hijackers" or a description of the "hijackers." She does not mention seeing or being informed of any stabbing, dead passengers or injured crew members. She does not either mention passengers being moved to the back. She does not mention participating in a counter-attack or in helping wounded passengers. In reporting that the plane was hijacked, her testimony remains abstract, failing to indicate any specific action that would reflect the hijacking.

In the light of all the aforementioned omissions, it is not far-fetched to suspect that her sobbing, heard on her publicly released phone call, was acted. This may have elicited the soft observation, "You did great!" discerned by some listeners.

The redaction by the FBI of two documents relative to CeeCee Lyles' call does not allay doubts about the purpose of her calls.

(12) Honor *Elizabeth* Wainio's Phone Call

According to the FBI, Honor *Elizabeth* Wainio, a passenger aboard flight UA93, made a single telephone call from an Airfone located in Row 33 ABC at 9:53:43, lasting 269 seconds. [2]

(a) FBI document IN-28689

On September 12, 2001, the Washington Field Office (WFO) of the FBI received information from the San Francisco Field Office regarding telephone calls from flights UA93 and UA175. This prompted WFO agents to contact Benn Wainio and his wife Esther Heymann. Heymann advised that she received a call from her step-daughter Elizabeth Wainio aboard flight UA93 at approximately 10:00 a.m. on September 11, 2001. After that call she immediately called emergency (911). Shortly thereafter, she was interviewed by FBI special agent [redacted] and special agent [redacted] from the Baltimore Field Office.

---

1   9/11 Commission documents. Team 7, Box 12. Flight 93—CeeCee Lyles. #1781
2   Overview of phone calls: Introduction to Part III of this book

(b) FBI document 302 84596. Interview with Esther Heymann. September 12, 2001

On September 12, 2001, FBI special agents interviewed Esther Heymann by telephone regarding a phone call she received from her step-daughter Elizabeth Wainio.

Heymann advised that she received the phone call at approximately 10:00 a.m. on the morning of September 11, 2001. Wainio said that the flight had been hijacked. After several minutes of personal conversation regarding her fate, Elizabeth told Heymann "they're going into the cockpit." Immediately thereafter, the telephone call terminated.

According to Heymann, Elizabeth did not provide any other pertinent information regarding the hijackers.

(c) Jere Longman's account

In Jere Longman's book ("Among the Heroes"), he devotes some space to Elizabeth Wainio's conversation with her step-mother, based on his interview with her. According to Heymann, Lauren Grandcolas had "handed her [cell] phone to [Elizabeth] and told her to call her family. Her stepmother said that Elizabeth had spoken calmly, but her breathing was shallow, as if she were hyperventilating."(Longman, 236)

According to Longman, Elizabeth's conversation with her step-mother lasted 11 minutes [the FBI claims the call lasted 269 seconds, or approximately 4 1/2 minutes]. Longman's account, however, accords with what Esther Heymann had earlier reported to the FBI, namely that most of her conversation with Elizabeth was of a private nature. Elizabeth did not provide any useful information about what was going on in the aircraft.

(d) Discussion

From the above accounts it is clear that Elizabeth Wainio did not report events taking place on an aircraft. Her statements remained at the level of abstraction, suggesting that she was not reporting real events.

The discrepancy in the call's duration appears also far too great to result from a mistaken estimate by Esther Heymann.

According to an FBI report of April 24, 2002,[1] Grandcolas' cell phone "is believed" to have been used by ElizabethWainio. Were she using a cell phone at 9:53, as believed by the FBI, a successful call would have been improbable, as the aircraft was still flying—according to the official account—at approximately

---

1   FBI OUT-2969. April 24, 2002.

11,000 feet.[1] If she made her call from a cell phone, it was done from an aircraft flying at lower altitude or from the ground. In its overview of phone calls, the FBI listed Wainio's phone call as having been made with an Airfone. It is surprising, to say the least, that on April 24, 2002, the FBI was still uncertain from which type of phone Wainio's call had been made.

Finally, it is inconceivable that while a counter-attack was proceeding aboard the aircraft, Elizabeth would not mention anything about it.

(13) Unidentified Callers

According to the FBI, an unidentified flight attendant made four Airfone calls from flight UA93, one from Row 33 and three from Row 34 to United Airlines System Aircraft Maintenance Control (SAMC), through the so-called Star Fix system:[2]

At 9:31:14	2 seconds
At 9:32:29	95 seconds
At 9:35:48	4 seconds
At 9:35:56	4 seconds

(a) FBI document 302 1880. Interview with Andrew Lubkemann at SAMC. September 11, 2001

Andy Lubkemann was interviewed by FBI agents at his place of employment, United Airlines, San Francisco International Airport. He said he received on 9/11, "shortly after 6:00 [9:00 EST]" a call on the STARFIX phone system from a female flight attendant of UA93, aircraft 5491. She said the plane "had been hijacked." Lubkemann gave the FBI agents the following written statement:

> "While answering calls from the STARFIX station, I was contacted by a female flight attendant. She spoke to me in a hurried and scared voice. I was informed that she was on Flight 93, Aircraft 5491. She said that the plane was being hi-jacked. The hi-jackers were in the cabin and Flight deck. I informed her that we had run into similar problems and were aware of the situation. I told her to remain on the line and I was going to transfer her call directly to my shift manager...We [...] were able to contact a manager who then came to the STARFIX table. He took over the call to Flight 93. All specific information regarding where the hi-jackers were on the aircraft and how the aircraft was flying, were then taken."

The report then adds that Richard Belme was the manager who had taken over the phone call from the flight attendant of UAL Flight 93. Information "was received that everyone was removed from first class seating and that the hijack-

---

1   UA93 Flight Path Study, *NTSB*, February 19, 2002, #126
2   Overview of phone calls: Introduction to Part III of this book

ers had knives and were in the cockpit." Lubkemann had no further identifiable information of weapons used. Note that Lubkemann did not mention in his *written* statement the allegation that "everyone was removed from first class seating" and that the hijackers "had knives."

(b) FBI document 302 1888. Interview with unidentified operator at SAMC, most probably Richard Belme. September 11, 2001

An unidentified person was interviewed at his place of employment, United Airlines, San Francisco. He provided the following information:

> On the same morning, at approximately 6:40 (Pacific time), an UAL System Aircraft Maintenance Controller took control of a phone call by an unidentified female flight attendant of UAL flight 93 initially received by [redacted]. [Redacted] was on the phone with the attendant for only a couple of minutes. The female flight attendant said that two male hijackers who had knives were on board, one of which was in the first class section of the plane and the other was possibly in the cockpit. The first class section was secured, no passengers were able to leave or gain entrance to the first class seating area.

The interviewed person provided a hand written statement that did not mention the last sentence—that first class section "was secured"—but added the following comments:

"One man [on the plane] attacked a flight attendant but no passengers or crew were hurt."

"I asked the condition of the aircraft, she said a few dives but OK. Then I lost contact."

Note also that the time given by Belme for the call (approximately 6:40 Pacific) is significantly later than that provided by Lubkemann (shortly after 6:00 Pacific). Belme did not apparently disclose to the FBI agent that this was his last working day at United Airlines before leaving for a new job. This fact was revealed only ten years later in a CNN interview.[3]

(c) MFR 04017218. Interview with Andrew Lubkemann, SAMC, by staffers of the 9/11 Commission. November 21, 2003[4]

Lubkemann [whose name is redacted in the released document] began working as a Star-Fix operator for United Airlines SAMC less than two weeks before 9/11 (a fact he did not mention to the FBI in his interview). On the morning of 9/11, he was still in training. He came in for the day shift shortly before 6:00 a.m. (Pacific Time). At that point Marc Policastro got a very short call from flight UA175. Policastro "just listened to the caller and didn't say anything. Then he

---

3   "The footnotes of 9/11," *CNN*, September 11, 2011- 21:00 ET, #885
4   MFR 04017218. November 21, 2003. Interview with Andrew Lubkemann

took the headset off and said, "That flight was hijacked." Lubkemann asked him if it was a joke but Policastro said, "No, it's for real." His impression was that the call received by Policastro from the flight UA175 was "very short." He was not able to really say anything to the flight atttendant. It was like "good morning."

After receiving two or three subsequent calls, Lubkemann received a call from a flight attendant on UAL 93. He said he did not remember whether the flight attendant identified herself. He could, however, hear the apprehension in her voice but was impressed with how professional she carried herself on the phone. She was not hysterical by any means. She reported to him that the plane "was being" hijacked. To the best of his recollections, she told him the hijackers were in the cabin and the flight deck. Lubkemann said that he knew at the time his call was from a different plane than Policastro's caller. He thinks the call he received from Flight 93 took place "before the second aircraft hit." His notes weren't that detailed. He said his notes with the flight number and aircraft number ended up in the trash somewhere and he reported that he hasn't spoken to anyone about this since 9/11.

Lubkemann recalled that his portion of the call lasted a minute or two before he handed the phone off to the supervisor (Richard Belme). He listened in for part of the call once the supervisor took over. After that, United management personnel separated him and Policastro from the other staff members until the crisis was over and told them not to speak to anyone. At that time he prepared his written statement about the call.

(d) FBI document 302 20230. Interview with Dee Ann Freeman. September 11, 2001[1]

Dee Ann Freeman, employed by Continental Airlines Reservations, was at work at approximately 3:15 p.m. when she received a telephone call from Javis Johnson, an African-American customer who was scheduled to take a Continental flight from Chicago to Cleveland. She said: "He was upset, alternatively crying and screaming, and had called to discuss canceling his flight plans as a consequence of his fears about flying in the wake of what had happened to his best friend that day aboard flight UA93 which had crashed." Freeman spoke with Johnson approximately half an hour.

Johnson (the caller) said he was a Northwest flight attendant and told Freeman that he had received a cell phone call from his best friend, a male flight attendant on UA93 who told Johnson to "[t]ake care of my wife and kids. I'm a dead man. We're being hijacked." The conversation was then cut off. Johnson tried to call his friend back but the line was busy.

---

1   FBI 302-20230. September 11, 2001. Interview with Dee Ann Freeman

Johnson said he called the friend's wife after the flight crashed and was told by her that she had previously spoken with her attendant husband. He told her that the Captain and in-flight crew had been gathered in the back of the plane, where the Captain was held by a hijacker with a blade to his neck. She told Johnson that they said they were going to Camp David. They threatened to cut the Captain's throat with a box cutter if the crew attempted to intervene.

Johnson added "that UA93 had changed the flight plan from Los Angeles to Washington, D.C. just before the crash." He said "that another of the in-flight attendants was a woman who was married to a police officer. She called her husband during the hijacking and was told by him of the Trade Center plane crashes, so the captain and flight crew had knowledge that they might face a similar end."

Freeman told the FBI interviewers that identifying information concerning Johnson might be available on the computer system at Continental Airlines Reservations in Salt Lake City, Utah. Accordingly, Freeman and the interviewers drove together to her place of work in the vicinity of the Salt Lake City airport, where they arrived at approximately 11:58 p.m. With the assistance of Gene Savard, Operation Analyst, who was the supervisor on duty, Freeman looked up and found the manifest information contained in the Continental Airlines Reservation system concerning Johnson. Savard printed out a copy of the computer data concerning Johnson and provided it to the interviewers. The printout identifies Johnson's e-mail address as [....] and indicates that he made the reservation over the internet using a Discover Card, card number [....]. There is a September 11 notation entered by Freeman as a consequence of her conversation with Johnson.

On the FBI report, someone—possibly a staffer of the 9/11 Commission—wrote with a marking pen: "Bogus call." Yet the caller apparently knew far too much for what, under the circumstances, he could have known. The call was made when most of the information he provided was not yet in the public domain. Some of the information he provided contradicted the official account.

There was no male flight attendant on UA93. Yet, he said he talked to the wife of that flight attendant who said she had talked to her husband on the plane. Who was that woman? Other information he provided applied, indeed, to flight UA93.

No caller from UA93 said that the Captain was held in the back of the plane.

He reported that a flight plane change was made by UA93 shortly before the crash. This was true, but how could he have known that fact?

CeeCee Lyles, a flight attendant on UA93, was indeed married to a policeman. From that account, the following conclusions can be tentatively made:

- Johnson must have been an "insider" by virtue of the facts he related

- The story included sinister elements that were not included in other calls.

- The story contradicted the official account.

How can this call be explained? One possibility is that the call was staged to reinforce the legend of UA93 but was, in the end, suppressed as too difficult to reconcile with other stories.

In notes by John Raidt, a member of 9/11 Commission's staff, who reviewed the phone calls, we found the following comments regarding the above call:

> We need to determine if the FBI interviewed [the caller] or the flight attendant's wife; who was the flight attendant; we need to reconcile this story of the pilot being held in the back.

The notes were included in the documents of the Commission released to NARA in 2009. There is no indication that Raidt's observations were followed-up. Doing so might have opened a can of worms.

Chapter 11. Reporting Bogus Events From Aircraft

In this chapter we synthesize the detailed analyses of the phone calls found in chapters 7 to 10. Readers who wish to check the sources are invited to consult these chapters.

(1) Inexplicable omissions

(a) No one witnessed cockpit entry by "hijackers"

The 9/11 Commission noted in its Final Report: "We do not know exactly how the hijackers gained access to the cockpit."[1] It should be recalled that in each of the four aircraft, passengers sat in close proximity to the cockpit and could observe all movements to and from the cockpit. Some of these First Class passengers made phone calls but even they did not mention how the "hijackers" entered the cockpit. That no passenger and no flight attendant witnessed anyone enter the cockpit is inconceivable. It suggests that no "hijacker" had entered the cockpit and certainly not by violent means.

(b) Most callers did not describe the "hijackers"

Most phone callers failed to describe the alleged hijackers. The fact that four flight attendants who made phone calls to the ground—Ong (AA11), Fangman (UA175), May (AA77) and Lyles (UA93)—did not describe the "hijackers" is even more surprising, for it is actually their duty to report as thoroughly as pos-

---

1   9/11 Commission Final Report, p. 5. Note the qualifier "exactly," deceptively implying that the 9/11 Commission knew how the hijackers gained access to the cockpit.

sible incidents occurring on board. This would include at least a summary description of those who act violently. These flight attendants displayed moreover no apparent curiosity to find out who the "hijackers" were.

Betty Ong (AA11) and Mark Bingham (UA93) repeatedly avoided to answer a direct question "Who are they?"

Tom Burnett called four times his wife, yet he never described the "hijackers." Joseph DeLuca and Linda Gronlund were traveling together on flight UA93 in First Class. They had seats 2A and 2B, sandwiched between three "hijackers" (seats 1B, 3C and 3D). Both of them made phone calls, yet neither of them described these "hijackers."

(c) No mention of foreign accent or what the "hijackers" said

Numerous callers said that the alleged hijackers had made some kind of announcement (see individual accounts). It was reported that the "hijackers" *said* to have a bomb, *threatened* to blow-up the aircraft or *ordered* the passengers to move to the rear of the plane. All these verbs imply that *they* said something. Yet no caller quoted what *they* had actually said or mentioned their presumably Arab accent. Jeremy Glick (UA93) said to his wife that "the hijackers had herded the passengers into the rear of the plane and *told them* that if they did not crash into the World Trade Center, that they were going to blow-up the plane," yet he equally said to his wife that they "did not speak English." Did the "hijackers" announce their murderous plans in Arabic?

According to Lee Hanson, his son Peter (flight 175) claimed to have "overheard" the alleged hijackers "talking about eight planes being hijacked." Did Peter understand Arabic, or did they speak among themselves in English, so that the passengers could overhear their plans? (the other callers from flight UA175, incidentally, did not mention to have overheard anything).

Saying that the "hijackers" made announcements or gave orders to the passengers would have invariably revealed their foreign accent, had they been "Arab," as officially claimed. The fact that none of the callers mentioned their foreign accent suggests that no such announcements were made or that the announcers were no Arabs.

(d) Most flight attendants didn't bother to contact the pilots

When an incident occurs aboard an aircraft, flight attendants must immediately contact the pilot, for he carries the primary responsibility for the safety of the plane and its passengers.

Except for the flight attendants aboard flight AA11, no other flight attendant mentioned attempts to contact the pilots and report to them the hijackings. This omission by most flight attendants would be inconceivable in a real hijacking situation. It would only be plausible if no hijackings had taken place.

(e) No one observed the stabbing of Mark Rothenberg (UA93)

Some of the callers said that one passenger and two flight attendants on flight UA93 had been stabbed and even killed on flight UA93. Yet none of the callers actually said to have personally observed the stabbing or any other violent act committed by the alleged hijackers. Tom Burnett told his wife Deena in his first call at 9:27 that "they already knifed a guy" (not explaining who "they" were). Burnett's seat number was 4B. As all four "hijackers" had booked seats in First Class and all male First Class passengers made phone calls, the knifed guy could only have been Mark Rothenberg (seat 5B). Yet, none of the other callers from First Class (Mark Bingham, 4D; Joseph DeLuca, 2B; Edward Felt, 2D; and Linda Gronlund, 2A) mentioned this stabbing and apparently no one was warning the cockpit that someone had been stabbed. It is thus most probable that Tom Burnett did not report a real event. The same reasoning applies to other callers who claimed that a passenger or a flight attendant had been stabbed. Surprisingly, Glick (UA93), who had a long conversation with his wife, did not mention any violent activity aboard the aircraft. CeeCee Lyles, flight attendant on UA93, made her first call only at 9:47 and left a message, the contents of which have been publicly released. In that crucial message she did not either mention any act of violence, let alone that the pilots were lying, injured or dead, in the front of First Class, as some callers claimed.

(f) Nobody saw the killing of Daniel Lewin (AA11)

According to the calls made by Betty Ong and Madeline Sweeney from flight AA11, a former officer in an elite unit of the Israeli army, Daniel Lewin, was fatally slashed on that flight. It is speculated that the "hijackers" attacked him because he allegedly tried to interfere with their attempt to enter the cockpit. If this had been the case, he would not have been attacked by surprise but as a reaction to his initiative to prevent the "hijackers" from entering the cockpit or from attacking a flight attendant. This would have meant that he would have been prepared to defend himself, causing widespread awareness of the struggle and prompting attempts by others to come to his help. As this did not happen, the only alternative to the attack story is that he was caught by surprise. But this, in turn, would not make any sense from a tactical point of view. What could be the point of the attackers to slash the throat of a passenger at random? Such attack would only awaken the resolve of passengers to fight back. In any case, no passenger, including those sitting near him, is known to have witnessed the attack on Lewin. According to flight attendant Ong, passengers believed that a "medical emergency" had occurred in the plane.

Reporting a bogus attack on Daniel Lewin could, however, make sense from a propagandistic perspective. By claiming that he—an Israeli Jew—was attacked, the anti-Jewish slant of the alleged attackers could be "proved" and by claiming that they "slashed his throat," their ruthless nature would be further highlighted.

(g) Nobody saw the stabbing of a flight attendant

Madeline Sweeney (AA11) reported to Michael Woodward that a flight attendant had been "stabbed in the neck." She must, therefore, have been near the action. How could she observe such a violent action that no one else apparently noticed? Ong said in her long phone call that passengers believed the crisis to be a medical emergency. How could they entertain such a belief if someone, let alone a flight attendant, had been stabbed? Whoever was aware of this crime, and particularly flight attendants, would reasonably warn all passengers to be on their guard. To withhold that information from the passengers would have been criminally irresponsible. If passengers weren't aware of these incidents, it is highly likely that Sweeney did not report a real event.

An example of disinformation regarding the events "in the aircraft" is revealed in an article of the *Boston Herald*. In its third edition of September 12, 2001, an unidentified source is quoted to the effect that the terrorists "started killing stewardesses in the back of the plane as a diversion. The pilot came back to help and that is how they got into the cockpit."[1]

(h) No violence reported on flight AA77

One flight attendant (Renee May) and one passenger (Barbara Olson) made in total three calls from flight AA77. Both of them said the aircraft had been hijacked, yet neither of them reported any threat or use of violence aboard the aircraft. Neither explained in their calls how the alleged hijackers executed their "hijacking." Was such omission conceivable?

(i) Nobody saw how the pilots were overpowered

Madeline Sweeney (AA11) said in her call that "three men were in the cockpit and in control of the plane." As no pilot would voluntarily relinquish control over passenger aircraft to a stranger, it follows that that the "terrorists" must have removed the pilots by force from their seats. This could not, however, have happened without great violence and without risking to dislodge flight instruments' settings and endangering the flight. That the alleged removal of the pilots and

---

1   Ed Hayward, Tom Farmer and Cosmo Macero, Jr., "Attack on America: Suspects ID's in terror strikes," *Boston Globe*, September 12, 2001 (3d edition), #162

co-pilots of flight AA11 (and the other three flights) had occurred without hitch and without anyone noticing, is inconceivable, even if the door of the cockpit was locked. One must not forget that the "hijackers" had to simultaneously over-power two people in the cockpit. No one, and least of all the 9/11 Commission, has yet proposed a plausible scenario that could explain how the cockpits of these four airliners were or could have been overtaken.

(j) No impact sound was heard at the end of calls

In the end of Beamer's, Felt's and Glick's calls from flight UA93, the line re-mained open but no listener heard any impact sound of the aircraft crash. Some listeners said they heard something resembling a wind sound at the end of the call. This suggests that the aircraft did not crash, or that the calls were not made from an aircraft.

(k) Flight attendants on flight AA11 didn't mention the radical turn of the aircraft

According to the official account, flight AA11 made a "dramatic turn to the south," i.e. diverged radically from its planned route, between 8:26 and 8:28 a.m. Neither Betty Ong nor Madeline Sweeney, both veteran flight attendants who used to fly this route, reported, however, this turn. This suggests that no such turn was made by that aircraft towards New York City.

(l) The only pilot among UA93 passengers wasn't mentioned

One of the passengers of flight UA93 was Donald F. Greene, an experienced pilot.[1] Despite his being aboard, none of the callers mentioned his presence on the plane, as one who could take over the plane if the alleged hijackers were overruled. He was not mentioned by any caller and did not, himself, make any phone call. This suggests that there was no reason for him to make a call and to volunteer to pilot the plane.

(2) Reports which didn't make sense

(a) Mace or pepper-spray that affects only one person

Betty Ong (flight AA11) repeatedly mentioned mace or pepper spray and complained about breathing difficulties, but at the same time claimed that the passengers were not aware of the hijacking. Her colleague Madeline ("Amy") Sweeney from the same flight did not mention in her 13-minute call any mace or pepper-spray in the air. How could these two testimonies be reconciled? If mace

---

1   Obituary of Donald F. Greene, *Remember September 11, 2001 website*, #1007

or pepper-spray had been spread in First Class, the alleged hijackers would also have had difficulty to breathe and carry out their murderous tasks.

(b) The pilot of AA77 was allegedly aware of the "hijacking" but did not bother to report it to the ground

According to Ted Olson, the husband of AA77 passenger Barbara Olson, his wife told him that the "pilot had announced that the plane had been hijacked." She actually asked her husband what she should tell the pilot, a rather surprising question. Assuming that Barbara actually made this statement and asked that question in her call, this would mean either that the pilot made the above announcement, thereby raising the question why he did not squawk the hijack code, as required; or that she was told by "someone" to make this statement, regardless of the facts. In that case, her statement would have been deliberately deceptive. Barbara's message is, actually, one of the most significant statements made by any of the callers: However her statement is looked upon, it undermines the official legend of the hijacking.

(c) Red bandanas to represent Islam?

According to *some* callers from flight UA93, the "hijackers" put on red bandanas. Did they need bandanas in order to carry out their murderous tasks? Or were they trying to appear as Muslims, forgetting that Al Qaeda operatives are considered Sunni Islamists, whose color is green. Someone thought that the more the better, so a bandana, unscathed, was conveniently found at the alleged crash site of flight UA93 at Somerset County. It emerged in mint condition at the trial of Zacarias Moussaoui.[1] This bandana was, incidentally, just one item among a long list of personal objects and documents said to have been found in perfect condition at the crash site, where no aircraft wreckage, bodies or blood were sighted (see chapter 4).

(d) "We may have crossed the Mississippi"

According to the first FBI interview with Sandra Bradshaw's (UA93) father, she said to him that she thought the plane might be around the Mississippi river because they had *just* passed over a river. If she could notice a river from cruising altitude, it was certainly a large one, suggesting that she might have guessed correctly. It could, however, also have been the Ohio River. In both cases, this observation would have meant that the aircraft did not crash at Somerset County. As reported in chapter 6, flight UA93 did not crash at Somerset County, but flew west past the Ohio River and was identified in the vicinity of Toledo and Fort Wayne.

---

1   Trial of Zacarias Moussaoui, Prosecution Trial Exhibit PA00111. #1782

(e) *"We will crash in 20 seconds"*

In her call, starting at 9:49, Marion Britton (flight UA93) said to her friend Fred that the plane "will crash in 20 seconds." According to the FBI, her call lasted 232 seconds, i.e. nearly four minutes, but she apparently did not find the time to explain why the plane would crash, did not describe the alleged hijackers, how many they were, what weapons they held, who was flying the aircraft, what the plane's destination was, or what other passengers were doing. Her call took place before any "counter-attack" had allegedly started. According to the official timeline of flight UA93, the aircraft was still at 18,000 feet when her call started and was descending at approximately 20 feet a second, which at 500 mph represents a very mild descent. She also gave to her Fred a cellphone number from which she said she was calling, expecting him to call back. But when he immediately tried to call that number, he got a message that the phone was not in service. All of that suggests that her report was fictitious.

(f) *Peter Hanson: "They intend to fly into buildings"*

Peter Hanson (flight UA175) said that the "hijackers" announced their intent to "fly into a building." Why would hijackers announce such an intent, which would do nothing but alert the passengers to their doom and prompt them to rise up? And did they make this announcement in English, so Peter could hear and understand? If so, why did no other passenger or flight attendant mention this announcement in their call? Or did Peter Hanson understand Arabic and was sufficiently near these murderous hijackers to overhear their private conversation? Or was Peter asked to tell this story in order to buttress the official legend of "Muslim hijackers flying into buildings"?

(g) *Only three hijackers were reported by UA93 callers*

The 9/11 Commission acknowledges that all callers from flight UA93 reported only three "hijackers." According to the official account, they were four. The Commission suggested the following explanation why the fourth "hijacker" was not seen by anyone:

> We found no evidence indicating that one of the hijackers, or anyone else, sat [in the cockpit] on this flight...We believe it is more likely that Jarrah, the crucial pilot-trained member of their team, remained seated and inconspicuous until after the cockpit was seized; and once inside, he would not have been visible to the passengers (Final Report, 12).

This explanation begs two questions: (1) Why did no one observe "suicide-pilot" Ziad Jarrah entering the cockpit? (2) What was the purpose of his publicized combat training in a US gym,[1] if it was not his role to subdue the pilots?

We suggest tentative answers to these questions: (1) No one saw Jarrah enter the cockpit because he never boarded the aircraft (see chapter 2). (2) Jarrah's combat training—assuming that it was he and not his double[2] who did the training—was later publicized with great flourishes[3] in order to promote the legend of hijackers preparing for deadly combat. But the real Ziad Jarrah obviously did not prepare to die on 9/11: On August 29, 2001, he got himself a Virginia driver's license. And on the following day he booked a ticket for September 11, 2001, on flight UA93 to San Francisco with a connecting flight on flight UAL 2301 to the Sin City, Las Vegas.[4]

(3) Puzzling conduct reported

(a) Callers reported murder with a calm voice[5]

Numerous recipients and listeners of phone calls noted the calmness of most callers. Some recipients found such serenity puzzling, or even shocking, considering the murderous events described by the callers:

Betty Ong (AA11)

Her "emergency call" lasted approximately 25 minutes, "as Ong calmly and professionally relayed information" about the murder of a passenger and the contemporaneous stabbing of her colleagues (Final Report, 5).

Madeline Sweeney (AA11)

Sweeney "*calmly* reported on her line that ... a man in first class had his throat slashed [and that] two flight attendants had been stabbed..." (Final Report, 6).

---

1   According to Bert Rodriguez, trainer at US-1 Fitness, a gym in Dania Beach, Florida, Ziad Jarrah trained there in May 2001. Rodriguez said in the Frontline show on PBS, January 17, 2002 (#1008): "The course that [Jarrah] wanted to train is called Close Quarter Aggressive and Defensive Tactics. It entails everything from grappling to choking to striking to knives to guns."

2   Paul Thompson, "The two Ziad Jarrahs," August 24, 2002, http://www.juscogens.org/english/fake/1010

3   Dennis B. Roddy, "Flight 93: Forty lives, one destiny," *Post-Gazette*, October 28, 2001, #712

4   FBI Working Draft Chronology of Events for Hijackers and Associates, November 14, 2003 (entries 2975, p. 95 and 2992, p. 97), #1783

5   This section is based to a large extent on blogger Shoestring's original analysis

Robert Fangman (UA175)

According to Marc R. Policastro of United Airlines (SAMC), Robert Fang-man, a flight attendant, called him and told that "both pilots had been murdered and a flight attendant had been stabbed." He added, though, that "he was reluctant to believe him because [he] was calm and there was no background noise." (See section "A call by an unidentified flight attendant," chapter 8.)

Todd Beamer (UA93)

According to Lisa Jefferson, Beamer reported that the pilot and co-pilot were lying on the floor of First Class, injured or dead.[1] Yet his voice "was devoid of any stress. In fact, he sounded so tranquil it made me begin to doubt the authenticity and urgency of his call."[2] According to the transcript of Jefferson's conversation with Lisa Beamer of September 15, 2001, Jefferson said that Todd Beamer was "calm, very calm. You wouldn't've thought it was a real call because he was, um, he wasn't nervous at all. He was speaking in a normal tone of voice, he never got upset, not one time."

Sandra Bradshaw (UA93)

Richard Belme, the UAL manager who took Bradshaw's call at SAMC, described Bradshaw as being "shockingly calm" while she was telling him that "two hijackers ... had attacked and killed" her colleague" (Staff Report, 40).

Thomas Burnett (UA93)

In his first call to his wife, Tom Burnett told her that "they just knifed a guy." In the second call he told her that the "guy they knifed is dead." Deena Burnett later described his third call: "[I]t was as if he was at Thoratec [the company he worked for], sitting at his desk, and we were having a regular conversation. It was the strangest thing because he was using the same tone of voice I had heard a thousand times. It calmed me to know he was so confident" (Burnett, 66). According to journalist and author Jere Longman, in his fourth call, Tom was also "speaking in a normal voice, calm"(Longman, 118).

Jeremy Glick (UA93)

Jeremy Glick called his wife, Lyz, and told her his plane had been hijacked by three "Iranian-looking" males who told passengers that they intend to blow-

---

1   Lisa Jefferson, p. 33
2   Ibid. p. 33

up the plane.[1] She recalled, "He was so calm, the plane sounded so calm, that if I hadn't seen what was going on on the TV, I wouldn't have believed it."[2]

(b) The puzzling passivity of passengers and crew

The number of passengers and crew members on flight AA11 (except for the alleged hijackers) was 87. According to both Betty Ong and Madeline Sweeney, murderous violence took place in the aircraft: Flight attendants were stabbed and a passenger had been slashed and killed. According to Betty Ong mace or pepper-spray additionally made breathing difficult. Under such circumstances, one would have expected everyone on the plane to cooperate in order to subdue the attackers. There is no evidence of any effort by passengers and crew members to overwhelm the alleged hijackers, to try to engage them in talk or to find out what they wanted. Such conduct is totally incomprehensible. Compare this passivity with the following examples of violent conduct on aircraft:

- On July 19, 1960, TAA flight 408 was hijacked in flight over Brisbane, Australia, by a man with a bomb who wielded a fully loaded sawn-off .22 calibre rifle. He even fired a shot, but was successfully subdued by a passenger and the captain.[3]

- According to a report in the Miami Herald of July 22, 1983, a Cuban named Rodolfo Bueno Cruz, 42, attempted to hijack a plane on a Tampa-Miami flight. He "asked a stewardess for a drink. As she brought it, he grabbed her arm and threatened her with a hunting knife." Two passengers grabbed him, a third slugged him and other passengers piled on averting what was about to become the ninth successful hijacking in eleven weeks. After subduing him, the passengers tied his hands behind his back with a belt and buckled him into a seat with two seat belts.[4]

- On April 7, 1994, a FedEx employee named Auburn Calloway attempted to kill the crew of cargo jet FedEx flight 705 and crash the aircraft. Calloway was a former Navy pilot and martial arts expert. He carried with him on the plane a guitar case containing several hammers, a knife and a speargun. Despite severe injuries, the crew was able to fight back and subdue the attacker. The crew survived the attack to tell the world exactly what happened[5]

- On July 23, 1999, a Japanese hijacker carrying a 20-cm. long kitchen knife forced a flight attendant on flight ANA 61 to allow him enter the cockpit. He then forced the co-pilot out of the cockpit and attacked the

1   FBI 302-11722. September 12, 2001. Interview with Elizabeth Glick

2   Matthew Brown, "Hero's family perseveres," *The Record* (Bergen County, NJ), October 5, 2001 [not anymore freely available on the internet]

3   Wikipedia: "Trans Australia Airlines Flight 408"

4   Helga Silva and Arnold Markowitz, "Passengers' tackle foils knife-wielding skyjacker," *The Miami Herald*, July 22, 1983, #1012

5   Wikipedia: "Federal Express Flight 705"; see also Penny Rafferty Hamilton, "Life changer—the horrific story of FedEx Flight 705," *State Aviation Journal* (undated), #901

pilot, who still managed to notify air traffic control about the attack. The attacker stabbed the pilot, who later died of his wounds, and took control of the plane but was then finally disarmed and held down by crew members.[1]

- On March 17, 2000, an agitated and incoherent passenger attacked the pilot and co-pilot of a San-Francisco bound Alaska Airlines jetliner, intending to crash the airliner. The man was subdued by crew members and several passengers.[2]

- On March 28, 2000 a man forced his way into the cockpit of a Boeing 737 (Flight LTU from Tenerife, Spain, to Berlin, Germany) and attacked the pilot in command. The pilot called for help and the crew members and four passengers were able to subdue the offender before the aircraft landed safely.[3]

- On December 29, 2000, a man broke into the cockpit, fought the pilots, and tried to seize the controls during a flight from London to Nairobi. Fellow travelers were woken at around 4:30 a.m. by screaming. Passenger Benjamin Goldsmith told Sky News that the "whole plane was hysterical. I don't think there was a single person on the plane who didn't think we were going to crash."[4] The man was eventually forced out of the cockpit and subdued by business class passengers and flight attendants.[5]

- On February 14, 2007, a man armed with two pistols hijacked an Air Mauritanian flight but was subdued by two passengers.[6]

- On January 5, 2011, a passenger on Turkish Airlines flight 1754, flying from Oslo to Istanbul, attempted to hijack the airliner. He said he had a bomb and would blow up the aircraft unless the plane returned to Norway. Some passengers overpowered him.[7]

- On April 24, 2011, a hijacker using a sharp weapon (some reports indicate the suspect was armed with a razor blade, while others say it was a nail clipper) threatened a flight attendant and demanded that the aircraft be flown to Tripoli, Lybia. This occurred on Alitalia Flight AZ329 from Paris to Rome. He was overpowered by crew and passengers and sedated by a doctor who was among the passengers.[8]

---

1 Nicholas D. Kristof, "Pilot of packed Japanese airliner dies after subduing hijacker," *New York Times*, July 23, 1999, #898; see also "ANA pilot slain during hijacking," *Japan Times*, July 23, 1999, #899.

2 Chuck Squatriglia, "Passenger enters cockpit, attacks pilot of jet near S.F.," *San Francisco Chronicle*, March 17, 2000, #1013

3 "Hijacking Report," *Aviation Safety Network*, March 28, 2000, #1014

4 "British Airways Passenger Fights Pilots in Cockpit," *Bloomberg*, December 29, 2000, #1015

5 "British Airways pilot fights of mid-air passenger attack," *Airline Industry Information*, January 2, 2001, #1016

6 "Passengers subdue armed hijacker," *CNN*, February 15, 2007, #1017

7 Daniel Baxter, "Passengers overpower hijacker on Turkish Airlines Flight TK1754," *Aviation Online Magazine*, January 8, 2011, #895

8 "Man attempts to hijack Alitalia Paris-Rome flight," *BBC*, April 25, 2011, #897; and "Passenger wanted flight to go to Libya," *USA Today*, April 24, 2011, #896

In all above cases, passengers and crew had admittedly only to deal with one dangerous person, not three. Assuming that this would explain the reluctance of the passengers aboard flights AA11, UA175, AA77 and UA93 to overpower the "hijackers," what would explain their failure to engage the alleged hijackers in conversation, make phone calls to report the events or prepare immediately a counter-attack? The above examples demonstrate that any attempt by a passenger to act violently on aircraft is invariably noticed and collectively resisted, most often on the initiative of crew members.

The alleged success of the alleged 9/11 hijackers to take over the aircraft was commented upon with surprise by 9/11 Commission staffer Dieter Snell. On December 1, 2003, 9/11 Commission's Vice-Chairman Lee Hamilton interviewed Dieter Snell on the progress of Commission's Team 1a.[1] According to the Notes of this interview taken by Ben Rhodes, "Dieter [found] it remarkable that [the hijackers] gained cockpit entry and *controlled passengers* even though none were physically imposing—the tallest was probably 5'8", and weight averaged 120–130 lbs."[2] But Snell did not pursue the matter.

The passivity of flight AA11 passengers and those of flights UA175 and AA77 goes far in proving that no violent action had taken place aboard these flights. This in turn suggests that the phone callers did not report real events.

(c) The puzzling nonchalance of three veteran flight attendants

Betty Ong and Madeline Sweeney (AA11) spent 27 and 13 minutes respectively on the phone relaying information about murderous events allegedly occurring aboard the plane. Assuming that both were veteran, conscientious and compassionate flight attendants, it is inconceivable that had their colleagues been really attacked and stabbed a few feet away, they would sit quietly and chat on the phone. The only explanation for their conduct is that they were not relating real events.

We also note that neither Ong nor Sweeney attempted to find out how the alleged hijackers entered the cockpit. This cannot be attributed—as in some of the other calls—to the short duration of their phone calls. During the nearly half an hour Ong chatted on the telephone, she had ample time to find someone on the aircraft who might have told her how the "hijackers" entered the cockpit, how many they were and who they might be. Assuming their sense of responsibility, these omissions are totally implausible and suggest, therefore, that the story of "hijackers" committing murder and entering the cockpit was fictitious.

---

1   MFR 030012997. December 1, 2003. Meeting of Team 1a: Dieter Snell with Chris Kojm and Vice-Chairman Hamilton

2   Ibid. Emphasis added

Renee May, a flight attendant on flight AA77, instead of calling the airline to report the hijacking, called her parents asking *them* to call the airline. She even had to ask "someone" on the aircraft for the airlines telephone numbers. Yet she was a veteran flight attendant with American Airlines and should have known which numbers to call in case of an emergency. Flight attendants are trained how to proceed when experiencing an incident or a hijacking aboard the aircraft. This can hardly include calling dad and mom. The fact that she called her parents instead of the airlines indicates that "someone" had the power to overrule the ordinary hijacking procedure and order her to call home.

(d) The puzzling conduct of passengers Beamer and Glick

Passengers Beamer and Glick (UA93) spent an inordinate time to chat on the telephone while reporting alleged attacks in the plane. Beamer even indulged in telling a telephone operator about his wife and children and then they recited in common the Lord's Prayer on the phone, as if there was no more urgent things to do on the plane. Some other callers, apparently, also spent most of the time on the phone talking about private matters while only providing scant information on the incident. Such conduct suggests that the callers were not experiencing a real hijacking.

(e) The lack of curiosity of flight attendant Madeline Sweeney

In her call, Madeline Sweeney (AA11) said the "hijackers" had a bomb with yellow wires. According to another report she reported to have observed "two boxes connected with red and yellow wire." According to a third report the men merely "said they had a bomb." Whichever of these stories is true, Sweeney, as a responsible flight attendant would try and find out what this box or these boxes were, and whether there was really a bomb on the aircraft. Apparently she did not attempt to find out, because nothing was mentioned later about this "bomb." Assuming she was a responsible person, her reports suggest that there was no bomb on board, that she was aware of this fact and that she had been asked to relay a bogus bomb story.

(f) Almost no callers from flights AA11, UA175 and AA77

Officially, the number of passengers (except the alleged hijackers) on flights AA11, UA175 and AA77 were, respectively, 76, 51, and 53, many of whom known to take initiatives in their private and professional lives. Yet no passenger from flight AA11, only two from flight UA175 and only one from flight AA77, made phone calls to someone on the ground. This omission can neither be explained by their fear or by their belief that it was not possible to make calls. They saw flight attendants on flights AA11 and AA77 and in the case of flight UA175 two passengers, make successful and even long phone calls without any problem. It is particularly strange that Barbara Olson was the only passenger from flight AA77 to make calls, whereas –according to her—all passengers had been herded into the back of the plane, and would have been highly motivated to make calls after seeing her, a nationally known television-commentator, repeatedly call her husband to tell him that the aircraft was hijacked. That is to say, many would have emulated these few callers, if there was a real crisis on board. Presumably there was none.

Rowland Morgan correctly pointed out (Morgan, *Voices*) that at the time flight UA93 was allegedly hijacked, it was known to the passengers that the WTC had been hit. Yet, only 11 passengers from that flight choose to make phone calls.

(4) Unexplained contradictions

(a) When was the cockpit of flight UA93 overtaken?

According to the official account, the cockpit of flight UA93 stopped responding to messages from air traffic controllers at about 9:28 a.m. From that fact, supported by the contents of the dubious cockpit voice recorder, the 9/11 Commission inferred that the cockpit of that flight had been overtaken around that time.

This official time was undermined by Lisa Jefferson's testimony. According to Jefferson, Todd Beamer, calling from flight UA93 said in his call that started at 9:43 a.m., that "the airplane was *about to* be hijacked" by three individuals who "were *preparing* to take control of the flight"(emphasis added). She said that she spoke with Beamer for seven minutes "before" two of the hijackers entered the cockpit. (see section devoted to his call). Her testimony, which is missing from her later interviews, contradicts the official legend.

A second account also contradicts the official timeline: According to the husband of Sandra Bradshaw (UA93), with whom she spoke, the "hijackers" did not yet enter the cockpit at 9:50. All three of them were still sitting in the cabin.

A third account also contradicts the official timeline: According to Jeremy Glick (UA93)—as reported by his wife to the FBI on September 12, 2001,—the "hijackers" entered the cockpit only after his call started, that is after 9:40 a.m.

We have here three testimonies, which contradict the official hijacking timeline.

(b) Was there or wasn't there a doctor aboard flight AA11?

Madeline Sweeney (AA11) said a doctor and nurse were caring for a stabbed passenger (Daniel Lewin), while Betty Ong (AA11) said there were none. Sweeney and Ong apparently sat near each other in the rear of the plane. Why did their reports contradict each other?

(c) Were passengers herded to the rear of the plane or not?

Betty Ong (AA11) said that passengers from First Class on the same flight had been moved to Coach. This was not mentioned by her colleague Sweeney. On flight UA93, two callers (Bradshaw and Glick) said that the passengers had been moved to the back of the plane. Yet no other caller mentioned this glaring fact, not even Burnett who called four times his wife and Beamer, who had a long conversation with Lisa Jefferson.

(d) Where did the "hijackers" sit in the plane?

Betty Ong (AA11) reported that the "men that are in the cockpit with the pilots" sat at 2A and 2B. Madeline Sweeney of same flight reported their seats as 9C, 9G and 10B. The 9/11 Commission said the "hijackers" sat at 2A, 2B, 8D, 8G and 10B. These are three versions. The difference in seat numbers given by Ong and Sweeney can be attributed to mistakes and should not be considered as significant. More significant is that neither Ong nor Sweeney mentioned seat 8D, which was assigned to Mohamed Atta, the alleged suicide-pilot. When asked about the seat numbers of the "men that are in the cockpit," Ong answered immediately 2A and 2B, but did not mention Atta's seat number.

According to Beamer (UA93)—as reported by Lisa Jefferson—one of the three hijackers, to whom a bomb with a red belt was strapped, "remained in the main cabin with the passengers after closing the privacy curtain between the First Class and Economy Class."[1] Beamer is said to have reported later that the passengers were preparing to "to jump on the hijacker with the bomb and try to get him down," thus confirming the presence of a single "hijacker" with the bomb in the cabin.

In Burnett's (UA93) four calls to his wife, no mention is made where the "hijackers" were seated. The only mention of their location is in the second call, where Burnett says "they're in the cockpit," not specifying how many they were. He repeatedly said, however, that the hijackers (plural) made announcements.

Glick (UA93) said to his wife that there were three "hijackers" and that all three "entered the cockpit of the plane." He also mentioned various announcements allegedly made by the "hijackers," who he also said, "did not speak English."

---

1   FBI 302-95630, September 11, 2001. Interview with Lisa Jefferson

According to the first FBI interview with Sandra Bradshaw's husband (UA93), she said that one of the "hijackers" was seated in First Class, whereas the (two) other "hijackers were seated in the back of the plane." According to the second interview with Sandra's husband, "all three" hijackers were seated in First Class. According to the official account, at least two of the hijackers should have been at that time in the cockpit, controlling the plane.

Comparing the various reports from flight UA93, we have one report having all three "hijackers" sit in First Class, two reports putting all of them in the cockpit and one report in which two of them are said in the cockpit and one is standing guard outside the cockpit with a bomb.

(e) Were there guns on board?

The Federal Aviation Administration (FAA) issued on the very day of 9/11 an executive summary, which included the following statement regarding a gun aboard flight AA11:

> The American Airlines FAA Principal Security Inspector (PSI) was notified by Suzanne Clark of American Airlines Corporate Headquarters that an onboard flight attendant contacted American Airlines Operations Center and informed them that a passenger in seat 10B had shot and killed a passenger in seat 9B at 9:20 a.m. The passenger killed was Daniel Lewin, shot by passenger Satam al Suqami. One bullet was reported to have been fired.[1]

The FAA subsequently changed its report, removing the reference to a gun.

Peter Hanson (UA175) said to his father Lee that he had seen a stewardess being shot. His comment was ignored by the FBI.

Mercy Lorenzo, an employee of AT&T called the FBI on the morning of 9/11 after she received a phone call from a caller, later identified as Barbara Olson (AA77). Barbara reportedly told Lorenzo that the "hijackers" were armed with guns and knives. The comment was disregarded by the FBI.

A gun was reported by Tom Burnett (UA93), calling his wife Deena. Deena said to the *London Times*, "[Tom] told me one of the hijackers had a gun. He wouldn't have made it up. Tom grew up around guns. He was an avid hunter and we have guns in our home. If he said there was a gun on board, there was."[2] The comment was ignored by the FBI.

---

1   James Ridgeway, "The 9-11 Gun," *Village Voice*, February 8, 2005, #894
2   Sarah Baxter, "Widow of hijack hero breaks ranks to sue United Airlines," *London Times*, August 11, 2002, cited by James Ridgeway, ibid.

Chapter 12. Cover-Up

Readers will probably have by now come to envisage—if they had not yet done so earlier—that there exists evidence for suspecting the US government of covering up the mass-murder of 9/11.

It does not require great efforts to notice the cover-up of 9/11. Virtually all mass-media and politicians refuse to ask the most elementary questions regarding 9/11. Some go even further by actually inventing facts regarding the events or slandering citizens who seek the truth on these events.

The present chapter presents a non-exhaustive list of attempts to cover-up the real nature and role of the 9/11 phone calls. Readers might discover further examples. The evidence presented herein would in legal parlance amount to *probable cause*, sufficient to justify subpoenas of suspects and documents but not for their conviction.

(1) Apparent forgeries

Forgery can be a federal offense and is also recognized as a felony in all the states of the Union. It can lead to conviction up to 10 years in jail. Evidence described herein strongly suggests that the FBI has forged documents in order to cover-up what really happened on 9/11.

(a) Betty Ong's audio recording and its transcript

In chapter 7 the existence of two distinct versions of Betty Ong's phone call from flight AA11 was revealed. The differences between these versions could not be explained by inaccurate transcription, clerical mistakes or communication problems. The evidence of forgery is there in plain sight, as demonstrated in that chapter.

(b) Ed Felt's audio recording and its transcript

Ed Felt's call (UA93) presents a similar case of suspected forgery. According to Glenn Cramer, the supervisor of "911" who monitored Felt's conversation with John Shaw, Felt mentioned both an explosion aboard the plane and white smoke. Cramer consistently maintained this testimony, including in media interviews. He then was gagged by the FBI. A transcript of Felt's call was later released by the FBI, that does not include any mention of an explosion and white smoke. Unless Cramer invented those observations and could thereby risk his career, the only conclusion left is that the FBI had doctored the audio recording of Felt's call and released a transcript conform with that doctored version. Circumstantial evidence supports this conclusion, including the secretiveness surrounding the audio version of Felt's call and the fact that Cramer was not allowed to listen to that recording (which he originally had monitored himself).

(c) Cell phone calls misrepresented as air phone calls

Deena Burnett, Tom Burnett's wife (UA93), consistently maintained that she received four phone calls from her husband, most of them using a cell phone. She insisted having seen his cell phone number on the indicator of her phone. She also meticulously wrote down the exact time of the calls and made immediately notes of what Tom told her. She said what he told her and what she saw with her own eyes. Mrs. Burnett had no motive to lie about the number and timings of her husband's phone calls, nor about what she saw on the indicator. Due to her conservative political views, she even had an incentive to adopt the government's view on the phone calls and suppress her own knowledge. The repeated interviews by FBI agents to which she was subjected, suggest that efforts were made to make her change her testimony. The fact that she stood her ground, speaks in support of her credibility.

Four other callers from flight UA93 made cell phone calls: CeeCee Lyles, Edward Felt, Marion Britton and Honor Wainio (see sections dealing with their calls).

As discussed in the section dealing with Burnett's calls (chapter 10), it was practically impossible in 2001 to make sustainable cell phone calls from passenger airliners flying at cruising altitudes. This means that Burnett, Lyles, Felt, Britton and Wainio made their calls either from an aircraft flying at substantially lower altitudes than 8,000 feet or from ground level. To admit this would have shattered the official version regarding flight UA93, undermined the justification for the war on Afghanistan and put to rest the dream of US global hegemony.

In order to help illustrate what the FBI did to save the official legend, please consult the following table. It lists the approximate start times of the calls made by the aforementioned persons, as reported by their recipients, and the altitude of flight UA93 at those precise times (as reported by the NTSB and depicted in chapter 10 under Burnett's section).

Name	Start time of call	Official altitude of UA93
Burnett, Call 1	9:27	35,000
Burnett, Call 2	9:34	35,000
Burnett, Call 3	9:45	20,000
Britton	9:49	17,000
Burnett, Call 4	9:54	11,000
Wainio	9:54	11,000
Felt	9:58	5,000
Lyles	9:59	5,000

In the weeks and months following 9/11, the question of cell phone calls from the allegedly hijacked airlines did not appear to be an issue. It was taken for granted that some of the callers from the allegedly hijacked aircraft made their calls with cell phones. Even the FBI did not dispute these reports. The FBI probably learned about A.K. Dewdney's experiments, discussed in chapter 10, and realized the threat they represented to the official 9/11 legend. For if cell phone calls could hardly be made from cruising aircraft, the question would arise from where the calls had been made. Adding to the suspicion that the flights did not crash at the known landmarks, such findings would have prompted the sinister suspicion that the passengers and crew did not call from hijacked planes but from an unidentified location and had been made to "vanish."

The FBI solved this challenge by accepting, as it were, that Felt and Lyles had made cell-phone calls, because the aircraft was at the time listed at 5,000 feet, an altitude from which cell phone calls could be made, and simply dismissing the testimonies by the next-of-kin of the three other callers, Britton, Burnett and Wainio. In FBI submissions to the 9/11 Commission and the Moussaoui trial, it presented data according to which the calls by Burnett, Britton and Wainio had been made with air phones.

An examination of the list of UA93 phone calls released by the FBI to the 9/11 Commission reveals, however, an exception precisely regarding the calls of Burnett, Britton and Wainio. One column on this list is entitled *Manual Entry Ind.*[1] Mark Rugg, Manager of Network Operations, GTE Airfone Inc. provided to the FBI on July 1, 2002, a spreadsheet detailing the GTE Airfone records from flight UA93. Those records were subsequently made part of the Events of 09/11/2001 Investigative Summary (Appendix A-3) produced by the Newark [FBI] Division.

---

1   9/11 Commission documents, NARA, Team 7, Box 13 Flight 11 Calls Folder—Response from DOJ to Doc Req 14 Calls, #779

Rugg was asked to revisit those records and provide an understanding of the various fields that were depicted in the spreadsheet. He explained that *Manual Entry Ind* is a "true or false field identifying whether a patron manually entered a credit card number."[1] Significantly, only the phone calls of the three individuals who, according to their next-of-kin had made cell phone calls on 9/11, were marked T (for True), whereas all other Airfone calls were marked F (for False). This raises the question why *precisely* Burnett, Britton and Wainio reportedly entered their credit card numbers manually, whereas all other Airfone users simply swept their credit card. Was this a clue to a grand deception?

Having to opt between two opposing claims, one made by three family members who received phone calls from their next-of-kin and another made by the FBI, the claims by disinterested family members seem far more credible than those of the FBI. On that base, it would follow that the FBI had forged data on the phone calls of the aforementioned three callers in order to suppress the fact that these calls were made with cell phones.

(d) Burnett's cell phone bill

Deena, the wife of Tom Burnett (UA93) was interviewed by staffers of the 9/11 Commission on April 26, 2004. Among the facts the staffers mentioned in their report, was that the cell phone call [sic] made by Burnett "did not show up on the cell phone bill, neither did the one he placed to his secretary before take-off." The report does not indicate who informed the staffers of this fact and whether they verified this allegation. In the light of the problems caused to the official account by Burnett's cell phone calls, it is likely that either the aforementioned phone bill had been forged, or that the story about the absence of entries for Burnett's various cell phone calls on that phone bill, was fictitious.

(2) Suppressed evidence

A common cover-up method is to suppress evidence. Governments regularly suppress evidence to conceal malfeasance but usually attempt to justify their suppression by invoking national security, business confidentiality, privacy considerations, or other apparently legitimate grounds.

Suppressing reports, interviews and other documents relative to the phone calls of 9/11 is surprising, however, because none of these calls was supposed to contain sensitive information requiring confidentiality. While information of a private nature (such as addresses and phone numbers of private people) can be easily redacted by blanking out sentences or words on documents, it is difficult to understand why entire pages or entire interviews are redacted or even their

---

[1] FBI 302-116622, July 1, 2002. Interview with Mark Rugg

existence suppressed. The suppression of audio recordings of phone calls, for which the transcripts have been released, is equally surprising. For if the transcripts are faithfully representing what is said on the recording, there should be no reason to conceal the corresponding recording. Such suppression of information relative to the phone calls suggests efforts by the authorities to cover-up facts that might have revealed official malfeasance.

Here are a few examples of suppressed evidence.

(a) Wilesca Martinez' call

Wilesca Martinez, a passenger on flight UA93, apparently made (or attempted to make) a call to her friend and roommate Angela Lopez, who worked at Dratel. This fact was confirmed to an FBI special agent on October 19, 2001, by the president/owner of Dratel Group Inc. (DGI).[1] Yet, on the FBI compilation of phone calls made from flight UA93 and presented at the Moussaoui trial, Martinez' call to Dratel is listed to have lasted 0 seconds.[2] According to telephone logs cited by the staff of the 9/11 Commission, the call lasted 138 seconds.[3] Angela Lopez was interviewed by the FBI on April 25, 2002, and claimed that she did not receive any call from Martinez on 9/11.[4] She said she was not in the office at the time of the call and received no message that Martinez had called. She expressed her belief that Martinez' call could have been placed on hold. Did Martinez talk to someone else within Dratel? Was the FBI falsifying records? Was Lopez coerced to deny the call? The FBI apparently did not follow up the claim by Dratel's president that such a call had taken place and suppressed in its submission to the Moussaoui trial the fact that the call lasted 138 seconds.

(b) Peter Hanson's testimonies were suppressed

Peter Hanson (UA175) told his father, Lee, that a flight attendant was shot and that he heard the "hijackers" mention eight hijacked planes. This testimony was suppressed in all but the first documents released by the FBI.

(c) Evidence about Javis Johnson, a phone call recipient from flight UA93 with a strange story, was strictly suppressed

Javis Johnson called Dee Ann Freeman at Continental Airlines Reservations on 9/11 and told her that a friend of him, male flight attendant from flight UA93,

---

1   FBI Serial 62621. October 19, 2001. Interview with William Dratel, DGI
2   Flight UA93, telephone call by Waleska Martinez (graphical presentation from Prosecution Exhibit at Moussaoui's Trial), #1019
3   John Raidt, Op. cit., #758.
4   FBI Serial 111535. April 25, 2002. Interview with Angela Lopez.

had called him from the aircraft and asked him to take care of his wife.[1] According to official reports, no male flight attendant was on UA93. Additional information Johnson provided showed that he had "inside information" about the events that he could not have gleaned from mass media. Yet the FBI either did not interview him and the wife of his friend or completely suppressed all evidence regarding these interviews.

(d) Suppressed audio recordings of phone calls

Recordings of phone calls made by passengers and crew represent primary evidence of what they said about the events on the aircraft. It has slowly emerged that a number of phone calls were recorded but remain concealed by the authorities. The standard justification for suppressing these recordings is "privacy." This explanation is not compelling, because (a) some recordings that contain private expressions have been released; and (b) some recordings whose transcriptions have been released, are suppressed. Privacy considerations do matter, but do not necessarily override the right of the public to know the facts on a national calamity. When an event occurs that is invoked to justify foreign war, the details of that event is no private matter. The nation, which pays for the war in money and blood, is entitled to know every detail of the event that triggered the war. In view of other official attempts to suppress information regarding the events of 9/11, it is probable that the following recordings were suppressed in order to hide statements that might undermine the hijacking legend.

- Nydia Gonzalez relayed on 9/11 her conversation with Betty Ong (AA11) to Craig Marquis (see chapter 7). Her call to Marquis was recorded and a transcript of that call was later released.[2] However the FBI has not released the audio recording of that call, which would allow the verification of the transcript's accuracy.

- Deena Burnett (UA93) made a call to "911" emergency that was recorded. In that call she reportedly said, "My husband just called me from United Flight 93. The plane has been hijacked. They just knifed a passenger and *there are guns* on the airplane."[3] The recording of this call has been suppressed. It is also likely that the FBI recorded her husband's second to fourth calls because she reportedly contacted the FBI immediately after his first call, informing the FBI of the hijacking.

- According to Robert Combs, Director of Technical Operations for GTE Airfone, he relayed Beamer's conversation with Lisa Jefferson in realtime to an unidentified FBI Special Agent. To do so, Combs must have monitored the conversation on a parallel line or sat near Lisa Jefferson

---

1   FBI 302-20230. September 11, 2001. Interview with Dee Ann Freeman. NARA. Team 7, Box 19. Key 302s Folder.

2   9/11 Commission documents. NARA. Team 7 Box 13 documents, #634

3   Jere Longman, "Cockpit Tape Offers Few Answers but Points to Heroic Efforts," *New York Times*, March 27, 2002, #890

(in which case he would only hear what she said). One must presume that executives of GTE Airfone and of the FBI can record their phone calls and that either Combs or his interlocutor at the FBI or both recorded this call. Neither Combs nor the FBI have confirmed or denied the existence of a recording of this call.

- Edward Felt made a call from flight UA93 to 911 Emergency. His call was recorded. An FBI memo from FBI New York to FBI Newark of March 22, 2002 (document 265A-NY-280350-OUT, Bates 000000341) is composed of two parts: The first part of the memo (approximately 15 lines) is completely redacted. The second part contains the following sentence: "Under no circumstances is Newark to provide [the family] FELT with a copy of the recording or a copy of the transcript. Any questions regarding this matter should be immediately brought to the attention of SA [redacted] at [redacted] or [redacted]."[1] The audio version of Felt's call was never released. What in Felt's call was so sensitive to compel such stringent measures? And why is it suppressed?

- Immediately after being contacted by his son, Peter, Lee Hanson called the Easton Police Department and told Captain James Candee about his son's call. Captain Candee told Hanson that "he would secure the tape of Hanson's ... call and copy it onto a separated cassette tape."[2] The recording of this call remains suppressed. According to other FBI documents mentioned in chapter 8, Lee Hanson related in his first calls that his son "had heard the hijackers talking about 8 planes that were hijacked." This testimony disappeared from later Hanson interviews. Did he mention this fact in his first call, made to Captain Candee?

- A puzzling call was made by Lauren Grandcolas (UA93) to her husband around 9:00 a.m. in which she mentioned some problems aboard the aircraft but that "they are being kind." According to the official timeline, the hijacking of flight UA93 began only at approximately 9:28. The call was recorded on the answering machine. It has not been revealed to whom she referred by "they." Neither the recording nor a ranscript thereof were released.

(e) Evidence of Marquis' direct contact with flight attendants was suppressed

According to the official account, Craig Marquis of American Airlines only obtained information about Betty Ong's (AA11) call through Nydia Gonzalez who relayed to him what Ong reported. Yet, on the transcript of Gonzalez' call to Marquis (which was recorded), Marquis says at minute 20:00 "I'm talking to the flight attendant in the back of the plane and she says the plane is descending." The transcript does not contain any mention of Ong saying that the plane is descending. Such an observation was made by Ong's colleague, Madeline Sweeney. Marquis' observation would mean that he was either talking directly to Ong,

---

1   FBI OUT-2526. March 3, 2002. FBI New York to FBI Newark, #1780, p. 113
2   FBI NH-3718. September 11, 2001. Interview with James R. Candee

without this fact being revealed, or monitoring directly Sweeney's call to Michael Woodward. If this was the case, why did Marquis withhold that information from the FBI and the 9/11 Commission and suggested that he only obtained indirect information from Betty Ong? Or did the FBI and the 9/11 Commission suppress his truthful account?

(f) An FBI agent was interviewed and told not to make a report

An unidentified FBI agent conducted on 9/11 a telephone interview with the father of Peter Hanson (UA175). No record of that interview was released. The agent himself was later interviewed by another FBI agent. The first agent was later told he would not need to make a 302 form about his interview with Peter's father. What was going on here?

(g) An FBI interview with Mercy Lorenzo was suppressed

Mercy Lorenzo, a employee of AT&T, was interviewed twice by the FBI after she received a call from Barbara Olson on flight AA77 who told Lorenzo that the "hijackers" were armed with "guns and knives." Only one of the interviews was released. The other interview—Serial 4082—is suppressed.

(h) The initial interview report of Phyllis Johnson (UA93) is probably suppressed

Phyllis Johnson was the person who initially took a widely reported phone call from Todd Beamer (UA93). She talked to him. Yet, according to publicly available information, she was only interviewed by the FBI in June 2002. In the light of the fact that virtually all phone call recipients were interviewed by the FBI on September 11, 2001, or in the subsequent days, sometimes repeatedly, it is inconceivable that Phyllis Johnson was only interviewed 9 months later. It is likely that her initial FBI interview(s) has/have been suppressed.

(i) Lisa Jefferson's first interview report was suppressed

Lisa Jefferson, who talked with Todd Beamer (UA93), was interviewed by three FBI agents around 1:00 p.m. on 9/11. The report of that first interview with her, has been suppressed.

(j) FBI interviews with Joseph DeLuca's parents have been suppressed

Joseph DeLuca (UA93) made two calls from the aircraft to his parents. The FBI suppressed its interviews of DeLuca's parents.

(k) The FBI concealed from Cramer the recording of Felt's call

Glenn Cramer, who took the call from Ed Felt (UA93) and monitored that call throughout said that Felt reported an explosion and smoke aboard the plane. While the recording of the call was played to Felt's family and to his assistant, John W. Shaw, Cramer himself was not given an opportunity to listen to the recording which contradicted his testimony.

(l) Three FBI documents relating to CeeCee Lyles are heavily redacted

One of the callers from flight UA93 was flight attendant CeeCee Lyles. Information about her two calls has been published, including an audio recording of her first call. But three FBI documents about her—Serials GJ-514, 96092 and 108562—are heavily redacted.

(3) Suspected attempts to influence witnesses

(a) Was there an attempt to modify Lisa Jefferson's testimony?

Lisa Jefferson (see chapter 10, Tom Beamer) had a long conversation with Todd Beamer (UA93). Todd Beamer asked her specifically to call his wife. She promised to him to do so. Yet Jefferson was prevented by the FBI of doing so until September 14, 2001. It is not known why the FBI withheld for three days the evidence of his call from his wife.

In her FBI interview of September 11, 2001, Jefferson said that Beamer had told her the "airplane was about to be hijacked" and that the hijackers "were preparing to take control of the flight," which they did, according to her, seven minutes into his call. In her interview she did not mention Beamer making a prayer, let alone that she prayed with him.

In a synopsis of September 14, 2001, attributed to her, she did not repeat the above testimony, which implied that the cockpit had been taken over after the beginning of Beamer's call, but we read that the "hijackers went into the cockpit and locked the door." In that synopsis, Beamer's prayer is mentioned for the first time, though not her participation in the prayer: Beamer is said there to have recited the Lord's Prayer, and then "someone" said " let's roll."

In later interviews and in her own book, the prayer is said to have been recited by both of them together and it is Beamer who says "let's roll." Jefferson's testimony took also other changes.

Was Jefferson continuously inventing facts about this call or did someone induced her to modify her testimony in order to create and maintain a hero-cult of Todd Beamer?[1]

(b) Felt's family monitored while listening to Ed Felt's recording

The FBI feared to leave a recording of Felt's emergency call (UA93) with his family and insisted to have its agents attending the playing of this short call. Were they sent there to convince Felt's family that Ed's recording was not doctored?

(c) John W. Shaw was interviewed three times by the FBI on 9/11

John W. Shaw, a telecommunications officer for Westmoreland County 911 Emergency Center, was interviewed three times by the FBI on 9/11. He was one of the two persons who listened to Ed Felt's call (UA93). While Shaw's supervisor, Glenn Cramer, monitored the call and told the FBI that Felt had mentioned an explosion and smoke aboard the plane, Shaw told the FBI that he did not *hear* any explosions or gunfire in the background. This apparent contradiction between their testimonies was never resolved. Were these repeated interviews conducted to induce the cooperation of John W. Shaw?

(d) Repeated interviews of Michael Woodward

Michael Woodward who took a call from Madeline Sweeney (AA11), was repeatedly interviewed by the FBI and even by the CIA and the State Department. In the released reports of Sweeney's calls there is nothing of particular value to the CIA and the State Department. Did Michael Woodward possess sensitive information from his conversation with Madeline Sweeney (flight AA11) that he was not supposed to reveal?

(e) Lee Hanson was repeatedly interviewed, including by Assistant US Attorney David Novak

The father of Peter Hanson (UA175) was repeatedly interviewed by the FBI, including once with Assistant US Attorney David Novak attending. Was this an attempt to ensure that he would not repeat the puzzling facts he initially reported?

(f) Renee May's parents were repeatedly interviewed, including by

---

1 "Todd Beamer—Hero Of Flight 93," *San Francisco Bay Area Flight 93 Memorial* (undated), #1020

Assistant US Attorney Robert Spencer

The parents of Renee May (AA77) were repeatedly interviewed by the FBI, including once with Assistant US Attorney Robert Spencer attending. What was the purpose of such repeated interviews in the presence of an Assistant US Attorney?

(g) Three lawyers attended interviews of United Airlines employees

On November 21, 2003, Marc R. Policastro and Andrew Lubkemann, two employees of United Airlines SAMC in San Francisco, who received phone calls from flights UA175 and UA93, were interviewed by staffers of the 9/11 Commission. The interview was attended by no fewer than three United Airlines lawyers. What was the purpose of their presence, if not to intimidate the interviewees into keeping silent about "certain facts"?

(h) Glick's wife retracts certain facts

On 9/11, Glick's (UA93) wife told the FBI that her husband Jeremy advised her that "one of the hijackers told the passengers to call their loved ones." Later, when she was interviewed by the staff of the 9/11 Commission, she said that her former statement had been wrong: Her husband had only said that "they" did not seem to care that the passengers were on the phone. Was she induced to change her story because what she initially told the FBI might have given rise to unwelcome questions about the motives of those who urged passengers to make these calls?

CHAPTER 13. DEVIL'S ADVOCATE

While the findings in the preceding chapters strongly suggest that the phone callers did not report real hijackings, three types of evidence are adduced here to debunk this conclusion:

- Callers on flight UA93 reported that passengers planned to attack the hijackers;
- Shouting and yelling was heard in the background
- Intercepted radio messages were imputed to the "suicide pilots."

(1) Reports by callers on flight UA93 about passengers' plan to attack the hijackers

Five phone callers mentioned a planned counter-attack on the alleged hijackers by passengers of flight UA93.

(a) Todd Beamer

According to the FBI, Beamer's call started at 9:43:48 and lasted beyond the alleged crash time of flight UA93.

Lisa Jefferson told the FBI on September 11, 2001, that at approximately 9:00 a.m. Central Time (10:00 EST), Beamer reported that the passengers were about to attack the hijackers.[1] Jefferson said she heard another passenger [in the background] give the go-ahead to make their move. After that point, she heard nothing.

---

[1]   FBI 302-95630. September 11, 2001. Interview with Lisa Jefferson

Robert Combs, who apparently listened to the entire conversation between Todd Beamer and GTE supervisor Lisa Jefferson, did not, however, mention to the FBI any observations by Beamer about a plan to counter-attack the "hijackers."[1]

In 2004 Lisa Jefferson told John Raidt of the 9/11 Commission's staff that a few of the passengers were getting together to jump "the guy with the bomb."[2] Shortly thereafter, she said she heard *Beamer* say to someone near him, "Are you ready? Okay! Let's roll!" That's the last she heard.

(b) Sandra Bradshaw

According to the FBI, Sandra Bradshaw, a flight attendant, made two calls from flight UA93, to United Airlines SAMC in San Francisco at 9:35, lasting approximately 6 minutes, and to her husband, starting at 9:50, lasting approximately 8 minutes.

In her call to her husband, Philip G. Bradshaw, starting at 9:50 a.m., she said, that the "passengers were getting hot water out of the galley and were going to rush the hijackers." At the end of the call, Sandra told her husband that "everyone was running up to First Class and she hung up the telephone."

(c) Tom Burnett

In the first interview conducted with Deena Burnett on September 11, 2001[3], she advised that her husband, Tom, called her three to five times. During his *last* call Tom told Deena that "a group of us are getting ready to do something" and he may not speak to her again. According to Deena, his last call was made at 9:54 (the FBI puts Tom's last call at 9:44).

According to the transcript of Tom's four calls, posted on the website of the Tom Burnett Family Foundation[4] and replicated in Deena Burnett's book (Burnett, 61-67), Tom mentioned already in his third call at 9:45 a plan for a counter-attack: "There's a group of us, Don't worry." Yet in his last call, at 9:54, he said they are still waiting to be flying "over a rural area" to start the counter-attack, implying that they do not wish to crash the plane over an urban area.

(d) Jeremy Glick

Jeremy Glick's call was the longest single call from flight UA93. It began at 9:37 and was never terminated.

According to an FBI interview with Lyz Glick, his wife, conducted on September 11, 2001,[5] the "hijackers" were three Arabs who did not speak English. Ac-

1   FBI 302-95682. September 11, 2001. Interview with Robert Combs
2   MFR 04020031. May 11, 2004. Telephone interview with Lisa Jefferson
3   FBI 302-535. September 11, 2001. Interview with Deena Burnett
4   "Transcripts of Tom's Last Calls to Deena," *Tom Burnett Family Foundation website*, #653
5   FBI 302-6390. September 11, 2001. Interview with parents of Elizabeth Glick

cording to Glick, they "took over the cockpit." Thereafter no communication to the cockpit was possible. At least one of them, said Glick, held a knife. Another held what appeared to him to be a bomb. The passengers "were forced to the back." He said to his wife that a decision had been made to resist the terrorist(s) and take back the airplane. The summary of the interview compiled by the FBI agent is extremely brief and cannot represent a conversation that lasted over 20 minutes. In that interview, no mention is made of a counter-attack.

On September 12, 2001, Jeremy's wife, Lyz, was again interviewed by an FBI agent.[1] In that interview Lyz said that at the end of his call, Jeremy said that "he and the other males were organizing to 'rush' the hijackers."

(e) Honor Elizabeth Wainio

Esther Heymann, Honor Elizabeth Wainio's step-mother, who received a call from Honor on the morning of 9/11 at 9:53:43—lasting 269 seconds—was interviewed by unidentified FBI agents on September 12, 2001.[2] According to these agents' report, Honor Wainio had several minutes of *personal* conversation with her step-mother regarding her fate before saying: "They're going into the cockpit." Immediately thereafter her call terminated.

According to author Longman, who later interviewed Esther Heymann, the FBI report was not accurate: After the personal chat, Wainio reportedly said: "They're getting ready to break into the cockpit. I have to go. I love you. Good bye"(Longman, 242).

(f) Discussion

Many passengers were fit, trained and courageous

According to the official account the cockpit of flight UA93 was overtaken by "hijackers" before 9:30 and was preceded by a "hijacker" stabbing a flight attendant, then slashing the throats of the pilot and co-pilot and finally removing their bodies from the cockpit. Yet, no passenger or crew member intervened to stop these murderous actions and neutralize the assailant(s). How can that be?

If these acts of violence, reported in phone calls, had been real, it would follow that at least some passengers and/or flight attendants would have observed these acts and react without delay. Were the passengers and flight attendants perhaps cowards? Not at all. Some of them were not only physically fit but had previously demonstrated their courage and initiative in crisis situations, including in overpowering muggers. They would have easily overruled collectively the one or two hijackers allegedly left in the cabin with short knives to guard the

---

1   FBI 302-11722. September 12, 2001. Interview with Elizabeth Glick
2   FBI 302-84596. September 12, 2001. Interview with Esther Heymann

passengers. Should anyone doubt about the collective capabilities found among passengers and crew, here are some details:

1. Mark Bingham, 6' 5" tall was a former rugby star, helping the Berkeley rugby club win national championships in 1991 and 1993. Once, unarmed, he fought off two muggers, one of whom had a gun. On another occasion he waded into a bar brawl to help a waiter beset by rowdies.[1] He saved his uncle from drowning, fought armed muggers, rescued a little girl from a busy street.[2] He was clearly a courageous man who would not hesitate to protect people being assaulted. In July 2001, his spirit of adventure induced him to don a red bandana and run with the bulls at the legendary Encierro festival in Pamplona, Spain—not once, but twice.[3]

2. William Cashman, an ironworker from New Jersey, had trained in martial arts.[4]

3. Jeremy Glick was an American National Collegiate Judo champion.[5] He was trained by Nagayasu Ogasawara, 8th degree Black Belt, who was head judo coach at West Point United States Military Academy Judo Club from 1989 until 1996.[6] Celita Schutz, a third-degree black belt and five-time national champion, trained with Glick when they were younger. She said of him, "He had no fear when he competed against anyone.... He was definitely willing to take chances, yet he was very careful about what he did."[7] Once when a man accused him and his friends of kicking garbage cans, the man—claiming to be an off-duty police officer—pulled a gun on one of Jeremy's friends. But Jeremy was not intimidated. He threatened, "If you don't put that gun down, I'm going to rip off your face."(Longman, 215)

4. Lauren Grandcolas kept fit through various sports such as sky-diving, kayaking and skating, activities about which she wrote a book.[8] She had also earned emergency medical technician's (EMT) credentials that she could have used (but apparently did not have to) aboard flight UA93.

5. Linda Gronlund was a karate brown belt and a certified emergency medical technician (EMT) whose skills were apparently not needed on flight UA93. Her varied interests included sailing, scuba diving and

---

1 Ruth M. Pettis, "Bingham, Mark (1970-2001)," GLBTQ (Encyclopedia of gay, lesbian, bisexual, transgender and queer culture), #1021

2 "A Life Remembered—Mark Bingham," *Sunday Morning Coffee*, September 11, 2011, #1022

3 Ruth M. Pettis, Op. cit, #1021

4 Jere Longman, "Flight 93: Refusing to give in without a fight," *New York Times*, September 11, 2002, #928

5 "Jeremy Glick," *Wikipedia*

6 Nagayasu Ogasawara, "We Will Never Forget 9/11 American Hero And Judo Champion, Jeremy Glick," *The Martial Art Reporter*, February 6, 2010, #1023

7 Ibid.

8 Cited from *Newsweek* in Amazon Review of Lauren Catuzzi Grand, *You Can Do It!: The Merit Badge Handbook for Grown-Up Girls*, #1024

gardening and cars.[1] Would she not offer her emergency skills to care for stabbed passengers and crew?

6. Richard Guadagno had been trained in close-quarter fighting and anti-hijacking measures.(Longman) Would he refrain from using his skills in a hijacking situation?

7. CeeCee Lyles, a flight attendant on UA93, was respected for her willingness to tackle fleeing criminals. Before joining United Airlines she worked for six years as a police officer in Fort Pierce, Florida.[2] She loved to dress up, but wasn't afraid to confront a gun-toting perpetrator.... For years she patrolled that city's crack-cocaine alleys as a beat cop, working up to detective.[3] After CeeCee Lyles became a detective, she and her colleague Wendy Burstein passed a 40-hour course in Miami called "Advanced Officer Survival": Drills included hand-to-hand fighting, take-down moves and the kind of police maneuvers usually seen only on television.[4] Would a flight attendant with such a background sit and duck while a passenger and pilots are murdered on the plane and merely call her husband to report the incident?

8. When a man once tried to snatch Hilda Marcin'spurse, "she beat him over the head with her umbrella. So she wasn't afraid to stand up for herself."[5]

9. Deborah (Debby) Welsh, a six-foot tall senior flight attendant, was not meek either. She once overpowered a drunken passenger and shoved him into his seat.[6]

The failure by *these* passengers and flight attendants to act *immediately* after they noted murderous violence aboard the aircraft suggests that no such violence had taken place.

Flight attendants did not participate in the counter-attack

According to the calls, none of the flight attendants actually participated in planning a counter-attack or in executing it. Is it plausible that flight attendants, whose professional duty is to assist the passengers in a crisis, would leave passengers to plan and execute a counter-attack all by themselves, and remain mere observers? Even after the stabbings, no one reported an attempt by flight attendants to find a doctor or nurse. Such omission would have been inconceivable, had real stabbings taken place.

---

1   Cited in *World Memorial Medic Tribute*, #1025
2   "Flight Crew: CeeCee Lyles," *Post-Gazette*, October 28, 2001, #1026
3   Linda Shrieves, "Appointment With Fate: Ceecee Lyles Was Soaring Through Life, Then Destiny Came Calling," *Orlando Sentinel*, September 29, 2001, #929
4   Ibid.
5   "Dateline NBC, No Greater Love: The Story of Flight 93," *NBC*, September 3, 2002, #1027
6   Ibid.

Flight attendants did not attempt to contact the cockpit

According to the above testimonies, no flight attendant attempted to contact the cockpit in order to ascertain what was going on there. Such omission would have been highly unlikely, had they really suspected that the pilots were not anymore in control of the airplane.

The counter-attack as a fictitious event

If the callers reported fictitious events—as appears to have been the case—there would be no reason to presume the truth of the legend of a planned counter-attack.

(2) Shouting and yelling heard in the background

We now examine the testimonies by recipients of calls made at or after 9:50 for evidence of shouting or yelling in the background. We chose this time frame because it is after 9:50 that an alleged counter-attack took place.

The following callers made substantive calls at or after 9:50, i.e. calls in which information was transmitted and background sounds could have been heard: Beamer, Britton, Burnett (fourth call), Bradshaw (call to father), Felt, Glick, Lyles, Wainio.

Here is what recipients of the calls reported:

(a) Beamer's call (starting 9:43:48, not terminated)

Robert Combs did not report any shouting in the background. Phyllis Johnson did not report any shouting in the background. She recalled "the absence of the usual background sounds created by the activity and conversations of other passengers." Lisa Jefferson reported, however, that she heard "screams, prayers, exclamations, and talk of subduing the hijackers." Then there was silence. She heard no impact sound of an aircraft crash. In her book *Called*, she dramatizes this point as follows:

> While these questions were going through my head, I began to hear profoundly disturbing sounds coming from the cabin of the plane. What was that? Then I realized what I was hearing: screams, bloodcurling screams. These innocents aboard Flight 93 were crying out for their very lives, and I couldn't help them...The shrill screams of fear, the human cries of terror and disbelief. These were people forced to suffer at the hands of tyrants who commandeered their flight...This was too much for me. But I knew I was Todd's lifeline. I couldn't leave him, and I knew God wouldn't leave me...Then I heard a woman screaming. It was a piercing scream. We all recognize a yell or a cry of pain. But this was different. It was clear these were desperate, anguished cries for help, from people clinging to a sheer thread

of life. A man with a baritone voice near Todd then said, "Oh no! No! God, no" What was happening on that plane?[1]

Was Lisa Jefferson a reliable witness? And does her narrative fit with what most callers reported?

(b) Bradshaw's call to her husband (starting 9:50, lasting 470")

Sandra Bradshaw's husband did not report any shouting or yelling in the background.

(c) Marion Britton's call (starting 9:49, lasting 232")

Fred Fiumano, Marion Britton's friend, who received her call, said he heard "a lot of screaming" and then the phone went dead."[2]

(d) Tom Burnett's calls (the last one occurring at 9:54, probably 1-2 minutes)

Deena Burnett, Tom's wife, who took all four calls from her husband "never noted any background noise other than one would normally expect on an airplane."[3]

(e) Jeremy Glick's call (starting 9:37, not terminated)

In the first interview with Jeremy's wife, Lyz Glick did not mention any shouting or yelling in the background. In her second interview, one day later, she said she could not hear any unusual sounds in the background of the call and the connection was extremely clear, "as if he was calling from the next room." In a subsequent MSNBC interview Lyz Glick said: "I was a little bit, I think, surprised by the aura of what was going on on the plane. I was surprised by how calm it seemed in the background. I didn't hear any screaming. I didn't hear any noises. I didn't hear any commotion."

Richard Makely, Lyz' father-in-law, who took over Jeremy's call from Lyz, said that he "only heard silence on the telephone, then three, four, or five minutes went by, and there were high pitched screaming noises coming over the telephone, that sounded like they were coming from a distance." Makely described the noises as "sounding similar to the screams coming from individuals riding a roller coaster," suggesting that the sounds were a reaction of the passengers to erratic flying. There was then several minutes of silence on the telephone. Then

1   Lisa Jefferson, p. 45-46
2   FBI 302-25306. September 17, 2001. Interview with Fred Fiumano, boyfriend of Marion Britton
3   FBI 302-535. September 11, 2001. Interview with Deena Burnett

Makely heard a series of high pitched screaming sounds again, followed by a noise which he described as "wind sounds."

(f) Cee Cee Lyles' second call (starting at 9:58, lasting about one minute)

After talking with his wife, CeeCee, Lorne Lyles said he heard screaming in the background and the phone went dead. He said he did not hear anyone giving commands.

(g) Honor Elizabeth Wainio's call (starting at 9:53, lasting 269")

Esther Heymann, who took Elizabeth's call, did not report hearing any shouting or yelling in the background.

Discussion

Shouting and commotion were reported by: Lisa Jefferson (Beamer's call); Fred Fiumano (Britton's call); Lorne Lyles (Lyles' second call); Richard Makely (Glick's call)

No shouting and background noise were reported by: Philip Bradshaw (Bradshaw's second call); Deena Burnett (Burnett's last call); Esther Heyman (Wainio's call); Lyz Glick (Glick's call)

Can these contradictory reports be reconciled?

Assuming that the shouting and commotion accompanied the counter-attack of the cockpit that, according to the CVR transcript began at 9:58:00,[1] only three recipients were connected to callers at that time: Lisa Jefferson (Beamer's call), Richard Makely (Glick's call) and very briefly Lorne Lyles (CeeCee Lyles' call). This would explain why shouting and commotion were not mentioned by most other recipients, whose communication terminated before that time. But how, then, are we to explain Fred Fiumano's report of shouting in the background at approximately 9:53? At that time the following recipients were in contact with callers: Lisa Jefferson, Philip Bradshaw, Lyz Glick and Esther Heymann. Yet none of them mentioned hearing any shouting or yelling in the background.

There is no reason to dismiss *what* recipients of calls told. Some of them most probably did hear screams and Lisa Jefferson hardly invented the screams she mentioned. What reveals the nature of these screams is a particular omission by the callers: Not only did most of them display unusual calm when reporting murderous events, but none of them reported that the *other* passengers were fearful, panicky, screaming, yelling or crying. This omission would have been inconceivable, had the aforementioned yelling and screaming originated in the cabin. So from where did the screams originate? The answer will be suggested in chapter 14.

---

1   The authenticity of the CVR is examined in a separate chapter. It is my considered view that the CVR and its transcript were forged.

(3) Intercepted radio messages of statements and shoutings

A number of radio messages intercepted by ground personnel on the morning of 9/11 were attributed to the allegedly hijacked aircraft. It must be emphasized at the outset that the sources of these messages—in terms of geographical coordinates—have not been determined by the US authorities.

(a) Flight AA11[1]

At 8:24:38 an unknown voice was recorded on the ATC radio frequency stating, "We have some planes. Just stay quiet and you'll be O.K. We are returning to the airport." (BOS 1204-1233 Sector 46R)

At 08:24:56, an unknown voice was recorded on the ATC radio frequency stating "Nobody move. Everything will be okay. If you try to make any moves, you'll endanger yourself and the airplane. Just stay quiet." (BOS 1204-1233 Sector 46R)

At 08:33:59, an unknown voice was recorded on the ATC radio frequency stating, "Nobody move, please. We are going back to the airport. Don't try to make any stupid moves."(BOS 1204-1233 Sector 46R)

According to *The New York Times*, the pilot of flight UA175 reported at 8:41 over radio: "We heard a suspicious transmission on our departure from BOS (Boston). Sounds like someone keyed the mic and said everyone stay in your seats."[2] What he reported to have heard was attributed to flight AA11.

All four communications were assumed by ground personnel to have been made by the alleged pilot of flight AA11, claimed to be the one and true Mohamed Atta. The 9/11 Commission tried to attribute this fluke to Atta's clumsiness:

> The hijackers probably did not know how to operate the cockpit radio communication system correctly, and thus inadvertently broadcast their message over the air traffic control channel instead of the cabin public-address channel.

In other words, the hijackers who outsmarted the US air force, had pushed the wrong button.

According to Huffman Aviation's director, Rudi Dekkers, however, the voice on that ATC recording did not resemble at all that of *his* Mohamed Atta. He said on the Erskine Overnight show about this recording:

> "I swear on my life, that's not [Atta's] voice. This is NOT ATTA SPEAK-ING. The guy that is on this tape, issued by the government, is in my opinion a black guy from the Bahamas speaking not with a monotone tone but

1   "Flight Path Study, Flight AA11," *NTSB*, #127, p. 6
2   Matthew L. Wald and Kevin Sack, "'We have some planes,' hijacker told controller," *New York Times*, October 16, 2001, #891

flowing like.... Atta was 'dead man walking,' Atta had a voice that was just
MO-NO-TONE."[1]

There is no need to rely solely on Dekkers' testimony in order to reject the official guesswork, for there is no evidence that *any* Mohamed Atta boarded flight
AA11.[2] This fact alone indicates that someone fabricated the radio messages in
order to help build the official hijacking legend.

(b) Flights UA175 and AA77

No unusual radio messages were said to have been intercepted from flights
UA175 and AA77.

(c) Flight UA93

According to the FAA Timeline of UA Flight 93,at 9:28:19 a "radio transmission of unintelligible sounds of possible screaming or a struggle from an
unknown origin was heard over the ZOB[3] radio."[4] At 9:28:54, "a second radio
transmission, mostly unintelligible, again with sounds of possible screaming or
a struggle and a statement, "get out of here, get out of here" from an unknown
origin was heard over the ZOB radio."[5] At 9:31:57, a third radio transmission,
"mostly unintelligible, may sound like an individual out of breath, more unintelligible words and what sounds like "bomb on board" from an unknown origin
was heard over the ZOB radio." At 9:32:31, a fourth radio transmission asked,
"Did you hear that transmission that reported a bomb on board?" from an unknown origin was heard over the ZOB radio. At 9:39:12, a fifth radio transmission, mostly unintelligible, stated words that may sound like "captain...bomb on
board...our demands...remain quiet."[6]

While the FAA timeline described the third transmission as "mostly unintelligible," the 9/11 Commission had no qualms to report as fact that "a hijacker,
probably Jarrah, made or attempted to make the following announcement to
the passengers of Flight 93: 'Ladies and Gentlemen: Here is the captain, please
sit down keep remaining sitting. We have a bomb on board. So sit.'"(Final Report, 12) Similarly, the FAA was apparently unable to transcribe most of the fifth
transmission, designating it as "mostly unintelligible," while the 9/11 Commission did not hesitate to affirm that FAA Cleveland Air Route Traffic Control

---

1   "Rudi Dekkers drops some bombshell: 9/11 revelations on the tenth anniversary of the at-
     tacks," *Erskine Overnight Show*, September 11, 2011. ‹http://www.erskineonradio.com/ar-
     chives/archives2011.html› [scroll down to 09-10-11] At minute 27:15,

2   See chapter 2 of this book

3   ZOB is the three-letter airspace designator for the airspace managed by the Cleveland
     ARTCC

4   Summary of Air Traffic Hijack Events, September 11, 2001, FAA, p. 20, #1028

5   Ibid.

6   Ibid. p. 21

Center "overheard a second announcement indicating that there was a bomb on board, that the plane was returning to the airport, and that they [*sic*] should remain seated."

The 9/11 Commission speculated that "while it apparently was not heard by the passengers, this announcement...was intended to deceive them. Jarrah, like Atta earlier, may have inadvertently broadcast the message because he did not know how to operate the radio and the intercom."[1] Apparently Jarrah's phantom, like that of his colleague Atta, was clumsy enough to push the wrong button and ensure that his message would be down-linked to the US authorities, so they could, as it were, prove their case. The 9/11 Commission explained why the "guys" were so clumsy: "To our knowledge none of them had ever flown an actual airliner before." Indeed!

Conclusions of Part III

As mentioned in the Introduction to Part III, the official account of 9/11 bases largely on the phone calls. These calls "proved," as it were, that the attacks were committed by "Arab or Islamic looking" men, that the attacks were executed by stabbing or slashing passengers, flight attendants and the pilots, and that passengers in the last hijacked plane tried heroically to overcome the "hijackers."

Readers of the preceding chapters could not remain oblivious to the fact, that what the public—acting as it were as the jury on 9/11—has learned about the events on board the aircraft, were shreds of third- or fourth-degree hearsay. Callers from the aircraft would communicate information to a recipient on the ground. That recipient would be interviewed by FBI agents, who would then— from notes taken—compile a report that summarizes what the recipient of the call has told. That report is never a verbatim record of what the recipient has said, but what the FBI agent finds interesting to note in his or her own words. These reports do not provide a clue to what the recipient had actually said or what he or she was asked by the interviewing agents. Some of the FBI reports were then repackaged as press releases that appeared in modified form in mass media with journalists variously tweaking the wording or meaning of the message.

In Part III we examined whether the reports from the phone callers—with due regard to their hearsay nature—could prove the official account on the hijackings. Here are the salient conclusions from this examination:

According to the preponderance of the evidence, phone callers did not report real events.

---

1   Ibid.

Numerous testimonies by recipients of calls have been suppressed or disregarded by the FBI, if they contained elements that might have undermined the official account of 9/11.

Circumstantial evidence exists to the effect that the FBI engaged in forgery with regard to some of the phone calls (Betty Ong [AA11], Edward Felt [UA93] and Thomas Burnett [UA93]), as well as regarding the Cockpit Voice Recorder from flight UA93. We suggest that the intent of this forgery was to cover-up the real function of these flights on 9/11 and reinforce a contrived legend of Islamic hijackers.

PART IV. THE DECEPTION

Chapter 14. Fake Hijackings and Real Mass-Murder

In Chapters 3 and 4, I demonstrated the failure by the US authorities to produce evidence that flights AA11, UA175, AA77 and UA93 had crashed at the known landmarks of the WTC, the Pentagon and in Somerset County, Pa. If they did not crash at the known landmarks, what happened to these flights?

Air traffic controllers can generally track an aircraft whose transponder has been deactivated by reverting to so-called primary returns, particularly when air traffic in the area is not dense. As traffic density increases and multiple aircraft turn off their transponders simultaneously it becomes very difficult, if not impossible, to determine which blip belongs to which aircraft.

(1) The military war games of September 11, 2001

(a) Evidence of a huge confusion

It appears that air traffic controllers had to contend with far more than four suspected hijackings on the morning of 9/11. According to the 9/11 Commission, "[d]uring the course of the morning, there were multiple erroneous reports of hijacked aircraft".(Final Report, 28) Alan Scott of NORAD told the 9/11 Commission that Delta Flight 89 was first reported missing, then that it had been hijacked and finally that it had not been hijacked but had landed safely in Cleveland. Scott described the flight as "the first red herring of the day, because there were a number of reported possible hijackings that unfolded over the hours immediately following the operation."[1] Other sources refer to that flight as Delta

---

[1]   Alan Scott (NORAD), 9/11 Commission Hearing, May 23, 2003

Flight 1989.[1] Was this the same flight? Other flights suspected of having been hijacked included American Airlines flight 43, which left Newark International Airport shortly after 8 a.m. bound for Los Angeles and made an emergency landing in Cincinnati, and American Airlines flight 1729 from Newark to San Antonio, departing at 8:50 a.m. and forced to land at St. Louis.[2] According to the BBC, however, flight AA43 was scheduled to fly from Boston, not Newark, and was "grounded due to a mechanical problem."[3] According to the Chicago Tribune, flight AA43 "was cancelled just minutes before its scheduled 8:10 a.m. departure from Boston due to a mechanical problem."[4] I have found no explanation for these conflicting reports.

According to the Daily Telegraph, "[A]s many as nine aircraft may have been part of the original plot."[5] At approximately 9:09 a.m., the FAA Command Center reported that 11 aircraft were either not communicating with FAA facilities or flying unexpected routes.[6] NORAD Major General Larry Arnold claimed that, on the morning of 9/11, a total of 21 planes had been identified as possible hijackings.[7] He added that, "We were receiving many reports of hijacked aircraft. When we received those calls, we might not know from where the aircraft had departed. We also didn't know the location of the airplane."

In a statement made to Leslie Filson, as contained in her notes, General Arnold again explained that there were at one time 21 suspected hijacks in the system and that there was "a lot of confusion, as you can imagine."[8]

Colonel Robert Marr, the NEADS battle commander, was informed that "across the nation there were some 29 different reports of hijackings."[9] Even Assistant Secretary of Defense for Public Affairs, Victoria Clarke, who was in the Pentagon during the morning of 9/11 and remained there for most of the day, admitted: "There were lots of false signals out there. There were false hijack

---

1   Ben Fenton, "Five planes may have escaped," *Daily Telegraph*, September 20, 2001, #517

2   "Investigation: Could it have been worse?," *National Journal, The Hotline*, September 19, 2001, #519

3   "FBI probes 'attempted fifth hijack'," *BBC*, September 18, 2001, #1055

4   Stephen J. Hedges and Naftali Bendavid, "FBI probes 5th flight for hijackers Plane grounded on day of attack," *Chicago Tribune*, September 18, 2001, #1054

5   Ibid.

6   William B. Scott, "Exercise Jump-Starts Response to Attacks," *Aviation Week & Space Technology*, June 3, 2002, #1053

7   Eric Hehs, "Conversation with Major General Larry Arnold," *One Magazine*, January 2002, #1052

8   Interview with Maj. Gen. Arnold and Leslie Filson, 9/11 Commission, September 11, 2002. Team 8, Box 22, p. NCT0068077, #1050. See also Miles Kara's comment, July 13, 2010, #1051

9   Robert A. Baker, "Commander of 9/11 Air Defenses Retires," *Newhouse News Service*, March 31, 2005, #1049

---

squawks, and a great part of the challenge was sorting through what was a legitimate threat and what wasn't."[1]

Apart from the four aircraft designated as the "death flights"—AA11, AA77, UA175 and UA93—and those mentioned above, the following flight numbers were considered possible hijackings at some point during September 11, 2001: AAL2247, USA41, DAL89, DAL1989, NWA197, UAL641, UAL57, USA633,[2] UAL163,[3] UAL177,[4] Continental 321,[5] AA189[6] and KAL85.[7] This list is far from exhaustive.[8]

According to Donald A. Robinson, an American Airlines dispatcher interviewed by the FBI on 9/11, AA189 was the only flight he knew to have sent a hijack message back to the dispatchers via ACARS, although he noted that it was unknown why the cockpit had sent this message.[9]

Andrew P. Studdert, the Chief Operating Officer and Executive Vice President of United Airlines on 9/11, testified before the 9/11 Commission on January 27, 2004. When speaking about the confusion that prevailed during 9/11, he said that "around 10:00 a.m we los[t] contact with United Flights 641, 415 and 399," and "[f]rom 10:55 to 11:15 United flights 103, 634, 57, 2725, 1211, 1695, 2101, 2256 and 2102 [we]re also reported missing but [we]re eventually located at various airports."[10]

Another unexplained source of confusion concerns the multiple ELT signals intercepted in various locations on 9/11.[11] ELT signals are broadcast by radio transmitters carried aboard aircraft and are supposed to activate only in the event the aircraft crashes, their function being to facilitate searches for the aircraft wreckage. According to Paul Thumser, an operations supervisor at the FAA's New York Center, ELTs on Boeing 767 aircraft cannot be activated by a pi-

---

1   "Chilling Audio From 9/11 Hijack Played at Hearing," *Paula Zahn Now*, CNN, Transcript, June 17, 2004, #1048

2   9/11 Commission Team 7, Box 7, "Other Flights," page 5, #1047

3   Ben Fenton, "More planes may have been targeted," *The Daily Telegraph* (UK), September 20, 2001, #563

4   MFR 03009986. October 8, 2003. Interview with Mark Randol, TSA Federal Security Director, Missoula MT, p. 5

5   Transcript of East NTMO tape, prepared by Miles Kara (9/11 Commission staff), November 4, 2003, #1784

6   FBI 302-22919. September 11, 2001. Interview with Donald A. Robinson, Jr.

7   Wikipedia: Korean_Air_Flight_85; see also Zaz Hollander, "High Alert," *Anchorage Daily News*, September 8, 2002, #1045

8   Blogger 'shoestring' posted on April 10, 2011 a long list of "false hijackings," #520

9   FBI 302-22919. September 11, 2001. Interview with Donald A. Robinson, Jr.

10 Statement of Andrew P. Studdert to the National Commission on Terrorist Attacks Upon the United States, January 27, 2004, #1785

11 Shoestring (pseudonym), "The 9/11 Time Discrepancy Oddity: Distress Signals Indicated Planes Crashed Minutes Before Flights 11 and 175 Hit the WTC," September 8, 2010, #903

lot and only activate if there is a serious impact.[1] According to the official account two Boeing 767 aircraft crashed at the North and South Towers, respectively, of the WTC. No ELT was triggered by the impact of the aircraft, however, although ELT signals were picked up a few minutes before the impact in each instance. In a Memorandum issued by the staff of the 9/11 Commission after interviewing Paul Thumser, the staffers wrote, "We visited the Rescue Coordination Center (RCC) [operated by the Air Force] and they receive all ELTs; so many in fact that they are a nuisance and they have special procedures and software to manage that."[2]

This confusion was also reflected in the news on 9/11. It was initially reported in media and "confirmed" by American Airlines that flight AA77 had crashed at the WTC while United Airlines announced at 11:30 a.m.—more than two hours after its reported crash at the South Tower of the WTC—that flight UA175 was still missing and could not be located. Only at 12:05 p.m. did ABC News quote United Airlines as confirming that one of its planes had crashed, although the aircraft was not identified. At 1:00 p.m., it was still believed that Flight AA77 had crashed at the WTC. At 2:30 p.m., ABC News announced that the FBI had claimed AA77 had crashed at the Pentagon; American Airlines remained reluctant to confirm this fact.[3] These anecdotes represent only a random sample of the confusing reports broadcast on 9/11.

Even when American Airlines issued a press release mid-day on 9/11 in which they confirmed that they had "lost" two airliners designated as Flights 11 and 77, they did not indicate *where* these airliners had been lost.[4]

It is still surprisingly unclear as to who gave the unprecedented order to ground all air traffic in the United States on 9/11. According to Wikipedia, Ben Sliney "is credited with giving the order to land every plane in the air over the US at the time, roughly 4,200 aircraft, and effectively shutting down US airspace." September 11, 2001, was Sliney's first day as National Operations Manager. In his testimony to the 9/11 Commission in 2003, Secretary of Transportation Norman Y. Mineta claimed *he* had given the order to ground all air traffic over the US, saying: "At approximately 9:45 a.m. ... I gave the FAA the final order for all civil aircraft to land at the nearest airport as soon as possible. It was the first shutdown of civil aviation in the history of the United States."[5]

1   MFR 04016821. October 1, 2003. Visit of FAA New York Air Route Center and interview with Paul Thumser. NARA Team 8—FAA—Thumser Paul

2   Ibid.

3   September 11 Television Archive, ‹http://archive.org/details/sept_11_tv_archive›

4   "Remaining aircraft account for, American confirms," Press Release, *American Airlines*, September 11, 2001, #544; see also "American Airlines Statement on Plane Crashes," *The Washington Post*, September 11, 2001, #1034

5   Norman Y. Mineta, "Statement before the National Commission on Terrorist Attacks Upon the United States," May 23, 2002, #1044

Staff members at NORAD's Northeast Air Defense Sector (NEADS) had difficulty locating American Airlines Flight 11 and other aircraft on their radar screens. Lt. Col. Dawne Deskins of NEADS said that, when the FAA first called to report the first hijacking, the FAA "gave me the latitude and longitude of that track ... [but] there was nothing there."[1]

Author and pilot Lynn Spencer explained in more detail why it was so difficult to locate the aircraft:

> To identify American 11, the surveillance and ID techs must go through a grueling process. Their radar scopes are filled with hundreds of radar returns not just from aircraft but from weather systems, ground interference, and what's called anomalous propagation—false returns caused by conditions in the atmosphere, or by such obstructions as flocks of birds. The technicians must first determine which radar data on their screens is for aircraft, which they do by monitoring its movement, which is distinctive for planes. The technician must observe for at least 36 seconds to a minute just to confirm that a blip is in fact an aircraft track. The tech must attach what's called a tactical display number to it, which tells the computer to start tracking and identifying the target. If the target is in fact a plane, then over a period of 12-20 seconds, the computer will start to generate information on the track: heading, speed, altitude, latitude, longitude, and the identifying information being transmitted by the transponder [if the transponder is on]. With the hundreds of pieces of radar data filling their screens, and little information as to the location of the flight, [the task of locating it] is daunting.[2]

(b) The reason for the confusion

There was ample reason for the above confusion, although this was not reported at the time: On the morning of 9/11 the US military had been scheduled to conduct multiple war games (or exercises, or drills) in the very air space where Operation 9/11 took place. At least one of these exercises included simulated "live-fly" hijackings.[3] As part of these exercises, electronic blips representing simulated hijacked aircraft were inserted onto the scopes of air traffic controllers, leading them to wonder whether the blips they saw moving on their screens belonged to bogus, simulated aircraft or to real aircraft. For a more detailed discussion of these exercises and how they relate to the actual events of 9/11, see the sub-section (c) below.

---

1   Liza Porteus, "Air Defenders Learn Lessons From Sept. 11," *Fox News*, September 8, 2002, #1043

2   Lynn Spencer, *Touching History: The Untold Story of the Drama That Unfolded in the Skies Over America on 9/11* (Free Press, New York, 2008), p. 31-32

3   "Live-fly" exercises mean exercises using real aircraft, not just table-top simulations. See NORAD News, Release 090708-00, July 8, 2009, #1786

In light of the confusion prevailing on 9/11, it is understandable that air traffic controllers could not realistically determine the identities of supposedly hijacked aircraft and their locations after the transponders of multiple aircraft were turned off or had changed their codes. They were thus unable to reliably track the four aircraft alleged to have been hijacked and crashed on 9/11. It was therefore similarly difficult to determine, based on observations made by air traffic controllers, which aircraft had actually crashed and if so, where.

The National Transportation Safety Board (NTSB) released Flight Path Studies for three of the 9/11 flights in 2006[1]: Flights AA11,[2] AA77[3] and UA175.[4] According to the NTSB report on flight AA11, transponder returns from that flight ceased at 8:21 a.m.[5] The NTSB's reconstructions of the flight paths were based on "radar data obtained from the FAA's Terminal and Route Traffic Control Centers and from the US Air Force 84th Radar Evaluation Squadron." The Radar Evaluation Squadron *reconstructed* the flight path from undisclosed data. Col. Alan Scott of NORAD confirmed to the 9/11 Commission that much of his radar data for the "primary targets" on 9/11 was not seen that day, confirming that "it was reconstructed days later by the 84th Radar Evaluation Squadron, and other [unidentified] agencies."[6]

NEADS Battle Commander Col. Robert Marr briefed the staff of the 9/11 Commission on October 27, 2003.[7] During his briefing, he acknowledged that when the crime unfolded, NEADS "was preparing for the day's NORAD exercise." He told the Commission staff that "at one point on 9/11 there were up to 11 unaccounted for aircraft in NEADS airspace."

Due to this confusion, a formal identification of the wreckage found at the officially-declared crash sites of the WTC, the Pentagon and Somerset County, Pa., was necessary in order to remove any doubts as to the identities of the aircraft that had crashed at these locations. The FBI, however, which had jurisdiction over the crash sites, decided not to forensically determine to which aircraft the wreckage belonged. Exceptionally, for the largest aircraft incident in US his-

---

1   Barbara Elias (ed.), "Complete Air-Ground Transcripts of Hijacked 9/11 Flight Recordings Declassified," National Security Archive Electronic Briefing Book No. 196, August 11, 2006, #1042

2   "Flight Path Study, AA11," *NTSB*, February 19, 2002, #127

3   "Flight Path Study, AA77," *NTSB*, February 19, 2002, #129

4   "Flight Path Study, UA175," *NTSB*, February 19, 2002, #128

5   According to Col. Robert Marr, head of NEADS, the transponder was only turned off some time after 8:30 a.m. (*ABC News*, Sept. 11, 2002)

6   "Major General Larry Arnold's Testimony," Public Hearing, *9/11 Commission*, May 23, 2003, #1040

7   MFR 03012970. October 27, 2003. NEADS field site visit. Briefing by Col. Robert Marr

tory, no formal identification of aircraft debris was carried out by the appropriate authorities.[1]

(c) The hijacking exercises of 9/11

1   Aidan Monaghan, "FBI Counsel: No records available revealing ID process of recovered 9/11 plane wreckage," *911blogger.com*, March 17, 2008, #1041

As the above Power Point diagrams show, the US military had envisioned various exercises, including terrorist attacks using aircraft as missiles planned by Osama bin Laden, *before* 9/11. More relevant to the subject at hand, however, is the fact that a number of military war games were scheduled to be conducted by the US military on the day of September 11, 2001, at precisely the same time as the murderous events occurred.[1] These war games included exercises involving aircraft hijackings and crashes. Were the exercises and the murderous events in some way related?

A central feature of the simulated war games conducted on 9/11 was for the military to feed electronic blips representing airliners into military and civilian radar. As the events of 9/11 unfolded, radar operators had no way of knowing whether the blips they were observing on their screens represented real or simulated aircraft. There were in fact three types of blips the controllers had to confront: Those representing virtual aircraft, possessing no physical existence; those representing real aircraft which were scheduled to participate in the simulated hijackings; and, all other blips representing real aircraft.

Similar exercises had been conducted just days prior to 9/11, all working with the same scenario of terrorists hijacking a London to New York flight with plans to detonate explosives over New York.[2] Air traffic controllers and others responsible for flight security in the Eastern part of the United States thus had good reason to believe that at least some of the input on their screens was part of a similar if not identical exercise.

The Final Report of the 9/11 Commission mentions such an exercise in passing, in connection with a notification received by NEADS at 8:37:52, saying that flight AA11 "had been hijacked." The following conversation is quoted by the Commission:

> FAA: Hi. Boston Center TMU (Traffic Management Unit), we have a problem here. We have a hijacked aircraft headed towards New York, and we need you guys to, we need someone to scramble some F-16s or something up there, help us out.
>
> NEADS: Is this real-world or exercise?
>
> FAA: No, this is not an exercise, not a test (Final Report, 20).

Upon receiving notification from Boston regarding the possible hijacking of flight AA11 NEADS commander Col. Robert asked if the notification was part of the exercise. Lt. Col. Dawne Deskins also received word of the possible hijacking from Boston. She, too, initially assumed it must be part of the exercise. Major

---

1   "NORAD Exercises—Hijack Summary," 9/11 Commission's documents, Team 8 Box 20, #240

2   Ibid.

Kevin Nasypany, the NEADS mission crew commander, had helped design the day's exercise. Thinking the reported hijacking was part of it, he was reported to have said, "The hijack's not supposed to be for another hour."[1]

Three NEADS technicians who were following the news—Stacia Rountree, Shelley Watson and Maureen Dooley—looked forward to an exciting exercise:

> 08:37:56
>
> | | |
> |---|---|
> | *Watson:* | *What?* |
> | *Dooley:* | *Whoa!* |
> | *Watson:* | *What was that?* |
> | *Rountree:* | *Is that real-world?* |
> | *Dooley:* | *Real-world hijack.* |
> | *Watson:* | *Cool!*[2] |

The above conversation is excerpted from recordings made in the control room of NORAD's Northeast headquarters, obtained by the magazine Vanity Fair.[3]

The expression "real-world" is used by the military to denote live-fly, as opposed to table-top exercises, not a "real attack". This can be ascertained from a comment made by Major *James Fox*, leader of the NEADS weapons team, at 8:43 a.m., after it had been made known within the system that flight AA11 had been hijacked: "I've never seen so much real-world stuff happen during an exercise."[4]

Had Shelley Watson, quoted in the above dialogue, believed that "real-world" meant a real attack, she would hardly have exclaimed, "Cool!"

Similarly, NEADS Battle Commander *Robert Marr*, upon observing his personnel reacting to the news of the hijacking, reportedly thought the day's exercise was "kicking off with a lively, unexpected twist." Even after a colleague informed him of the situation—"real life, not part of the exercise"—he continued to believe his colleague was playing a part in the exercise by attempting to mislead him. Marr said he thought that "this is an interesting start to the exercise. This 'real-world' mixed in with today's simex [simulated exercise] will keep [my staff members] on their toes." (Spencer, 26)

Even Major General *Larry Arnold* later said that, when he heard of the hijacking, his first thought was to ask, "Is this part of the exercise?"[5]

When United Airlines' Chief Operating Officer *Andy Studdert* arrived at the airline's System Operations Control (SOC) center on the morning of 9/11, at around 9:00 a.m., he had to repeatedly assert to employees that the unfolding

---

1   Michael Bronner, "9/11 Live: The NORAD Tapes," *Vanity Fair*, August 2006, #308
2   Ibid.
3   Ibid.
4   Ibid.
5   "Major General Larry Arnold's Testimony," Public Hearing, *9/11 Commission*, May 23, 2003, #1040

crisis was not a training exercise: "This is not a drill!"[1] Ten days prior, he had surprised the staff with a crisis-training exercise, where he'd told them a flight over the Pacific had broken radio contact and suffered a potentially disastrous engine failure. The staff believed the story for 30 minutes before he told them the truth.[2]

As late as 9:04:50, after both WTC towers had been hit, the following conversation took place at the Battle Cab, the glassed-in command area overlooking the ops floor at NEADS:

> *Is this explosion part of that that we're lookin' at now on TV?*
>
> *Yes.*
>
> *Jesus... And there's a possible second hijack also—a United Airlines ... Two planes? Get the f.. out...*
>
> *I think this is a damn input, to be honest.*[3]

The last sentence reveals that the unidentified speaker thought that what he was seeing on television was also an "input," i.e., a fabricated image being fed to "his" television set. This suggests that he was not the only participant to believe that everything he or she was being fed had been faked.

In a detailed analysis, the blogger *Shoestring* demonstrated that some locations carried the exercises past the crash times of the four aircraft.[4] They apparently believed the stories about the crashes, including what was being reported by the television networks, to be fake.

It bears mentioning that most major NORAD exercises conducted previously had included a hijack scenario. NORAD officials have acknowledged that "scriptwriters" for the drills had included the idea of hijacked aircraft being used as weapons in past exercises.[5]

As *Vanity Fair* reported, audio recordings from the operations floor at NEADS reveal that "there was no sense that the attack was over with the crash of United 93." Instead, "the alarms go on and on. False reports of hijackings, and real responses, continue well into the afternoon [of 9/11]." The fighter pilots over New York and [Washington] DC (and later Boston and Chicago) would spend hours darting around their respective skylines intercepting hundreds of aircraft they

---

1   Alan Levin, Marily Adams and Blake Morrison, "Terror attacks brought drastic decision: Clear the skies," *USA Today*, August 12, 2002, #794

2   Ibid.

3   Michael Bronner, Op. cit., #308

4   *Shoestring*, "'Let's get rid of this goddam sim': How NORAD radar screens displayed false tracks all through the 9/11 attacks," 911blogger.com, August 12, 2010, #800

5   Steven Komarow and Tom Squitieri, "NORAD had drills of jets as weapons," *USA Today*, April 18, 2004, #1039

deemed suspicious.... No one at NEADS would go home until late on the night of the 11th."[1]

The FBI and the 9/11 Commission showed no inclination to investigate the relationship between the exercises and Operation 9/11. US authorities refused to disclose the identities of those coordinating these exercises, and why September 11, 2001, had been selected.

Numerous authors have examined public evidence surrounding these exercises. An encyclopedic overview of similar exercises carried out prior to 9/11 is available on the website History Commons.[2] Michael Ruppert, the first to investigate these exercises, strongly believes that they provided the necessary cover for the actual operation. His view is supported and enhanced by Webster G. Tarpley, who provides a detailed analysis of no fewer than 46 separate exercises and drills that may have been carried out with the events of 9/11 in mind.[3]

Tarpley explains how military exercises represent a classic method to prepare a sneak attack, a coup or a provocation:

> The aggressor army announces that it is holding its summer maneuvers near the border of the target state. The deployment takes place under the cover of press releases announcing that they are merely maneuvers. When the troops are in position, they receive an order for a real attack. If field exercises can be used for fooling the adversary, then staff exercises are more useful for deceiving one's own side...Staff exercises or command exercises are perfect for a rogue network which is forced to conduct its operations using the same communications and computer systems used by other officers who are not necessary party to the illegal operation, coup or provocation as it may be. A putschist officer may be working at a console next to another officer who is not in on the coup, and who might indeed oppose it if he knew about it. The putschist's behavior is suspicious: What the hell is he doing? The loyal officer looks over and asks the putschist about it. The putschist cites a staff maneuver for which he is preparing. The loyal officer concludes that the putschist's activities are part of an officially sanctioned drill, and his suspicions are allayed. The putschist may even explain that participation in the staff exercise requires a special security clearance which the loyal officer does not have. The conversation ends, and the putschist can go on with his treasonous work. (Tarpley, 204-5)

Within the framework of a live-fly hijacking exercise, the military would seek to employ reliable participants to play the role of hijacked passengers and flight crew. Participants would be told they had been selected for their trustworthiness and discretion, and would be invited to participate in an anti-terror

---

1   Michael Bronner, Op. cit., #308
2   "Military Exercises Up To 9/11," *History Commons website*, as of June 25, 2012
3   Webster Tarpley, "The Forty-Six Exercises and Drills of 9/11," (from *9/11 Synthetic Terror: Made in USA*, 5th Edition, Progressive Press, 2006), August 2011

exercise. Most of them would probably accept to participate in such an exercise as a civic and patriotic duty. Those reluctant to make fake calls to their next-of-kin would be offered the option of calling unrelated persons, such as security officials. With such a scenario, the plotters would be able to establish the future legend of Islamic hijackings.

(2) Did the phone callers participate in hijacking drills?

Having mentioned the multiple military exercises being conducted on the morning of September 11, 2001, including live-fly hijacking drills, and the fact that the phone callers reported bogus and implausible events, the question that immediately springs to mind is: Were the callers participating in the hijacking drills? It should come as no surprise that, had this been the case, it would be treated as a mortal secret never to be revealed. The conduct of the callers strongly suggests, indeed, that they were acting rather than relaying real events.

Serious attempts to explain the incongruities of the phone calls were undertaken by Rowland Morgan, David Ray Griffin and blogger John Doe II, with each identifying numerous contradictions and anomalies surrounding the phone calls. All three agree that the phone calls were faked or fictitious.

(a) The voice morphing theory

One theory presented by Prof. David Ray Griffin suggests that the phone calls may have been faked via *voice morphing*,[1] a technology developed in the Los Alamos National Laboratory to simulate the voice of a person. To create such fabrications, a 10-minute digital recording of the voice to be simulated is sufficient. A template is created from that original, permitting the morphing software to transform the speech of the actual speaker into the voice of the original speaker, thus allowing that person to be impersonated.

Morphing phone calls would offer a logistical advantage over other means of fakery. Operators impersonating passengers or flight attendants could be recruited from competent military personnel with high security clearances. From a management perspective, such a method of fakery would be preferable. The method does present serious problems, however, particularly when applied to real-time dialogue.

In a critical essay examining Prof. Griffin's theory, Erik Larson pointed out the difficulties of using voice morphing in *real time*, which would have to have been the case if the calls made on 9/11 had been faked with said technology:

> [T]he inventor [of this technology], George Papcun, has commented that voice-morphing a conversation in near real time would be more complex

---

1   David Ray Griffin, "9/11 Live or Fabricated: Do the NORAD Tapes Verify the 9/11 Commission Report?," *911Truth.org*, September 4, 2006

than fabricating a simple recorded statement, and would require an extensive recording as a sample. It would be even more difficult to fool the subject's family members, who, in addition to being familiar with the person's voice, would be familiar with their unique communication style and intimate details of their lives.[1]

Even if such voice morphing technology had been available in 2001, attempting to impersonate a next-of-kin in an interactive dialogue could risk exposing the scam. The caller might, for example, be confronted with questions that only a true husband or wife would be able to answer. While a skillful impersonator could have learned the names of all family members, even pet names, ahead of time, and successfully sailed through any potentially embarrassing questions, the call recipient might become suspicious if the impersonator repeatedly avoided answering certain questions, or made mistakes with names, dates, facts or terms of endearment. Morphing technology could have been used for calls made to strangers, but it is improbable that it would be used to call husbands, wives, parents or intimate friends.

Another problem, mentioned by Prof. Paul Zarembka, is that a number of callers were late arrivals to flight UA93. This means that the plotters did not have the opportunity to record the 10-minute voice sample necessary for the morphing software to function effectively or to collect the family details needed to fake such a call. Unless all the callers had been selected in advance, morphing the voices of late travelers would have been impossible.

A parsing of the phone calls for which details are available suggests that at least some of the calls, particularly those lasting more than a minute or two, would have posed serious challenges to potential impersonators, with the corresponding risk of raising their interlocutors' suspicion.

(b) The hijacking drill theory

Enter a theory sketched out years ago by blogger John Doe II, but which apparently has not since been explored systematically. According to this theory, the phone calls made by passengers and crew members were genuine, meaning they were made by the named persons and not by impersonators. The callers would have been asked to participate in a live-fly hijacking drill in which they would enact, as realistically as possible, the role of passengers and crew on a hijacked aircraft. Their main task would have been to call selected recipients on the ground and report the mock hijackings, including the alleged conduct of the alleged hijackers, their alleged Middle Eastern background and other details that would later become building blocks of the official 9/11 legend. The volunteers would have been told that the military needed civilian volunteers to participate

---

1   Erik Larson, Op. cit, #1038

in a yearly hijacking drill, the purpose of which is to find out whether the information provided by the phone calls would trickle through "the system" quickly enough to trigger a military response to the hijackings.

Before proceeding, it must be emphasized that asking participants in an emergency exercise to make bogus phone calls is not uncommon. In fact, such a procedure was envisaged for 9/11, as related below.

The National Reconnaissance Office (NRO)[1], one of the least-publicized US intelligence agencies, had scheduled an exercise for the morning of September 11, 2001. The scenario of that exercise revolved around a corporate jet crashing into one of the four towers of the NRO Headquarters in Chantilly, Virginia, just four miles from Dulles International Airport.[2] The scenario was meant to test the evacuation protocols of NRO's headquarters after such a crash. Participants—in this case, NRO employees—were given cards with simple tasks to be carried out, including *making phone calls* to various recipients and telling them about the bogus crash and ensuing fire. To lend the exercise as much realism as possible, a smoke-generator was used to fake the burning wreckage of the downed aircraft.[3] According to the head of the NRO, the exercise was canceled at the last minute due to Operation 9/11, with most NRO employees being sent home. NRO spokesman Art Haubold said, "It was just an incredible coincidence that this happened to involve an aircraft crashing into our facility."[4]

According to the instructions distributed for the NRO drill, participants were to inform their listeners that their call was part of an exercise. This is not ordinarily the case, however, as a true exercise is carried out without letting the majority of participants realize it is an exercise. Only in this way can their response be tested and properly evaluated. Emergency exercises are therefore designed to appear as realistic as is possible. The NRO account does not prove that the 9/11 phone calls served a similar purpose. It does show, however, that such a method of conducting an emergency exercise had previously been envisioned by a US government agency, and it is therefore a plausible theory that must be seriously considered with respect to the 9/11 phone calls.

Let us recall that, throughout chapters 7 to 10, we found callers reporting actions or circumstances which they did not see or which contradicted what others had said; we found also numerous inexplicable omissions, multiple implausible statements and unexplained contradictions. We summed up these findings

---

1   "About the NRO," National Reconnaissance Office webpage (www.nro.gov), #1037
2   John J. Lumpkin, "Agency planned exercise on Sept. 11 built around a plane crashing into a building," *Boston Globe*, September 11, 2002, #555
3   NRO Emergency Response to a Small Aircraft Crash, Exercise Concept, 9/11 Commission documents, Team 8, Box 16, Misc-Work-Paper-Fdr-NRO-Exercise-Plane-Crash-Into-Building, #809
4   Ibid.

in a single sentence, namely that *the callers did not report real events.* Such conduct, inexplicable in view of the official account, would fit well the hypothesis of a hijacking drill. The callers would report either what they were told to report or improvise on the basis of keywords or themes given to them on a script sheet. It is likely, though not absolutely necessary for this theory, that the players for the drill were selected in advance of 9/11. There exists circumstantial evidence that such a selection process may have occurred.

While the findings in this chapter conform to this theory, there exists additional supporting evidence.

Calm callers

The calm demeanor of callers reporting stabbings and killings that occurred within their lines of sight is incompatible with ordinary human behavior. Even battle-hardened persons would express fear if they were to witness a murder a few feet away, in an environment where person-to-person violence would be so unexpected. The calm tone used by several callers in reporting dreadful events surprised even those who knew them. Their conduct would be plausible, however, if the callers were reporting fictitious events from a script. In such a case, they would actually have to exert themselves to fake their own fear. Not all callers were good actors or attempted to fake fear.

Puzzling conduct by crew members

Air carrier responsibilities for security and anti-hijacking training for flight crews were laid out in the Air Carrier Standard Security Program prior to 9/11. In addition to specifying several hours of security training, it provided an outline of in-flight hijacking tactics for both the cockpit and cabin crews. Among other things, this outline advised air crews to *land the aircraft* as soon as possible, to *communicate with authorities*, and to *try delaying tactics.*[1]

According to the official narrative, crew members initially had every reason to presume that this was a classic case of hijacking. From that perspective, it is puzzling as to why none of the flight attendants aboard flights UA175, AA77 and UA93 attempted to contact the pilots, or why they or the pilots did not attempt to contact the appropriate authorities. Betty Ong (AA11) called the AA Southeastern Reservation Office in Cary, North Carolina. Madeline Sweeney (AA11) called the AA administrative office at Logan. Robert Fangman (UA175) called SAMC, a UAL maintenance center in San Francisco. Renee May (AA77) called her parents. Sandra Bradshaw (UA93) first called SAMC in San Francisco and then her husband. CeeCee Lyles (UA93) called her husband. None of them called security personnel.

---

1   9/11 Commission. "Staff Statement Nr. 4 (The Four Flights)," p. 1 (emphasis added)

It is also puzzling, too, that none of the flight attendants tried "delaying tactics" towards the alleged hijackers, such as engaging them in small talk or trying to find out whether the alleged hijackers actually held a bomb, as they claimed. Such a dereliction of duty would be incomprehensible had there been real hijackers and something resembling a bomb.

From the perspective of a real hijacking and stabbings, it is puzzling that both Betty Ong and Madeline Sweeney (AA11) would sit for a long time and chat on the telephone while their colleagues were being stabbed. This is certainly not normal conduct of a responsible flight attendant.

From the perspective of a real hijacking, it is puzzling, too, that the pilot of flight AA77 would announce to passengers that the flight had been hijacked, yet not report that fact by radio to the ground.

All of the above puzzling conduct would, however, be perfectly normal within the framework of a hijacking drill.

The reason for secretive conduct by American Airlines officials

American Airlines officials were described in chapter 7 as intending to conceal the evidence they obtained from the AA11 phone calls. Families of 9/11 victims, who learned of this concealment later on, were furious. They were justified in considering this conduct as almost criminal. On its face, suppressing information about real hijackings instead of immediately informing all appropriate authorities would have been at least a terrible mistake for which these individuals should have been fired, if not prosecuted. There is no evidence, however, that these individuals were investigated, let alone punished.

Why did these airline officials act so strangely? The most plausible explanation is that they had been informed of impending hijacking drills and believed that the phone calls were part of such drills. Under such an assumption, it would be reasonable for them to not seek to unnecessarily alarm too many people. A significant fact is that they even refused to relay information to Madeline Sweeney, a flight attendant on flight AA11, strongly indicating that they were not concerned about a real threat, but were instead trying to "play the game" as faithfully as possible. The lack of any investigation into this conduct suggests that the US government did not wish to have these individuals testify in public.

Were passengers urged to call their loved ones?

According to Jeremy Glick's (UA93) wife in her testimony to the FBI on September 11, 2001, he reported to her that one hijacker had urged passengers to call their loved ones. Such advice by real hijackers would have been self-defeating, because (a) passengers would be induced to fight back; and (b) doing so would introduce the risk of earlier interception by the Air Force. This advice was, however, consistent with the scenario of a hijacking drill in which participants are urged to act the role of "hijacked passengers." This reported advice was apparently too troublesome to be included in the official account: Mrs. Glick never repeated it in subsequent interviews. In 2004, she even told the staff of the 9/11 Commission that her husband had never said that, only that the "hijackers" did not mind passengers making phone calls.

An "operation" on board flight AA11

The first version of Ong's call included the following question, asked by Craig Marquis: "What operation, what flight are we talking about? Flight 12?" First, note the fact that this sentence does not appear in the second version of the call, where the word "operation" is never mentioned. Second, note that Marquis corrected himself immediately, as if sensing that he had blurted out something he wasn't supposed to say by mentioning an "operation." The term "operation" would fit a military exercise, because such exercises are ordinarily referred to as an *operation*.

"You did great"

Some acute listeners claim to be able to hear someone whisper to CeeCee Lyles at the close of her tearful call to her husband, saying, "You did great." Were this true, it would support the view that she was acting within the framework of a hijacking drill.

(3) The enforced disappearance of the passengers and crew of the four flights

As documented throughout this book, the phone callers were duped into deceiving the recipients, including their husbands and wives, though they did so for a legitimate reason, namely participating in a counter-terrorism drill. There is no evidence that they survived.

Absent definite evidence as to where passengers and crew were taken after they had checked in at the airports, the airlines and ultimately, the US government, bear the responsibility of providing a credible and verifiable account about their fate. Even if they are believed to have been murdered at the behest of the US authorities, their legal status under international law remains that of *enforced disappeared persons*.

Under international law, governments are obliged to investigate enforced disappearances. According to Article 2 of the International Convention for the Protection of All Persons from Enforced Disappearance:[1]

---

1   "International Convention for the Protection of All Persons from Enforced Disappearance," adopted by the UN General Assembly on December 20, 2006, entered into force on December 23, 2010. #1787

For the purposes of this Convention "enforced disappearance" is considered to be "the ... abduction or any other form of deprivation of liberty by agents of the State or by persons or groups of persons acting with the authorization, support or acquiescence of the State, followed by a refusal to acknowledge the deprivation of liberty or by concealment of the fate or whereabouts of the disappeared person, which place such a person outside the protection of the law."

Although the United States has not yet signed and ratified the above Convention, enforced disappearances involve violations of treaties binding on the United States, including the International Covenant on Civil and Political Rights and the Convention against Torture and Other Cruel, Inhuman or Degrading Treatment or Punishment.

Because the fate of a person who is "disappeared" remains unknown, international law considers an enforced disappearance to be a continuing violation. It is ongoing until the fate or whereabouts of the person becomes known.

Beyond the legal status of the disappeared passengers, it is the moral duty of decent Americans to help the families of these passengers in discovering the fate of their loved ones.

Concluding Reflections

In the Introduction to this book, I made it clear that it does not purport to cover all aspects of 9/11. Those familiar with the subject are certainly aware of a large body of literature regarding the preplanned destruction of the Twin Towers and of WTC Nr. 7.[1] Mainstream media have extensively reported about the reluctance of the Bush administration to investigate 9/11,[2] the destruction of criminal evidence from Ground Zero[3] and other facts suggesting a government cover-up,[4] but they stopped short of connecting the dots.

In the preceding chapters readers were presented with numerous examples where US authorities suppressed crucial information, appear to have forged and planted evidence, attempted to intimidate witnesses and publicized deceptive and contrived reports. Such conduct would not have taken place if US leaders

---

1   David Ray Griffin, "The Destruction of the World Trade Center: Why the Official Account Cannot Be True," *Global Research*, January 29, 2006, #989; David Ray Griffin, "The Destruction of the World Trade Center: Why Have Otherwise Rational Journalists Endorsed Miracles?" in *9/11 Ten Years Later* (by same author), (Haus Publishing Ltd., London, 2011), pp. 32-83; Kevin R. Ryan, "The NIST WTC 7 Report: Bush Science reaches its peak," September 10, 2008, #958; Steven E. Jones, "Why Indeed Did the WTC Buildings Completely Collapse?" *Journal of 9/11 Studies*, September 2006/Volume 3, #959; "Interview with Dr. Niels Harrit on Discovery of Nano-Thermite in WTC Dust," *Foreign Policy Journal*, March 7, 2011, #960

2   "Interview with 9/11 Widow Lorie Van Auken," *Buzzflash.com*, October 21, 2004, #961

3   "WTC Steel Removal: The Expeditious Destruction of the Evidence at Ground Zero," *9-11 Research* (no date given), #962

4   "Able Danger Questions," *Washington Times*, August 21, 2005, #963; "Navy Captain Backs Able Danger Claims," *Fox News*, August 23, 2005, #964; "Specter: Pentagon may be obstructing committee," *CNN*, September 21, 2005, #965; John Crewdson and Andrew Zajac, "Atta known to Pentagon before 9/11," *Chicago Tribune*, September 28, 2005, #966

had been acting in good faith, felt compassion towards the victims of the mass-murder and considered themselves accountable to the American people.

(1) An unprecedented propaganda coup

When the sun rose on New York and Washington on September 11, 2001, the official legend of 9/11 lay ready to be promoted worldwide. It was conceived before the events and confirmed by the U.S. Congress—give and take minor details—within 24 hours of the deadly events.

While this book concentrates on a relatively narrow aspect of 9/11, there is a need to address a far larger picture, including the facility with which entire nations were deluded within hours to believe in what can be designated as a surreal legend. For the official 9/11 narrative—had it not been systematically and intensively promoted by all major media—could have provided a perfect synopsis for a book on religious miracles:

> Nineteen young and pious Moslems with short knives succeeded to hijack within minutes of each other four Boeing 757 and 767 airliners and maintain all forty to eighty passengers and crew in each plane docile as sheep. To do so, they first slashed the throats of passengers and flight attendants without anyone noticing. They then sneaked unobserved into the cockpits and silently massacred the pilots and co-pilots, who did not fight back. The pilots among the terrorists, who had previously trained on single-engine Cessnas, sitting in a pool of blood, found their way to their targets, hundreds of miles away, by looking out of the window. Allah, who heard their prayers, ensured to them a clear day. Their very religious team leader, the one and only Mohamed Atta, who four days previously got drunk in a Florida bar, managed to hit the North Tower of the WTC, a building only slightly wider than the wingspan of his aircraft, at over 500 mph. He accomplished what non-Muslim pilots found difficult to repeat on a simulator, and thus proved what deep Islamic faith can accomplish. Allah also ensured the confusion of US air defenses and that President Bush would dawdle in a class room while America was attacked. The great Usama Bin Laden later said that, thank to Allah, the consequences of 9/11, which surpassed all human expectations and measures, included the miraculous free-fall collapses of the Twin Towers and of WTC Nr. 7.[1] He thus summed it up: "God has struck America at its Achilles heel and destroyed its greatest buildings."[2]

---

1   "Osama bin Laden, The Towers of Lebanon," October 29, 2004. Video message attributed to Osama bin Laden delivered to Al-Jazeera. In *Messages to the World: The Statements of Osama bin Laden*, edited and introduced by Bruce Lawrence (Verso, London, 2005), p. 240

2   "Osama bin Laden, The Winds of Faith," October 7, 2001. Video message attributed to Osama bin Laden delivered to Al-Jazeera. In *Messages to the World: The Statements of Osama bin Laden*, edited and introduced by Bruce Lawrence (Verso, London, 2005), p. 104

The readiness of wide sections of Western society to swallow this legend hook line and sinker, is difficult to comprehend. Yet, this is an undeniable historical fact that cries for an explanation.

When examining the potency of this myth, we discover that it did not emerge from an immaculate conception. The crash of the second aircraft was timed to take place exactly 20 minutes after the first crash. This interval was necessary to allow television networks to reach the site and focus their cameras on the burning North Tower while catching the images of the second aircraft hitting the South tower. Within a short time all major networks around the world transmitted the events in real-time. The interval between the crashes—20 minutes—was optimal: Neither too short, not too long.

The grisly television spectacle included scenes of people jumping from the burning floors to their deaths and apocalyptic scenes of collapsing skyscrapers. The towers had to be destroyed while everyone was glued to television, in order to cause the requisite mental trauma. Had they been destroyed too early, questions might have arisen as the reason for their demise. Had they been left burning an additional hour, many viewers would have switched off their television sets. Timing was an essential ingredient in this carefully staged and staggered operation. The plotters designed the horror show to last no longer than an average feature film, that is just under two hours. Indeed, some commentators actually compared the events to a grand spectacle.

The dramaturgists of 9/11 must have envisaged that the events, played out real-time on television, would serve to unite the American people and rally it behind the flag. These effects were duly observed by journalists early on. Caryn James, for example, writing in *The New York Times* on September 13, 2001, observed that

> television does for the national psyche what wakes and funerals do in personal situations...That communal function is a crucial today as it was when John F. Kennedy was assassinated...A similar pattern united the country after the Oklahoma City bombing and the shootings at Columbine High School...[A]s the images [of 9/11] were replayed and the conversations continued, the reality sank in.[1]

The role of the media in promoting the official account on 9/11 is by now notorious.[2] Today's mass media are increasingly perceived as *weapons of mass deception.*[3] Some mainstream publications have spent since 2001 substantial resources,

---

1   Caryn James, "Television; huge events are close to home," *The New York Times*, September 13, 2001, #166

2   Several websites such as Media Monitors Networks, TVNewsLies.org, PRWatch and Project Censored are dedicated solely to exposing and fighting media lies as a general phenomenon. Specific lies by media are exposed daily by civil society activists.

3   "Weapons of Mass Deception" is the title of a book by Shelton Rampton and John Stauber (Penguin,2003). It is also the title of a documentary film by Danny Schechter (2004)

both in time and money, to promote the foundational myth of 9/11 and the fear of Islamic terrorism and continue to do so.[1] Jack Leslie, chairman of the one the world's largest P/R agencies—Weber Shandwick Worldwide—said in a hearing before the US House International Relations Committee after 9/11: "There has been no greater challenge for communications professionals in my lifetime that [sic] explaining the importance of the war on terrorism."[2] Indeed, in the light of the fact that more people die in their own bathtub than in terrorist attacks, selling the "war on terror" represents a real challenge for P/R professionals!

Here is a personal example of how an eminent journalist reacted to a challenge with regard to 9/11. On October 31, 2007, after attending a lecture at the London School of Economics, I happened to meet Richard Norton-Taylor, a senior journalist of The Guardian. One day earlier, he wrote an editorial in The Guardian in which he stated that 15 of the 9/11 perpetrators had come from Saudi Arabia. In the presence of two witnesses I offered him £10.000 if he could present—given two weeks time—evidence for his allegation. Instead of looking forward to earn a neat sum by meeting this challenge, he silently walked away. I reiterated my offer to him later in an email, emphasizing that this was no joke, but he did not respond. I made this offer to other, less known, journalists, but none of them felt confident enough to meet the challenge. As I do not assume that most journalists are wealthy, I presume that they simply fear to reveal their inability to prove their allegations or their doubts about the official account on 9/11.

Like millions of spectators, I admit that I too was transfixed by the images that were disseminated world-wide on 9/11 and believed for over a year in the official legend. It was my fortune, however, to be warned early on, that the official account was dubious. This warning piqued my curiosity, leading me eventually to engage in intensive research of this issue.

(2) The dereliction of academia

Not all scholars have been so fortunate or so curious as myself in questioning 9/11. I parsed a random sample of approximately 100 articles published after 9/11 in English-language law journals about terrorism-related issues. None of the authors of these articles questioned the official myth of 9/11 or the spurious claim that terrorism represents a serious threat to world peace or to the security

---

1   Popular Mechanics and National Geographic Magazine in the United States and Der Spiegel in Germany, have issued colorful special issues and DVDs to promote the official account of 9/11 and debunk "conspiracy theories." US officials, on the other hand, have been reluctant to defend the official account.

2   The "War on Terror is [the] 'greatest communications challenge of generation'," *The Holmes Report*, November 19, 2001, #377

of Western nations.[1] None of the authors provided evidence or just references to substantiate these two legends. These omissions appear to affect virtually all academic publications, all specialities included. It is no exaggeration to say that nearly the entire academic community, worldwide, has espoused these two myths and lent them a scientific garb in academic literature.

Failing to substantiate factual claims is rightly regarded in the academic world as bad science. When such dereliction, observed with regard to 9/11, is so massive and systematic, it transcends individual failure. This massive dereliction by the vast majority of the intellectual elite may be regarded as a symptom of a fundamental civilizational crisis: the demise of the Age of Reason.

Attempts to engage tenured academics in debate about the events of 9/11 have repeatedly and consistently failed. I am not aware of any tenured academic who is willing to publicly defend the official account of 9/11. The willful avoidance of the questions surrounding 9/11 by the academic community verges on the pathological.

(3) The dereliction of the Left

The Socialist and liberal leftist sections of Western societies espouse a similar willful avoidance regarding 9/11 as the academic world, though probably not for the same reasons. The similarity manifests itself in the persistent and sometimes forceful refusal to examine the facts of 9/11 and engage in debate.

While the failure of academics to question the official account of 9/11 may be attributed to fear of dismissal or of losing funding, that of the established Left is probably based on other considerations. Traditionally, the Left has opposed war and US imperialism. One would have, therefore, expected Leftists to be in the forefront of those who question a US-generated narrative. Leftist writers have, however, tried to explain the events of 9/11 as a retribution by Muslim warriors against US foreign policies, including its support for Israel, designating it as a "blowback."[2] Typical in this respect is former UK member of parliament George Galloway, who ten years after 9/11 said that "the planes didn't come out of a clear sky but emerged from the swamp of hatred the west had sown over many years [among Muslims]" and that "our role in the Palestinian catastrophe and the

---

1   "[Y]our risk of dying in a plausible terrorist attack is much lower than your risk of dying in a car accident, by walking across the street, by drowning, in a fire, by falling, or by being murdered" (Ronald Bailey, "Don't be terrorized," *reason.com*, August 11, 2006, #1124); Professor Peter Rez of Arizona State University, says that for the average passenger, the risk of dying from body-scanner induced cancer is about equal to the risk of dying from a terrorist attack – 1 in 30 million (Jason Mick, "Pilots Unions Boycott Body Scanners Due to Health Risks," *Daily Tech*, November 15, 2010, #1125)

2   See, for example, Jack Hunter, "Did 'Blowback' Cause 9/11?," *Charleston City Paper*, September 19, 2007; Patrick Foy, 9/11: "Blowback for US Foreign Policy," *Taki's Magazine*, September 10, 2011; "Interviewing Chomsky," *Counterpunch*, September 18, 2001

propping up of the dictators who ruled almost all of the Muslim world [were] the twin reasons that some enraged Muslims were being drawn to Bin Laden."[1]

While this explanation may appeal to some Leftists—who may relish that "someone" was finally retaliating against the US—it is not grounded on evidence. When the war on Afghanistan was debated in various European parliaments in 2001, no leftist fraction demanded to see hard evidence that Afghanistan had anything to do with 9/11.

This failure to ask questions about 9/11 did not, however, stop in 2001. Despite the publication of serious critical literature on the events since 2004 and the growth of the 9/11 truth movement, Leftist organizations remain firm in their refusal to critically tackle 9/11. The usual justifications for not dealing with 9/11 are either that questioning the official account amounts to a "conspiracy theory," or that 9/11 has lost its actuality. Such answers do not explain, however, the determination displayed by many leftists to remain ignorant about 9/11, or their attempts to slander the 9/11 truth movement.

Indeed, some prominent leftist publications were not content with merely ignoring the issue of 9/11. *The Nation*(US)[2], *CounterPunch* (US)[3], *The Progressive* (US)[4] and *Le Monde Diplomatique* (France)[5] have actually engaged in slander of 9/11 truthers. Respectable citizens who have questioned the official account on 9/11 have been derided by these publications as loonies or conspiracists. Attempts are even made to imply that 9/11 skeptics are covert antisemites. In fact, the overwhelming majority of 9/11 skeptics are known to oppose war and racism, support justice and engage in investigating 9/11 because of their strong sense of civic responsibility. Among these are hundreds, if not thousands, of eminent personalities from the fields of humanities, science and government. Some are even former military and intelligence officials.[6]

The probable reason for the Left to avoid dealing with 9/11 appears to that leftist parties and organizations hope to join the fold of "the establishment" in order to enjoy the ensuing material and psychological benefits. Some leftist organi-

---

1 Simon Jenkins, et al, "What impact did 9/11 have on the world?," *The Guardian*, September 5, 2011, #1154

2 Christopher Hayes, "The Roots of Paranoia," *The Nation*, December 8, 2006, #973; Alexander Cockburn, "The 9/11 Conspiracy Nuts," *The Nation*, September 7, 2006, #972

3 Alexander Cockburn, "The 9/11 Conspiracists: Vindicated After All These Years?" *CounterPunch*, September 2-4, 2011, #967; Alexander Cockburn, "The 9/11 Conspiracists and the Decline of the American Left," *CounterPunch*, September 28, 2006, #968; Alexander Cockburn, "The 9/11 Conspiracy Nuts," *CounterPunch*, September 9-11, 2006, #969

4 Matthew Rothschild, "Enough of the 9/11 Conspiracies, Already," *The Progressive*, September 11, 2006, #975

5 Alexander Cockburn, "The Conspiracy that Wasn't," *Le Monde Diplomatique*, December 2006, #970. Alexander Cockburn, "Hinter wem sie wirklich her sind," *Le Monde Diplomatique in German*, December 2006, #971

6 See "Military, Intelligenge and Government Patriots Question 9/11," ⟨patriotsquestion911. com⟩

zations are already the recipients of foundation grants or of government largesse and might endanger such funding by asking embarrassing questions on 9/11.[1]

(4) The futile demand for a new, independent investigation of 9/11

In 2004, the 9/11 Commission issued its Final Report. While initially hailed as a breakthrough, it is today widely recognized as a huge whitewash.[2] This was admitted belatedly by the chairmen of the Commission, Thomas H. Keane and Lee Hamilton who revealed in their joint book *Without precedent* that the Commission was "set up to fail," that it was seriously misled by senior officials of the Pentagon and that it was not given access to crucial data, such as transcripts of interrogations of 9/11 suspects.[3]

In an attempt to appear reasonable, the 9/11 truth movement articulates the demand for a new, independent investigation of 9/11.[4] This morally legitimate demand is largely supported within the movement. But is a new investigation of 9/11 at all necessary? And is it feasible?

(a) Is a new investigation of 9/11 necessary?

Those who consider a new 9/11 investigation necessary must apparently believe that existing evidence is not sufficient for rejecting the official account. Investigations carried by volunteer citizens since 2001 have, however, assembled reams of evidence establishing probable cause regarding US government lies and complicity in orchestrating 9/11. If criminal law could be enforced, such evidence would largely suffice to issue arrest warrants against suspects among US leaders, subpoena documents and force depositions. There is, therefore, something disingenuous for those who are convinced that the Twin Towers of the WTC and WTC Nr. 7 were destroyed with explosives, to demand a new, independent, investigation of 9/11. If these individuals and groups are convinced of their findings—and there exists no reason to doubt their sincerity—there is no need for a new investigation but rather for criminal proceedings against the suspects. The evidence presented in this volume vindicates this view.

---

1   An overview of foundation funding of "leftist" media is found on http://911review.com/denial/imgs/left_gatekeepers.gif, #1788

2   Benjamin DeMott, "Whitewash as public service: How the 9/11 Commission Report defrauded the nation," *Harpers Magazine*, October 2004, #976. Also David Ray Griffin, *The 9/11 Commission Report: Omissions and Distortions* (Olive Branch Press, 2005)

3   Ivan Eland, "9/11 Commission Chairmen Admit Whitewashing the Cause of the Attacks," *The Independent Institute*, August 7, 2006, #977. Also wikipedia: "Criticism of the 9/11 Commission"

4   Search the internet for the string "9/11 Truth Petitions"

(b) Is an independent investigation of 9/11 feasible?

It has been demonstrated in this book and elsewhere that the main suspects for the mass-murder 9/11 are US officials. Those who conceived, planned and carried out the mass-murder of 9/11, did certainly not act to satisfy their personal whims. Whoever conceived the mass-murder of 9/11 did so, obviously, in the long-term interests of Empire. The operation was designed to wake up the American people (and more generally the Western public) from its complacency and ensure its active support for the Project of a New American Century, in which the United States would reign supreme and lead the world.

Professor John Lewis Gaddis, a noted historian of the Cold War and of Grand Strategy, explained already in 1989 that an external threat is needed in order to rally the populace behind a proactive foreign policy that would allow the US to capitalize on the global opportunities available with the demise of the Soviet bloc:

> We have great opportunities that could be taken advantage of if we could define our strategy a little more clearly. The problem is that we may not be able to define a clear strategy in the absence of a clear sense of danger [...] If the Gorbachev strategy of depriving us of an enemy continues, then that element is not going to be present, and it may be more difficult to formulate something.[...] You require a crisis, like the one that we had in 1947, or like what we had in 1940 to '41, where the security of the country really is in danger, and people have to think and they have to think fast. Those are the situations where you normally get vision beginning to emerge [...] There clearly has to be an ability to move the public and to sustain public support. You have to be able to convince the public that this vision, whatever it is, is the right thing to do and that it's going to advance the national interest. If you can't sell it, then you're not going to get very far with it.[1]

A similar perspective was formulated by former presidential advisor Zbigniew Brzezinski in his book *The Grand Chessboard*, published in 1996:

> The pursuit of power is not a goal that commands popular passion, except in conditions of a sudden threat or challenge to the public's sense of domestic well-being. [...] Democracy is inimical to imperial mobilization (Brzezinski, 22).

Brzezinski also summed up his strategic recommendations relative to Central Asia that the US began implementing immediately after 9/11:

> [F]or the United States, Eurasian geostrategy involves the purposeful management of geostrategically dynamic states and the careful handling of geopolitically catalytic states, in keeping with the twin interests of America in the short-term preservation of its unique global power and in the long-run

---

1   Harry Kreisler, "Conversation with John Lewis Gaddis," Berkley University, May 8, 1989, #978-982

transformation of it into increasingly institutionalized global cooperation. To put it in a terminology that hearkens back to the more brutal age of ancient empires, the three grand imperatives of imperial geostrategy are to prevent collusion and maintain security dependence among the vassals, to keep tributaries pliant and protected, and to keep the barbarians from coming together.[1]

The need for the United States to capitalize on the opportunity that arose by the demise of the Soviet bloc was duly recognized by leading members of the American political class. Conservative leaders, including Dick Cheney, Donald Rumsfeld and Paul Wolfowitz, together with other members of the Project for a New American Century (PNAC), issued on June 3, 2007 PNAC's Statement of Principles. These Principles, or aims, were to "rally support for American global leadership," to "increase defense spending significantly" and to "accept responsibility for America's unique role in preserving and extending an international order friendly to our security, our prosperity, and our principles."[2]

In 2000, PNAC issued its report *Rebuilding America's Defenses: Strategy, Forces and Resources for a New Century*, under the heading Key Findings we read:

> This report proceeds from the belief that America should seek to preserve and extend its position of global leadership by maintaining the preeminence of U.S. military forces. Today, the United States has an unprecedented strategic opportunity. It faces no immediate great-power challenge, it is blessed with wealthy, powerful and democratic allies in every part of the world....At no time in history has the international security order been as conductive to American interests and ideals.... Yet unless the United States maintains sufficient military strength, this opportunity will be lost.

The report refers repeatedly to the need to revolutionize the nature of conventional armed forces by capitalizing on information and space technology, an effort requiring huge investments. The authors warn, however, "The process of transformation [of the military], even if it brings revolutionary change, is likely to be a long one, absent some catastrophic and catalyzing event––like a new Pearl Harbor."[3] The events of 9/11 were visibly a "catastrophic and catalyzing event" comparable to Pearl Harbor.[4] The events of 9/11 justified immediately a vast increase in resources for the transformation of the US military and for multiple US wars. As proposed by PNAC, the US military has gradually become a global constabulary force, ready to intervene whenever the ruling circles demand.

---

1   Ibid. p. 40
2   "Statement of Principles," *PNAC*, June 3, 1997, #385
3   "Rebuilding America's Defenses: Strategy, Forces and Resources For a New Century," A report of the *Project for a New American Century*, September 2000, p. 51, #1789
4   Michael Streich, "Pearl Harbor and 9/11 Attacks Compared," *American History Suite 101*, March 5, 2009, #983; Donna Miles, "Pearl Harbor Parallels 9-11," *Military.com*, December 7, 2006, #446

Had the crime of 9/11 been carried out by rogue elements of the US government or the armed forces against the vested interests of the US ruling class, its perpetrators would have been long ago exposed and punished. The truth is, that no one has been convicted for 9/11, that the ruling elite has prevented the truth on 9/11 to be established and that US-led wars have been extremely profitable for corporate America. This demonstrates that the ruling elite stands united behind the cover-up of this crime. In such circumstances, an independent investigation of this crime cannot take place, absent a regime change.

The same considerations extend to the pipe-dream that an honest US judge would somehow volunteer to issue warrants for the arrest of US leaders as suspects for 9/11. The well documented deference of US judges to the wishes of the US administration in questions of national security as well as in cases dealing with 9/11[1] should chill the hope of anyone who believes in the integrity and independence of the current US justice system.

It is equally moot—and for similar reasons—to expect governments allied to the US or dependent upon the US, to support or demand an international investigation of 9/11. Even if a majority of UN members were to demand such an investigation, a Commission of Inquiry mandated by the United Nations would hardly be allowed to enter the United States, let alone interrogate US public officials and subpoena official documents. While the Security Council of the United Nations has given lip-service to the obligation of states to cooperate in view of prosecuting the planners and participants in 9/11,[2] it did not and cannot enforce this demand. The interests of many UN members are not only intimately linked to those of the US elite, but have themselves skeletons in their closets. They are, thus, not in a good position in making moral demands upon the United States.

The current political situation is not conductive for establishing the truth on 9/11. Both mass media and parliaments in the Western world have been unwilling to demand that the US produce evidence to prove its accusations regarding 9/11. Most political parties and virtually all mass media in Western countries have for over 10 years passively and actively engaged in the cover-up of the mass-murder. The *extent* of the deception by Western parliaments and the media with regard to 9/11 has no precedent in modern history. It is moot to expect those who participated in this systematic cover-up to concede voluntarily their persistent dishonesty.

---

1   Mary-Rose Papandrea, "Under Attack: The Right to Know and the War on Terror," *Boston College Third World Law Journal*, Vol. 25, Nr. 1 (2005), p. 35-80; Jon Gold, "District Judge Alvin K. Hellerstein—The 9/11 Judge," *911blogger*, July 17, 2009, #986

2   According to UN Security Council Resolution 1368 of September 12, 2001, the Security Council "calls on all States to work together urgently to bring to justice the perpetrators, organizers and sponsors of [the attacks of 9/11]."

Critical authors, such as myself, are sometimes expected to produce a "smoking gun" regarding the alleged complicity of the U.S. authorities in 9/11. Such expectation is, however, not realistic. The U.N. Human Rights Committee addressed the asymmetry between ordinary citizens and States in its 1994 report: "The burden of proof cannot rest alone with the author of a [complaint], especially considering that the author and the State party do not always have equal access to the evidence and that frequently the State party alone has access to the relevant information."[1] What an understatement!

(5) The revolutionary potential of 9/11-truth

The events of 9/11 demonstrate, perhaps better than any other contemporary issue, the limits of parliamentary and judicial remedies to cases of high state criminality. Those who have recognized that 9/11 was a state crime, will inevitably discover that they cannot rely on established procedures to achieve justice. Existing political, financial and military institutions have become so entwined with those of the US regime, that a break with that regime may be viewed by those depending on these institutions as an existential threat to their own privileges.

If the mass-murder committed on 9/11 had been the result of individual malice, it could have been disposed of as the sole "rotten apple" in an otherwise healthy heap. The massive cover-up of 9/11 proves, however, the central role this crime was supposed to play in the strategy of the Western elite. The mass-murder of 9/11 was the natural outcome of an imperial strategy that required the creation of a new epochal enemy, for which it was necessary to sacrifice thousands of "one's own citizens." Absent a defeat of US imperialism in coming years, we may bear witness to, or become victims of, ever larger crimes committed against the peoples of the world by the imperial powers and their auxiliaries.

Instead of defending their right to dissent, as they have done hitherto, 9/11 skeptics can and should now raise an accusing finger against governments, politicians, journalists and academics for their complicity in systematic deception used to justify wars and the erosion of democracy. The accused have no defense available. They will certainly ignore the accusations, as they have done hitherto. They will avoid debates and refuse to attend public meetings where they could be heckled and challenged. But their cowardice cannot be concealed forever. They possess no defense against a coordinated and offensive campaign by 9/11 truthers.

---

1   1994 Report by the United Nations Human Rights Committee, Vol. II, Annex IX, AA, para. 9.2 (*Albert W. Mukong v. Cameroon*, case 458/1991)

Accusing those who cover-up the 9/11 crime is not only a sound strategy; it is also morally and legally justified. The families of 9/11 victims are entitled to know what happened to their next-of-kin. Society is entitled to have the perpetrators, planners and facilitators of the mass-murder identified, prosecuted and convicted. Justice must be *seen* to have been done. The right to the truth about a mass murder is recognized as a legal right under international law.[1]

The probability that the US government ordered the mass-murder of 9/11 gives also rise to security considerations. The risk exists that loyalists of the US government, whether acting under the auspice of US state institutions or under those of other states, can be expected to commit new murderous crimes in the future, if they consider such crimes imperative for maintaining their own power. The physical security of ordinary citizens worldwide is at risk as long as military, intelligence and law-enforcement officials cooperate with the rulers of the murderous US regime or its domestic stooges in other countries.

It appears to me that only a revolution can save our civilization from a terrible ordeal; not a revolution by an enlightened minority who has found "the truth"; nor a suicidal armed insurrection; but a cultural revolution based on moral integrity, refusal to obey immoral orders, grass-root solidarity across the globe and genuine commitment to a social order in which human dignity and compassion prevails over greed and the quest for power. Such a revolution can only be achieved by peaceful means.

If this book has contributed to awareness of the revolutionary potential of 9/11 truth, it would have served its purpose.

---

1   Elias Davidsson, "The Events of 11 September 2001 and the Right to the Truth," *The Wisdom Fund*, April 14, 2008, #988

Bibliography

Ahmed, Nafeez Mosaddeq: *The War on Truth and the Anatomy of Terrorism* (Olive Branch Press, 2005)

Bin Laden, Osama: *Messages to the World: The Statements of Osama bin Laden*, edited and introduced by Bruce Lawrence (Verso, London, 2005)

Brzezinski, Zbigniew: *The Grand Chessboard: American Primacy and its Geostrategical Imperatives* (Basic Books, 1996)

Burnett, Deena: *Fighting Back* (Advantage Books, 2006)

Clarke, Richard A.: *Against All Enemies* (FreePress, 2004)

Final Report of the National Commission on Terrorist Attacks Upon the United States, 2004 ("Final Report")

Fink, Mitchell and Lois Mathias: *Never Forget, An Oral History of September 11, 2001* (Harpers Collins, 2002)

Griffin, David Ray: "The Destruction of the World Trade Center: Why Have Otherwise Rational Journalists Endorsed Miracles?" in *9/11 Ten Years Later* (by same author), (Haus Publishing Ltd., London, 2011)

Griffin, David Ray: *The New Pearl Harbor: Disturbing Questions about the Bush Administration and 9/11* (Olive Branch Press, 2004)

Griffin, David Ray: *The 9/11 Commission Report: Omissions and Distortions* (Olive Branch Press, 2005)

Huffman, Suzanne and Judith L. Sylvester: *Women Journalists at Ground Zero: Covering Crisis* (Rowman & Littlefield, 2002)

Jefferson, Lisa and Felicia Middlebrooks: *Called* (Northfield Publishing, 2006)

Kashurba, Glenn: *Courage After the Crash* (SAJ Publishing, 2002)

Longman, Jere: *Among the Heroes: The True Story of United 93* (Harpers Collins Publisher, 2002)

McCall, David: *From Tragedy to Triumph* (Noah's Ark Pub. Co, 2002)

Meyssan, Thierry: *L'effroyable imposture* (Editions Demi-Lune, 2002) and *Le Pentagate* (Editions Carnot, 2003—in French)

Morgan, Rowland: *Flight 93 Revealed: What really happened on the 9/11 'Let's Roll' Flight?* (Robinson publishers, 2006)

Morgan, Rowland: *Voices—40 phone calls changed the world that day* (ebook, 2010)

Murphy, Tom: *Reclaiming the Sky* (AMACOM Books, 2007)

Rampton, Shelton and John Stauber: *Weapons of Mass Deception* (Penguin, 2003)

Ruppert, Michael C.: *Crossing the Rubicon: The Decline of the American Empire and the End of the Age of Oil* (New Society Publishers, 2004)

Scott, Peter Dale: *Deep Politics and the Death of JFK* (University of California Press,1996)

Scott, Peter Dale: *The Road to 9/11: Wealth, Empire, and the Future of America* (University of California Press , 2008)

Scott, Peter Dale: *American War Machine: Deep Politics, the CIA Global Drug Connection, and the Road to Afghanistan* (Rowman & Littlefield Publishers, 2010)

Spencer, Lynn: *Touching History: The Untold Story of the Drama That Unfolded in the Skies Over America on 9/11* (Free Press, 2008)

Staff Report of the 9/11 Commission ("The Four Flights"), 26 August 2004 ("Staff Report")

Tarpley, Webster Griffin: *9/11 Synthetic Terror Made in USA* (Progressive Press, 2006)

Trento, Susan B. and Joseph J. Trento: *Unsafe at any Altitude: Failed Terrorism Investigations, Scapegoating 9/11, and the Shocking Truth about Aviation Security Today* (Steerforth Press, 2006)

Trost, Cathy (Newseum) and Alicia Shephard: *Running Toward Danger: Stories Behind the Breaking News of 9/11* (Rowman & Littlefield Publishers, 2002)

Von Bülow, Andreas: *Die CIA und der 11. September: Internationaler Terror und die Rolle der Geheimdienste* (Piper Verlag, 2003, 2004, 2011—in German)

Wisnewski, Gerhard: *Operation 9/11, 10 Jahre danach* (Knaur Taschenbuch, 2011—in German)

Wisnewski, Gerhard: *Mythos 9/11—Die Wahrheit auf der Spur* (Knaur Taschenbuch, 2004—in German)

Zarembka, Paul (ed.): *The Hidden History of 9/11* (Elsevier, May 2006)

Zwicker, Barrie: *Towers of Deception: The Media Cover-Up of 9/11* (New Society Publishers, 2006)

INDEX